NOT TILL WE ARE LOST

Like the best kind of long walk, *Not Till We Are Lost* unfolds organically and in unexpected directions, taking the reader through diverse and vividly drawn ecosystems and neighborhoods. We are joined by many fellow travelers for stretches of the road: not only Thoreau and Emerson, but also Herbert Marcuse, Rachel Carson, Pierre Hadot, Gregory Bateson, Martin Buber, and Carl Jung, to name just a few. But the real joy of this book is the ambling narration of our companion, William Homestead, whose humility, humor, and ready ease in making unanticipated connections are gifts that will long outlast the journey. This is a vital book for anyone interested in thinking deeply about the twin arts of teaching and learning and how they might be mobilized on behalf of the planet.

—Kristen Case, author of *Keeping Time:*
Henry David Thoreau's Kalendar

William Homestead offers a compelling meditation on what it means to teach students whose world is beloved but bewildering, wild but warming. At once pedagogical guide, spiritual autobiography, and climate-grief narrative, *Not Till We Are Lost* illustrates how embracing Thoreau's dictum to "live deliberately" transformed one teacher's intellectual journey, shaping both his life and his lessons for the next generations.

—Rochelle L. Johnson, president of The Thoreau Society

Thoreau may be the crucial American author, and this lively and engaging book reminds us why: the questions he raised are the questions that trouble us still. Or perhaps they trouble us more now than ever, in a dispirited and lonely country, where a tonic reminder of human possibility like this is always welcome!

—Bill McKibben, author of *The End of Nature*

William Homestead's magnificent memoir is an enriching educational, environmental, and spiritual journey. He uniquely follows the patterns of Thoreau's life to illuminate the challenges we all face as educators and informed citizens.

—Mitchell Thomashow, author of *To Know the World:*
A New Vision for Environmental Learning

NOT TILL WE ARE LOST

Thoreau, Education, and Climate Crisis

William Homestead

MERCER UNIVERSITY PRESS
Macon, Georgia

MUP/ P701

© 2024 by Mercer University Press
Published by Mercer University Press
1501 Mercer University Drive
Macon, Georgia 31207

28 27 26 25 24   5 4 3 2 1

Books published by Mercer University Press are printed on acid-free paper that meets the requirements of the American National Standard for Information Sciences—Permanence of Paper for Printed Library Materials.

Printed and bound in the United States.

This book is set in Adobe Caslon.

Cover/jacket design by Burt&Burt.

ISBN   978-0-88146-948-6   Print
            978-088146-949-3   eBook

Cataloging-in-Publication Data is available from the Library of Congress

To the memory of my parents, Herb and Ruth Homestead,

whose love transcends time.

MERCER UNIVERSITY PRESS

Endowed by

TOM WATSON BROWN
and
THE WATSON-BROWN FOUNDATION, INC.

Contents

Acknowledgments

Many thanks go to Maura MacNeil, who provided feedback on two full drafts. Maura's insights greatly informed the revision process; I was fortunate to have such a generous colleague at New England College.

Thanks also go to David Gordon from Loyola University Maryland, who did a late reading of the manuscript that led to added context and clarification; Diane Gruber, from Arizona State University, who did an early encouraging reading that kept me going; and Richard Panek from Goddard College, where I received my MFA, who did a very early reading that helped shape the narrative.

And many thanks to Marc Jolley, a fellow Thoreauvian and the director of Mercer University Press. I deeply appreciate his feedback and support.

Not Till We Are Lost has gone through many iterations over a ten-year period, especially as I attended Thoreau Society Annual Gatherings and learned from new scholarship. More thanks go to the Thoreau Society, then, as well as the man himself, Henry David Thoreau, who becomes more relevant, rather than less, when we learn about his struggles.

Thoreau's responses to his lostness, and the lostness of his times, are rooted in inner genius, conscience, and sympathy with the more-than-human world. These responses cascade over two centuries, providing much guidance to educators in our age of climate crisis. I receive them with gratitude and hope others will as well.

"Every man has to learn the points of the compass again as often as he awakes, whether from sleep or any abstraction. Not till we are lost, in other words, not till we have lost the world, do we begin to find ourselves, and realize where we are and the infinite extent of our relations."

—Henry David Thoreau

Introduction

Not till we are lost, Thoreau argues, do we learn the most important things—who and where we are—before becoming lost again, ready for more learning, re-finding the compass. And then the process repeats. Sounds like a lot of work but it's just the lot of those living a full life of endless discovery.

As a college teacher for twenty-seven years, I encounter lost students all the time, as well as those who need to recognize their lostness so that they may find their inner intelligence.

A colleague at New England College once stated that the teacher is like a psychopomp guiding souls to their destination. Mythologically, the psychopomp escorts the dead to the afterlife, but the psychopomp as teacher is adept at guiding souls to new life, to new transformations by dying to old selves. I love this analogy because I have had two mentors who have provided this guidance—you will meet them within these pages—and I try to provide such guidance to students.

Teaching is truly a labor of love, of mind and heart, and not all are up to it—sometimes I am not up to it—but it's an important job. Or rather, it's a calling and only the called should teach. But feeling called does not make teaching easy. We make mistakes and must work to recover the compass. Still, it is a privilege to do what I do; that is, when I recognize the inherent dignity of the student and embrace the possibility of guiding them from one state of awareness to another. Guiding students to new life does not occur by instruction, though, but by gently prodding them to listen to themselves, or their daemon or inner guiding spirit that supplies instruction. The psychopomp escorts us to the afterlife, but for the ancient Greeks, the daemon guides us here, to life on earth, and continues to guide us throughout our lives, if we are willing to listen.

One may doubt the existence of the daemonic. Students certainly do, but perhaps that is because they have been socialized out of their souls, and, tragically, their education is the main reason.

This book is about the education of an educator. It's about personal failures, a journey of redemption, and the failures of an industrial educational system of general soullessness that, while seemingly beyond redemption, may be saved by the soulful pursuit of what is true, good, and beautiful. It is, I hope, a provocative example of what Jung called the process of individuation, of living our inner life outwardly, and the good work and difficulties of trying to instill this process in others. It's a story of listening: to students, to logos and critical rationality, to nature, to the daemonic and call of vocation, and to mysteries beyond rational comprehension informed by experiences both beautiful and trying; or rather, the trying experiences—our struggles and dark nights—become beautiful when they lead to growth.

This book is also about books and writers that have acted like guides, both personally and pedagogically, especially the work of Henry David Thoreau, whose life was wholly original yet influenced by his mentors, Ralph Waldo Emerson and other transcendentalists (whom you will also meet within these pages). It's a defense of the liberal arts, whose worth has been questioned in a time of economic downturns and high tuition. And it's an exploration of material excess and eco-social crises, rooted in the Cartesian split between mind and nature, but also excessive spirituality expressed as detachment from the needs of the world; as such, it illustrates the search for middle ground where the spiritual and material meet.

It is, ultimately, about the blessings of being lost such that we may learn what we need to learn. Only through such learning will we walk our path, a spiritual path, rather than a proscribed one, and find fulfillment and contribute to others. In doing so, we recognize our collective lostness and potential for awakening while hopefully finding a calling in a career and taking care of the material demands of modern living. Or we shun modern definitions of material demand to live a life that addresses key questions of our climate crisis times.

Such is the measure of education, is it not?

Many may say "not" in a world dominated by financial markets, job markets, and market-model universities. "Finding yourself" is frequently mocked as a luxury for those without student loans or as an excuse for slackers who deny economic realities; but while financial realities must be considered, especially for first generation college students striving to help their families, can we afford to allow what Emerson termed "the lucrative standard" to deny spiritual realities? Or the material realities of rising CO_2 and other greenhouse gases?

In fall 2021, the first part of the UN IPCC 6th Assessment Climate Report was released: no surprise, the scientific facts are not pretty, with UN Secretary-General Antonio Guterres calling it "code red for humanity." The third part, released in spring 2022, provides a "now or never" warning. We need bold action now to keep warming to 1.5 degrees Celsius, which is still deeply destructive, with more deadly storms and wildfires, more extreme heat, more biodiversity loss. Most likely, we will continue where we are heading: an even more destructive and deadly 2.0 C (or higher) in coming decades, leading to failed harvests, scorching temperatures making many places too hot to live in, melted ice caps swamping major cities, and numerous other eco-social disasters.

Sometimes I don't know what to teach; I am lost, or at a loss, given that there is so much to teach and so little time to do right by the earth and ourselves to change course. The lucrative standard, which drives most students, is driving us to the brink of societal collapse. Transition to a far different standard and way of living is inevitable, but how will we navigate that transition? There are lots of options, including better, bad, and ugly.

Better is obviously best, but what to teach to get there? That question returns me to *Walden* and Thoreau's writings generally and the far from perfect Thoreau himself because much-needed insights and actions are there: the integration of the sciences and humanities and practice of the naturalist; criticism of dominant technology and embrace of appropriate technology; a vibrant and vital inner life inspired by the daemonic and practiced as self-reliance; simple living and reshaping economy and work; staying put and contributing to community; civil disobedience fueled by conscience in response to systemic injustice; learning by listening beyond the human; and, most importantly, the value of lostness and pursuit of not only knowledge but spiritual transformation.

All are called by inner intelligence in sympathy with ecosystem intelligence, and still further, the soul of the world.

Using my life as guide, this book attempts to show that we desperately need an educational system that mirrors this reality, embracing the infinite extent of our relations in an age of climate crisis.

Chapter 1

Voice

"Good as is discourse, silence is better, and shames it."
—Ralph Waldo Emerson

Jeff seethed in his seat in the basement classroom of our high tech, ten-story building, his eyes hiding under a baseball cap, face red. I stood at the front of thirty undergrads, nervous at the start of my first full semester of teaching but soon enjoying the stage, except for the scowl in the center row. I oversaw a section of the infamous Com 114, a required public speaking course at Purdue University. Required, meaning students of every major were forced to take the course. Required, meaning no one wanted to be there, at least not initially.

Jeff did not want to be there.

"Are you following the presidential race?" I asked, hoping to warm up the class before preparing them for their speeches.

A smattering of heads nodded.

"If you watch Bill Clinton speak, and then watch his wife, Hillary, you might ask if she should be running."

Many students smiled, especially the women. Jeff wore his usual glare.

"Why haven't we had a woman president?" I continued. "Why are there so few women in Congress, or heading corporations?"

The class looked attentive now, intrigued. Jeff looked more than warm.

"Why does Hillary get flack for pursuing a career rather than staying home and baking cookies?"

This, apparently, was too much.

"There's nothing wrong with a woman staying at home," Jeff blared in a those-are-fightin'-words voice.

"I didn't say there was anything wrong with a woman staying at home; I asked why our culture doesn't seem to think it right for women to have positions of power."

I was trying to stir things up, awakening students both figuratively and literally, but Jeff had caught me off guard.

"My mom stayed at home and baked cookies," he retorted.

"That's great," I laughed, "but why can't men bake cookies too?"

Jeff was heated now, ready to unleash his stocky, coiled frame. The laugh, which slipped out, seemed to have stoked his rage.

"What do the rest of you think?" I said, quickly, the typical get-everyone-to-talk phrase transformed into more of a flight response. I was hoping for help to deflect Jeff's building anger and quell my own defensiveness and desire to fight.

It was 1992—Nirvana and grunge were rampant, multiculturalism was fervent, and Jeff was a stew of discordant energy sitting at a desk. Although new to teaching, I was not new to the classroom and the fact that vocal students made class interesting—the last thing I wanted was for everyone to easily agree—but this was different. Jeff disrupted the flow, the magic, fleeting and rare, when passion for a topic leads discussion into unexpected and potentially transformative terrain, or at least small insights.

Jeff's classmates challenged his views in class and avoided his anger before and after class. A one-on-one conversation was overdue, but I had no teaching tools for dealing with a student like Jeff. Every imagined conversation began as a confrontation and ended as a lecture, leading him to become more entrenched. At the midpoint of the semester, however, students were required to visit with me to discuss their persuasive speeches. We would have to meet.

My students gave speeches on issues such as abortion, alternative energy, school violence, or the presidential run of Bill and Hillary, who were pushing health care and women's rights, and I wanted to make sure they had considered all possible views. Little did they know, but, to me, the core content of the course was not speaking in public but practicing higher order rationality and ethical discernment, and ultimately, finding your voice and changing the world—clichéd and idealistic, sure, but I did not know a better reason to teach.

On a practical level, our one-on-one meetings were an act of mercy. Earlier rounds of speeches revealed that prepared students would pepper

5

the poorly prepared with tough questions, leaving dumbfounded speakers looking like they'd just been to a paintball tournament without a gun. I hoped for group dialogue, not group sacrifice.

I held meetings at a woodsy café in the student center, the walls covered with dated, black-and-white photos of athletes, mostly football players from their glory years, posed to accentuate agility and brawn. I used the café because the professors took all the offices. I was a mere "adjunct lecturer"—being an adjunct is like being in a ditch in front of the first rung of the academic ladder—and office space, or health care, or any perks, were not in my contract. But I would have chosen to meet students amid the café's more relaxed atmosphere anyway, knowing from undergraduate experiences that a stuffy office didn't lend to deeper conversations, especially if an insight was bouncing around within, rearranging the way they understood themselves and the world.

Jeff was five minutes late for our afternoon meeting—five minutes of bracing for battle—but he seemed contrite when he arrived, fingering his baseball cap and avoiding my eyes. I reiterated the basics of the assignment: students should choose a topic that elicited their passion, something that made them happy, sad, or enraged; something that made them want to speak out.

"My father is an alcoholic," Jeff said softly, taking off his baseball cap and looking me in the eyes for the first time. "I want to do my speech on alcoholism."

This revelation started the flow.

"Good," I said, returning his gaze, "I'm sure you feel a lot of passion about that. You can use that in your speech, if you want. If you're comfortable, you could grab the audience's attention by opening with a story about your dad. What's he like?"

"He's a bastard, that's what he's like."

"How so?"

"He yells…" Jeff said, his voice trailing off and eyes drifting to photos of grinning athletes celebrating their success as if strangers to struggle.

"What does he yell about?"

"He just yells. He drinks and gets pissed off. He tells everyone what to do. He tells me what to do."

"What does he do?"

"Like, for a living?"

"I meant at home, but yeah, what does he do for work?"

"He's an engineer," Jeff smirked, "and he wants me to be an engineer."

"But you don't want to?"

"Hell no, but you try telling that to my father."

Jeff's anger flared, like it had so often in class, but then he softened again.

"What do you want to do?"

"I don't know. Maybe major in psychology..."

Jeff put on his cap and stopped talking. I followed his eyes and saw that the next student had arrived early and stood near our table. I asked if he wanted to set up another time to chat. He nodded, and we agreed to choose a time tomorrow in class. He slid out of his seat, the athletes a blur as he hurried to the exit.

That evening, I couldn't stop thinking about our meeting. Jeff's admissions felt like a mix of confession and apology, as well as an explanation for the previous two months. He knew he had isolated himself and found the courage to begin making amends. Things became clear when he mentioned his father's alcoholism: Jeff had been like a tape recorder in class, replaying the lessons he had learned at home.

I sat on the front porch of the rental house I shared with grad students, sun fading, insight emerging, a remembering more than a rearranging: the university places artificial limits on the classroom.

I called Jeff at his residence hall to see if he wanted to go for a walk. He was shocked to hear my voice but agreed to meet outside the student center. It was a crisp, autumn night—stars distant yet close, like a witnessing presence—and we began strolling across the plush, manicured lawns of campus.

"What were you doing when I called?" I said, innocently.

Jeff winced, as if forced to admit a secret, "Sitting in my room playing with a knife."

I nodded my head.

"So, tell me more about your dad?" I said, changing the subject, albeit slightly.

"What do you want to know?"

"You said your father was a bastard. Does he hit?" I asked, knowing it wasn't a softball question but that he had already made hard admissions.

"Sometimes. Lots when I was growing up. First with a belt, as punishment…I deserved it. I got in trouble a lot. At some point he switched to using his hands."

"You mean punching?"

"Mostly he slaps. It's the alcohol."

I nodded again, listening while also aware of the starry night. It was expansive and beautiful while Jeff was constricted and oblivious. We walked without speaking, reaching spacious athletic fields where a water tower sat serenely on a moonlit rolling hill.

"You know, despite your father's demands you might want to change your major. You should read books on psychology and take some courses. And there is free counseling at the health center. Counseling will help you to learn about yourself, which would help you to counsel others later."

This idea seemed to stir something within him, but then I really got his attention.

"Are you thinking about suicide?"

Jeff turned and stared at me, as if it was one thing to think it but quite another to have someone say it. I paused, making sure I didn't add more weight to the burden he already carried, and then smiled, pointed to the night sky, and spoke without affectation.

"If you committed suicide you would just rejoin the energy of the universe. But you're already the energy of the universe, so you might as well find a creative way to express it."

Jeff continued to stare, unable to utter a reply, and then looked up, noticing the night for the first time. I assumed that no one had spoken to him that way before. It was not words that I hoped to convey, but silence prior to utterance, to all the noise that filled up his head, allowing him to be present to an expansive cosmos.

We stood, together, without words. I continued to smile, hoping to induce one in return, and it slowly emerged.

After more talking and walking in silence—taking it all in—we reached his residence hall. I asked if he was okay, wondering if I should contact campus safety or his RA. He assured me that he had no intention of hurting himself, and then thanked me, saying he would see me tomorrow.

The night sky and shared silence seemed to have loosened him up; looking into his eyes, I intuited that he would be fine.

What if I was wrong?

Walking home, I imagined the front page of the student newspaper the next day: "Student Kills Himself after Walk with Teacher." But I also recalled a quotation from William James: "No man is educated who has never dallied with the thought of suicide."

ଔ

Purdue is a "Big Ten" university in West Lafayette, Indiana. When I taught there were over forty thousand undergraduates, and the departments with the most students were engineering, business, agriculture (agribusiness), and forestry (industrial forestry). Students from the largest major, engineering, were only required to take three courses in the humanities, two in English composition, and Com 114. Once an engineering student passed these minimal requirements, they were free to specialize in a particular branch of engineering, graduate, and be considered educated. On the other hand, those who majored in the humanities had little to no impetus for taking courses in the sciences. They were free to graduate and be considered educated without foundational knowledge in how the ecosystem works.

This bifurcation of knowledge became particularly troubling to me when more than sixteen hundred world scientists, including most living Nobel laureates, published a 1992 "Warning to Humanity" documenting a myriad of eco-social ills—destruction of forests, loss of soil, water resource exploitation, species extirpation, and, most troubling since it exacerbates all problems, global warming—stating that humans and ecosystems were on a collision course. I saw a report on the warning in a newspaper, thinking that something essential was missing from education, and that something essential was missing from *my* education.

It was within this context, at age thirty-two, that I began a seven-year run of teaching four or six sections of Com 114 per semester for a paltry twelve thousand dollars a year. The Communication Studies department structured the syllabus (the book, the assignments, the final exam), but, to my deep pleasure, they couldn't structure the core content.

I began the first day of class with a simple question: Why are you in college? After typical responses—money, career, learning a specialty so they could have money and a career—I shared my own path to graduation, a tragicomedy of three New Jersey schools, seven years, and four majors. I started college in 1978 as a computer science major because I was decent at math and the field promised a future with numerous job opportunities and substantial salary. These are understandable reasons for choosing to study computer science, I said; there is certainly logic present. But I also asked, what is the logic? Where did it come from? And who, or what, legitimizes this logic? I told students I had no clue what I wanted to do with my life when starting college—my choice was based on an outer, socio-cultural logic, not an inner logic—and given the pressure in our society to be "successful," cluelessness was a logical result.

While I spoke—and I spoke with the passion of having lived it—many students would shake their heads up and down in acknowledgement, especially when I used the word "pressure." I began classes in this manner for many reasons, but the main one was because I imagined myself as a seventeen-year-old first-year student sitting in the back row needing to hear someone speak as if they knew what was in my heart.

After my passionate talk, discussion would ensue with students sharing concerns, fears, and stories, as if big questions and feelings, which they often don't know what to do with, were finally let loose and allowed to enter the classroom, creating a reciprocal energy. Some claimed they knew exactly what they wanted in life and defended their desire for money and material comfort. I replied that I was happy for them, and even a bit jealous of their certainty, but added that if they became the authors of their education, rather than passive receivers, the university was a wonderful place to explore diverse fields of knowledge, and, if they were open, new insights might emerge. My teaching strategy was simple: expose students to Emersonian self-reliance, challenging them to "learn to detect and watch that gleam of light which flashes across his own mind from within."

It seemed to work with Jeff. He was attentive and humble the next day in class, treating me with a deference I didn't need, although it was sweet. He soon gave a personal and passionate speech on alcoholism, endearing him to fellow students. At the end of the semester, he filled out his class evaluation by writing three words, all in capitals, with an exclamation point: BEST TEACHER EVER! He also changed his major to psychology.

Let's be clear: I'm hardly the best teacher ever. I've made many mistakes and bored my share of students over the years, but this early teaching experience suggested that lessons learned from pre-college and college struggles with formal education and post-college spiritual searching were of some service. This experience also suggested that helping students to find their voice helped me to more fully express my own, and that I may have found a long sought-after career, or better yet, a calling to teach after years of blue-collar work.

I often worked closely with engineering majors, as Purdue drew students with high SAT scores from all over the US and world. They were a smart bunch, earning high marks in math and quantitative thinking. They especially excelled at taking multiple-choice exams. Many of them, such as Jeff, chose the major for future monetary rewards. I had nothing against engineering students or their desire for money as long as they also had a real interest in the field and in understanding themselves.

Another of my first students, Ken, was especially bright. He was in the engineering program but also interested in literature and philosophy. After my first-day spiel, we struck up a semester-long conversation; he was troubled by the specialized focus of his major, which didn't provide room in his schedule for exploring other fields. His senior year would supply a bit of freedom, but that was still a few years away. Before entering college, he considered a career as an English teacher but decided teachers were too poorly paid. I couldn't argue with him there but suggested an impractical solution: taking an extra year to finish school so that he could explore more of his interests. This idea assumed privilege, as if financial resources were available, but he didn't find my idea appealing because of finances but because his family would view a delay as a failure. If his family was right, he couldn't have found a bigger failure than me.

Ken began to consider a move to the English department, but then I inadvertently cured him of his idealism. I was also working part-time at an independent bookstore that was a hub of social and intellectual activity, and one night he came up to the register with a book and found his teacher working as a minimum-wage clerk. I tried to start a conversation about his purchase, but his response was stilted, as if he couldn't handle the switch in roles. I was suddenly diminished in his eyes, like gourmet chocolate melted on the sidewalk, and he approached me sheepishly the next day in class, stating that he had decided to commit himself to engineering. I laughed to myself while assuring him that he made a fine decision and had a lifetime for reading and learning.

Our bookstore meeting taught Ken that following your ideals has financial consequences; it was a good lesson to learn. For me, the bookstore was a great place to meet people, make extra cash for microbrews and conversation at the pub, and revel in the Christmas-like pleasure of opening boxes of new books on postmodern culture, eco-philosophy and environmental ethics, and Buddhism and other spiritual traditions.

I continued to be Ken's source for discussing philosophy and literature that semester, and he thanked me when it ended. But not all dealings with students had happy endings.

My teaching style was sarcastic and playful. Sarcasm allowed me to have fun while being critical, and playfulness removed the invisible wall that often arises between teachers and students. I played with my authority, taking ideas seriously but not myself, which made students respect and like me. Their reaction, in turn, gave me authority, but now it was a willful act on the students' part and not an act of coercion on my part. However, there were times when I thought I had to demand respect.

Com 114 had a mandatory attendance policy created by the department. One of my best students, Sarah, missed a lot of class and was getting dangerously close to the automatic fail-the-class number of absences. I went out of my way to excuse many of her absences even though her reasons were often no better than she was picking someone up from the airport. But as the semester progressed and absences increased, she took advantage of my kindness.

Sarah was thoughtful and buoyant and sensitive. She did her first speech on the author Sark, who writes creative books on surviving sexual abuse. Sarah courageously told the class that she was a survivor of abuse and that Sark had been a great help in her healing process. I worked to create a comfortable space where students could take risks, and Sarah, like Jeff, had taken a big one, teaching others and empowering herself in the process. I had helped with her speech, so it bothered me when she didn't respect my teaching style. I was supposed to be a good listener and confidante, and in return she was supposed to want to come to class.

I hated having an attendance policy and feared that it would turn the teacher-student relationship into one of warden-prisoner, bound together by the ever-present punishment of a poor grade. I told students that they should come to our required class of their own volition because they never knew when someone might say something that they needed to hear. Or better yet, they never knew when their insights might be what others need to hear. Something was at stake, and it was the quality of their lives. I also decided to trust students. If they successfully lied about absences or late papers, their "win" was really a loss. I hoped to model the world view articulated in class—listen and learn by pursuing the true (scientific investigation, critical rationality), good (contemplation, ethics), and beautiful (aesthetics, spiritual experiences)—and doubting their characters sucked me into a whirlpool of suspicion that didn't reflect what I taught. Still, as her absences grew, I decided to confront Sarah.

When she finally came to class, I asked her to stay afterwards to talk. It was near the end of the semester—a semester of teaching six classes—and students swarmed like pollinating bees, eager to ask questions about an assignment or the final exam, receive information, and then move on to their next class for more of the same. I learned to be direct, beginning with quick questions and then moving to more elaborate needs. When it was finally Sarah's turn, I raised my voice slightly and tersely asked her where she had been, accusing her of treating the class and me poorly.

She might have had a good excuse, but I didn't find out because she shut down when she heard an accusatory tone: face flushed, body cowed. I neglected to consider her years of abuse from male authority figures. I tried to change my tone, but it was too late. That was the last day I saw Sarah.

ॐ

Who were Jeff, Ken, and Sarah before compartmentalized education, outer ideals of success, and abusive parents marked their identities and damaged their ability to simply listen to themselves? How should one teach, given the power of overspecialization, economics, and patriarchy to drown out our calls to deeper intelligence and experience, to finding voice and changing the world?

I don't have certain answers to these questions. I do know that I have dealt with them throughout many years of teaching, especially the tension between making a living and making a life. I also know that during my undergraduate years, I often felt I had nothing of value to offer, and that formal education provided little to assuage this opinion. I further know that the spiritual traditions that explore a deeper intelligence and experience in relation to identity and life path are rarely discussed in school, and when they are, they're treated as knowledge to be tested and forgotten rather than internalized and lived.

Academia can be hostile to the spiritual dimension of life. It can be hostile to the playfulness that comes from identifying with the mysterious source of all things (playfulness because we are unburdened when we discover that we are much more than we thought), and to the purpose that comes from identifying with individual and world soul (purpose because we become responsive to inner voice and the voices of others, including nonhumans, recognizing them as fellow Thous rather than objective Its). The university, at its best, challenges students to form academic voices for critical thought and respect for difference, but too often this academic voice precludes the play and purpose that come from exploring deeper wells where spiritual unity and material diversity know each other intimately. The cliché of "finding our voice" is a dynamic metaphor for the continual challenge of expressing deeper wells, or what we, as whole human beings, are called to do when conscience conflicts with circumstance, including the human collision course with our own ecosystem, or own home.

The hostility toward spirituality, labeling it anti-rational, fundamentalist, or New Age rather than discriminating between foolish and genuine practices, leaves us sadly short in the educational quest to transform ourselves and our world. It's a shortsightedness that dogged and fogged my formal education, and which I have tried to defog for students.

Emerson's "Self-Reliance" acted as a defogging spiritual guide for me, and I re-read his treatise against conformity and the "hobgoblin of little minds" whenever disconsolate concerning my life path. Emerson's voice stimulated my own and reminded me that "virtue and vice emit a breath every moment." But it was Thoreau who became a kindred spirit. I tried inhabiting his spirit during my Purdue years, arriving at a "dress up as your favorite dead radical" party as Thoreau, with a beard and no moustache, well-worn and rustic coat, pants, and shoes, and a copy of *Walden*. I forced Margaret Fuller and Malcolm X to listen to passages.

Emerson called for a revolution of intellect and Spirit, an "original relation to the universe" in America, not following England, not following tradition, not following the crowd. Thoreau would embody those words, but not without confusion and crisis, not without being lost, asking himself, Which way to go?

In Com 114, I often shared Thoreau's desire at Walden Pond to confront the "essential facts of life" and not, when he came to die, discover that he had not lived, as well as Thomas Merton's advice that life path guidance comes from "consulting our death." Thoreau and Merton remind us that we should weigh decisions against ultimate questions and realities. To confront life and consult death is to embrace everything and realize what matters most.

That is all I was trying to convey to Jeff, Ken, and Sarah. My desire was to teach what I had experienced: There is much more to life than we are socialized to think, and when we discover deeper wells, our voices are expressed in our decisions and actions, in a life well lived.

Formal educational struggles made me an unlikely candidate to become a college teacher, and these struggles with school, or rather, "lucrative standard" industrial education, began long before college. A blue-collar background also made me an unlikely candidate; I was the first one in my family to earn a college degree. The only reason I was initially allowed to teach was because I was an adjunct, instructing an introductory course at a cheap cost. But the informal education I received from two mentors prepared me to share the play and purpose of life, as did reading books, especially Thoreau's transcendentalist writings. Practices such as meditation led me to share the value of stillness, at least in better moments, including the awareness that silence provides the ground for thoughtful speech.

The more I taught, the more it seemed that my spiritual searching and discoveries were what made me most useful to students. I knew that crises, including long nights of death contemplation, may be transformed into some semblance of a gift. I understood the despair of arriving at college insecure about the future and ignorant of talents. I believed—not dogmatically, but with passion—that the ultimate question for education is not "Why are you in college?" but "Why are you here on earth?"—a living earth that also has a voice, and we must learn to listen.

After I read the "Warning to Humanity," it was clear that our myriad eco-social crises were the manifestation of a spiritual crisis in which we are collectively and individually lost.

A lostness I knew all too well.

Chapter 2

The Bottom Drops Out

"I have frequently seen people become neurotic when they content themselves with inadequate or wrong answers to the questions of life. They seek position, marriage, reputation, outward success as money, and remain unhappy and neurotic even when they have attained what they are seeking. Such people are usually confined within too narrow a spiritual horizon."
—Carl Jung

"What does education often do? It makes a straight-cut ditch of a free, meandering brook."
—Henry David Thoreau

Like Jeff, I had lots of issues during my undergraduate years, including anger, although I was not sure what I was angry about, other than not fitting in with societal expectations. School, work, love—why were these so important?

In *Young Man Thoreau*, Richard Lebeaux writes that Thoreau needed an "extended adolescence" to address such questions, but this phrase suggests immaturity rather than time to search for something other than what industrialization was offering: materialism, class structure, conformity.

The summer prior to attending Harvard University, Thoreau spent his spare time in the woods. He was already gaining a reputation as "the one who did not fear mud or water." He also floated on Walden Pond on his first handmade boat; he paddled to the middle, lay on the seat, and gazed skyward, allowing rippling waters to take him where they will and finding that "idleness was the most attractive and productive industry." Such sweet, drifting idleness led to contemplation and opened him to spiritual experiences, ecstasies, and to what is possible: living in sympathy with higher laws and the highest learning.

What happens when the rest of life fails to measure up, including the demands of school?

Which way to go?

Lebeaux writes that an 1837 college graduate would be expected to join the "emerging bourgeois capitalist order" and immediately find a job, or they could rebel against that order. Whatever the choice, guilt would likely accompany the decision. Thoreau was confronted with a more basic question: to stay put in his hometown of Concord, Massachusetts, or follow westward "Manifest Destiny" expansion and exploitation. Concord, like most villages, was diversifying but valued convention over autonomy and provided little opportunity to experiment with identity and callings, unless, despite self-doubt, one carved out time and space or stumbled into it. So, he stumbled, with Emerson and other transcendentalists in town providing much needed support, a refuge, as well as a vision of a different world.

Young Thoreau was most certainly in need of growth, of learning beyond formal schooling, but classifying his search or rebellion as immaturity merely secures the status quo. Fast forward: everything has changed, yet not much has changed. The seeds of industry in the early to mid-1800s led to critical questions about work and livelihood, and their dispersion over decades has intensified those questions.

For Thoreau, the core question of why we are on the planet was not seriously addressed, nor was it seriously addressed in my classes. The lucrative standard ruled.

After seven years, three colleges, and four majors—computer science, business, general studies, and communication studies—I was on the verge of receiving my passport to a money-making future: a bachelor of arts degree from Rutgers, a respected, quasi-Ivy League university. It was supposed to be *the* accomplishment out of which the rest of my life spiraled.

It was 1985—MTV and British New Wave were rampant (Flock of Seagulls, Psychedelic Furs, Duran Duran); greed was fervent (recall Gordon Gecko's claim that "greed is good" in *Wall Street*); Ronald Reagan, our B-movie president who took down Jimmy Carter's solar panels, was vacant (before being lionized after death); and I was taking seven spring-semester classes to finally graduate while working thirty hours a week at a hotel.

"Roooom service," I bellowed, over and over, while knocking on doors in brown polyester pants and vest, ruffled white shirt, and shiny bow tie. My job was to play the role of happy employee whose purpose in life was to deliver overpriced food to the daily influx of business clientele. This clientele always seemed happy to see me, probably because they charged their Marriott burgers and imported beers to their expense accounts and spent their evenings with the hotel's selection of soft porn.

My all-time favorite customer was a Swedish businessman who, while not viewing porn, answered the door naked, laughing hysterically. He was watching *Stripes* with Bill Murray and emitting high-pitched giggles—imagine the Swedish Chef Muppet after inhaling helium—the entire time I was in the room. He took my pen to sign the check, pointed toward the TV, threw out some high-pitched giggles, leaned over to sign the check (mooning me in the process), righted himself, pointed toward the TV, threw out more high-pitched giggles, and gave me a wave goodbye in a Promethean display of good cheer and body positivity.

I was also passionately in love with Jennifer, the young woman working in the gift shop at the hotel. I introduced her to New York City: Broadway shows, art exhibits, Tower Records, funky eateries and cafes, thrift shopping at the Antique Boutique, the Strand Bookstore and its "eight miles of books," and lots of independent film. She was five years younger than me, eighteen when we first met, and viewed me as the older brother she never had.

Jennifer stayed over at my small, close-to-campus apartment whenever she wanted, and since I wasn't her brother, she slept in my bed, legs intertwined with mine, breath shared, but no sex. *No sex!* I lost my virginity with my first girlfriend during a summer spent at the Maryland shore working at a boardwalk arcade. I didn't love her—whatever love was, it wasn't that—I wanted sex. When I finally had it, after years of fantasizing, it was freeing but not as special as expected.

Jennifer, though, was special, so I kept telling myself that she was worth waiting for, worth fighting my arousal for during nights intertwined and happy yet sleepless while she slept.

I also started to drink.

One frigid night, thoroughly buzzed, I left the always-packed Melody bar in downtown New Brunswick with Ralf, an endearing free thinker and fellow room-service waiter who introduced me to pricey German Dab beers. I lost one of my gloves after leaving another bar earlier in the night, so with the bare hand I held my car keys in my pants pocket. When I slipped on a patch of ice, my gloveless hand reached high for balance, and my keys flew into the air and landed in a sewer drain. Amazed at the sequence of events, we peered at them through the grate. Lost glove, hand in pocket, ice patch, instinct for balance, keys in drain: what were the odds? I spent the night at Ralf's apartment watching *Valley Girl* on TV and drinking more beers until we passed out. We fetched my keys the next afternoon with a stick.

On another night, I drank cheap frosty mugs of Budweiser at a local working-class tavern with Pat, a history major and room servicer who introduced me to Mrs. Pac Man. I drove home at 3:00 a.m. on an empty, winding road, and a rabbit darted in front of my car. Fearing I hit it, I turned around to check. No rabbit. Pleased, I turned back around and ran over a rabbit. I stopped my car, the carcass lifeless, my buzzed brain incredulous: "What the fuck is up with this world?"

Spring break arrived, and Pat organized a four-day trip to Fort Lauderdale. While I was doing my share of drinking, I wasn't the type for spring break stupidity. Pat did all the arranging—all I had to do was fork over four hundred dollars—and I imagined spending my time lying on the beach, free of cares and at peace.

"Just what I need," I thought.

The arrangements included sharing a hotel room with Pat and two other Rutgers students I hadn't met. This arrangement was fine until I discovered that my roomies invited several friends to sleep for free on our floor. No one cared about this apparently typical spring break practice except me; the room was always active and sleep impossible. That left the beach, except the beach was like my room—filled with people, or lotion lathered people sandwiched on the sand blaring boom boxes, each competing with the next, creating a cacophony of noise.

There were people—students, drunk students—everywhere, the infrastructure of Fort Lauderdale bursting at the seams, the four lane main drag filled with a traffic jam of cars, the air with exhaust.

My many roomies started stacking up their empty beer cans in the window of our room, a kind of pyramid to drinking egos, to manly accomplishment.

The only place to eat was a McDonald's, and the lines stretched out the doors all day long. The crowded sidewalks smelled of sunbaked urine and puke.

There was no peace in my room. No peace on the beach. No peace anywhere, certainly not in my head. Pat and I were friends, but he joined his other buddies on a search for sex, leaving me alone amid the horny, drunken masses. They saw good times; I saw decadence and decay and a replay of high school years, of the parties where I didn't belong.

Hoping to get away, I walked down the sidewalk. Six miles later: a movie theater and what I thought would be a brief respite watching a matinee showing of *Mask*, the based-on-a-true-story drama starring Cher as the mother of a disfigured teenager afflicted with lionitis. I struggled to keep it together through every tear-inducing scene in the near-empty theater, wanting to cry for the teenager, Rocky, who struggled to fit in and suffered ridicule, but also for myself.

A week earlier I had spent a drunken evening staring at myself in the bathroom mirror, wondering who I was, thinking, over and over, "Why are we all here?" and "Why does it matter if I live or die?" while digging at skin with my fingernails, as if trying to find someone, some answer, and then, finding nothing, daring myself to draw blood.

I left the theater and bought a six pack of Budweiser.

"God, this beer is terrible when it's not in a frosty mug," I said to no one.

I began drinking my way, slowly, back to the hotel, thinking of Rocky, who died at the end of the movie after suffering from severe headaches. He had real problems, I thought, feeling pathetic. I threw my last two beers against telephone poles, hoping to see them explode.

When I arrived at the room, I put on a mask, pretending to be fine while my many roomies stacked more empty beer cans in the window, a replacement, I assumed, for their inability to find sex. I watched as each can was placed on the next, desperate for uninterrupted sleep in my paid-for half of a double bed.

On my first night back in my Jersey apartment, I laid on my futon in boxer shorts, feeling the heat. My art student roommate, Joe, collected snakes and lizards, and he kept the thermostat at eighty, fearing his pets would die from cold. The only light came from aquariums—Joe had so many creatures that I let him put a few snakes in my room—and Ry

Cooder's atmospheric score for the film *Paris, Texas,* set in a desert land-scape, played on my stereo. My mind drifted, and I laughed, freely, when a renegade iguana ran across my chest.

"Why did I ever leave," I thought, "when peace was in my room?"

I had another laugh the next day watching *Monty Python* on TV. Dead parrots, the twit Olympics—"Yes, yes, the world is absurd. Why search for any other meaning? Just laugh at the randomness of keys down drains, roadkill rabbits, and the masks we all wear."

Just laugh.

Then the seven classes started again, and thirty hours of room service, and Jennifer.

Jennifer went on a date with another guy and asked the young stud to pick her up at my apartment. I shook his hand and threw in a mock, "Have a nice time, but make sure you drive safe and have her home by midnight." I was somehow OK with it, thought it amusing, because I had a plan. She was supposed to get over the brother thing and realize we were perfect for each other. Devotion would count for something, as if the willingness to forgo sex would win me karmic relationship points. This willingness also had other roots. I continued to spend time looking at myself in the mirror, wondering who I was, feeling detached from my body.

Perhaps detaching from sex led me to detach from my body? Perhaps I was more than my body? Perhaps I was screwed up? The latter seemed most likely. But if I was "something more," what was it? Consciousness?

I knew one thing for sure: my self-consciousness was Promethean, and I turned forgoing sex into an act of will, a monkish mind over bodily desire, telling myself that I was better than mere mortals who could not control sexual appetite. But when Jennifer got serious with one of the dates, and I found out she was having sex with him, my body shook and shuttered, as I lay, alone, on my bed. No tears. That I fought to control. The rest of my body had a mind of its own.

I hung on for a couple weeks, but finally, in a bluster of bravado—showing no emotion—I told Jennifer that I never wanted to see her again, even though, lost in first-love fever, the opposite was the truth. I knew she loved me, in her way, and figured refusing to see her would make her shoulder some of the hurt. And it hurt. I replayed, over and over, a ques-tion she once asked me, a question that made me wonder if she could be swayed to my reality, my fantasy: "If we got together, you would never leave me, would you?"

The combination of an insanely busy school schedule, inane employment, a spring break that wasn't a break, sexual and identity questioning, and unrequited love took me to the edge, but it was the prospect of graduation that spiraled me downward. Most communication graduates from Rutgers sought advertising and public relations jobs in nearby New York City. I assumed I would do the same, but as the end of the semester approached, thoughts of working in the city twisted me inward.

I decided to take a practice commute.

I had taken the hour-long train trip from New Brunswick to Penn Station in midtown Manhattan numerous times but never with the early morning work crowd. I arrived at the station on a mild, early May morning with the requisite look: to-go coffee in right hand, *New York Times* folded and wedged into left armpit, and my version of a business suit, a black jacket bought for five dollars at a Catholic mission, hundred-dollar black shoes bought from a trendy Greenwich village store, black "WilliWear" slacks, white button-down shirt, and skinny black tie with a touch of silver glitter (it was the mid-eighties, don't forget).

The 7:15 express arrived on schedule, and I found a window seat next to a seasoned commuter, his pedigree obvious because he completely ignored me. I, on the other hand, was checking everyone out. And "everyone" was like my seatmate: butt cheeks securely planted on the drab yellow and orange vinyl bench seats, coffee and headlines guiding a slow ascent into the day.

New Jersey's nickname is "The Garden State," and this moniker is not just false advertising, thanks to the Pine Barrens, ocean beaches, and manicured lawns; but large swaths of the northern landscape along the turnpike support Jersey's reputation for unrepentant industrialization. The mechanical torsos of oil refineries dominate the land and spew dark smoke into the air. When the conductor squeaked out "Elizabeth" over the static-filled intercom, the smell of burnt oil had already announced the stop. Like all Jerseyans, my friends and I spoke geographically in terms of exits on the Turnpike and referred to the putrid scent of Elizabeth as "eau de exit thirteen."

The train arrived at Penn Station, and I began navigating the chaotic mass of bodies and making my way up the escalator to the street. The assault was immediate—people everywhere, angular buildings reaching toward the sky, a man begging for change and smelling of liquor and piss.

A memory triggered from when I was ten years old. My parents took me to the Broadway musical *Jesus Christ Superstar*, and while looking out the car window, I saw a dirty and disheveled man sprawled on the concrete slabs of the sidewalk. I don't recall saying something. I hardly remember anything from that day other than Pontius Pilate's outrageously high platform shoes, the colorful antipasto platter at Mama Leone's, and the image of passersby dodging that man lying on the side of the street. My ten-year-old self didn't understand how, in Jesus's name, that could happen, but now I was doing the dodging.

I soon became part of a phalanx of workers heading east toward Madison Avenue, bobbing and weaving through the crowd, pretending to be late for an early morning meeting. At one point, I got stuck behind a wall of suits, and another image flashed, this time from *Koyaanisqatsi*, a film I had recently viewed at the Rutgers Student Center. *Koyaanisqatsi*—a Hopi Indian word meaning "life out of balance"—is a montage of fast- and slow-motion images juxtaposing shots of nature, industrialization, and urban life, set to the pulsating rhythmic drone of the modernist composer Philip Glass.

Life out of balance: atmospheric CO_2 was at 346.12 parts per million (ppm), getting closer to 350 ppm, the threshold that climatologists argue we dare not cross if we hope to have a habitable planet, a planet to which life adapted and spawned civilization.

Who knew, other than a smattering of scientists and policy makers who were unable to influence policy?

The Hopi prophesized that people and planet were not in sync, and thus we were profoundly and disturbingly and tragically lost, a disconnection the film illustrated with fast-motion shots of comfortably numb people mindlessly scurrying along the streets of the city like tiny worker ants. In one segment, the image of mobs of commuters scrambling up an escalator was paired with gobs of Oscar Meyer hot dogs shooting along a mechanized assembly line.

I scurried and scrambled to the office building of Ogilvy & Mather, one of the largest ad agencies in the world, but couldn't bring myself to go in the door. I just kept walking back and forth along the huge city block, looking at the other hot dog people, getting in their way. Until this point, I had been having fun with my practice commute, but the imposing physical structure of the building induced an instinct for protection, and my body once again had its way: heavy breathing, light-headedness, speeding pulse rate. I stopped walking, unable to move for five minutes.

There was no way I was going to get a job in the city. I stayed in New York for lunch, but no longer. I didn't want to deal with the evening rush hour.

The next morning, a radiant sun-filled Saturday, I walked in a nearby park hoping for a few moments of sweet, drifting idleness, but then I questioned whether I would take final exams and write final papers demanded by my classes. Lilac trees dotted the landscape, the tiny, fragrant flowers creating a visionary field of lavender. Their scent, strong and diffuse, weakened meager defenses, and I dropped to my knees, taking long, labored breaths, and then fell flat, crying, finally, violently, my face wedged into the turf.

I couldn't believe I was on the verge of fucking up. The thought of ending the semester with seven Fs was intolerable, but, with one more week of schoolwork left, earning a diploma meant nothing. I had tied the value of a degree with a career, and now that the latter was in doubt, I just didn't care.

As the youngest son of a factory worker and secretary, I had internalized the lucrative standard and expected my college education to lead to financial freedom. This expectation was an amorphous part of growing up blue collar, asserting a subtle, but continual, pressure. There was no mention of the value of a liberal arts education or mention of the "liberal arts"— I never heard the words. My parents labored to pay for my education; it was time for me to prove they had made a wise investment.

I did love some of my classes, or rather, liberal arts classes that I finally could fit in my schedule during my senior year. In an art, music, and literature class, we listened to Beethoven's triumphant *Eroica Symphony*, originally dedicated to Napoleon until Beethoven decided that the general had betrayed the heroic archetype. In my French film class, we viewed Jean Renoir's *The Rules of the Game*, which portrays the inequities and absurdities of corrupt society. In a class called "Theory of Narrative," we read Jose

Luis Borges's "The Garden of Forking Paths," exploring themes of destiny, life path, and coincidence. In theater appreciation and for reasons I do not recall, the professor discussed Carl Jung's idea of the collective unconscious, and I felt a connection when he uttered those words.

The quest for high grades and a cushy career was a race. I had circled the track only to approach the finish and find that I had spent seven years chasing an unwanted goal.

I continued crying on the ground, thinking how nice it would be to wander for a while, reading and pondering with no specific goal in mind. This desire pulsed through my veins, gathering blood and transporting it to the surface of my skin. My head became light, conjuring up yet another memory.

Earlier in the semester, I was walking amid the large trees and ivy-covered, red brick buildings of the Rutgers campus, which often seemed alive with the palpable presence of learning, when a bubbly recruiter for the financial planning industry greeted me and launched into her sales pitch, stating her company was looking for ambitious individuals to train. Without missing a beat, I looked into her eyes and replied that I was sorry, but I had absolutely no ambition. The image of her startled, horrified look, as if I had sucked out her life force with a toothy kiss, came back in vivid detail. I laughed as violently as I had been crying, the sweet scent of lilacs filling the air, my face still burrowed in the earth.

I felt no sense of accomplishment when I managed to complete final work to earn my degree, only a momentary sense of relief.

Chapter 3

When the Student Is Ready

"The misery of man is to be baulked of the sight of essence and to be stuffed with conjectures...the fairest that can befall man is to be guided by his daemon to what is truly his own."
—Ralph Waldo Emerson

"As for conforming outwardly, and living your own life inwardly,—I do not think much of that....It will prove a failure. Just as successfully can you walk against a sharp steel edge which divides you cleanly right and left. Do you wish to try your ability to resist distension? It is a greater strain than any soul can long endure."
—Henry David Thoreau

"I wake up every morning wondering why I am alive."

I was sitting on the floor of my reptile-filled apartment with Preston, a fellow Rutgers graduate, four months after my practice commute on a late September evening in 1985. Preston was not a drinking buddy; he was my intellectual buddy and one of the few friends whom I could tell anything. We spent most nights at a local diner sipping coffee, talking about ideas and what stirred our souls, and labeling ourselves the "diner guys," yet he recoiled at my emotionless words.

"I think I know someone who can help you," he replied after some thought. "The poet I have been working with on the poetry index, Rafael Catala—he's a professor at Lafayette College but also a spiritual teacher. Do you want me to call him?"

"I don't know. What's he like?"

"You should meet him. He also writes what he calls sciencepoetry. I think you would like him. I'm surprised I haven't suggested you meet before."

Now I was thinking. I wasn't the type to seek help from a "spiritual teacher," but Preston knew me as well as anyone and seemed sure it was a good idea.

"Okay, call him," I said, not expecting to leave the apartment.

Within minutes we were walking on streets near campus, past tightly packed row houses and across a two-lane main drag with pizzerias and taverns to his blue-gray condo.

Rafael, a smallish man with a kind face, dark hair, and aristocratic nose, greeted Preston with a hug, leading him to give me one as well: my first surprise of the evening.

Preston and Rafael began to chat while I scanned the books that covered every inch of his living room walls and spotted a shelf filled with titles by the 20th century Indian spiritual teacher J. Krishnamurti. I had discovered Krishnamurti's *Think on These Things* at a used bookstore a week earlier and thought he was an obscure, little read, Eastern sage. I was unaware that he authored so many books.

"Who the hell is this Rafael?" I wondered.

At first opportunity I pointed towards the shelf. "I see you have a lot of books by Krishnamurti. What do you think of his writings?"

Rafael smiled as if I had just pitched an easy one into his spiritual wheelhouse.

"Have you read Krishnamurti?"

"I just picked up a copy of *Think on These Things*. I haven't read very much, but I like his criticisms of religion and education."

"Krishnamurti criticizes religion and education because they are stuck in a world of separation, while he perceives unity. You see, we are like waves that are inseparable from the ocean. Each one of us is unique, yet the waves are one with the whole ocean, and the ocean is fully present in every wave."

These ideas sounded appealing, but I was distrustful, fearing he was lost in sixties nostalgia or a New Age guru—Shirley MacLaine's reincarnation book *Dancing in the Light* was popular at the time.

"I've read similar things in other books, but ideas of unity are just ideas," I countered matter-of-factly, as if my truth deserved equal merit. "You're sitting over there, and I am sitting over here—we are separate. That's reality too. That's my reality. I just graduated, and I'm working at a factory, which I hate, and spend my days feeling separate, not like an ocean wave."

Rafael continued speaking, this time about God, and I was immediately turned off, the word having nothing to do with the awareness we were discussing. To me, God was a geezer on a cloud that fools unquestioningly worshipped, or a supposed meddler in human affairs, like when professional boxers look skyward after having just finished pummeling their opponent, praising God for their victory.

"Why do you have to use the word *God?*" I asked, my countenance shifting from interest to disgust.

Rafael smiled again, as if he had these conversations before.

"God is not separate from you or anything. God is omnipresent, within every earthly expression, and when this is experienced we realize that we are God made manifest."

"But that's not what people mean when they use the word," I protested.

Rafael pointed to a single stalk of wheat sticking out of a vase.

"Call it 'wheat' then, and this wheat is the intelligence of the universe manifested as the homeostasis of the planet, as the birds and trees, as you and me and all things."

Rafael's comment took me aback, causing me to question my negative fixation on "G-o-d." It was, after all, only a word.

"If you don't like the word," Rafael continued, "you can read Krishnamurti or Whitman or Emerson—writers who don't reference God much but lead to the same place, a place of peace where you don't feel separate, a place of oneness, a place that is your birthright."

We talked into the night.

When Preston and I left, I was too wound up, so we strolled to the Rutgers campus, circling a tree-lined oval that passed ivy-covered brick buildings and the spot where I told the financial planning recruiter that I lacked ambition. On nights that we didn't go to the diner, we often went to this pathway to take "academic laps," walking, talking, thinking.

We had never walked this late, and I had never been so stirred, mostly because I had never thought of the concept of God as anything other than a concept or made-up fantasy. We walked round and round until rays of red sunlight peeked in the distance. I got home just in time to change into work clothes.

Preston and I started going to Rafael's condo once a week for talks and meditation. On one occasion, Rafael surprised us by getting out a tape recorder. He was working with students in New Mexico but could not be there as often as they wished. Tapes of his disembodied voice, apparently, were the next best thing to his physical presence.

"You must fuk-us," Rafael seemed to exhort in his Cuban accent, the tape recorder spinning to preserve nuggets of wisdom.

Preston and I nodded in agreement, trying not to laugh as we sat on the couch opposite him, a portrait of a Latin American scholar on the wall above his head.

He sensed something was up, so he repeated himself.

"You must fuk-us in the mystical life."

This time we lost it.

"What?" he queried.

"You're saying *fuk-us* instead of *focus*," Preston said.

"Oh my God, stop the tape," he roared.

I hit the stop button, happy we had it recorded.

Rafael talked through his laughter. "I once told someone about a former student who studied hard and went to Yale, but he thought I said jail."

We were silly now.

"What if I don't want to *fuk-us*? Or study and go to *jail*? Can I still follow the mystical path?" I said.

"No, no, you don't have to *fuk-us* or go to *jail*, you don't need to do anything other than love."

Rafael didn't tape after that. The incident was funny but also strange: taping yourself seemed a bit much, a bit too egotistical. His face, though, often displayed a radiance associated with mystics, with an expansive sense of self, although this time rather than some transcendental understanding being the catalyst, it was simply the willingness to laugh at yourself and feel unabashed joy.

Preston soon stopped coming to our meetings. He was more philosophically inclined, finding solace in the life of the mind, but I was intrigued by the life of Spirit. Something about Rafael affected me: his confidence and lightheartedness, for sure, but something else too. It was as if I had walked into a Herman Hesse novel, with me, the young protagonist, living the spiritual cliché "When the student is ready, the teacher will appear."

I accepted Rafael's offer to meet twice a week to study mysticism. I wanted to understand how he could be mystically minded *and* a critically minded academic. Like most brooding undergraduates, I was influenced by existential philosophy, which, according to Sartre, states that existence precedes essence, so we are responsible for creating ourselves without the comfort of religious assertions of predetermined souls or birthrights. But while I was suspicious of comfort, a part of me desired something more than existential courage or Monty Python absurdity in the face of a meaningless universe.

ಬ

There are differing stories about how and when Emerson first met Thoreau. We know that Thoreau read Emerson's influential first book, *Nature*, after borrowing it from the Harvard library twice, and that Emerson gave a commencement address during Thoreau's graduation, although Thoreau, not a fan of crowds and pomp, did not attend. We know that Emerson's sister-in-law spent time boarding at the Thoreau home, and she brought Emerson some of his poetry. We know that he was open to mentoring promising young men because the promise of America would not be fulfilled if not "dictated by high sentiments of human nature."

Reading *Nature* was a balm to young Henry because it explored nature's "service to the soul," as well as its many uses as commodity, which are "temporary and mediate" by comparison. Emerson's nature delivered the goods yet inspired the high sentiments of the good and beautiful.

Early 1600s European colonizers, however, found a new-to-them natural world of useful abundance in New England and didn't understand why the Native people seemed to live in poverty. Already bound by the lucrative standard, settlers saw "merchantable commodities" everywhere, with landscapes broken down into separate, commercial units. Timber from oak, hickories, chestnut, and pine; wild meat such as bear, moose, deer, and turkey; fish of all types, cod, bass, alewives; and endless birds, including flocks of doves and pigeons that could block out the sun. And so many berries. Little did summer settlers know that after gorging on giant wild strawberries, they would find the fall and winter to be fallow and that the "poverty" of Natives allowed them to survive by moving to the food. Settlers, after much die-off, eventually settled by imposing agriculture on the land.

Natives in the South did some planting, including intertwined corn and bean mounds and other permaculture-type arrangements that looked messy but preserved soil and provided protein. They also set intentional fires, which removed brush, making the forest more park-like and easier for hunting. Whether known to Natives or not, the fires had the added benefit of enriching soil and propagating plant growth, which attracted animals and further aided hunting. Up north, colder climates and less fertile soil led tribes to remain hunter-gatherers, but the Native way of living, using the land in multiple ways but never reducing it to commodity, was increasingly overrun.

The pre-colonial New England ecosystem, like all dynamic ecosystems, had been in flux, including because of changing climate. What was glacial tundra 12,500 years ago had become forests of various species with fire, wind, and disease altering its composition. While Natives altered the ecosystem, becoming a part of this history of flux and change for thousands of years, they were intimate with the land, understanding ecological processes that the colonists did not, or refused to understand, as they were bent on imposing their Manifest Destiny.

Emerson criticized this use of nature, which "all men apprehend," without also perceiving interdependency, beauty, and Spirit, themes that Thoreau would explore in his writings and life. Emerson and Thoreau were impressed by industry but also perceived devastating downsides. Two hundred years after the first colonists, Thoreau would catalogue the loss of species and changes to the land, including hard-to-find wild currants and large strawberries, which were tamed by cultivation. He would write of a fallen world, a lost world increasingly dominated by manufacturing while his compatriots saw progress and immeasurable gains.

After missing the Harvard address, Thoreau received tickets from Emerson to attend his "Human Culture" lecture series in Boston. He walked nineteen miles to hear Emerson question how citizens could be "blind to a beauty that is beaming on every side of them," why we don't love both poetry and mathematics, and why we don't turn to wild nature, rather than trimmed gardens, to awaken sense and sensibility.

Thoreau, prepared by his college education but also by experience and struggle, found a kindred spirit. When Emerson heard that Thoreau walked all the way to Boston to hear him speak, he soon invited his Concord neighbor to his home. This much is clear: Thoreau was ready to meet Emerson, perhaps because he was guided by his daemon to what was truly his own.

The same may be said for my meeting Rafael; however, he did not know what he was getting himself into.

ဆ

After receiving my degree, I combined room-service earnings with graduation money and went to Europe with my snake-charmed roommate for two months of summer travel. Traveling by Eurail passes and staying at hostels, we visited the Van Gogh museum and ogled red-light district prostitutes in Amsterdam; had our vision expanded by magnificent fjords in Norway; received directions from an older gentleman in Munich, who sardonically remarked that I spoke English quite well for an American; watched children play soccer with a tattered, makeshift ball on a street outside the Coliseum in Rome; did our best to relax on the fleshy beaches of the Cote D'Azur; and had my hand slapped by a wrinkled French woman when I squeezed an apple she was selling. The diversity of each day diffused the frustration of my final semester and released energy for creative pursuits: I took photos of landscapes and people and experienced both detachment and participation in the nuances, colors, curves, and angles of moments unfolding into the next.

Halfway through the trip, I found a copy of Robert Pirsig's *Zen and the Art of Motorcycle Maintenance* left behind on a train. I read it slowly, stopping to reflect on Pirsig's claim that we need to cultivate the peace of mind that does not separate self from environment, including, in his case, a motorcycle. Ruminating, I realized that traveling and taking photos were Zen practices of sorts: I was detaching from old thoughts of a troubled self and finding some peace by embracing a new life of adventure in new countries with new people.

Why couldn't I be this "self" all the time, beholden to high sentiments?

The book was a gift that seemed meant for me, or at least I interpreted it that way. I gazed out a train window at the rolling landscape and gave thanks to the unknown soul who left it behind.

I returned home in late August alert and alive, as well as penniless and clueless as to how I was going to make a living. My dad called to tell me they were looking for temporary help at Proctor and Gamble, his employer on Staten Island, N.Y—"Crisco department, $15 an hour." "Nothin' to sneeze at," he said. I had worked there before in the detergents department where I drove a forklift, unloading trucks filled with empty cartons for Tide, Cheer, Oxydol, and Spic and Span, and then delivering them to the appropriate assembly lines, discovering that most detergents come from the same factory and corporation, while commercials claimed there was a significant difference among products.

The illusion of choice, I thought. Or worse, the illusion of freedom.

I also drove into a window, crashed into the Comet conveyor line, and nearly flattened the head manager. The job was a kick in the ass—I either finished college and found a tolerable profession, or I worked in a factory. It was hard, repetitive work but also a respectable means for making a living, especially if you have a family to feed like my dad. After three months of forklift follies, I swore I'd never work there again.

I choked hard and told Dad I could be ready by six in the morning.

We soon made the first of many trips from Jersey to Staten Island, the hour-long drive providing ample time to ponder the ironic fact that I was commuting to New York after all—not to the big city, but to my place of birth and Manhattan's favorite trash dump.

We drove past the Great Kills dump, which stretched for miles along the highway. Bulldozers graded mountains of refuse while seagulls picked through rotting fruit and vegetables, disposable diapers, and last week's chicken. The odor, which no car window could withstand, woke me from my groggy, early morning haze. It also signaled that we were twenty minutes from work, assuming we left early enough to avoid the daily traffic jam. We arrived and split up at the plant parking lot. My dad headed for the food warehouse where he was a general warehouseman, meaning "you name it, he did it," and I walked apprehensively down the sidewalk toward Crisco. Silos dominated the landscape, emitting nonstop puffs of white that drifted softly into the sky as if they were manufacturing clouds.

Few illusions remain once you're on the Crisco Oil gallons assembly line. Take plastic bottles out of cardboard carton, lean over, place 'em on the conveyor belt—making sure they're in proper alignment—and then send the empty carton along another conveyor belt to the end of the line. Then do it again. Do it again. Proper alignment. Keep it running. Or on the third floor. Lids. The plastic lids that crown the top of Crisco shortening are placed on a revolving carousel that periodically turns and dumps a row onto a pair of spinning rods, which then shoots them, one at a time, down to the second floor where they are combined with a can into a finished product. That's the job. Place plastic lids on the carousel, except when you're at the other end of the floor loading up metal lids, the kind you take off with a can opener.

The most relevant description of my new job was "temporary" although factory work had its benefits. I got paid and once again experienced why my dad came home from work so tired, needing a nap before dinner. On one of our return commutes, he asked about my day. I revved up a whiny voice, contorted my face, and told him that I had to mop the bathroom and clean toilets and urinals. "So what?" he replied, looking me straight in the eyes. "That's just another day for me."

Commuting with Dad was an education, but despite lessons, the assembly line was eating away at the energy experienced in Europe, a Europe that had embraced urban ecology expressed as brick-laid city streets for walking without cars and trains connecting everything. But also a Europe that had denuded its landscapes centuries before America, losing its wild places, thanks to a factory system that had crossed the pond and within which I somehow found myself. During a fifteen-minute mid-morning coffee break I sat under one of the few trees on the plant property reading an article in the *New York Times* about ozone holes and the clear-cutting of forests. I dropped the paper in disgust, providing a clear view of pollution spewing from my building and my participation in what felt like a cycle of death and self-destruction.

I was also angry about the structured schooling I had endured—college had mostly consisted of memorize-the-book, spit-it-back-out on the multiple-choice exam grading—as well as what I learned in some of my better classes: we are habituated to an over-consumptive, hyper-individualized, environment-destroying, techno-industrial-capitalist society.

In my Language and Behavior final semester course we read Herbert

Marcuse's *One-Dimensional Man*, in which he made Marxist-Freudian arguments that techno-industrial inhabitants are characterized by "repressive desublimation," or the failure to creatively express individual and collective energies because we are ground down by the dominance of the machine over a more organic life. This idea, which Thoreau was already lamenting in the mid-1800s, was depressing enough, but Marcuse further argued that the commodification of everything contains social change. Dissenting discourse from those awake to an inner life is often undermined by the assimilating discourse of consumerism. For example, it's hard to resist the "machine" when The Beatles' "Revolution" is used to sell Nike sweatshop-labor sneakers. For Marcuse, the language of transformation is co-opted, leading us to enact a "happy consciousness" that attempts to buy its way to joy while repressing instinctual, sensuous, and relational needs that bring true happiness.

Reading Marcuse contributed to my soon-to-enter the work world angst, and things got worse when I did enter even if it was temporary. I was doing deadening work at a polluting factory for a mega-corporation known for animal abuse in product testing, spending days noticing how ugly everything looked while wondering why I was alive. The uses, and abuses, of nature were all too clear, and the vibrant, palpable presence of life experienced while traveling increasingly gone, along with the good and beautiful. Add neuroses—introversion that slid into alienation—and Rafael realized that he needed to do some counseling, with me overcoming a resistance to help that my blue collar background deemed a sign of weakness, before we could study mysticism and practice meditation.

 number of

Rafael began by asking about my childhood and found the lever he was looking for when I recalled an experience in third grade. One morning, the individual voices of noisy classmates merged, grew, and echoed in my ears and overtook my thoughts. The waves of sound traveled outward, enveloping the room, and "I" rode the sound until feeling outside myself and completely outside my thoughts. I slipped into a dreamlike state, witnessing classmates, the room, and myself from a perspective that felt more real than anything experienced before. While I perceived distinctions, there was no separation between others and myself because there was no filter of words and thoughts creating separation. If the experience had been a test question, I would have marked it "true."

This memory unearthed another, this time from second grade when I played outside. The sun shined radiantly on everyone and everything, and I zoned out, once again floating among the noise of children. "I" was gone, for I don't know how long. When "I" returned, my teacher told me that she had been calling my name, but I did not respond.

Both experiences were peaceful while they were happening but not when they were over. I knew something major had occurred: things were not as they seemed, not as I'd been taught, not as we all pretend.

Rafael was enthused by these responses, asking if I had other experiences beyond words and thoughts in childhood. I recalled time in nature, especially the Adirondacks of Upstate New York where my family vacationed at a cabin camp for the first fifteen years of my life, which provided a counter-balance to the busyness of Staten Island and New Jersey, including the busyness of thought and incessant doing rather than just being.

The camp seemed to have everything: a lake nestled within pine trees and mountains, a dock filled with old wooden rowboats, horseback riding just down the street, and a slew of games—tennis, ping pong, shuffle board, horseshoes. But it was more than games that made this place so alluring. The deep, soft piles of randomly placed brown pine needles were a stunning contrast to the meticulously manicured lawns of suburban New Jersey. The water was clean, the first clean body of water I had ever seen, and it was safe to swim in, as well as fish for bass, perch, and bluegills. And the air was a fragrant, intoxicating presence, which led to the amazing early-age discovery that all air was not the same.

Earth, water, air, and fire.

At night, everyone staying at the cabin camp—including friends we knew from vacationing during the same weeks every year—gathered by a pavilion near the lake. We brought up chairs from the beach and sat around an outdoor fireplace, the kids roasting marshmallows while the adults drank Utica Club, a cheap beer from a regional brewery in Utica, New York. The cabin camp was a wondrous world to childhood eyes, but its function for our parents is difficult to measure. They left their jobs behind: carpenters, phone company installers, firemen, secretaries, factory workers, all looking for two weeks of freedom and peace. And sure enough, as the nights gently progressed, cragged, tired faces would begin to shine along with the fire's glow.

I also recalled playing sports. I was a natural on the playground as a kid, in basketball, football, baseball, or anything that required agility. Play was spontaneous and effortless—no thoughts emerged to block the flow of movement when I ran for a touchdown or snagged a grounder. I seemed to have an innate detachment from my body: imagining the particular move allowed me to use my body as an instrument.

When I began organized sports, my imagination was disrupted and rhythm compromised. I still knew the feeling—what athletes call "the zone"—but it came less often due to too much coaching advice, or too much teaching and thinking, as well as increased pressure and sudden self-doubt. The worst thing that ever happened to my athletic abilities was the praise from coaches that what I was doing was not natural but extraordinary. I knew the zone so well from the playground that I got frustrated when it was absent, and frustration merely assured that it would stay absent. I dealt with this paradox continually in organized sports. My biggest battles occurred in high school and college tennis, and they took place within my head.

In high school, I was talented enough to play the top spot, and I would sometimes win tight, high-pressure matches. This talent would also disappear, like the time I lost a three-set match against a top rated-player. He was from a wealthy town—their entire team had the luxury of expensive lessons and indoor court-time in the winter—and it was an away match held at a private club. His privilege amused me, and I was supposed to lose, so I relaxed and easily won the first set. But then the score got announced, leading a crowd to gather near the court. Instead of embracing the attention, I began thinking that I wasn't supposed to beat him—and then how badly I wanted to beat him. Lightness transfigured into thinking, thinking, thinking; normally free-flowing movements became stiff as quick-drying cement. After I lost, my teammates congratulated me as if I had won since I gave the rich kid a tough match, but I knew that was bullshit.

By the time I was playing for my first college, Montclair State, a counselor was needed, or someone to help me understand the paradox of thought: the more I wanted to win, the less it happened. Instead of having a consistent mental approach, my process varied depending on who I was playing. I still found the zone against top players I wasn't expected to beat, letting it fly free and lose the entire match since it was okay if I lost. I won some and lost some, but the match was great every time, like a dance of competitive cooperation. My sense of using my body as an instrument would merge with the image of the shot—the angle serve, the flick topspin forehand, the point-ending overhead slam—and it felt like I was being who I am, who I was meant to be.

The opposite would happen when playing poor players. I'd struggle with the expectation of winning, and instead of a natural detachment supported by positive image, I found myself detached and drowning in thoughts: *Who is my opponent? Why is winning important? What is it all about?* I'd swirl in a downward spiral, missing shots, screaming at myself for missing shots, slamming my racket on the court, losing points, games, matches. My coach wanted to know what the hell was happening. Did I lack killer instinct, competitive fire, and drive? That is what I was told. But that criticism paled in comparison with the moments when the paradox dissolved into silent, harmonious action.

I was searching for something, in fits and starts, without being fully aware of what it was. I knew that a strong ego could take one far; I witnessed it in better opponents all the time, like the rich, club kid. But my insecure blue-collar self often thought them jerks, confident jerks full of themselves. Perhaps I knew intuitively that peak moments and naturalness were the opposite of egotism, and so I couldn't bring myself to fully participate in that self-delusion. Or rather, I tried but it was always an uncomfortable fit because it didn't untangle the paradox.

Rafael listened to my stories, nodding as if I were discovering clues to a larger life. Childhood revelations had lain dormant during my teenage years and early twenties, but now, with Rafael's help, I was exploring their potential as life-altering experiences.

Could it be that spiritual revelations had long been part of my sensibility, even though I couldn't make sense of them? Did the silent, peaceful reality discovered at an early age operate unconsciously, contributing to later dissatisfaction and despair? Had I been searching to understand the mystery of second and third grade with no language, no instruction—certainly none from school—no way of figuring it out until now, until I somehow found my way to Rafael?

Questions led to questions.

Was I confused about what really mattered, about the purpose of life, and then played this confusion out by struggling with school and on the tennis court? Why did I fear both career failure and success? Why was I overcome with physical symptoms—a speeding heart rate and shortness of breath—when I stood on the sidewalk outside of Ogilvy & Mather? Why did I end up crying, face down in the turf amid the scent of lilacs? Why was the assembly line grinding down, day after day, the aliveness experienced in Europe? Why did grades always seem false, as artificial as a can of Cheese Whiz?

I wondered if the answers might include the fact that my experiences of these material realities failed to mirror the spiritual reality of unity-in-diversity discovered at early ages, a reality that suggests that there is deeper meaning to life.

Both Emerson and Thoreau wrote of "double consciousness," of ecstatic, mystical moments inspiring devotion to higher laws such as unity-in-diversity and more frequent mundanity when we are not quite feeling it. Or, as Emerson put it, "our faith comes in moments, our vice is habitual." We may be God made manifest, expressing "likeness to God" and inner light, but, too often, we are "a God in ruins." Emerson supplied a way out, a daily spiritual practice to keep the "sweetness of solitude" amidst the crowd: turn within, listen, and act on what emerges. Thoreau wrote that "moments of inspiration are not lost though we have no particular poem to show for them; for those experiences have left an indelible impression, and we are ever and anon reminded of them."

Thoreau also wrote that he would not exchange "an expansion of all my being for all the learning in the world," and he had a talent for such expansion from an early age, aided by the stars and expansive night sky of the nineteenth century. Subsequent twentieth- and twenty-first century students experience instead a sky marred by light pollution, leading to a loss of correspondence between humans and cosmos.

Rafael supported my moments of expansion and inspiration by referencing William James's *The Varieties of Religious Experience*, while adding that religious experiences are significant because they feel significant to those that have them. They're potentially transformative, enhancing our psychological development towards increased connection, love, and compassion. He also emphasized that while religious experiences can be denied, ignored, and poorly interpreted, they are not figments of our imagination. Rather, they enlarge our rational life, opening us to mystery and not-knowing as well as a deeper knowing of who we are and what we can know.

Rafael further argued that such experiences mean little unless we bring them to awareness and strengthen our insights with study and practice.

℀

Rafael suggested we begin our studies by reading the work of Joel Goldsmith, a Christian mystic who traveled the world in the 1950s and 1960s teaching a spiritual practice called "The Infinite Way." "The Infinite Way" sounded like a cult, but I withheld judgment until we began reading. We began and it still sounded like a cult. There was too much world denial, and, for me, too much oft-putting Christian language. Rafael explained that "The Infinite Way" had no organization, no outreach, no rules, but was passed on to anyone who expressed interest—Goldsmith insisted that it remain nondogmatic and transmitted by word of mouth. He further explained that Goldsmith's work was useful because it provided spiritual principles in a clear, step-by-step fashion and that contemplating our deeper identity, which he called the "infinite invisible individualized," led to inner fulfillment expressed outwardly as genuine service. Fulfillment leading to service was compelling since alienation was not my natural state of mind, and the phrase "infinite invisible individualized" reflected what I had experienced in second and third grade—that reality was spiritually unified and materially diverse at the same time.

Rafael and I also discussed Jungian psychology, especially synchronicity, shadow, and the individuation process; quantum physics, a hot topic at the time due to Fritjof Capra's *The Turning Point*; James Lovelock's Gaia hypothesis (now theory); and Rafael's own "sciencepoems," which integrated scientific principles and language with poetic-spiritual process. A larger vision of knowledge and self was the focus of our time together, and he began and ended each meeting with a guided meditation, inviting me to watch my thoughts without judgment. This practice initially led to more judging and thinking—"I need to stop thinking about not thinking"—but later to moments of silence that dissolved, at least temporarily, worries and anxieties.

Our meetings lasted four to five hours. I walked home around midnight past the pizzerias, taverns, and row houses, once again alert and alive like when traveling in Europe. I would glance toward the night sky, and the town suddenly felt small, as if within one of those Christmas-time snow globes. A new reality was emerging, yet it felt unreal because it was so new. Everything was beautiful for the simple fact that it existed.

Rafael became my counselor, teacher, and eventually, friend. He demanded nothing in return, neither money nor obedience, only a commitment to study that matched his own.

When we first began working together, my doubts concerning mysticism prevented our conversations from progressing. Rafael suggested that we make friends with our doubts since they are constant companions. This amused me but also made me more receptive because it signaled that he also lived with doubts. So, I listened to my doubts without letting them rule me, especially when we discussed knowledge of some type of transcendent reality. It helped considerably when Rafael argued that "God" was omnipresent and thus an awareness and attitude rather than a separate entity. When we reside within the presence of this mystery, we are freed from constantly striving. We become sensitive to everything, separate from nothing.

Embracing religious experience led me to understand that a transcendent dimension, while known most fully via experiences of unity, is an intrinsic part of our contemplative life. We evoke the transcendent as soon as we explore our cosmic origin, or why something exists rather than nothing, or why we are here on earth.

I also discovered that silence and stillness are called forth by an identification with Mystery, or God made manifest, or the infinite invisible individualized, or Spirit unfolding, or whatever words we choose to name what cannot be named—Emptiness, Tao, Brahman, Being—providing a peaceful place within to perceive the world with more clarity. A meditation practice made residing within this place easier, and a more habitual aspect of daily life, freeing my thinking mind to become a wondrous tool rather than the center of identity. Formal schooling makes the mind the center, Rafael suggested, excluding spiritual modes of knowing and self-understanding. Students then lose their connection, naturally known in childhood, with the life force, the intelligence, the subtle energy that continually forms and reforms, organizes and re-organizes, and drives creative consciousness and transformation.

Studying with Rafael didn't make mopping floors at the factory any easier, but it did expand my perspective. My sense of self changed dramatically when I identified with transcendent Spirit unfolding as immanent matter, life, mind, and soul. With each meditation my anger receded, and the world became more amusing, something to be enjoyed no matter the circumstance. By identifying with Spirit unfolding rather than alienation, I was free to explore multiple dimensions of life. I still saw the pervasive ugliness of our techno-industrialized, one-dimensional world, as well as societal structures that perpetuate collective despair, but I also perceived ugliness and despair as the result of a lack of awareness. Krishnamurti referred to this lack when he wrote that in the distance between the subject and object lies the whole misery of humankind. For him, when an awareness of unity is absent there is fear instead of compassion.

My lostness prepared me to meet Rafael, as did traveling in Europe, reading Pirsig on Zen, and discovering Krishnamurti's writings in the used bookstore. Preston was insightful enough to introduce me to Rafael, and in a twist, I introduced him to a former professor who guided him to his doctoral program in philosophy and communication at Purdue. Emerson wrote that friendship is marked by two qualities, truth and tenderness, and Thoreau argued that friends should be complements, not doubles without difference. These qualities defined my relationship with Preston.

The greatest gift I received from Rafael was his insistence that I had something to offer the world. He saw the awakening of talent, ability, and character where I saw failure expressed in poorly chosen university majors and wasted time pursuing unwanted careers. I had wasted no time, he told me; my so-called mistakes provided lessons and growth. His message was clear—your life is your continually unfolding project—so I was patient with all that was unresolved in my heart and relieved from feeling I had to figure everything out.

Meeting Rafael led to a new education, and it was painful to imagine where I would be without his mentorship and Preston's friendship. I continued working at the factory because it provided funds for future freedom while I followed a call to explore the spiritual dimension of life.

What could possibly go wrong?

Chapter 4

The River Knows

"A river, with its waterfalls and meadows, a lake, a hill, a cliff or individual rocks, a forest and ancient trees standing singly. Such things are beautiful; they have a high use which dollars and cents never represent. If the inhabitants of a town were wise, they would seek to preserve these things, though at a considerable expense; for such things educate far more than any hired teachers or preachers, or any at present recognized system of school education."
—Henry David Thoreau

Indiana is farming country, known for its rich soil, conservative values, and love for basketball—no barn is complete unless it has an old iron hoop where farm kids can hone shooting skills. Purdue University is rooted in this rural culture, its identity shaped by the Morrill Act of 1863, which provided federal land for universities devoted to teaching agriculture. The Indiana General Assembly voted to take advantage of this act in 1869 and established Purdue with the help of a $150,000 donation from John Purdue, a local business leader. In 1887, the Hatch Act charged land-grant schools to create a research arm to advance science and solve problems for the food, agricultural, and natural resource system. Purdue owns thousands of acres of agricultural land and actively participates in this research mission.

During some of my years of teaching Com 114, I lived in a three-room apartment in Lafayette, two miles from the university in West Lafayette, and crossed the Wabash River on daily walks to work. I would saunter down Main Street past the Lafayette Brewing Company, a microbrewery built in a former furniture store and my favorite watering hole, and a block later past Kokoro (meaning "heart"), a Japanese restaurant known for its owner and chef, "Crazy Tony." When overwhelmed with orders for California rolls, tuna rolls, and the like, he drank imported beer from his own tap and shouted while waving his knife in the air. The first page of the menu pleaded with patrons to please not ask Tony questions while he was slicing the sushi.

After Kokoro, came the historic courthouse, the center of downtown and the site of annual Christmas protests over the lack of an appropriate nativity scene. It also once attracted a KKK rally, and, on another occasion, an old pick-up truck filled with large drums of gasoline attached to a trigger switch that didn't fire, most likely a gift from a disgruntled felon or a local militia group. My walk eventually led past the Java Roaster, a café in another renovated old building and hangout for young would-be poets, and then to an attractive, brick-laid pedestrian bridge that took me over the river.

The initial path through West Lafayette had a different aesthetic. The sight of historic buildings and small businesses was replaced by traffic and fast-food chains: Wendy's, Long John Silver's, and of course McDonald's. On one walk I witnessed a man being carried out of Mickey D's on a stretcher with the "billions and billions served" sign in the backdrop. I hungered for a camera, imagining a public service announcement that read, "You deserve clogged arteries today…at McDonald's!"

The path to Purdue proceeded up a hill and past shops and eateries, including the Triple X, an early-morning and late-night breakfast spot for locals and students that, despite greasy food, always seemed to be crowded. The path continued to Von's, the independent bookstore where I worked for two years, and then to a series of bars, the most popular being the Chocolate Shop, where howls blasted through the front door and drunken undergraduates plastered their sloppy faces against the windows.

The sights on my walk to campus define the towns, but none more than the river. The name "Wabash" comes from the Miami Indians, who called the river "Wah-Bah-Shik-Ki," or "pure white." But there was no longer anything pure about the Wabash; it was brown and polluted. The Department of Natural Resources gave the Wabash its highest pollution rating, and swimming and eating fish were strongly discouraged. The sources of the pollution were typical: factories, sewage plants, and pesticide run-off from farms, or more precisely, farms that have adopted agricultural practices formulated and encouraged by land grant universities. New technologies and chemicals have seduced most Indiana farmers. Once hooked, they are like drug addicts craving short-term highs.

Lafayette upgraded its sewage treatment plant, but in heavy rains it overflowed like a gigantic backed-up toilet. The river was expected to clean up the mess without anyone noticing, but it was difficult to ignore the stench on humid summer days. The polluting factories along the length of the Wabash are many, but Lafayette has a special polluter, Eli Lilly, the largest drug company in the world and maker of the antidepressant Prozac. The Lilly plant is a huge complex, running a New York City block or two along the east bank of the river. Other than the university, it's the town's biggest employer, as well as a frequent supporter of various Lafayette institutions and cultural events. Many consider Eli Lilly to be a good corporate citizen and benefactor.

During my walks to and from school, I often stopped on the walking bridge to gaze toward the Wabash in search of some type of aesthetic connection. The only connection I found was a downward spiral between our psychological health and treatment of the river.

The systems thinker Gregory Bateson argued that we experience a relational and communicative exchange between mind and nature in our perception of beauty, which he called "the pattern that connects." But what happens when this exchange is muddied and beauty muted? Bateson, writing in the early 1970s, focused on polluted Lake Erie to explain his insight. He wrote that when we decide that Lake Erie is a good place to get rid of the byproducts of human life, we "forget that the eco-mental system called Lake Erie is part of our wider eco-mental system—and that if Lake Erie is driven insane, its insanity is incorporated in the larger system of our thought and experience."

To Bateson, we have separated our individual minds from the system of mind and intelligence within which they are embedded. This separation is an illusion, a product of ill-health and disconnected thinking, and we pay a stiff price when we create institutions and a way of life based on this illusion.

The polluted condition of the eco-mental system known as the Wabash is no different. Gazing outward from the walking bridge—in silence and stillness—I perceived a vicious cycle in which we turn to drugs such as Prozac to trigger chemicals in our brain, making us happier and more resistant to stress, while we continue to dump chemicals into the environment, polluting the water, air, soil, and psyche. Many people do suffer chemical imbalances, and anti-depressants can help to correct this imbalance, but as I gazed at the murky Wabash, receptive to its secrets, I saw Eli Lilly, with its large pipe discharging effluent directly into the river, creating its clientele by contributing to the depressive and unbalanced state of the planet, and then providing a profitable antidote in the form of a pill.

Lafayette and West Lafayette would not exist without the river, as its clear, flowing waters brought settlers to the area who then used it as a shipping route. But as the towns have grown, the role of the river "Wah-Bah-Shik-Ki," the source of the community, is forgotten and disrespected by the farmer, the town, industry, and the university, which operate under a limited definition of mind and intelligence.

❧

I once lived near a clean river in Old Town, Maine.

It was 1987, two years after graduating from Rutgers, and one year after a US Senate committee held two days of hearings on "Ozone Depletion, the Greenhouse Effect, and Climate Change." The CO_2 count was 349.19 ppm, just shy of the threshold. In the hearing, Senator John Chaffee, a Republican who convened the meeting—that's right, a Republican before climate became a partisan political issue—stated, "The scientific evidence…is telling us we have a problem, a serious problem." Then Senator Al Gore, citing a statement from the 1985 Villach, Austria Conference, a meeting organized by the International Council of Science, the World Meteorological Organization, and the UN, added, "[A]s a result of the increasing greenhouse gases it is now believed that in the first half of the next century a rise of global mean temperature could occur which is greater than any in man's history."

During the two years after graduation, I worked at the CO_2-spewing factory for eight months and then as a printer in my brother's small quickprintshop. I was also studying with Rafael and becoming a three-times-a-day meditator more in touch with the workings of my inner life. Rafael taught students to listen to and follow intuitions that emerged from meditative silence, or our "still, small voice," even though we don't know where they will lead. My intuitions led me to enroll as a graduate student in the Communication Studies department at the University of Maine.

There was a paper factory in Old Town, my new Maine home, which sometimes fouled the air with a wretched stench, but overall Old Town and neighboring Orono, home of the university, were small communities surrounded by forest and cut through by rivers. I lived with a graduate student couple, Alan and Judi, and my walk to school was a two-mile path through dense forest, an invigorating prelude to academic study.

There was one problem: I dropped out after one month due to another intuition, bound up with and forged by doubts. Rafael's teachings were not easily lived.

My classes were relatively interesting, and the professors thoughtful and kind, but something else was gnawing at me, and calling to me. I was drawn to the Maine woods and a book, Henry David Thoreau's *Walden*. I had never read Thoreau and thought my arrival in Maine signaled the right time. My initial interest began with an off-handed remark. I was chopping wood to earn a reduction in rent and turning red-faced from placing all my strength into the downward thrust of an eight-pound maul. Alan looked me over and laughed, "Chop your wood and it warms you twice." It was the perfect remark, which he quickly attributed to Thoreau.

Walden was written with my disposition firmly in mind, and the aphoristic quotations, while old hat for Thoreau scholars and common on calendars, left me cackling like fresh wood on a fire.

"The mass of men lead lives of quiet desperation." Harsh words, but deadly accurate to a desperate soul such as myself who spent the previous two years doing tedious work in a factory and printshop.

"To be a philosopher is not merely to have subtle thoughts, nor even to found a school, but to so love wisdom as to live according to its dictates, a life of simplicity, independence, magnanimity, and trust. It is to solve some of the problems of life, not only theoretically, but practically." Manna to those who believe that ideas are for living, not for tests and grades.

And the stirring, "If a man does not keep pace with his companions, perhaps it is because he hears a different drummer. Let him step to the music which he hears, however measured and far away." Or the lesson behind his two-year-and-two-month stay at Walden Pond: "I learned this, at least, by my experiment; that if one advances confidently in the direction of his dreams, and endeavors to live the life which he had imagined, he will meet with success unexpected in common hours."

All of it music to me, given my newfound call to explore the spiritual dimension of life. And embedded within the quotations was a clear claim: our deepest discoveries were to be found within ourselves and nature, not in school.

I had other problems with graduate school: receiving a grade for expressing intellectual development always felt idiotic, and having to give them was worse. In exchange for tuition and a stipend of seven thousand dollars a year, I started teaching an interpersonal communication course. I was filled with nerves the first day of class, partially because of self-doubt and partially because learning meant too much to me. I couldn't bear the thought of being like many of my teachers, turning fascinating topics into drudgery.

Despite bursts of passion, I was distinctly average during my month of teaching (a C!); I was poorly organized and had little faith in the assignments. The first paper was a short reaction to a reading. I skimmed over the lifeless papers, knowing they had written what they thought I wanted to hear in the bland style that had been hammered into them—not the slightest hint of transformation, of the assignment having any meaning—and I was supposed to slap on a grade, encouraging more lifeless work in the future or leaving bewildered students searching outside of themselves for the proper formula to academic success.

So, I quit. I apologized to the department chair, acknowledging my inadequacy while explaining my concerns as best as I could, and then read Thoreau and headed to the woods.

Alan and Judi became friends and empathized with my reasons for leaving school, but it was their nearly two-hundred-pound black Newfoundland, Mac, who became my closest companion. Newfoundlands are amazing swimmers with an instinct to save you if they think you're struggling in the water. We went swimming in the clear, cool Penobscot River, and Mac would paddle his huge paws toward me until I grabbed his tail and allowed him to drag me to shore. We performed the rescue mission over and over, and I thanked him every time. He seemed to love the ritual, as if taking pleasure in helping a fellow being.

One time, while walking along a forested path, Mac suddenly bolted left, off trail and out of sight. I stopped, staring at the opening in the brush where he disappeared, and then called his name in a joking voice, "Hey

Mac, where you goin'?" I always used a leash when we walked through town but let him loose as soon as we hit the woods, but, fearful that they would disapprove, I never told Alan and Judi. I didn't think they'd mind, but we were having so much fun with our freedom that I didn't want to risk having it shut down. Minutes passed with no Mac in sight, and my joking tone turned to a nervous, "O-kaay, I may have lost Alan and Judi's dog." I began calling to Mac more seriously, and then with a touch of panic, wondering whether to follow his path through the woods or stay and keep hollering. Before I could decide, he burst through the brush and onto the trail—fifty yards ahead of me. If I had kept walking at our usual pace, I would have been at that exact spot.

When I caught up his look seemed to say, "What were you doing back there?" It was a lesson, not only that Mac was a special dog but also in trust and in a kind of nonverbal communication rarely explored in academia. Panic had caused me to fail to listen this time, but Mac and I had bonded in a language beyond words and thoughts.

Thoreau knew this silent communication well, or the "language which all things and events speak," expressed as a grounded transcendentalism. He experienced the force and flow and energy of nature, allowing it to be his teacher. Transcendentalism, as a theory, has many influences: the panentheism of Hinduism, Plato's focus on ideas behind forms, the life of Jesus rather than institutionalized Christianity, Goethe's vision of a unified but continually changing nature, Kant's privileging of subjective knowledge and perception beyond the senses, Romantics such as Coleridge, Wordsworth, and Carlyle, who furthered Kant's inquiry, and Emerson's call for self-reliance—exploring voice and what one is meant to do on earth. It was Thoreau who so loved wisdom that he embodied these ideals and lived the transcendentalist vision.

❦

Thoreau was twenty years old when he graduated from Harvard in 1837. He was a good student, especially in languages. He could read and write five of them well, two reasonably well, and dabbled in local Native languages; his education provided foundational knowledge that would eventually serve him in his writing. It turns out, however, that formal education inanities have a long history; he despaired over the regimentation and rote learning at Harvard, not to mention the hateful grading system. The president of the college had established an elaborate marking system, attaching points to every facet of student life, including missing curfew and absence from chapel. The totals were used to figure class rank and scholarships, which were crucial to students such as Thoreau who did not come from a wealthy family.

Thoreau barely got into Harvard because of financial difficulties and because he was busy studying the woods, wetlands, ponds, and rivers of Concord instead of prepping for entrance exams. Once in, he was forced to toe the line to stay in—such behavior was out of character, especially given the later, civil-disobedience Thoreau—but many Harvard professors saw students as enemies; no getting to class late or getting to class early or asking questions; all led to a loss of points and scholarship money. His exacting writing teacher provided a good lesson on lessening excess but a bad one on lessening emotion, wit, passion. He did rejoice in the extensive library and in his classmates and learning from each other.

Due to a decent class rank, despite losing points for taking a term off to earn money, he gave one of three pre-commencement student addresses on a key question of his time: the commercial spirit. Thoreau, finally freed from points and rank, responded, "The order of things should be somewhat reversed,—the seventh should be man's day of toil…and the other six his Sabbath of the affections and the soul."

The seeds of *Walden* were already firmly planted, but, upon graduation, he faced the same daunting question I faced and today's awake students face—the tension between ideals and practicality. He wanted to just live but needed to make a living while hopefully keeping his soul. There were parental expectations: his family had moved to a smaller house to help pay for his education, and few had been educated at Harvard.

After much searching, Thoreau lucked into a position as a teacher at a public school near his home in Concord. It paid five hundred dollars a year, a substantial amount, especially since there was a growing financial crisis that would lead to years of depression. Out of twenty or so public-school teachers in Concord, he was one of the two best paid when good jobs were hard to find. He quit after two weeks, unwilling to administer discipline in the form of daily canings.

Thoreau had as "many trades as fingers," as he put it. He worked intermittently for his father's pencil-making business, where he used engineering skill to redesign machinery and pencil lead. He worked as a surveyor, carpenter, magazine salesman, speaker, and editor. He joked in his journal, or perhaps he wasn't joking, of finding work picking huckleberries or gathering herbs. He sarcastically commented on carrying evergreens to villagers so that they could be reminded of nature, before remarking that trade inevitably curses what it handles, and his greatest skill was to want little.

He also worked as a schoolteacher again, this time with his older brother, John, in their own school, which initially had only four students. It was in threat of closing until more enrolled once word got out about the Thoreau brothers' innovative teaching philosophy inspired by transcendentalist principles: students should not be punished as sinners or merely trained as workers but educated to unfold inner divinity, inner light, inner fire. The results were student field trips, passionate and engaging talks from Henry on topics such as the changing of the seasons, and bright spirits and friendly conversation from the outgoing John. The brothers encouraged students to journal and write on what they knew, and to translate texts into their own words, such as found poems. There were recess parties with melons from the brothers' famous patch and mixing with students outside the classroom—John playing with groups, Henry talking with individuals, children catching him by the hand and walking to hear more. John and Henry brought lessons from the street, from the community, into the classroom.

On August 31, 1839, Henry and John took the boat they had built in the spring, the *Musketaquid*, on a two-week journey down the Concord River and then up the Merrimack River to the White Mountains of New Hampshire. On the first day, they traveled seven miles, camped on shore—their sail doubling as a tent—and picked huckleberries to go with their dinner of bread and hot cocoa made with river water. Over the next week, they would pass Wicasuck Island, former home of the Penacook Indians, Nashua's factories with mountains in the distance, and Manchester, a village going industrial, as well as woods, pastures, and agricultural fields. At the canal locks in Cromwell Falls, they found arrowheads on the bank and listened to stories from the lock tender; soon, the march of "progress" would make the canals obsolete as the railroad took over the job of moving commercial goods. In Hookset, they pitched their tent where Maine Penobscot Indians had camped two years prior, and then they stowed their gear in a friendly farmer's barn and scaled Mount Washington.

The trip back took a mere two days, thanks to friendly currents and winds, with the brothers setting shore back in Concord late in the evening, tying their boat to the same wild apple tree that held it before they left. Emerson, upon hearing of their adventure, sang their praises, remarking that his young neighbors had not only built their own boat but "lived by their wits," dining on fish from streams and berries in the woods. In contrast, long years of formal education led to a "bellyful of words" and not knowing a thing about edible roots or telling one's "course by the stars or the time by the sun." For Henry and John, the trip was just fun, and a bonding experience, but Thoreau would later realize its literary possibilities in his first book, *A Week on the Concord and Merrimack*, where the river, and water generally, reflected heaven, quieted negative passions, and preserved equipoise, keeping us from "secret violence" and absolving "all obligations to the past."

John and Henry returned to teaching, and John's buoyant personality led him to become head teacher despite Henry's Harvard education. But the school would not last. John fell ill with the scourge of New England: tuberculosis. As John increasingly weakened, it became clear they would have to close the school. Less than a year later, on New Year's Day 1842, he cut his finger while shaving. The cut led to infection with tetanus spores that led to lockjaw. John died in a bereft Henry's arms eleven days later at age twenty-six. Henry experienced an intense loss and lostness that would leave him bedridden for a month as he searched for new ways to understand nature's cycles and to take his next steps. The closing of the school was a major loss for their students, yet the brothers' mission to make education pleasant, even joyful, was radical then, and sadly, radical now. A former student said Thoreau never ceased to teach after leaving the classroom.

Thoreau wrote and wrote—his journals would tally over two million words—but he struggled to get paid for writing. It took years for him to find a voice generally and a writer's voice specifically. There are many excellent biographies detailing the unfolding of his voice, with Walter Harding's *The Days of Henry Thoreau* and Laura Dassow Walls's more recent *Thoreau: A Life* being the most acclaimed. Paul Dann's *Expect Great Things: The Life and Search of Thoreau* has a unique angle exploring the daemonic expressed in his life. In his first public speech at the Concord Lyceum in 1838, only a year after graduation, he remarked that "the world he is hides for a time the world that he inhabits" and "that which properly constitutes the life of every man is a profound secret."

Thoreau, due to early struggles to find vocation, or because he was lost, did his best to attend to his secret world. He consciously dwelled within larger forces while literally dwelling at his family's homes. He also lived with Emerson where he helped run the household and played with Emerson's kids, with Emerson's brother in Staten Island for a short period while he tried to shop his writing in New York City, and at the tiny house he built near Walden Pond on Emerson's land. Along with writing, he spent much time reading, contemplating, hiking in Maine, and sauntering through the woods. These were spiritual acts as he left the town behind to re-find the compass and commune with his secret world and the secrets of nature. Later in life, he would study nature's secrets via an embodied scientific practice. He was passionate about the classics of history and literature but without nostalgia for past ages; the classics were nothing unless they stimulated new knowledge and awoke the daemon, the genius, that was already within, allowing him to experience more fully the present moment.

The myth, of course, is that Thoreau was a crotchety hermit, yet his tiny Walden house was not isolated but near a road and popular fishing hole. Travelers were curious: what was he up to, giving up comforts for simple living? That curiosity provided an opening for conversation and learning. He wrote that he had more visitors when living in the woods than at any other time in his life, having three chairs, "one for solitude, two for friendship, and three for society."

Thoreau was ultimately a townie and intimately involved in the social happenings of Concord: he curated the lyceum lecture series for several years, spoke at the lyceum, met transcendentalists at Emerson's home, met all kinds of travelers at his parents' homes (which were also boardinghouses), and conversed and walked with many friends. All were part of his education as he sought to live his inner secret life outwardly as a spiritual path.

ɔ

I was seeking too, trying to live Thoreau's realization that we can "elevate our lives by a conscious endeavor." I continued to meditate three times a day and sometimes danced at night near the river, giving praise to the stars and moonlight. I also practiced seeing God in and as everything and everyone, including two graduate student friends with whom I could have had romantic relationships, but the meditating and God awareness dissipated desire. In another annoying paradox, the more I lacked desire, the more interested they became. Why do we so often want what we can't have and not what we can? If I could fully liberate myself from desire, I thought, meditating away a need for everyone and everything while also embracing divinity, then the paradox would unravel, and perception would be clear.

Thoreau's life and insights mirrored lessons I learned with Rafael. His adherence to the transcendentalist principle that material life was Spirit unfolding led him to perceive harmony and pattern and higher laws in the details of nature as well as within human beings. To integrate the intelligence of outer and inner worlds was to finally awaken from our slumbers and participate in the poetic or divine life.

I longed for such a life, which I recognized as yet another desire, another paradox, another block to enlightenment.

Thoreau called himself a mystic, a label I was increasingly willing to embrace, and he stumbled upon mystical experience. During a time when agriculture was already growing in the direction of large farms and stultifying labor, Thoreau hoed his beans at Walden Pond as if conducting a concert: "When my hoe tinkled against the stones, that music echoed to the woods and the sky, and was an accompaniment to my labor which yielded an instant and immeasurable crop." Lost in his work, in reverie, he cultivated a loss of separate self: "it was no longer beans that I hoed, nor I that hoed the beans."

The Walden experiment, I realized, was essentially an education of deep listening leading to transformation. Thoreau not only attended to seemingly objective, physical facts of nature but also practiced a subjective intimacy with the bean field, woods, pond, and rivers, as well as animals, who were often like friends, and whose voices were songs, oratorios, leading him to the daily experience that we are part and parcel of the natural world. If the masses were desperate, it was because they did not have ears to hear the concert, had forgotten how to listen, or worse, had been socialized and educated out of it. They had dismissed such practice as romantic yearning rather than what it truly is: a profound openness to mystery, to wildness, and the ground of a life well lived.

I was also pleased to discover that he embraced paradox. He extolled a vegetarian lifestyle while also celebrating his instinct to grab a woodchuck and devour it whole. He found within himself a predilection towards a "higher, or as it is named, spiritual life," and another towards a "primitive rank and savage one." The spiritual and the primitive expressed dimensions of freedom, and he relished them both.

Thoreau, like Bateson, explored the integration of mind and nature. Or, as he stated in a stirring quotation from his essay "Walking": "The highest we can attain to is not Knowledge but Sympathy with Intelligence." His sympathy knew no bounds, which he expressed in a quotation from *Walden*: "Shall I not have intelligence with the earth? Am I not partly leaves and vegetable mould myself?"

Thoreau also likened Walden Pond to earth's eye, "looking into which the beholder measures the depth of his own nature." The pond mirrored soul, I surmised, because it reflects sky and land, heaven and earth, the spiritual and the material. For the theologian, the words are transcendent and immanent, but they are only words; in his life they represented a creative tension between poetic imagination and the sweat and dirt of simple living.

Rafael used the phrase "creative tension" when I spoke of frustration with paradox, with wanting to figure everything out; he said we learn and grow from embracing differing poles of our nature rather than denying them. Was I in denial by not embracing romantic relationships? I did not know, but I did know that there are moments, religious to be sure, like Thoreau's experience in the bean field, or when he floated in a boat under the moonlight, casting his awareness upward toward transcendent mysteries while the immanent tug of nature lured him downward to the elements, in which we feel whole, having "caught two fishes as it were with one hook."

Reading Thoreau led to the realization that I had come to Maine for a different kind of schooling: my Maine experiment, informed by spiritual study with Rafael. Had my still, small voice led me here, to learn through experience? Or was such chatter a willful act of giving after-the-fact reasons for choices, reading into randomness, finding order? I again didn't know, but purpose and play were present, and they displaced the drudgery of the factory and printshop.

Along with swims and walks with Mac, I also took solo journeys off trail, walking miles into dense forest to test intuitions and sense of direction. I intentionally got lost, and then sat on the forest floor pondering next moves. I learned I had no sense of direction, no idea where I'd find the trail or town. I would continue to sit, this time meditating, and, like a flowing river, let my thoughts and fears wash away so that fresh insights could emerge. I'd eventually receive a mild assurance of which way to go, and then run, making quick, intuitive decisions on where to place my steps as I angled and slashed through pine. I either found my way back to the trail or an unfamiliar road, proving perhaps nothing but good fortune or that there were plenty of trails and roads. But I was in the woods, taking risks, exploring, having fun.

I once ended up on Penobscot land, foolishly not knowing anything about their existence; intrigued, yet feeling like an intruder, I retraced my steps. Only later did I learn that Thoreau had come to Old Town—had we stood on the same patch of ground? He had visited with some Penobscot his first time in Maine when he stayed with relatives while looking for a teaching job prior to getting one in Concord.

Thoreau loved all things Native, or "Indian," as they were educated by place, knowing far more about the land than European agrarian latecomers. Finding an arrowhead stirred his imagination and prompted his research into Native history and lifeways. What one learns is a story of death. The Native population in New England was reduced by 90 percent due to exposure to diseases such as smallpox, displacement for those who survived, and attempts at Christian reeducation. Tahatawan, a Musketaquid leader, supposedly sold the land that became Concord to the English, but since land could not be owned, it could not be sold; Tahatawan thought payment was for usage rights.

An unfortunate lesson of colonization.

There would be more.

The "commercial spirit" took over Natives and land, with trade turning everything into commodities, including beaver and deer, which led to overhunting, which led to a loss of deerskins and the need for English clothing. Beaver dams rotted, turning wetlands into fields, and then a domesticated economy of pigs and cattle. Money was necessary to buy clothing and livestock, and axes and hoes and guns. Out went an eleven-thousand-year-old wild strawberry, ecological economy—imperfect, but sustainable—in went bustling commerce and industrialization, all justified, including the deaths, as Divine Providence made room for "civilization."

For Thoreau, arrowheads also reminded him of history prior to land stolen via renaming. He cherished Native names and used them whenever possible, including for his first handmade boat, and his second, *Red Jacket*, named after the Seneca chief who gave a speech to the US Senate demanding the Indians' right to practice their own religion.

My formal education led me to know nothing of this history. Instead, I explored the land from my cultural bias, and my rituals drifted into the absurd.

One day, I strolled down the aisle of the local supermarket looking for fresh-baked blueberry muffins when I spied a chicken twirling on an electric spit. I thought of Thoreau and the woodchuck and was overcome with not an intuition but an impulse to devour it out in the woods. I was no hunter, so it seemed like a good way to experience animal flesh in the wilderness. The impulse was so strong that it overcame critical resistance. It was an abused, agribusiness, soon to be bag-wrapped chicken for Christ's sake—but I wasn't dissuaded.

The worst part was that it took a half-hour to act on my impulse: wait in the fifteen items or less check-out line, drive my gas guzzling, fake wood-paneled station wagon to the trailhead, and then walk a mile until I found a perfect spot. But I did all of that, and then huddled over my prize, set on my haunches with my back touching the base of a giant pine, ripping the chicken apart with my hands, taking large, gulping bites, and whipping the bones to the side while keeping eyes attuned to the movements of potential predators. When finished, with juice on chin and hands, I stood up and let loose a holler, which was satisfying in its physicality but also because I was willing to be such a fool.

I was also fond of finding a secluded section of woods and stripping down for a naked jaunt. Thoreau often bathed in Walden Pond and walked in rivers clothed only in sun-protecting hat and shirt. This practice should be no surprise, despite the puritanical mid-1800s in which he lived. Thoreau sought freedom and ecstatic experience, and there is an undeniable eroticism to nature, to the scent of pine, a soft breeze on flesh, and the elemental, wild energy of which we are part and parcel.

A lack of clothes left me vulnerable, open, attuned. I became more attentive without protective second skin, free and yet aware of possibly being seen, not by human eyes but by plant and animal, as well as the divine in the form of sunlight and wind and invisible grace. My decision to disrobe was no nudist colony frolic, but a ritual of receptivity before forces my intellect could not comprehend.

〇〇

Rivers such as the Wabash and Penobscot, along with providing transportation, bounties of fish, and aesthetic pleasures, have always played a symbolic function in human knowing. We can never step in the same river twice, Heraclitus proclaimed, for flowing waters are ever-changing. Or Emerson: "Who looks upon a river in a meditative hour, and is not reminded of the flux of all things?" For Emerson, however, daily observation of the ever-changing natural world led to an unchanging spiritual revelation. "Nature always speaks of Spirit," he wrote; thus, to know the most important things we must be in sympathy with the divine energy that streams through all that exists.

For Thoreau, rippling rivers reflect the spiritual journey, restoring and uplifting as we embrace "new water every instant." The pond symbolized the conjoining of heaven and earth, inspiring possibilities of spiritual enlightenment. Or rather, listening to nature's diverse voices, apprehending beauty, nonverbal presence, and energy exchange, attunes us to the voice of Spirit.

Thoreau listened, finding the most reliable sources of guidance.

So, I pondered. Did the polluted Wabash River have a memory of the past and hopes for the future, of what it used to be and the possibilities for what it is meant to be? Does the river know the eternal now, silence before time, along with its gurgles and blurps and rapid rushings, melding stillness and sound in its dynamic currents? Do the sounds of the river reflect the purposeful utterances of primordial mysteries and the playful yips and yowls of youth? Perhaps asking these questions, to the river itself, is to know a little of these things. Perhaps small insights, transient and elusive, can transport us to new and vibrant ground.

My 1987 pre-Purdue Maine experiment, including "failure" as a teacher after a month, sauntering in the woods with Mac, and reading *Walden*, along with many other learning experiences on my newfound spiritual path, would eventually lead to silence and stillness when I stood on the walking bridge gazing at the Wabash five years later. And more pondering led me to realize a sad irony: university education, stuck in the Cartesian separation of mind and nature, made respecting the river harder to experience.

Such lack of respect is akin to anti-education, but out of that lostness we could be found. Out of that lostness we could teach; but first we must humbly acknowledge our lostness, asking necessary questions, like: How we can live in sympathy with the eternal now amid ongoing rapid rushings?

Fortunately, many are still drawn to the river.

Every fall in Lafayette a festival gathers along the Wabash's eroded banks. The Feast of the Hunter's Moon recreates eighteenth-century life at Fort Ouiatenon Historic Park—the French built the fort in 1717 as a military outpost to prevent British expansion, and it later became a trading post for Natives and White settlers. The Feast draws eight thousand costumed participants—from blacksmiths, soldiers, and French voyageurs in handmade canoes, to drum and bugle corps, Native American singers and dancers, and artisans and villagers—as well as sixty thousand visitors for the two-day event.

Participants take the event seriously, seldom breaking out of character, while enjoying their temporary escape from modern life. The visitors take it all in—the scents of burning wood and grilled corn fill the air—while bringing the modern world with them and leaving behind thirty thousand pounds of trash.

I once worked at the onion soup booth, which is popular on colder days. The soup was made in an iron cauldron on a wood fire and stirred with large wooden spoons. I wore a beret and antique white cloth shirt—nothing too special, but I wasn't a featured performer—and spent the day ladling soup at a dollar a cup. The proceeds went to a local animal shelter.

At night, the real celebration began. Visitors returned to their cars and homes, while participants gathered near the fort for a contra dance. My favorite performance was the paddle dance, with the French Canadian Bent Nickel Dance Band playing in the background. Three dancers stood in a row with the middle dancer holding a paddle while peering back and forth at potential partners. They handed the paddle to the one they didn't want and then danced off into the night with their new beau. The dancer left behind inherited the middle position, giving them the power to choose next.

The Feast was a mix of nostalgia, stabs at authenticity, and the ever-present modern world, as well as a longing for a simpler, more communal existence. The contra dance was especially lively when the night was clear and filled with stars. It was easy to ignore, at least for a while, the bright lights of Eli Lilly shining off in the distance, and to focus instead on the festivities and moonlight shimmering on the river.

Chapter 5

Open to Mystery

"The worship of the Great Mystery was silent, solitary, free from all self-seeking. It was silent, because all speech is of necessity feeble and imperfect.... Here is the supreme mystery that is the essence of worship, without which there can be no religion, and in the presence of this mystery our attitude cannot be very unlike that of the natural philosopher, who beholds with awe the Divine in all creation."
— Charles A. Eastman (Ohiyesa)

"The most beautiful experience we can have is the mysterious.... Whoever does not know it and can no longer wonder, no longer marvel, is as good as dead, and his eyes are dimmed...it is this knowledge and this emotion that constitute true religiosity; in this sense and in this sense alone, I am a religious man."
—Albert Einstein

"Any questions?" Mary asked spritely after soaking up applause from classmates.

No questions.

I looked around the room, waiting.

Mary had given a speech on her church's mission trip to a Native American reservation. She explained how they brought gifts of food, helped with upkeep, and made themselves available to talk about their Christian faith. She spoke with sincerity and good-heartedness, making it hard, I assumed, for her classmates to point out possible problems. Or perhaps they were unaware of problems.

She smiled and started to leave the podium.

"Do you know," I asked, "that Native Americans have a rich religious history, and that their culture gave much to ours prior to and after being decimated and made poor through conquest? And therefore, might it be wrong to proselytize?"

"Proselytize?"

"To convert Native Americans to your faith."

"We were not there to convert, but to help while sharing the Word of God," Mary insisted, her curly blond hair bouncing as if there was a breeze in the windowless classroom.

"But do you see my point? Can you imagine someone arriving at your church with gifts while sharing their faith?"

"We were just there to help," Mary smiled, radiantly.

As usual, I was trying to get a feisty and fun discussion going—this is college, damn it, not church, and we critically question here—but her good nature seemed to deflect my words.

It was the late 1990s, near the end of my seven-year run of Purdue adjuncting, and I had listened to and graded over two thousand Com 114 speeches. In terms of style, Mary was one of the best speakers I had witnessed, which may be another reason her classmates were silent. She spoke as if imbued with rightness gifted from her Creator, as if He were propping her up, making her a vehicle for His ministry. Every word was said with clarity and appropriate emphasis. She made no mistakes (and received an A).

Mary fascinated me, and I spent hours trying to figure her out. I wasn't trying to untangle the content of her speech, the problem there was clear: she thought she knew with certainty but there was much she didn't know. What fascinated was that her certainty seemed to be at the root of speaking skill. She displayed a strange assurance, as if God was watching over her, and public speaking fears were absent and confidence present. Faith worked—there was evidence—and thus she believed. To challenge faith with rationality would be an affront to her experience of what worked.

Mary also displayed passion; she cared about Christian service, which I was happy to praise. However, the ancient Greeks argued that logos is necessary to liberate us from the excesses of pathos, expressed as emotional appeals. Mary's speech was not soaked in pathos, but logos was lacking, evidenced by a lack of critical inquiry into the context of Native American history. It was likely lacking because it is not practiced by her church. It was no surprise that a devout Christian might be remiss in practicing logos, but most students, including those devoted to science and technology, were remiss as well, as the fullness of logos is not practiced in industrial education.

After listening to so many seemingly diverse students, one thing became clear: their speeches frequently reflected either a religious or techno-scientific voice. But Rafael had led me to the realization that our voices are larger, more encompassing; the Word was made flesh, after all, instilling in us the potential to integrate religious feeling with rational inquiry.

慘

Mary was relatively open to growth. She resisted questioning her Christian faith, but her experience of the reservation, even through a limited lens, opened her to learning about Native American culture. I recommended Jack Weatherford's *Indian Givers*, which details Native American contributions ranging from agriculture to political structure and decision making; *Black Elk Speaks*, which provides a powerful example of a religious voice different from her own; Leslie Marmon Silko's novel *Ceremony*, which illustrates the lostness of Native Americans when their rituals and stories are replaced by colonist narratives; and Charles Eastman's (Ohiyesa) *The Soul of the Indian*, in which he states that the transcendent and immanent Great Mystery speaks via silence, and experiencing this silence develops one's character. I didn't expect her to read these books, but I wanted her to know that they existed. What I really wanted to share with Mary, and the whole class, and all my classes, was the fullness of logos.

Preston, whom I followed to Purdue, introduced me to the work of Calvin O. Schrag, his professor and a respected philosopher. In *The Resources of Rationality*, Schrag writes that modern readings of logos are far different from the ancient Greek view, which bound the rational soul to the rational structure of the cosmos. The Greek concept of logos eventually devolved into technical rationality, shifting logos to logic characterized by calculation and control, with science becoming our privileged mode of knowing. Modernity reduced the once-powerful logos, displaying a Thoreauvian sympathy with intelligence, to scientism.

Reading Thoreau led me to read environmental philosophy, and I had come to realize that such reductionism was taught to us, without us being aware, by dominant narratives that separate mind from nature, including myths of linear progress (history as a straight line of bigger and better stuff), unlimited economic growth (more and better stuff leads to the good life), and technology as savior (minor problems from progress and growth will be solved by more and better technology).

These myths, within which we are educated and asked to find our place, result in exclusionary clubs that often literally club others into submission. Indigenous cultures that do not adhere to the strictures of dominant narratives have been systematically devalued and destroyed.

Oh, and these myths also cause and perpetuate ecocrisis, with the shift from logos to techno-logic a marker of our lostness.

Schrag does not critically question the shift from logos to logic to support theistic religious narratives (or scriptures), which divide God from creation and separate mind from nature, devalue Indigenous cultures, and lead to ecocrisis. Rather, he argues that postmodern citizens should traverse our pre-modern past and glean insights from Greek logos to better pursue the good. Questions concerning the good are traditionally the province of philosophy, and, as Thoreau reminded, true philosophers are lovers of wisdom who live according to the dictates of this love. But how, exactly, are we to live?

Indiana didn't have Jersey diners, but Preston and I were "diner guys" again, talking about philosophy, religion, everything. Thinking I had found some essential, beyond-any-time-period truth, I was trying to live a mystical life, to bring an awareness of unity, and a resulting peacefulness, to daily affairs. However, thanks to Preston, I was aware of the postmodern deconstruction of absolute notions of "Truth," whether centered in spirituality or logos, so I was still questioning, still trying to figure it out. He pointed me toward more books, Pierre Hadot's *What Is Ancient Philosophy?* and *Philosophy as a Way of Life*.

Hadot states that wisdom is something we move toward without ever achieving, yet—and this is the exciting part, the part that leads us to live our love—ancient philosophers provided spiritual exercises, such as dialogue, intuitive contemplation, and the perception of beauty, which led to inner transformation. The rational soul practices these exercises to explore our developmental capacity.

Hadot's emphasis on spiritual exercises, or practices, resonated with me. Ancient Greek philosophers, along with propagating rationality as logos, were spiritual too. Thus, just as Rafael intimated, rational and religious orientations toward the world, and rational and religious voices, were not necessarily mutually exclusive. But I was still left with the ethical question of defining the good, and the pedagogical question of how to teach the good to students. Hadot engages these questions by turning to Socrates and his dictum, "All I know is that I know nothing," which the Oracle of Delphi claimed made him the wisest man. Socrates questioned citizens and students, leading them to realize their ignorance, especially those whose education and culture persuaded them that they possessed knowledge, while midwifing *moments* of knowing to emerge from within.

This all sounded right—my goal as a teacher was to help students unlearn as much as learn, and to realize, along with Socrates, that everything human is highly uncertain. We desire to know but cannot fully know, and to take this situation seriously is to find an ironic humor and playfulness, which Socrates modeled by living a rational life marked by the love of wisdom. Hadot argues that Socrates was a happy man, no matter his circumstance, and he taught equally with his words and presence. He knew silence and stillness well—students often found him in a meditative posture, seemingly lost within himself—and he embodied a healthy nonattachment toward petty or superfluous things. He was able to live a simple, contemplative life with few needs.

Socrates managed to untangle a difficult paradox: wisdom is an ideal we cannot possess, but we express more of it by admitting our limitations, including the limitations of rationality. This awareness left him with no compunction to prove his worth and made him, paradoxically, a worthy model of the pursuit of the good.

Education in the ancient academy celebrated learning via contact with teachers such as Socrates who practiced philosophy as a way of life. Students were trained in rational dialogue and speaking, but they also learned to live as they spoke. Hadot writes, "Professors did not merely teach, but played the role of genuine directors of conscience who cared for their students' spiritual problems."

My questioning of Mary was not meant to lead her to reject her faith or merely prove myself right (my knowledge of Native American cultures and spirituality was certainly limited). It was meant to start a dialogue respectful of the postmodern "truth" that no single perspective is final, whether religious or scientific or Indigenous. Of course, I wanted students to respect diverse cultures, but my main pedagogical goal was to goad them into willingly tolerating uncertainty, seeing not-knowing as the rational ground for self-discovery.

I also wanted students to take another step. Although no perspective is final, living in sympathy with intelligence means that divergent perspectives might be on speaking terms. Rafael, my spiritual director of conscience, was also president of the Ometeca Institute, a nonprofit devoted to exploring the relations between the sciences and humanities. "Ometeca," taken from Aztec language, means "two into one," and the institute was critical of academic overspecialization that creates scholars ignorant of discoveries outside their narrow fields.

Ometeca affirmed the need for specialists, whether poets or climatologists: the humanities, even when severed from the sciences, teach us to think critically and ethically while the sciences, despite too often ignoring the humanities, serve up a baseline of material facts. But in 1959 C. P. Snow wrote that the humanities and sciences had separated into "two cultures" with education modeled after a factory assembly line. Snow lived through the Atomic Age, so the danger of divorcing scientific and technical knowledge from pursuit of the good was easy to see, but the problem was even broader: Specialized humanists often did not know what other specialized humanists were up to, and specialized scientists were befuddled by other specialized scientists.

Emerson put it this way: "The reason why the world lacks unity, and is broken in heaps, is because man is disunited with himself." The marriage of self and world, which would allow us to see the "miraculous in the common," was increasingly lost in Emerson's fragmented time of burgeoning industrialization. In Snow's time, with industry operating at full force, this disunity, this alienation from nature, was even more extreme—and we had nuclear weapons.

A confirming moment occurred when I found that Einstein, our icon of science, wrote that a "cosmic religious feeling" of wonder, unity, and beauty motivated his investigations. Scientists and humanists need not be half-human, beholden to an assembly line approach to knowledge; rather, we may pursue the true via science with a whole heart informed by pursuit of the good and beautiful. Science and religious feeling, then, are very much in dialogue, informing not only exploration of the cosmos but also core questions of education: Why are we on earth, and further, what are we to do?

Ometeca invited such dialogue, hoping to create a new logos among academics since, as Einstein is oft quoted, we cannot solve world problems, especially wicked ones such as nuclear proliferation, the climate crisis, and the loss of traditional ecological knowledge, with the same consciousness that produced them in the first place.

Preston's nudge to read Schrag and Hadot led me to learn that logos has a long history, it's been thought of as an ordered cosmos, the mind of God, and the abstract mind of modern humans. A re-thought logos integrates all three, encompassing science, technical rationality, and critical thinking while remaining open to religious feeling, to aliveness and sacredness, to the mystery of existence and a gifting cosmos. Such a logos partners with pathos to express an expansive ethos and allows us to discern the downsides of the myths of bigger, better, and more while making a commitment to *phusis*, to inner growth in harmony with the nature of things.

For students to develop, I surmised, they must practice the fullness of logos, engaging in spiritual exercises, questioning themselves and others, and sharing via dialogue diverse insights as well as discoveries held in common. They must expose the human tendency to be deceived by shallow passions and follow a deep desire for the unreachable good.

Simple. Right?

Teaching undergraduates consistently reminded one that it takes years of struggle to embody a fuller rationality, assuming we ever do.

ભ

Mary had a gift for public speaking, no matter the source, but she needed to let new ideas mingle with the old, with traditions that are worth embracing at the same time as we question them. I had a bigger challenge with Ruth, a fundamentalist Christian whose faith commanded that the flock not watch videos. If I showed a video in class, she shielded her eyes because the ban against graven images of God was extended to all images. Because I showed few videos, this restriction initially did not affect her ability to pass the class, but, in addition to their speeches, students were required to do a group project, which I crafted into a cultural and communicative analysis of a film.

Students were instructed to show scenes of high- and low-quality interpersonal interactions, then analyze them using criteria inspired by Socrates's dialogic method (conversations characterized by listening, questioning, the subject matter rather than the wills of the participants leading the conversation, and ultimately, learning and transformation) and by Buber's I-Thou/I-It ontology (Thous are honored as speaking subjects; Its are silenced). Students were then asked to rewrite and act out the scenes—thespians in the class were pleased—using their analysis to fix poor communication and ruin the quality communication. Finally, students were instructed to do a Cultural Studies analysis of values communicated by the film and the growth of characters in relation to cultural blocks to communication: race, class, gender, sexual orientation, age, geographical location, education, and, of course, religion.

A creative assignment, I thought, but not to Ruth. At this point I was unaware of her eye shielding, thinking she was resting her head on her desk, so I was surprised when she stayed after class and asked for an alternative assignment due to her church's prohibition, which, like alcohol in the 1920s, I couldn't imagine working.

Didn't the faithful sneak a few glances, or even a wide-eyed visual dollop before crumbling like a dieter at a dessert bar? Ruth, with thick round glasses and tightly braided hair, was earnest; she desperately desired to keep the faith. My brain ricocheted—respect student difference or challenge close-mindedness? I was unsure how to respond. After all, I also saw plenty of problems in our techno-visual, disinformation overload age of images, but pretending that these images didn't exist was disturbing. I told her I would think about it and get back to her.

Next class arrived, and I asked Ruth a few questions, like how realistic is it to avoid images in an age of images? Aren't we indirectly affected by images even when we don't view them, as we inevitably interact with others who watch images and are affected by them? I argued that it was impossible to shield ourselves from images, and thus wasn't it better to critically interpret them? Ruth replied that she had the right to follow the teachings of her church. I mentioned that she was in college and not in church, but I ultimately offered her an alternative assignment. I asked if she was a member of any groups that she could analyze in a paper using the communication criteria from class. Her eyes glistened and face shone—this was the first time I saw her smile—as she stated that she was a member of her church's youth ministry.

I was a fool for not seeing that one coming. Perhaps I was also a fool for relenting. But I didn't see the point in arguing with her, thinking she would back even further into a corner, defending religious territory. Ruth likely needed a crisis to develop, but I didn't sense pushing her to the edge would help the process. I also thought it would be uncomfortable for classmates to work with her. Such discomfort might lead to learning for everyone, or, more likely, alienation for Ruth and frustration for the group.

Ruth's paper was well written but poor in content. I commented that given that group members were so much like her, she really didn't have the experience of critically analyzing diverse values, communication, and self-development. She seemed chagrined, and more receptive, the rest of the semester; perhaps she recognized that I had given her a break by not forcing her to do the film assignment, or perhaps she recognized that she was shielding herself not only from images but also from others. Her well-researched informational speech on diabetes, including appropriate pathos regarding personal struggles with the disease, was compelling, making her part of the class. She even showed the spot on her belly where she received insulin shots—now *that* was an image.

Religious students presented difficulties, but students devoted to a techno-scientific identity and voice also presented challenges. Given that technical rationality is supported by dominant narratives, it is exceedingly difficult to get students to embrace scientific investigation and technological innovation while also being critical of scientism and the myth of technology as savior. At Purdue in the nineties, with its identity as a land grant university in the breadbasket of Indiana, this was especially true for students studying the technological advancements in agriculture.

Bigger, better, and more were the common themes for speeches on the future of farming or, more precisely, agribusiness. It wasn't surprising that there wasn't any sentiment for Thoreau, his bean fields, and religious experience, but students also resisted powerful agricultural voices such as Wendell Berry, a progressive Christian, and Wes Jackson, who both speak out against the destructiveness of agribusiness and supply healing solutions in the form of community-based farming, permaculture, and biomimicry. Berry, I was told, had even come to Purdue prior to my arrival to give a speech; if he had, I saw no residue of his thought among students.

I learned about Berry and Jackson, and a host of other environmental thinkers and issues, from monthly meetings of The Tribe, an eco-spiritual group led by a well-rounded biology professor who taught environmental ethics. And working at the bookstore gave me access to the latest writings of Berry and Jackson and other authors who articulated a more encompassing logos. Berry argues that the good farmer is like an artist, performing within patterns of intelligence. In "Whose Head is the Farmer Using? Whose Head is Using the Farmer?" he laments the fact that conventional farmers tend to rely solely on techno-scientific knowledge while disregarding thought generated by their own experience. Jackson promotes transforming agriculture by mimicking nature's wisdom via no-till, no-pesticide plant arrangements.

Berry and Jackson, both rooted in science and the humanities, advise farmers to listen to experience and nature, or inner genius and the genius of place, while conventional farmers' daily decisions are made by listening to agribusiness corporations and techno-scientific experts.

For alternative voices such as Berry and Jackson, conventional agriculture tells a story of hubris, disconnection, and deafness in which the vocal cords of the land are severed. Industrialization has imposed patterns of its own making, and the results include soil loss, pesticides and cancer, the creation of super-pests, exorbitant energy expenditure from the over-reliance on fossil fuels, the loss of the family farm, the exploitation of farm workers, animal cruelty, genetically modified food, rivers polluted like the Wabash, and increased greenhouse gases in the atmosphere. I told students this list is the direct consequence of a narrow-minded logic that is utterly alienated from a larger logos and intelligence. Berry writes, "We had better respect the possibility of a larger, unseen pattern that can be damaged or destroyed and, with it, the smaller patterns."

Berry suggests that solutions will come from consulting the land in the spirit of dialogue, but even though I introduced students to Socratic dialogue and Buber's I-Thou ontology, they struggled to accept the concept of listening to the land. Such communion was not part of their experience or was a forgotten vestige from childhood; it certainly had not been part of their education. Besides, agricultural students felt we were winning, that our monologue with nature was producing abundance and increasing our standard of living.

I mentioned the publication of Rachael Carson's *Silent Spring* in 1962, a marker moment that influenced the modern environmental movement due to its criticisms of the indiscriminate use of pesticides, or biocides, as she called them because they kill life, not just pests. Our chemicals, Carson writes, are into everything, altering the chemistry of the planet. I also referenced Bill McKibben's 1989 *The End of Nature*, which, along with being the first popular book documenting the effects of global warming, argues that nature has ceased being a force independent from humans. Global warming is more than a wicked and root worldwide problem, it is a root metaphor for the age in which they lived and learned: Human hands, alienated from whole minds and hearts, were into everything.

We had crossed a line. What did they think of that?

Carson and McKibben anticipated the Anthropocene, the geological term that has morphed into sociocultural questions: Given that humans are the main force directing the future habitability of the planet, how should we use that power? How should we respond to the plethora of crises that we have, in our educated ignorance, created, misunderstood, and proliferated?

For Berry, when we fail to listen to the genius of place, we fail to perceive that we are on a treadmill of abuse. We make decisions within the limited context of objective science and technology in the service of profit, and then wonder why there is an increase in eco-social problems and a decrease in nutritious food.

I further shared that there is slack in the system, within the pattern that connects; problems don't always show up right away, but eventually we get messages—methane from manure contributing to climate disruption, or manure lagoons overflowing into waterways, destroying habitat and killing fish (for some reason I thought scatological examples would better get their attention), or cancer from living downstream from the runoff of biocide-rich fields—that stir the senses and intellect, raising the possibility that we might want to reconsider our agricultural habits.

It was not easy to convince students to recognize the deeper roots of problems, such as the separation between mind and nature and the divide between the sciences and humanities. Too abstract, I suppose, or too much perceived gain from jumping back on the treadmill and trying to fix things with the same limited techno-scientific awareness that created the problems in the first place.

℣

My views were influenced by Thoreau, who anticipated the Anthropocene long before Carson and McKibben and most other environmental thinkers.

In the last decade of his life, Thoreau increasingly embraced the scientific method, and facts brought him closer to nature, as well as to praising the ways of science: "Science is always brave; for to know is to know good; doubt and danger quail before her eye." However, while collecting species for Louis Agassiz, a leading scientist at Harvard, the "bravery" of science was not apparent, as recorded in his journal after he killed a box turtle: "I cannot excuse myself for this murder and see that such actions are inconsistent with the poetic expression...I pray I may walk more innocently and serenely through nature."

He put the matter bluntly in another journal entry: "The man of science, who is not seeking for expression but for a fact to be expressed merely, studies nature as dead language."

Thoreau, and Emerson, understood that exploring the way of things was poet's work. In a lyceum talk that rehearsed his arguments in "Nature," Emerson catalogued the "advantages" gained from studying natural history, including training the scientific mind, making useful economic discoveries, and the tonic of being outdoors for body and character, but the "highest benefit" was discovering knowledge that explained "man to himself." And that, to Emerson, was also the goal of the lyceum, a sentiment shared by Thoreau, who integrated these advantages by getting outdoors and calculating, using technological instruments along with heightened poetic perception.

Emerson stated that Thoreau's observatory powers, marked by silence and stillness, becoming a "log among the logs," suggested additional senses and sympathy, such that a "snake coiled around his leg; the fishes swam into his hand…." Over his life, as word spread of his knowledge and abilities, he became in demand among locals, especially farmers, whose land he seemed to know better than they—due to being adept at listening to inner genius and genius of the place—and he freely taught children, not just botany, but wonder.

In earlier years, he sent lots of species to Agassiz, including some he had never seen, filling him with questions before feeling dismay over killing for science. Later, in 1860, after being one of the first in America to read Darwin, only five weeks or so after publication, he found a theory to match his studies. Ironically, Agassiz's Christianity led him to reject Darwin's evidence for natural selection in favor of God's creation and placement of each species on the planet, with White men like himself at the top of the hierarchy—the kind of history that I wanted Lily and fellow students to be critical of—while Thoreau saw that everything evolved from the same source, everything was entangled, mirroring the Native view of "all my relations."

Thoreau, as it turns out, knew a few things about agriculture. After reading Darwin, he gave a talk on forest succession for an agricultural fair, stating, "I have great faith in a seed," which included the seeds of justice. The speech was well received; his audience praised him not only as a model citizen contributing to the community but also as an educator.

Thoreau spoke many times in Concord and throughout New England as part of the lyceum circuit, which was adult education of its day, and, along with conversation and print, how information was dispersed prior to telegraph, radio, TV, internet, texting, and social media. Not surprisingly, not all embraced his sensibility and intellect. Some lectures were duds or taken that way. When he spoke on "White Beans and Walden Pond," one reviewer wrote, "To be frank with you, you are better as a woodman, or say, a woodpecker, than as a cockney philosopher, or a city parrot, to mimic the voices of canaries or cat owls, of Emersons, or Carlyles…." The reviewer then suggested he quit speaking until he became more original. But a reviewer at a different talk, with an audience with ears to hear, wrote that Thoreau bewilders with the "mists of transcendental-ism," delights with "brilliant imagery," shocks by "irreverence," and sets off a roar by "sallies of wit."

Emerson was more of a sage as a speaker; Thoreau, while accused of mimicking Emerson, was more of a wry humorist. Both spoke to provoke, not just edify. Speaking, when at their best, was effortless effort, with words married to religious feeling and facts; they expressed their unique voices—a skill born of a certain faith, reflecting transcendentalist ideals but not certainty.

"The Succession of Forest Trees" was placed in the *New York Weekly Tribune* and became Thoreau's most widely read piece in his lifetime. Farmers knew they were destroying their woods and needed practical ad-vice. Applying Darwin, he explored the origin of all things in relation to the dispersion of seeds, including via animals, water, and wind instead of God. Yet divine intelligence was implicated, expressed as nature's design, or the patterns attended to by Berry and Jackson; when plants died, they nourished the soil, becoming receptive to more seeds, more growth.

Thoreau once considered killing a snake for Agassiz but came to an I-Thou realization that it was "not the means of acquiring true knowledge." Science, he realized, made the mistake of treating subjects merely as objects, as independent "its," an error he no longer made because his more poetic science perceived interdependency. Animals were killed all around Concord, for science and from hunting, while Thoreau communed with a flying squirrel and reached into a knothole to pet a screech owl. Teased by some about his new refusal to kill, he responded, "Do you think I should shoot you if I wanted to study you?"

Thoreau also told a Harvard librarian that science made another mis-take: not listening to and learning from Natives, who had fifty names for cedar, could locate a snake by sounds and call animals to them, and knew more habits of fish than Agassiz. For Thoreau, Natives were "damned, because his enemies were his historians."

Thoreau's ecstatic, mystical moments in nature came less often as he got older, but his panentheism—God in all things, all things in God—stayed with him as he increasingly turned to science, with his journals tak-ing on added importance as he catalogued the details of divinity on daily walks. Animal minds became a model: how to walk like a fox, how to have one's mind and senses wholly open. On the muskrat, he wrote, "he is a different kind of man, that is all," and when someone shot the summer ducks he cared for, he lamented that they considered it more important to "taste the flavor of them dead than I should enjoy the beauty of them alive."

The commons nourished and educated him yet were being lost while the masses became increasingly starry-eyed over new technology, which he questioned as "improved means to unimproved ends."

Thoreau became a member of the American Association for the Advancement of Science, and a Harvard president appointed him to the Committee for Examination in Natural History, yet he acknowledged the unavoidable subjectivity of science. The scientist should watch "the moods of his mind as the astronomer watches the aspect of the heavens," which may reveal more than what is studied. Still, his observations were rigorous and extensive, and his dated records of wildflower blossoming are used by current scientists to track global warming.

The biologist Richard B. Primack has gone as far as to call Thoreau a climate scientist, given his detailed records of more than three hundred plant species over a ten-year period, often walking many miles in a day to revisit specific species. He also recorded substantial baseline data on wild fruits, weather, migrating birds, insects, reptiles, mammals, and, of course, the succession of forest trees, with extensive study of botany, phenology, and seed dispersion—a huge contribution given the dominant view of special creation by God. All this data collection was directed toward his "Kalendar" project to catalogue the changing seasons over time. And, to top it off, near the end of his life, he took on a massive civil engineering and hydrology project commissioned by local farmers to study river systems around Concord. His findings were so accurate that he once again gifted a baseline of data to current researchers.

Thoreau did not just dabble in science; he was an ahead-of-his-time ecologist who died before he could complete his work, yet his scientific practice was informed by sympathy, expressed as the rational yet empathetic orientation of the naturalist, listening to the language that all things speak within the context of spiritual experience. Such inquiry led to objective facts and the realization that the facts "most astounding and most real" were "never communicated by man to man." He was incessantly wary of exchanging the microscope for "views as wide as heaven's cope," and thus he was incessantly open to mystery, mindful that claiming to know was an impediment to listening.

Emerson wrote, "Beware when the Great God lets lose a thinker on the planet." Thoreau was a graced thinker because he thought within the contexts of earth and cosmos and Spirit; he was a scientist among poets, a poet among scientists, living Ometeca's vision of the sciences and humanities embodied within the individual. He was one of the few, if not the only, of his time who could turn two into one.

In a word, Thoreau practiced logos while industrial education too often teaches students cognitive roadmaps that are narrow-minded and confused.

And we keep driving full speed ahead.

ᘔ

After hearing speeches on the necessity of large farms and pesticide use, satellite mapping systems, and genetic engineering—which were interesting; the students had learned their lessons well and taught me quite a bit— I would ask questions about local and organic farming (this was prior to the increased awareness and movement of buying local and organic) and if they had read Berry and Jackson in their classes. Their responses were that local food and organics were not realistic options given our large and growing population, and they had never heard of Berry and Jackson. The question of population would raise provocative class discussion. We were able to begin practicing logos by exploring the connections among global problems, but it often felt like the speakers had already decided; they were sure that industrial, high-tech solutions were the only way to go.

I'm sure my students felt that I had already decided too as I was happy to speak out passionately against agribusiness and university education that uncritically supports it. But here's the rub: I also argued that all world views are not equally valid. No perspective being final does not lead to relativism (to thinking and doing whatever we want) but to continual searching for situational ethical solutions informed by non-dogmatic universals, such as the reality that we are immersed within larger patterns of intelligence and exist in relationship to human and nonhuman others, and thus we have a responsibility to pursue the good.

None of these ideas, of course, lead to easy agreements. That was okay—dialogue is a spiritual practice—but students often resorted to relativistic "that's just my opinion" rhetoric when defending their views. I enjoyed exploring our techno-agricultural future with students, but I stated, in the spirit of logos, that mere opinion was not good enough. As Socrates suggested, citizens, and students, are not entitled to uninformed opinion; they are entitled to their position, their evolving world view, which they must rationally defend.

I asked students to critically consider the power of techno-scientific thinking and agricultural narratives to shape their biases and silence alternative narratives.

I tried to engage them in dialogue to question received opinion and add new knowledge to their positions.

I suggested they take up a spiritual practice.

I wanted too much.

Like the religious students, the techno-scientific students led me to much reflection and to another book recommended by Preston, Martin Heidegger's *Discourse on Thinking*.

Heidegger responds to the dominance of technical rationality by extolling logos expressed as meditative thinking, or "releasement towards things and openness to the mystery." Such thinking leads us to ponder the "meaning which reigns in everything that is" and demands that we "engage ourselves with what at first sight does not seem to go together at all." But our technological age is governed by a different kind of thought, which Heidegger called "calculative thinking." This type of thinking does not engage mystery and meaning, like the life force of animals or the rational order of the cosmos; rather, it only counts as knowledge what can be easily classified, like more efficiency and profit. Put simply, meditative thinking is open to connections, to I-Thou dialogue and relations while calculative thinking tends to objectify, separate, and dissect, treating everything like an It.

To Heidegger, calculative thinking is the essence of technology. Thus, technology is not merely a tool we use but has a bias that powers a particular type of thinking and way of being in the world. Both meditative and calculative thinking are necessary—Heidegger does not claim that technology does not have its place—but meditative thinking pushes us to ask deeper questions, such as *Why is technology so rarely connected to the genius of place?*

Heidegger argues that we don't ask such questions because we've been seduced by technology's amazing array of successes, making calculative thinking our dominant mode of thinking. We all enjoy technology's successes, and there has been much genuine progress in the technological age. The western enlightenment project, which brought so much scientific and technological advancement, also institutionalized such dignities as human rights, freedom, and equality, all played out in Thoreau's time, and all still being played out. However, there is a danger that technology's ability to "captivate, bewitch, dazzle, and beguile" will cause us to forget that our deeper nature is revealed in meditative thinking.

Heidegger reminded me of Marcuse, and I wondered if the bewitching and beguiling effect of our technologically-based consumer society caused students to happily dwell in this forgetfulness daily. When uncertain and therefore in the proper position for meditative thinking, students seemed to be repositioned away by the noise of gizmos, advertising, societal ideals of success, and techno-scientific experts masquerading as teachers, all of which kept them from opening themselves to mystery. They might sense something more, intrigued by something said in class, seduced, for a moment, by the practice of logos, but I feared that they settled for something far less as their desires were intermeshed with a one-dimensional society of bigger, better, and more of the same.

Students, understandably, had trouble seeing that they were entrenched in techno-consumerist narratives and thus hacked and colonized by inherent biases, including, as Heidegger argued, a bias against nature that turned the natural world into a "standing reserve" of resources. I wanted them not only to see their socialization but also to be seers, as Thoreau advised, not "students merely," reading "their fate" and walking "into futurity" guided by spiritual exercises, perceiving nature as both resources and source. When students are not motivated to question their biases—thinking it's all good rather than pursuing the good—they tend to comport themselves with an attitude of acceptance that is mirrored by the acceptance of others. Or: Whose head is the student using? Whose head is using the student?

I hoped my passionate words would fill their heads, creating some cognitive and heart-changing dissonance, but teaching alternative narratives often taught me the futility of such hopes. All I could do was challenge students to engage the world and their potential by practicing logos.

What happened next was open to mystery.

Mystery I was willing to accept, but sometimes the narrowness of student opinion approached the absurd.

Mike, a young agriculture major, insisted on doing all his speeches on pigs, or rather, the wonders of pork. He had his career mapped out—he was going to hawk pork—and he wanted to practice in Com 114.

Mike's speaking style was salesman, complete with inauthentic smiles and grand gestures. He had seen the future, and it was pork, which, he claimed, was healthier than beef; never mind the logical fallacy of turning eating decisions into a false dichotomy of pork versus beef, or the destructiveness of hog confinement farms and polluting manure lagoons, or the ethical options of eating locally and organically, or of reducing meat consumption or not eating meat.

Or that all decisions, all responses, had to be rethought within the context of the Anthropocene and climate crisis and our utter lostness.

Rational people ate pork.

愉

The Purdue I knew in the 1990s was the fount of much critical pedagogy despite being rooted in the mission of the land grant university, the Cartesian dualism between mind and nature, and the separation of the sciences and humanities. Numerous courses in the liberal arts and sciences were offered from talented professors for those with time in their schedule to take them. A group of graduate students and professors often met on Friday nights at the pub for conversation on a range of topics, including challenging students (in both senses of the phrase), restrictive university structures, and the radical continuation of Enlightenment ideals of freedom, rights, and equality. We also questioned the excesses of modernity and techno-rationality, as well as the excesses of postmodern deconstruction, which exacerbated our lostness by breaking everything in heaps without constructing wholes that better enable us to live in sympathy with intelligence.

I learned much of what I know of philosophy from the spiritual exercise of dialogue with Preston and others in the Purdue community. And the river-fed West Lafayette and Lafayette offered much in their Indiana sunsets, fertile land, and rural values, like friendly waves and hard work from the many farmers. Their crops of corn and soybeans, though, were not for human consumption and were shipped instead to factory farms to fatten cattle before being killed in nightmarish slaughterhouses.

On campus, intellectual and cultural events were numerous—concerts, films, speakers, including respected theologians and scientists such as the Anglican priest and physicist John Polkinghorne (who saw evidence for a theistic God), the evolutionist Stephen Jay Gould (who saw no evidence), and Guy J. Consolmagno, the pope's astronomer, who gave a slide show on what we know of the birth of the universe (providing evidence of something wondrous and mysterious, but with no mention of God). However, Campus Crusade for Christ, one of the largest evangelical organizations in the US, also sponsored frequent speakers. CCC drew hundreds to their events, and I often wondered how much Lily and Ruth and other religious students were influenced by them.

One presenter demonized environmentalists, arguing that God gave dominion to humans and therefore Creation was ours to do with as we pleased; we had God-given freedom to drive big cars and to consume generally. The speaker used an emotional tone: pathos, disconnected from logos, was intended to persuade. Environmentalists were preaching a gospel counter to God's will, and they had to be stopped!

Another CCC presentation demonized Native American culture and religion, while celebrating Christian-inspired progress that overturned the savagery of Indigenous life embedded in nature. Instead of breathing hysterical hellfire into his rhetoric, the speaker spoke softly and avoided eye contact with the audience, which included a few Native American students who sat stunned and saddened. The speaker's style was strange, but upon reflection, strangely appropriate; he seemed lost and dead to the world. Perhaps it was his conscience speaking, even if he was unaware, from deeper wells.

Students such as Mary and Ruth received mixed messages from various on- and off-campus events and the critical thought of their classes. These messages reflected different narratives, and in response, students needed to recognize those narratives that supply room for the pursuit of the good and those that do not—or those that dangerously deepen our lostness by dividing science and religious feeling rather than inspiring wholeness and healing and re-finding the compass.

More books that I mentioned to Mary were the Native American scholar Vine Deloria Jr.'s *Custer Died for Your Sins* and *God Is Red*—the titles themselves a wake up. Deloria argues that a Native view of religion is grounded in timeless experiences that connect us to specific places. The Great Mystery, or the eternal, is experienced in the present as a lived presence. In contrast, our Christian heritage provides a linear conception of time. God, or the eternal, is known in the future, and thus heaven is somewhere else, to be experienced after death. To Deloria, the dominance of the Christian narrative results in a faith in linear progress, which, along with attendant beliefs in unlimited growth and technology as savior, disregards the gifts of the earth.

Along with suggesting books, I should have suggested that Mary visit the town of Battle Ground a few miles west of campus. Formerly Prophetstown, Battle Ground is the site of a historic battle between Native Americans and William Henry Harrison's army. The Native American leader Tecumseh, along with his younger brother, the Prophet, founded Prophetstown in 1808 as a place to unite various tribes against the incursion of White culture. Midwestern Indians lived there, near the river Wah-Bah-Shik-Ki, building a resistance movement, which Tecumseh hoped to grow into a confederacy by visiting tribes between Canada and the Gulf of Mexico and persuading them to join. He left his brother in charge when he left Indiana, giving instructions not to attack the Whites.

The Prophet, however, had a vision foretelling that the army's bullets would not harm his warriors. The opposite, of course, was true, and the resistance was defeated before Tecumseh could return. Harrison lost more men in the battle, known as the Battle of Tippecanoe, but his troops held the ground, effectively ending the movement. The victory eventually helped to elect Harrison president.

There is a rock ledge overlooking the battleground where the Prophet reportedly sang to his warriors during the battle. The ledge, covered by overhanging rocks, creates a cave-like perch. The site is marked, and visitors can climb to the perch, imagining Tecumseh's leadership and instructions, the bloody historical scene, and the Prophet's mistaken prophecy, with him lost in a Socratic allegorical cave of shadowy one-dimensional thinking. In contrast, one can commence meditative thinking, reflecting on Tecumseh's practice of logos, the losses to Native American culture, and their struggle to resist.

Mary had a talent that needed to be heard, but to continue to explore her voice and develop speaking skill she needed also to listen to a variety of narratives, not just a linear Christian narrative within which she was born and expected to find her place. Reading Thoreau and eco-philosophy revealed that the sources of ecocrisis are many, and all religions may be greened through enlightened reading, but the claim that God gave man dominion, when interpreted as domination, is antecedent to Anthropocene angst.

If Mary did some research and went to Battle Ground, she would discover that there are content lessons to be learned from the history of Tecumseh and Prophetstown, as well as style lessons by imagining Tecumseh's rhetorical attempts to unite differing tribes to create a confederacy of resistance. There are also content lessons to be learned by critically considering the Prophet's vision and style lessons from the potential dangers of believing one is being spoken through by higher powers.

Still, we may well be empowered by a larger, more encompassing sense of self, a widened and wiser identity that is open to learning from Indigenous cultures, the ancient Greeks, progressive religiosity, and modern science, letting logos and the Great Mystery speak.

Chapter 6

World Soul

"We lie in the lap of immense intelligence, which makes us receivers of its truth and organs of its activity. When we discern justice, when we discern truth, we do nothing of ourselves but allow a passage to its beams. If we ask whence this comes, if we seek to pry into the soul that causes, all philosophy is at fault. Its presence or its absence is all we can affirm."
—Ralph Waldo Emerson

"With all your science can you tell how it is, and whence it is, that light comes into the soul?"
—Henry David Thoreau

Rafael told me early on that I was an old soul or reincarnated monk, and at times I bought into the idea since it made me sound wise beyond my years. But is there such a thing as "soul"? How far back do the seeds of voice go? We should be open to mystery, but how open must we be? Scientific and religious voices address these questions, agreeing that we are biological and cultural beings but differing on the mystery of whether we are also something more.

Rafael led me to read Carl Jung, which led me to read the Jungian James Hillman, and I often shared with students Hillman's argument that we are born with a daemon that makes its presence felt in childhood and with whom we may consult throughout our lives. Socrates, for example, claimed to have a daemon that spoke in no's; he proceeded along a path until he heard a voice within directing him elsewhere. Hillman further argues that we must "grow down" into our daemon, our "image in the heart" that holds the seeds of our potential, more than grow up, and that the daemonic is more influential than family circumstance. Or rather, no matter our family influence, or formal education for that matter, deeper development does not occur unless we listen to our daemon that arrives with us at birth.

Hillman distrusts transcendence or growing up that doesn't include growing down into soul; a distrust I also pondered. My meditation practice had helped me to find perspective and joy, even when doing monotonous work in the factory and printshop, but I found myself questioning if I was using my spirituality to accept work that was not right for me. I needed to make money and used the money to buy the freedom to think, read, and experience—a soulful desire—but I still wondered if I was transcending soul rather than listening to what my daemon, interpreted as my "still, small voice," wanted of me.

I shared Hillman's views, and Socrates's example, to stimulate class discussion once again. As far as I was concerned, the spiritual dimension of life was worthy of academic study, and academia was the best place to critically consider the possibilities of soul in relation to finding our voices. I also suggested that there is much to be learned from reading our lives backward, "growing down" by embracing moments and places that have most influenced who we are, as soul is tethered to land and community and embodied experience.

ೞ

What bothered me about the assertion that I was an old soul or reincarnated monk, and what bothers my students when we discuss soul and daemons, was that it leaves one feeling stuck, as if the direction of our lives is predetermined and that we don't have freedom to alter that course. The larger question is not predetermination; it's whether our identities are also formed by something providing guidance to our lives that is more than family circumstance, biology, and culture. That idea gets their attention and allows me to assert that we still have freedom: to pay attention or be asleep.

I never liked the word "soul" (as I never liked the word "God"), but Jung, Hillman, and others opened me to the complexity and power of the term. Still, during my Purdue years I hesitated to even write "soul" since it became the poor, overused, and degraded word that popular spiritual books, turning a creative force into milquetoast, associated with a heaping helping of chicken soup. For Jung, nothing rages more fiercely than soul, especially when its presence is felt but not given form in the world. The plethora of books that market a meager knowledge of soul mocks its true power and thus deserve the full force of its rage, a conscious, loving rage that fuels our passions.

Along with Jung, Rafael suggested I read Emerson, especially his essays "Self-Reliance" and "The Over-Soul." In Emerson's radical interpretation of soul, most humans exist in lethargy, unaware of the silence and stillness within connecting us to both the eternal One and the many shining parts and particles of manifest existence. This mystical realization— one in many, many in one—described in wisdom traditions East and West, led Emerson to follow Coleridge in making a distinction between reason and understanding, with reason reflecting universal soul and understanding the empirical (yup, the opposite of what you'd expect). As in meditative thinking, reason revels in finding connections, while understanding divides and calculates. With meditative thinking sidelined, Heidegger argued that calculative thinking had become thinking itself in the twentieth century just as Emerson felt that understanding had gotten the upper hand in the nineteenth century, despite reason being a necessary mode of being in the world.

Reason, which Emerson argued we belong to, may result in revelation, putting us in touch with the eternal, and the eternal in touch with us, such that we intuit spiritual principles, like divine play and purpose, which provide meaning to life. But commerce, linked with understanding, "has availed so far as to transfer the devotion of men from the soul to the material in which it works."

In 1834 at age thirty-one, three years after his beloved first wife, Ellen, died and then leaving the Unitarian ministry at Boston's Second Church, Emerson sat beside a tree in the Mount Auburn Cemetery in Cambridge, among living nature and the dead, opening his eyes and letting "what would pass through them into the soul." After Ellen passed, and no longer feeling the call of the pulpit, he sailed for Europe and spent ten months overseas. He was in limbo and lost yet sensed possibility as we are souls immersed within the life force of the Over-Soul standing on the "edge of all that is great." A few days after visiting Mount Auburn, he wrote in his journal, "Get the soul out of bed, out of her deep habitual sleep, out into God's universe, to a perception of its beauty, and hearing of its call," becoming "a god...conscious of force to shake the world."

In an earlier 1832 journal entry, when pondering his role as minister, he wrote, "The difficulty is that we do not make a world of our own but fall into institutions already made and must accommodate to them to be useful at all. And this accommodation is, I say, a loss of so much integrity, and, of course, of so much power." His disenchantment with his profession had been brewing, and the death of Ellen and traveling brought his soul loss to the surface and revealed integrity and power that had been there all along. He was soon following soul into more satisfying, and independent, work as a lecturer on the lyceum circuit and occasional guest preacher. At the same time, he devoted himself to his writing, a call that had not been fully heeded. Many on the outside saw failure in his decision because he gave up a secure position and substantial salary, but revelations guided by reason often include risk.

My readings of Emerson, Jung, and Hillman, along with life experiences, suggested that socialization and genetics cannot explain revelations of soul. More precisely, they cannot explain away revelations such that discussions concerning human identity begin and end with blank slates or selfish genes. When the invisible mystery we have come to call "soul" is drawn out, like rhizomatic roots in fertile soil, it looks like compassion, it looks like justice, and it looks like intelligence.

Or, in Thoreau's hands, it looks like the refusal to join the crowd, and it looks like civil disobedience, like soul in action, in which the freedom to follow inner life is given expression in the world. But the presence of soul is often misunderstood, and feared, so we end up ignoring it, or trying to kill it, whether with an assassin's bullet ripping flesh or a transnational corporation chain-sawing a five-hundred-year-old redwood. If we don't know how to live it ourselves, our utter emptiness leads us to try to destroy it.

Yet soul, being an immaterial force, cannot be killed.

It can only be repressed.

At Purdue, I came to see liberating students from repression as a core of education. Jeff, Ken, Sarah, Lily, and Ruth all had deeper desires that wanted expression. My job, as best I could, was to draw soul out of others and let it be drawn out of myself. For Emerson, the true teacher does not merely instruct, but ignites inner fire, soul attuned to Over-Soul. After all, "educate" comes from the Latin *educere*, to draw forth, and thus it does not mean we stuff as much information as possible into our neocortices, prop-ping up a Cartesian separate self, regardless of the usefulness of that infor-mation; it means there is already an unfolding intelligence within that needs to be cultivated and that interprets the advice and information we receive.

Teaching at Purdue seemed to confirm what Rafael had insisted: I had wasted no time because my lostness revealed lessons that bore fruit when working with students. But despite spiritual searching and feeling I had found a calling (or because of spiritual searching and remaining thor-oughly human, thoroughly prone to stumbling and folly), I had doubts about the possibility of enlightenment. I had doubts that so-called enlight-ened adepts were perfect and had complete knowledge, or that any soul could fully live in harmony with Over-Soul; not saints and sages, not Jesus, Buddha, Mohammed or Lao Tzu.

Instead, I embraced the possibility that experiences of spiritual unity, or the contemplation of unity, provide a baseline awareness for loving acts, just like science provides a baseline awareness of material facts. According to the spiritual philosopher Ken Wilber, spiritual and material methodol-ogies are similar: if you want to know this, do *this* (learn about a particular meditation practice or formulate a hypothesis); do the practice or experi-ment; and then compare findings with other competent practitioners or experimenters, seeking communal confirmation of one's discoveries.

Such methodologies engage the process of knowing more, but, as Hadot reminded, I did not see how one could fully possess wisdom. Tho-reau also honored our not-knowing, stating that our ignorance may be both useful and beautiful; however, he continually returned to the claim that we may live more consistently in sympathy with outward intelligence by consulting inner intelligence. Or rather, just as biological nature evolves into new forms, human nature may evolve new expressions of soul.

Some students did not like the word "soul," but, following Emerson, I suggested that soul does not pinpoint; rather, it means that we are irre-ducible. It's the word that proclaims that we cannot be fully defined by words, the force that ignites our actions when it is not forced. Obey soul and we are free from being defined by others, and thus freer to unfold by inner listening, keeping the "sweetness of solitude" amidst the crowd. I admitted that this may seem utterly impractical in a world governed by the lucrative standard, but the more we practice deep listening, the more adept we become at recognizing the presence and absence of soul, in varying degrees, discerning the potent mixture in all we do.

Self-culture is an "educating of the eye," Emerson argued, in which we perceive via reason rather than merely understanding—we must distinguish between what is real and what has been mistakenly taken to be real, such as spiritual virtues versus materialistic valuations. Thus, if Thoreau is right that the mass of men led lives of quiet desperation, and a characteristic of expressed wisdom is to not do desperate things, then it makes logical sense that we desperately need education that acknowledges the mystery of soul and draws it out again and again. We need education that does so even if the existence of soul is not provable by scientific methodology. We need education that embraces spiritual methodologies and experiential insights that enhance our ability to pursue the good.

We need education that is discerning enough to tell the difference between feel-good, marketed "soul" and the joyful experience when we meet in our collective depth, the soul of the world.

cs

All education was inherently religious for Emerson, in the esoteric sense of being transformed by spiritual insight, cultivating soul-awareness, finding our voice, and changing the world. Emerson participated in debates within the Unitarian Church, with some arguing for rational criticism of a literal interpretation of the Bible and stripping religion of ill-advised faith, especially Jesus' supposed miracles. Emerson agreed with this critical approach—he greatly valued rational understanding—but he also worked to save religious feeling and intuition from hyper-rationality, stating that all life was a miracle.

Most Unitarian ministers were influenced by William Ellery Channing, whom Emerson called "our bishop" and who espoused transcendentalist ideals, but Channing went to only one club meeting and did not label himself a transcendentalist. Channing preached that humans were defined by "likeness to God" and "inner light," not sin, and his church welcomed all, fought for human rights, and abhorred slavery, inspiring abolitionist and transcendentalist preachers James Freeman Clarke, Wendell Phillips,

William Lloyd Garrison, and early feminists and abolitionists Margaret Fuller and Elizabeth Peabody, among many others. Still, not all agreed on how to end slavery, how fiery to preach, and the best methods of protest. Ministers were also inevitably concerned with church membership, which was declining in response to calls for church and societal reform.

Emerson eventually resided on the outskirts of the church reform debates and focused more on the problem of understanding (calculative thinking) dominating or dismissing reason (meditative thinking and intuition); for him, the way to reinvigorate a decaying church was "first, soul, and second, soul, and evermore, soul." Young Thoreau, whose family regularly went to church, witnessed the debates over traditional Trinitarianism, which argued for the full divinity of Jesus, versus more progressive Unitarianism—or Unitarianism influenced by Transcendentalism—which argued that God was not three but one and everywhere. Thoreau thoroughly studied the Bible, but also Hindu, Islamic, and Buddhist writings, which led him to conclude that the true church was not contained in a building. Thus, he followed his soul and just stopped going.

For me, there was little soul at our family church growing up. Instead, my religious education was mostly forgettable, in the sense that it focused on exoteric ritual devoid of any connection to deeper wells and resembled the rote learning of school. I did recall causing Mom to cry when I refused to go to All Saints Lutheran. I sat in my bedroom closet in my Sunday best, cemented to the floor, ranting about how boring it was—had I been older, I would have said "soulless"—but then Mom shed a tear. That was the first time I ever saw her cry, and in a flash I was on my way to the car.

I also recall being unable to write a prayer in Sunday school (was I supposed to ask for things?), and a confirmation service in which I answered two Bible-related questions in front of the congregation. During my Q & A, the pastor mercifully asked questions from a practice session the previous evening, and I stood and feebly gave the requisite responses, but before I could sit down, he asked me to repeat my answers with more volume. I looked at him like Job confronting the Old Testament God of wrath and punishment and dribbled out a pathetic "What?" He chuckled, "never mind," bringing forth laughter from everyone present, including my family.

When the service was over, I was so flustered that I said "congratulations" when receiving handshakes from exiting parishioners. Why I was congratulating them, I did not know. But it was a day for laughter. Once I was confirmed, my parents agreed to stop forcing me to go to church.

I needed to look beyond my religious education, or beneath it, to explore a genuine religiosity.

Along with my spiritual experiences in second and third grades, I told Rafael three early memories from Staten Island that may have suggested the emergence of soul and a future path; memories that perhaps I needed to grow down into rather than transcend. I remember neither my exact age when these events occurred nor the order. I only know that they happened before the age of seven and were powerful.

There was an empty lot with a small, winding brook near our home. In the lot sat the shell of an old, abandoned blue-and-white Chevy sedan. Next to it was a tree with dangling branches. One day I was playing with neighborhood kids in the lot, and before long we began climbing on the car. I managed to crawl on top, stand up, and grab some of the branches, which bent like coiled bedsprings. I reached as high as I could, tugging on the sturdiest branch, and my feet lost contact with the car, leaving me bouncing four feet from the ground. I tried to reestablish footing on the car but had veered too far off the side. The other kids thought it funny, causing one on the ground to jump and grab at my feet, but I had lost my bearings and was overcome with panic. I pleaded with the smart-alecky kid to stop pulling my legs, but she didn't, and my grip soon failed, causing a backward tumble to the earth.

As soon as I hit the ground, I began to wail, and then hyperventilate, my standard practice as a child. Crying often led to a wheeze, and then to gasping breaths, as if I were struggling to get enough oxygen to last a lifetime. This time, however, I added another step to the process by fainting. My next memory is of waking up on a comfy chaise lounge on our back porch, with, of all things, a deep sense of peace. My mind was still as my mother explained that a neighbor had witnessed my fall and carried me home, and that after having plummeted into the unknown, I seemed to be physically fine. I was more than fine and spent the rest of the afternoon lying on the chaise lounge, with my eyes bright and breath slow and sweet.

The second memory centers on the winding brook. My mother told me, over and over, to never go near the thing. Too young to understand the meaning of sewage, I only knew that it was bad, off-limits, not to be messed with under any circumstances. I disobeyed though not intentionally. I was drawn to the gurgling water flowing around and over rocks. Everything else near our home was innocuous—the overarching oak trees in the back yard, our next-door neighbor's pool where we swam in the summertime, the red dirt and shale behind the garage where we dug a giant hole within which we could nestle and hide—it didn't make sense for the brook to be outside this orbit of innocence. My innocence was wiped away when I got home with wet, sopping shoes. I was in trouble with Mom, but that was nothing compared to when she took off my sneakers. My feet were covered with tiny white worms. I cried, wheezed, and hyperventilated as my mother took me to the bathroom and picked them off one by one. I had once again discovered terror—this time from feeling invaded on my body and within my safe world.

The third memory took place indoors. I was lying on the rug in our living room with colored pencils and blank paper, filling up a page with some form of script. I couldn't write yet, so it was pretend writing with lines and symbols of my own making. I got more and more excited with each pseudo-sentence, and then I gasped, as if making a profound discovery. Something had entered the activity, something mysterious but also real, like finding a long-sought-after prize. I was enthralled, as if accidentally stumbling upon an incomprehensible force. Was it untapped talent, the creative process, silence taking form in the world, the collective unconscious, or simply an early discovery of language? I don't know, but I filled up every inch of that page in my multicolored scrawl and could not have been happier.

These memories may be soul-less, centered solely in family circumstance, but soul works with materiality, with the actual world and in response to actual events. Reading Emerson, Jung, and Hillman made me wonder if I arrived in this world with predilections suggesting reasons for why I am here. These predilections may have shown themselves, like little games of hide and seek, in the more dramatic moments of childhood. It is easy to project onto events, but my early tumble into the unknown and peace, the sensuous allure and stunning disrespect of the earth, and the joy of discovery and writing are central to my character. Perhaps the circumstances were triggers for something within me—my daemon?—to emerge. Perhaps memories hold gifts, not just of family history, but of guidance that shows a way to a future path.

During my Purdue years, I taught as if passion and voice, and the fundamental educational question of why we are here on earth, are connected to the mystery of the "something more." Still, I also felt it best to hold some things lightly, realizing that we often develop more through meditative thinking than affirming or denying.

Rafael seemed to be open to all things religious and joined esoteric groups: the Masons, Rosicrucians, and Theosophical Society. He also argued for reincarnation, saying that you can find it in the Bible, and equated it to cosmic recycling. I found the former interesting but inconsequential and the latter amusing and appealing, but despite the appeal of being an "old soul," I did not know what to make of this claim. Despite loving solitude, I did not want to be, or live, like a monk.

I was sure that I had arrived in this world, like all children, like all students, with a talent for love and engagement with nature and the world soul, with the sources that have formed us and of which we are formed.

Chapter 7

Magnificent Misfits

"I confess myself utterly at a loss in suggesting particular reforms in our ways of teaching. No discretion that can be lodged with a school-committee, with the overseers or visitors of an academy, of a college, can at all avail to reach these difficulties and perplexities, but they solve themselves when we leave institutions and address individuals."
—Ralph Waldo Emerson

"I would make education a pleasant thing both to the teacher and the scholar. This discipline, which we allow to be the end of life, should not be one thing in the schoolroom, and another in the street. We should seek to be fellow students with the pupil, and we should learn of, as well as with him, if we were to be most helpful to him."
—Henry David Thoreau

"Give the soul free course, let the organization be freely developed, and the being will be fit for any and every relation to which it may be called."
—Margaret Fuller

"I'm Professor Homestead; I'm new here, so why don't you tell me about your school and why you are here."

It was my first day teaching at New England College, and I was facing the typical student silence, to which I responded with more silence and a smile while waiting for bravery: one of fifteen sitting in Fitch 12, an old classroom in a white New England–style house, finally spoke with a heavy Boston accent.

"NEC is the only place that accepted me."

His fellow students laughed. I soon found out that his name, or nickname, was "Southie" and that he was from South Boston.

"Why is this the only school that accepted you?" I asked, thinking him bold enough to handle the question.

"I *sucked* at high school. I got in trouble a lot and so they put me in a special school. I did better but my grades still sucked."

I was stunned, and amused, by how forthcoming he was.

"Do you think grades matter?"

They seem surprised to hear the question.

"Do they reflect who you are?"

"Hell no," Southie said, with an emphasis and surety that I would come to know well.

"Grades matter," said another student. "How else are we going to know how we are doing?"

"I could just give comments on your papers without a grade. Some schools don't have grades—they have a portfolio system. Students get a record of comments on their work throughout their college careers."

They looked intrigued, so I shot for more.

"The education scholar Howard Gardner argues that there are seven core intelligences, including logical-mathematical and linguistic intelligences, or logical thinking and language use, and that's what schools emphasize on tests and in grading, or in scores, like the SATs. But according to Gardner there are other intelligences, including musical, kinesthetic, or the bodily intelligence of athletes and dancers, and spatial, which is important for architects or others working in design, as well as two communicative intelligences, interpersonal and intrapersonal, which is another way of saying self-knowledge. He later added three more intelligences: naturalistic, existential, and spiritual, which address the big questions of our place on the planet, who we are, and how we should live. So, in formal schooling you are mostly graded on two intelligences, but there are ten."

"No wonder I flunked out of school," Southie said.

"Why? Aren't you good at logical-mathematical and linguistic intelligences?"

"I suck at math, but my writing is okay, and I can talk."

"I can see that."

The other students laughed again.

"Why do we have to take math?" another student asked.

"Or science," said another. "They make you take a course here called The Way of Science—I hated it."

"I liked that class," said a third.

"Math and science and logical-mathematical intelligence are important. The mistake students make when I talk about multiple intelligence theory is they think they have some of the intelligences and that the ones they struggle with don't matter. But the theory should help you to figure out your strengths and weaknesses and then to work on your weaknesses. I do want you to feel better about yourselves and to realize that you may have intelligences that school systems ignore, but not to the point where you ignore intelligences or rebel against the good parts of school."

"There are good parts to school?" Southie said.

More laughter. I set that one up, and I am sure others were thinking the same.

"School has its problems, but you are fortunate to be in college. You understand that, right?"

Blank looks.

"You need to take advantage of what college has to offer, exploring different disciplines and finding the courses that matter to you. There are so many learning experiences, and not only in the classroom. There are speakers all the time, films and other events, and you learn from each other. When I first went to college, I played ping pong with a student from Japan and a student from Kenya. They became friends, just because we liked ping pong, and I ended up learning about their countries. In my senior year, I used to go to a local diner at night with my best friend from college, and we drank coffee and talked about ideas, about what we were reading in classes, and what we hoped to do with our lives. We called ourselves the 'diner guys' and learned a ton from talking and thinking together."

"I still don't know why math matters," Southie said.

"Or science," said the science-phobe.

"They add to our understanding of our place on the planet. I know they often aren't taught that way—you just take tests on course material—but you should be connecting what you learn to life. The theologian Thomas Berry and cosmologist Brian Swimme wrote a book called *The Universe Story*, and they argue that evolution should be understood as a creation story that provides meaning to our lives. Science provides us with a great narrative, an evolutionary epic in which we commune with other species and celebrate our existence."

More blank looks. I had no idea if they were getting it, but I was too far gone to stop.

"We are the universe made conscious, and we have a responsibility to commune by listening and paying attention to each other, to other species, to the stars. Berry argues that most of us no longer gaze at the stars because of artificial light and our busy lives, and he calls this a soul loss. We watch screens instead of communing. In another book, Berry argues that participating in the unfolding earth and universe story is the 'great work' of our time. We all need to figure out our role in the story, how to celebrate and live in harmony with what we can know about the cosmos—via math and science and all disciplines—and then what we are here on earth to do. College is really about your great work, not grades—grades are not why you are here. College is about asking the big questions, or at least it should be."

Silence. They looked dazed. A student who hadn't spoken speaks.

"At first you used the word 'universe,' but at the end you said 'cosmos'—is there a difference?"

"Great catch," I said with playful exaggeration. "What's your name?"

"Matt," he said proudly.

Everyone smiled.

"The word 'cosmos' is used to denote the order of the universe. The opposite of cosmos is chaos. The universe, and evolution, is characterized by both order and chaos, or order and randomness, but by using the term 'cosmos,' I'm suggesting that we should use our intelligences to live in harmony with the intelligence of the universe and earth, to figure out why we are here and what we have to offer. But we should never forget that this intelligence includes randomness—randomness adds creativity to the evolutionary system, it makes it dynamic, allowing newness to emerge. And just to be clear, I am not talking about Christian 'intelligent design' here, which is creationism in another guise and leaves little room for chaos, or randomness, or science."

Quizzical looks.

"Are you with me or am I losing you? Look at your lives—aren't they both orderly and chaotic, sometimes very chaotic? Some of that chaos is good—it means you are being challenged by new knowledge and developing as a human being—but some of that chaos is bad, like the clutter that keeps you unfocused, like watching TV instead of communing with the stars."

"I like TV," Matt admitted.

"I know you do," I laughed. "I like it too, but I have also mindlessly flipped through the channels, going round and round, often finding nothing worth watching. But there are some good shows."

"What are your favorite shows?" said a young woman who, for the first time, looked interested.

"In a second we're going to go around the room and tell our names and some of our interests—and we can do shows and movies—but let's finish this conversation."

"How are we supposed to know what to do?" Southie said, this time with deep seriousness.

"We don't, but we can ask the big questions and receive insights that give us a sense of direction, and then the next thing you know, you're on a path of self-discovery. The poet Rainer Maria Rilke wrote a book called *Letters to a Young Poet*, and he gave this advice: 'Be patient toward all that is unsolved in your heart and try to live the questions themselves.' We need to ask good questions and see where they lead, which is what we are going to do in this class. And, since we are in a college classroom, we are going to do close readings of books, and I will have to give grades. I hate grading—I didn't become a teacher to give grades. If I had my way, I would just give comments, helping you to explore your intelligences and develop as human beings. But the evil institution of education makes me give you grades."

Big smiles, all around.

"Oh, by the way, the fact that I hate giving grades doesn't mean I'm an easy grader. If you have a problem with a grade, don't sulk, think about my comments for at least a day and then come talk with me."

CB

I first visited New England College, or NEC, in 2005 for a job interview. After leaving Purdue in 2000, having taught fifty sections of Com 114 and listening to, and grading, thousands of speeches, I decided to try graduate school again; more education was the only way I was going to teach anything other than speech class. I followed head and heart to the University of Montana and earned master's degrees in Communication Studies and Environmental Studies. The university was nestled at the base of mountains and along the Clark Fork River in Missoula, a location I was happy to call home. But jobs in Missoula were sparse, and so the nationwide search for work after graduation, doing what I felt called to do—teach college—began. Even a PhD, the golden ticket of academia, did not guarantee a position.

All I knew about NEC was that it was a small liberal arts college in Henniker, New Hampshire, and there was an opening to teach three courses in the Communication Studies department, again as an adjunct but with the possibility of stepping out of the academic ditch onto the first rung of the ladder. I asked my faculty tour guide about the students, and she said many didn't like to read. The conversation turned to other matters—the small student-teacher ratio, small town, small campus with newer buildings and several white clapboard and black shutter houses, and natural surroundings of woods, mountains, and Contoocook River.

I was soon at the pre-fall semester Robert's-Rules-of-Order-town-hall–style faculty meeting. The vice president of academic affairs, a Napoleonic man, made opening remarks and then took questions; it was clear that there was disharmony between in-the-trenches teachers and office-fixated administration. After ten minutes of tension, a faculty member proposed a motion to cancel the meeting. It was seconded, a vote taken, and the meeting was over. The VPAA looked dumbstruck. I was too. I had driven an hour for a two-hour meeting, relieved to have a teaching job, but now wondered if I was stepping aboard a train wreck.

NEC was created after World War II for students attending college on the GI Bill. Its financial viability is dependent on tuition, and I soon learned that the college had endured two financial crises, one in the early seventies, and a second in the late nineties when enrollment took an unexpected downturn; retrenchment forced painful decisions, including dropping some majors and delaying maintenance on infrastructure. The college had also endured a revolving door of administrators, including presidents and vice presidents (the one at the meeting was soon gone). But despite the demise of many small, rural, modest-endowment liberal arts colleges, a pulse was keeping NEC going: professional but personal teacher-student relationships, which provided plenty of opportunities for mentoring.

My first impression upon seeing the place and meeting colleagues was that it was a college of true teachers, some with master's degrees grandfathered into the system before PhDs became the academic norm, and set in a beautiful location, "the only Henniker on Earth," as the sign says as you enter town. I also loved the name. New England College sounded like a school where Thoreau would teach, or at least I would get to teach in his bioregional stomping ground.

I was most intrigued by the faculty characters, including a literature professor with long white hair and beard who reminded me of Walt Whitman. When he became the next vice president of academic affairs, he stabilized the position and college. He retired after forty years although he continued to teach a history of film course and adapted literature for the theater department. I also met an environmental science professor who eventually retired after fifty years that spanned his NEC undergraduate degree and teaching career. He had combined his background in engineering with a liberal arts sensibility to teach experiential learning courses in sustainability long before the term and movement became popular.

Faculty were devoted to the college—there had to be something special about the place to engender such deep feeling—and they were a feisty bunch, with creative research interests but whose primary focus was teaching.

I soon learned the challenges of teaching at NEC, like the fear of low enrollment and another financial crisis. At Purdue, and other big universities with big endowments, big campuses, and big class sizes, there is a "goodbye and good riddance" approach to students who are not measuring up. At NEC, there are multiple attempts to find out why they are struggling and provide support. Faculty try to keep students, or not judge them out of college too quickly, but some souls end up not being ready for the rigors of academia and may never be ready; their character and paths rightfully lead them elsewhere. The only way to know is to provide opportunity, including the opportunity to struggle. Some students have a learning difference, some claim to be visual learners (and thus they don't like to read), and some are dealing with ADD, a growing trend at all schools..

NEC is not an "elite" college based on the wrongheaded Ivy League definition—we don't get many applications from 4.0 GPA high schoolers or top SAT scorers—but we do get our share of magnificent misfits who struggled in high school for various reasons, including because they thought it stupid, but who have plenty of potential. If there is such a thing as a daemon, they have not been communicating with their inner intelligence.

Many are lost.

NEC is where some find themselves (both existentially and spiritually) or where they find what they need to find.

NEC is not the right fit for all professors. One new hire left due to not finding the students to be very magnificent, but, being a misfit myself, I began to see NEC as the "little engine that could." It upholds the ideals of the liberal arts in service of students who need a chance to find nascent abilities, and perhaps soulful predilections, during a time when the liberal arts, the core curriculum of an educated citizenry, is devalued in favor of the market-model university.

ଔ

There are reasons I relate to the struggles of students like Southie. My grades in formal education are etched in consciousness, marking me, so to speak, in ways that are difficult to measure. I was a high school honors student until I started to ask questions. I had done well out of fear of failure or being average—or being labeled by grades—but eventually refused. What, after all, had I learned and what did it have to do with anything? One thing I learned was how to memorize material and spit it out on the test, but without fear I often had little motivation.

My pedagogy is inevitably different from a professor who has only known academic success by specializing in a particular field and intelligence, not only because of grade questioning and being lost, but because Rafael showed me that the classroom is only one site for education. The mentor-student relationship taught me more than any course could possibly teach.

Reading Thoreau led me to research his mentor-student relationship with Emerson, with Emerson a mature thirty-four and Thoreau a magnificent misfit twenty at the time of their first meeting. I also researched mentoring relationships among other transcendentalists, particularly Margaret Fuller.

Emerson spoke widely in the US and had become the country's first public intellectual with a reputation for exciting young students. He heartily approved when he met Thoreau, stating that he was "spiced through with rebellion." When Thoreau began visiting the Emerson household, and meeting with New England transcendentalists, he found other misfits, in the sense that their thought, including on education and spiritual transformation, was more evolved than their fellows.

Emerson esteemed character over class rank and recognized Thoreau's nonconformity as a principled conscience. He also recognized his potential, and made sure Thoreau realized it too, an essential function of mentoring that Rafael provided for me, and which I try to provide for my students. Emerson suggested that Thoreau write in a journal, and he shared his library and lively conversation, including on walks and boat rides. In a late evening excursion with his "good river god" Thoreau, they "left all time, all science, all history" behind as Thoreau rowed them on the Concord River, entering into silence and stillness, the stars saying, "Here we are," their "ineffable beams" stopping human conversation.

Emerson's schooling included graduation from Harvard in 1821. A fair scholar by formal standards, he spent more time on independent reading than assigned texts. He loved to read, asking himself, "When shall I be tired of reading?" He responded, "When the moon is tired of waxing and waning, when the sea is tired of ebbing and flowing, when the grass is weary of growing, when the planets are tired of going." He loved great thinkers, like Plato, yet his education also blossomed via mentoring, especially from Aunt Mary Moody Emerson, with whom he corresponded via idea-filled letters.

Emerson claimed that Aunt Mary was the best writer in Massachusetts, and she was well-known as an articulate and outspoken conversationalist. Her obituary stated, "she was thought to have the power of saying more disagreeable things in a half hour than any person living." Not surprisingly, she was a devoted reader, but it was her lively spirit, originality, and force of character that were most influential. Emerson wrote that she fulfilled a function "which nothing else in his education could supply." A religious woman, she was uncomfortable with rigid belief or unbelief and was guided instead by passion for direct experience, or what Emerson called "reading God directly," which most occurred in nature. She also brought passion to reading and demanded that the written word measure up to her experiences rather than the reverse. Her central advice to Emerson and his brothers was to always do what you are afraid to do, and she displayed an interest in and a gift for speaking with and challenging young people.

Reading about their history led me to the conclusion that the largely forgotten Aunt Mary, while not a transcendentalist, embodied the spirit of transcendentalism in the form of energetic education. In her case, it was self-education, expressed as turning within and going her own way, and then expressing herself outwardly for the purpose of challenging received ideas and creating new human beings.

Another influence on Emerson and Thoreau was the "new woman" Margaret Fuller, the editor of the transcendentalist journal *The Dial*. The introduction to the first edition, written by Fuller and Emerson, made their mission plain: "We are to reconcile spirit and matter; that is, we must realize this atonement. Nothing else remains for us to do. Stand still we cannot. To go back is equally impossible." Strong words, and Fuller, a feminist pioneer, educator, journalist, political revolutionary, and revolutionary writer, was best suited for the task. She was also happy to challenge Emerson and Thoreau on gender or pretty much anything; their discussions on Goethe were particularly important, persuading them to ground transcendental leanings more fully in the "law of the leaf," in which we perceive evolving patterns of intelligence.

In "The Great Lawsuit," an essay published in *The Dial* and later extended to the groundbreaking *Woman in the Nineteenth Century*, she argued that women must have inward and outward freedom to grow, as there is "but one law for all souls." Like all transcendentalists, she focused on the liberation of the divine spark within; for women that meant arbitrary barriers must be struck down such that all paths were open. Not seeing the destiny of women was a defect in man's moral development as women were "taught to learn their rule from without, not to unfold it from within."

Education focused on making them better companions and mothers of men, yet for Fuller, masculine and feminine are fluid, passing into each other.

Fuller was taught by her father as if preparing a son for Harvard, which did not accept women. Instead, she went to Miss Susan Prescott's Young Ladies Seminary in Groton, Massachusetts; an advanced intellect, she had trouble fitting in and was disappointed in her education, which included classes on manners and sewing. She later declared that she considered Miss Prescott a mentor, and the school had a powerful effect on her character.

Fuller struggled to find her voice in a world that did not value women's abilities, or the fact that they too had souls. She wrote of her despondency in her journal. Afraid of disappointing her father and pressured by church to conform, she felt sad and weary from not having her gifts recognized. Miss Prescott may have seen her potential, but a whole society did not. Sustained mentoring was not available to help save her from her lostness, but a spiritual experience did: she "saw there was no self, that selfishness was all folly, and the result of circumstance; that it was only because I thought self real that I suffered; that I only had to live in the idea of the All, and all was mine...My earthly pain at not being recognized never went deep after this hour."

Fuller was a force influenced by larger forces. Paul Dann, in his Thoreau biography, writes that Emerson and others considered her "an incarnation of the daimonic." And she wrote in the preface of *Woman in the Nineteenth Century* that our destiny is to fulfill the law of our being, doing "holy work" by making "the earth part of heaven."

Fuller went on to teach at Bronson Alcott's Temple School in Boston. Alcott, a prominent transcendentalist and the father of Louisa May Alcott, used Socratic dialogue to draw out insights from young students, until scandal from subject matter on religion and sexuality led to his school's closure. Fuller also loved reading, and teaching allowed her to share that love; Barry Andrews, in his book on transcendentalism, states she was "without a doubt the most well-read woman in America," and she may have been the most well-read of either sex. She later taught at the Greene Street School in Rhode Island and mentored wealthy women (who were not allowed to be educated) in Boston at Elizabeth Peabody's bookstore and salon. Peabody, another early transcendentalist guided by the fire of soul, assisted Alcott at the Temple School and started *The Dial* with Emerson, within which she was the first to translate a Buddhist text for an American audience. Peabody advocated for early education for children and called the mistake of confusing ego and soul "egotheism."

At the bookstore, Fuller called her participatory pedagogy "conversations," and she pressed her compatriots to pursue the good and beautiful by asking questions such as, "What were we born to do?" and "How should we do it?" She introduced students to Sappho, Germaine de Stael, George Sand, and other accomplished women writers and thinkers who provided models for women and ignited their potential.

Fuller gave Thoreau a core piece of advice: "Nature is not yours until you have been more hers," but they tiffed over Thoreau's early submissions to *The Dial*, which she sometimes refused to publish. At the time, she was impressed with his character more than his writing, yet she offered him good criticism and advice. It was Thoreau who searched for her remains when her homebound ship crashed close to the Cape Cod shore as she returned from Italy. She had become a foreign correspondent covering the Italian Revolution and was returning with her husband and child, who also perished. She died at forty, and the country lost a soul committed to finding voice, changing the world, and eliciting such commitment from others.

Emerson and Thoreau were further influenced by other magnificent women—my research uncovered a theme—who changed their times by refusing to fit in. Emerson's second wife, Lidian, involved him in the antislavery movement and stimulated his social conscience. Thoreau was shaped by his mother and sisters and women relatives and boarders in the household generally. Many of these women formed the Concord Female Anti-Slavery Society, leading men into the cause. Thoreau's strong-willed mother, Cynthia, sheltered escaping slaves in their home as part of Underground Railroad, and Thoreau helped to escort them to safety. Abolitionism and women's rights were twin causes; Fuller had stated that men were too much under "the slavery of habit."

Thoreau respected self-reliant women: bold and smart women such as Fuller; his mother and sisters, who integrated, as Fuller argued, masculine and feminine qualities; and Mary Moody Emerson, whom he considered a genius. She reminded him "less often of her sex" than any woman he knew. It should be no surprise that some of Thoreau's views on women reflect his time; he considered genius in women rare. He also struggled with romantic love since Ellen Sewell rebuffed his marriage proposal when he was twenty-two. Ellen had stayed at the Thoreau boardinghouse for two weeks, leaving young Henry, and his brother John, smitten and ready to commit. She refused both of them, partially because they did not measure up to her minister-father's standards.

Losing Ellen had a deep effect on Thoreau. The rejection turned him more fully to nature, but it is unclear if it influenced his attitudes toward women. After all, even Mary Moody claimed that women were "frivolous, almost without exception"; to the degree that this was true, it was a function of education or its lack. None could go to college and next to none had mentors—a historical lesson that provides critical perspective for my students—yet all, according to transcendentalism as theory, had potential for inner genius and could learn by listening rather than conforming.

Both Emerson and Thoreau seemed to embrace the common conception that men represented the intellect and women the emotions. However, they also perceived that this binary was not rigid, and that the highest sentiment combined both. Thoreau stated that unless men and women are "both wise and loving, there cannot be either wisdom or love," which is another stirring quotation (Thoreau and Emerson are quotation machines). Thoreau was supportive of Fuller and the cause, calling "The Great Lawsuit" a noble piece, but he did not fight for women's rights like he did for nature and the antislavery movement. Emerson also forcefully praised "The Great Lawsuit," stating "it will teach us all to revise our habits of thinking on its head." Thanks to the women around him, Emerson's position on women's rights evolved from concern to commitment to advocacy.

Fuller, and all transcendentalists, participated in and led discussions on key questions of their time; Rafael, referencing a literary mentor, the Cuban educator and political revolutionary Jose Marti, argued that it was criminal for education not to do so. From my research, it also became clear that the transcendentalists all mentored each other and challenged each other—they most certainly did not easily agree. All, in their way, were educators mentoring a nation, especially the young, but perhaps no one more than Emerson.

In "The American Scholar," Emerson presented themes on education that occupied him and Thoreau throughout their lives: Study nature and your own inner nature, which are of one mind. The essay, first delivered as a commencement speech at Harvard in 1837, shook the audience because it criticized education devoid of self-reliance or inward inquiry into soul connected to Soul. He also decried "minutely subdivided" disciplines "spilled into drops." In response, he called for holistic education marked by reading nature, reading books but trusting our own thoughts, and applying what we have read via action; or rather, "we hear that we may speak." There was no praise for Harvard, or academic tradition, or anything associated with institutionalized education; instead, he attempted to liberate students from institutions, stating that they should "plant themselves in their own instincts." He argued that we do ourselves a disservice when we forget that great thinkers of the past were once not so great; they became great only by trusting themselves and listening to inner promptings.

Emerson gave his American Scholar speech at Thoreau's commencement, which Thoreau refused to attend because he did not want to be part of the crowd. Or, as he later stated in a lecture, he feared merging into the festivities of the day along with everyone else and "losing his identity in the nonentities around him." In a sense, however, they had already met because Thoreau had read and was influenced by Emerson's *Nature*; reading books may be considered another form of mentoring, especially when read with the force of Mary Moody.

A year later, in 1838, graduating seniors invited Emerson to speak at the Harvard Divinity School. He accepted, and his address attacked historical and organized Christianity, including its teaching at Harvard. Emerson revered Jesus and said that his finest quality was his ability to listen to and then act on his inner genius, but Emerson criticized the blind adoration of Jesus and the Bible because it removed divinity from within us and caused us to mistrust or ignore our own revelations and the miracles of everyday life in nature. Emerson, privileging religious feeling over rigid faith, advised students to "go alone" and not conform to deadening debates over theism and atheism or to mediators of religious truth. Instead, they should find their own truths. He also made his pedagogical argument that it is "not instruction, but provocation that I can receive from another soul."

The faculty, having their traditional commitments challenged, condemned his words, and Emerson was banned from speaking at his alma mater for more than twenty-five years.

Thoreau, critical of Harvard for its fixation on branches of knowledge without recognizing their roots, modeled the learning Emerson proposed in his talks. Emerson stated that Thoreau "gives me, in flesh and blood...my own ethics." But here my inquiry into mentoring was slowed by a seeming contradiction. To go alone, as Emerson knew well, requires that we are not alone, that we have a someone who acts as catalyst and guide, or at least supporter, especially when living our ethics does not initially lead to fulfillment.

After graduating and changing his name from David Henry to Henry David—no longer his parents' child but becoming his own man—Thoreau lived in Staten Island with Emerson's brother and tutored his child while shopping his writing in New York City. There were expectations associated with being Emerson's protégé, yet, homesick for Concord, he returned a "failure," unsure of what to do next. At times, their mentoring relationship was challenging and messy. In in his essay "The Poet," Emerson lamented, "I look in vain for the poet whom I describe."

Thoreau did not give up and consoled himself in his journal: "Defeat is heaven's success." He intuited that the cosmos and his daemon may have other plans that take time to unfold; all he could do was go alone, in the sense that Emerson meant in his address, by listening to and following inner genius as best as he could while recognizing that one is never truly alone when living in sympathy with intelligence.

Soon after, in 1844, Emerson bought a section of the Walden woods, and Thoreau's friend, Ellery Channing (the nephew of seemingly everyone's mentor, William Ellery Channing) suggested that he build a hut on the land, "devouring yourself alive. I see no alternative, no other hope for you." It was good advice; mentors and friends sometimes see our souls as well or better than we do. Thoreau soon made a deal with Emerson to plant cultivable land and build a small house, and he moved into his Walden cabin on July 4, 1845, a personal declaration of independence. Thoreau called Emerson's generosity an "infusion of love from a great soul."

He had gone to Walden Pond all his life and had crafted the poem "Walden" years earlier in 1838, in which he conversed with the pond; now he was living it. Life seemed to be leading him to this; a cabin built with his own hands, life and writing becoming one. He could open trade with "the Celestial Empire" and ask, "Life! who knows what it is—what it does? He meant to find out: "If I am not quite right here I am less wrong than before."

Thoreau was independent at Walden Pond. He needed less mentoring as life force took over the job. The world, though, remained in the form of the rambling train passing by daily and in visiting town and in friends visiting for walks—once members of the Female Anti-Slavery Society came for a visit. All the while, Thoreau experienced and recorded universals amid changing land. He left Walden after two years because Lidian Emerson needed him while Emerson was away lecturing in Europe. He helped care for the household and kids, and when Lidian got sick, he cared for her like a sister with spiritual love.

The offer to stay at Walden Pond was Emerson's greatest gift, and he began to repay it by helping his family. He likely could have gone back to the small cabin after Emerson's return but wrote "what is well done…is done forever," and that he had "several more lives to live, and could not spare any more time for that one." Next would come the further writing and rewriting of *Walden*, which would take many years. The deepest return gift to his mentor would be *Walden* itself, and teaching others through it, including its reverberations after their lifetimes.

The gift must move.

That is the deeper purpose of the liberal arts, that is why true teachers teach, that is the "little train that could" mentoring heartbeat that was keeping NEC going.

As my students graduated, they sometimes surprised me with emails telling me of their adventures and careers and even their great work. They also expressed gratitude for what they were given but did not fully appreciate until they found out more about life, what it is and what it does, and struggled with their lostness.

Thoreau would continue to go alone but would never again live alone, yet the Walden experiment would stay with him for the rest of his life. And his supposed failure in New York City led him to meet an important contact, Horace Greeley, publisher of the *Herald Tribune*, who would later publish many of his essays and support and promote him generally.

Emerson's mentoring was crucial to Thoreau's development, and early on he mimicked his mannerisms. But Thoreau did not just live Emerson's ethics and ideas, he lived his own, discovering depths of thought, and soul, via experiences of wilderness and wildness to which Emerson's temperament was unsuited. They most certainly did not always agree; Emerson cautioned against extremism and Thoreau argued, "I know of few radicals as yet who are radical enough."

Thoreau was already on the transcendentalist trail when he met Emerson, and he steadfastly followed his path. The key to mentoring, then, may be to help students to be less wrong when choosing which way to go.

ℛ

My formal schooling taught me that transcendentalist principles are ignored and mentors like Rafael are rare. Still, I often poll students about their high school years, and nearly everyone has one person who supplied much-needed support and guidance beyond the classroom. For me, it was my sarcastic and on-your-side tennis coach and senior-year math teacher, Gene Schnure, who had an almost leprechaun-like charm and easily won students over with a quick, high-pitched laugh.

Gene had master's degrees in mathematics and English. When I took his probability and statistics class, math was suddenly applicable to life. He never let his authority get in the way of a good time but was serious about learning, moving swiftly through problems, keeping attention and pushing abilities. Gene held up excellence as a worthy endeavor, and students liked him so much they wanted to show what they could accomplish. We weren't after grades; we were after his care and approval.

Gene was on earth for a purpose—to teach and have fun—and it came through, consistently, with strength and determination. I found myself modeling his character, especially his sarcastic wit and intense gaze; not to mimic, but as a means for exploring my own abilities. He followed his inner life with vigilance, and I wondered where this vigilance came from and if it was also within me.

Skilled teachers often work within antiquated systems. In his 2003 essay "Against School," John Taylor Gatto, a thirty-year educator and New York City Teacher of the Year, describes the eighteenth-century

Prussian roots of dominant educational structures: the division of students by age, class, subject, testing, and grades was designed to provide workers and a manageable citizenry. The intent was not to develop well-being or critical thinking skills, and certainly not to discover a meaningful inner life. As Thoreau put it, "What does education often do? It makes a straight-cut ditch of a free, meandering brook."

Gatto reviews functions of education described by Alexander Inglis in his 1918 book, *Principles of Secondary Education*, beginning with an adaptive function that inculcates a habitual reaction to authority (where else do you need to ask permission to use the bathroom, except prison?). Other functions further enforce the conformity needed to harness and ma-nipulate a large labor force by determining each student's role within the social machine using quantitative testing methods. And finally, the selec-tive function, as in Social Darwinian selection, weeds out the unfit via the humiliation of poor grades while training those with high grades as man-agers in charge of perpetuating the industrial system.

After reading "Against School," I wanted to dismiss this list as the product of a past age, especially considering the many skilled, and caring, teachers I knew existed. But reading my experiences as a student forward to my experiences teaching students like Southie, it was clear that these functions still have influence. Education, with its emphasis on specializa-tion and grades, may lead to narrow-mindedness and humiliation and "straight-cut ditches" more than it leads to "free meandering brooks" able to explore potential and pursuit of the good. And what of the criminality of not seriously addressing key questions of our time? Along with climate crisis, a key question is the structural bias of education: specialization and grading are expressions of I-It calculative thinking; a meditative-thinking pedagogy would focus on listening and wholeness and love of place or love generally.

Love, after all, mirrors the unfolding order of the cosmos, expressed as *agape*, self-giving unconditional love; *eros*, the ecstatic interconnecting energy of love; and *philia*, friendship love, which E. O. Wilson extended as *biophilia* to include our affinity with all species, with all forms of life. While Thoreau was never in a romantic relationship, or at least not in a consummated one, he experienced and wrote often of such idyllic forms of love. Instead of turning the crank of machinery in our work, he advised us to turn the "crank within," and wondered, "how many horse-power the force of love, for instance, blowing on every square foot of a man's soul, would equal." He continued: "Love is the wind, the tide, the waves, the sunshine. Its power is incalculable."

Thoreau was in love with the exuberance of nature as a force that expresses spiritual unity amid material diversity and calls us to action that moves the gift. Love most certainly could not be judged by the lucrative standard or reduced to buying things to prove love or win affection. "A man is rich," he wrote, "in proportion to the number of things he can afford to let alone." The American Dream narrative had not yet been institutionalized in Thoreau's time, but it was present and growing, and he responded with an "antimaterialist counterdream," as the Thoreau scholar Lawrence Buell puts it.

Lucrative standard reductionism is sold to student-consumers daily. Earlier "uneducated" generations knew the value of simplicity and thrift while today's "educated" students simply consume without simplicity and thrift being recognized as values. At Purdue, I had a student give a speech on attaining the five C's: career, cash, credit card, condo, and country club membership. I knew that most students come to college in pursuit of a high-paying job but had never heard these materialistic goals articulated so specifically. I told her that the material aspects of life are certainly important, especially for the impoverished, but her model left out other C's—commitment, compassion, creativity, community, and callings.

I loved hearing about the five C's because they exposed the cultural context within which we educate and learn. Some students in the class were shocked by this litany of goals, but if honest, they would admit to similar definitions of success, which societal narratives have hammered into them. Just before the famous "different drummer" line in *Walden*, in which Thoreau implores readers to "step to the music which he hears" rather than follow the crowd, he asks another key question: "Why should we be in such desperate haste to succeed, and in such desperate enterprises?"

Emerson also had plenty to say about genuine success, or "rules" for life, such as healthy living, both physically and psychologically; fulfilling work; friendship; deep conversation; and "[making] yourself necessary to somebody." "The high prize of life," however, is "to be born with a bias to some pursuit," which is another way of saying that our greatest good comes from listening to and following our daemon. Success as an educator comes from provocation that aids this individuation process. He put it this way: "All education is to accustom him to trust himself," becoming a "self-searching soul, brave to assist or resist a world" and "only humble or docile before the source of the wisdom he has discovered within him."

During my undergraduate years at Rutgers, I walked past a poster in a shop window that would have made Emerson squirm, or ill, or utterly confused at what gets deemed the high prize of life: bikini-clad women fondling a shiny sports car with a single-word heading "$UCCE$$." Such images are common for anyone who has watched beer commercials, but the starkness of the image stopped me and made me laugh—there was no mistaking its message, no pretending to have a conscience, no mix of ideals. Success equals access to money, shiny cars, and beautiful women, who are just another item in the list of desirable possessions.

The poster is absurd. It's instructive also to imagine Thoreau and Fuller coming across this image, yet the nexus money-women-sex-cars-consumption is the story Jeff learned before he entered a college classroom and struggled to find a worthwhile major and life. It was the story informing Ken's decision to be an engineer rather than an English teacher and the story contributing to Sarah's inability to heal from abuse. It was the story that influenced Southie to major in theater, not to be an artist, but so he could become a celebrity and be in commercials.

Thoreau intimated that words such as "success" and "failure" did not mean the same to him as they did for his neighbors. He wrote that "life is everything" and thus the proper measure of "destiny." He also advised that we go in the "direction of our dreams," and said that if we have "built castles in the air" our "work need not be lost"—we just need to "put the foundations under them." In doing so, we will "meet with success unexpected in common hours." He also asked his neighbors for their "original thoughts" coming from their life experience, or that they should go "a-huckberrying in the fields of thought and enrich all the world with his visions and joys."

Perhaps it's better to fail, then—not failure as an easy excuse, but failure to fit the dominant culture's definitions, like advertising depictions of the perfect life. Perhaps we should embrace being imperfect misfits, lost yet listening and going alone by coming home to ourselves and our great work.

Knowing that I would have soul-damaged students in my classes led me to change my first day spiel over the years. I made sure to convey to students my misgivings with grading, even though I would be grading them.

I also sometimes told students my New York City "practice commute" story, thinking it a kind of alternative parable that might inform their choice of major. They often missed the point, though. It is not a story about the evils of advertising or cities, and it is not a story about persuading them to do what I did. It's a story about the struggle to "go alone" by simply listening to ourselves. I admitted that it may be wise to listen to others, such as mentors and parents, who may have practical guidance to share concerning work and careers, but it's also important to return to *educere*. For learning to take place, we must interpret guidance through the filter of our inner life. This assumes, of course, that we have an inner life, that we invite solitude and intrapersonal conversations that lead to self-knowledge, and that we see such inquiry as a central part of education.

I received telling information from my unconscious during my practice commute in the form of memories and images, as well as from my body's reaction to standing outside of Ogilvy & Mather. I received more the next day from emotions, from crying and laughing in the park. I tell students that they might receive different messages from a similar commute, jumping for joy outside the impressive buildings and advertising agencies. Thoreau wrote, "I would not have anyone adopt *my* mode of living on any account; for, beside that before he has barely learned it I may have found out another for myself, I desire that there be as many different persons in the world as possible…." However, he continued, "but I would have each one find out and pursue his *own way*, and not his father's and his mother's and his neighbor's instead."

Do not follow my "practice commute" path, I implored, follow your own while recognizing that insights will continue to emerge from the fertile meetings of inner and outer worlds.

Or these worlds will crash. I had a lot more listening and learning to do.

I also told my practice commute story because I wanted students to know that I have lived the pressures that many of them are living. I wanted to remind myself of the pressures and display empathy for what it's like to be an undergraduate. Pressures, though, do not come only from false definitions of success, parental expectations, and anxiety over post-graduation careers; they come also from grades, the boon and bane of industrial education.

When my final Rutgers semester neared its end, I could have taken my practice commute and searched for an ethical profession in New York City. I could have worked for a nonprofit, creating public service ads that expose the emptiness of the five C's, or the fast-food industry's insipid purveyance of agribusiness beef and heart attacks, or Eli Lilly's pollution of the Wabash River and our psyches while offering Prozac as a cure for the right price. But my years of formal education didn't lead me to explore such directions, mainly because it never really directed me, with seriousness, compassion, and care, to explore my inner intelligence.

Like Thoreau, students need Emersonian mentoring to guide them to who they are and who they may become as beings of spiritual depth. Such mentoring frees them to perceive power structures with clarity, including the game of grading. Are A students successful if they graduate, move up the corporate ladder, make lots of money, and participate in the destruction of the ecosystem that gives us life?

If one were to argue yes, we would have to ask *On what grounds?* Certainly not the ground of Being, or silence and stillness, or life force reverberating within wild rivers.

Or the ground of love, including the love of matter, of land, water, air, animals, us, which we have "successfully" devastated each year I was in school as a student, and each year that I have taught.

A marker moment for me was the 1989 Exxon *Valdez* oil spill in the pristine Prince William Sound in Alaska; the images of the ocean on fire and oil-coated wildlife were hard to bear. Many of my students recall the 2010 *Deepwater Horizon* spill in the Gulf of Mexico, thanks to images of that underwater pipe incessantly pouring gallons and gallons of oil into the gulf, the rig on fire, and more oil-coated wildlife. There have been so many other spills before, in between, and after those we don't hear about or aren't publicized for long. In the Niger Delta, an estimated nine to thirteen million barrels have spilled over fifty years. During climate-disruption–influenced Hurricane Ida in 2021, nearly 350 spills were reported in Louisiana alone.

Real successes abound as rights have progressed, thanks to thought leaders and grassroots movements, such as Fuller, the Concord Female Anti-Slavery Society, and the long fight for equality generally. And the rights tradition has been expanded to animal rights and the rights of nature, including rivers. If Thoreau didn't call directly for these rights, such expansion was inspired by his wild expressions of *agape*, *eros*, and *biophilia*. But since Thoreau's time, the industrial revolution, and industrial education that supports it, has been a smashing success at burning fossil fuels and destabilizing climate, undermining the rights of the marginalized and impoverished across the globe. In my lifetime, we have successfully procreated, tripling human population and creating the sixth "great" period of species extirpation.

The so-called successes of the lucrative standard, of business as usual, are everywhere, and they increasingly trump real social justice and rights successes. Desertification, check. Sea level rise, check. Ocean acidification, check. Ocean plastic, check. And on and on and on. We have already produced dead zones, and each day we take further steps toward ecosystem and societal collapse fueled by more carbon-based humans burning carbon and producing and discarding more stuff as if there are no limits. And those "successes" can happen only when humans go along rather than go alone, learning that following status quo routines rather than Emerson's principled rules may get you the five C's.

Thoreau's writings, especially the "Economy" section of *Walden*, argue that finding our great work demands a redefinition of success, and thus the redefinition of what it means to be a productive human being, and thus a redefinition of work. Thoreau, Emerson, Fuller, and other transcendentalists took on this task. Another urgent question of our time is whether education, despite structural constraints, will as well, or if we can rid ourselves of such constraints and redefine education, mentoring misfit souls as if their lives, and all our lives, both human and nonhuman, depend on it.

ଔ

New England College does enroll top high school students, and I am over-joyed to have them in class—they have a strong work ethic and read, hope-fully for the right reasons. Anna, an initially shy young woman who at-tended my first class at NEC, was an A student from a local high school taking her first college course. She received a C on her first paper and nervously approached me to ask why. I read over my comments, pointing out writing errors, textual misunderstandings, and incomplete reasoning, and then repeated the purpose of the assignment: we read the text to go beyond the text, internalizing knowledge and making it part of our lives. I also told her not to worry—her identity was not permanently marked—and to work harder.

Anna desired A's but she also cared about learning and self-develop-ment. Such care can be hard to find given the five C's unless the student has had a high school teacher like Gene, a soul-nourishing family, or dae-mon providing guidance, even if consciously unaware.

Anna became an involved student at NEC, running the school news-paper as editor-in-chief; interning at New Hampshire NPR; and helping to organize political events, including talks by presidential hopefuls. With New Hampshire the first primary state, they all come to campus. I ended up having her in three courses and worked with her in my role as advisor for the newspaper. We also worked together on a directed study in inves-tigative reporting, and she produced a twenty-page report on underage drinking that explored legalities, police procedure, and student stories. Af-ter graduation, she got an entry-level job at a respected New Hampshire newspaper. They were impressed with her report, stating that they had never seen anything like it from a student. Then she had a better offer from NPR, but she left town, making a difficult decision to join her boy-friend who was attending college in Maine. She was lured by their long-term relationship as well as the plan to live a simple life, build their own log house, garden, and learn more than any text can provide.

I shuddered a bit when she told me that she turned down the NPR job. Anna also seemed to have regrets, but I quickly replied that she made no mistakes. She was doing her best to follow her own path, not a pro-scribed one. She was displaying intelligence because she was struggling to listen to deeper wells and take risks that would stimulate learning. What-ever happened, she would be okay, with post-graduation steps leading to the mystery of next steps.

Students like Anna would excel with any teacher, and our classes together were not always filled with brilliance. Plenty of students take my classes, seem unmoved, and I rarely see them again. But the small classes and chance to mentor at NEC allowed me to participate in a student's progression over several years, helping them to be less wrong while a witness to their next steps. When she graduated, Anna gave me a thank-you card that said she never forgot my first-day spiel. She also saved her first paper, remarking that I was right to give her a C.

Transformation is NEC's motto, and we enroll students who are ready to transform, even if they don't know it. Business is the largest major, as it is at most colleges, but the business professors participate in the liberal arts mission, and the general education program assures that students take a range of courses, including questions-of-our-time liberal arts seminars exploring the natural environment, civic engagement, and science, including "Anthropocene: The Age of Humans," "Is Capitalism Good for the Environment?" and "Communicating Nature."

NEC, like any college with a liberal arts mission, strives to produce inquiring human beings, both inwardly and outwardly, *and* future professionals.

The process is rarely smooth.

I ended up having Southie in five courses. He met with me the day after our first class interaction, bright-eyed and energized, telling me that he was changing his major from theater to communication studies. I tried to slow him down, stating that theater was a fine major, but then I learned that his heart really wasn't in it. He basically wanted to be Marky Mark (Mark Wahlberg), so I concurred that perhaps the change of major was a wise move and said that I would love having him in my classes.

So began many battles, with Southie always ready to defend his conservative street politics. But the battles juiced his classmates and led to dynamic conversation—there was never an awkward silence in a Southie class. The discussions provided opportunities for me to argue that our debates were not about politics, certainly not about the false dichotomy of conservative versus liberal, but were about the liberal arts tradition of practicing higher-order rationality, avoiding logical fallacies, and remaining open to mystery.

Southie embraced his Boston blue-collar identity and less than stellar academic standing. He was in the habit of doing average work and hovering near a probation-level GPA, but he was also more than street smart and had a critical mind and strong interpersonal, writing, and speaking skills that he refined with each semester. In our Feature-Writing Workshop, he wrote dynamic articles on Whitey Bulger, the infamous South Boston gangster, and drug use among old friends. He eventually earned A's. The high marks shook up his persona and added new dimensions to his identity.

Southie competed to be the senior speaker at commencement, a day he thought he would never see. He won due to his energy and flair and gave the best speech of the event, better than even the honored guests and doctorates. His speech began with humor as he described his first day at college questioning the cosmos in disgust when he found out his roommate was a diehard Yankee fan. But he soon turned serious, stating that even though he knew it was a cliché, he had become a man at NEC, and he was deeply grateful.

What would have become of Southie if he had not been accepted at NEC? His feature piece on drug use detailed friends in jail and dying from overdoses.

The last I heard, Southie had a good sales job in Boston that provided funds for tickets to his beloved Red Sox and Celtics. He tinkered with sports writing and wrote a screenplay but lamented that he wasn't writing a book. He may still have dreams of celebrity success, which is okay, since the desire to show the world our talents can be a powerful motivator. I told him to write for the right reasons, when he had something he needed to say, and that he might write a book when he was sixty or seventy.

My hope for him and all former students is that they seek rich experiences, stoking the fire of soul.

Chapter 8

Nature as Teacher

"In the woods, we return to reason and faith. There I feel that nothing can befall me in life,—no disgrace, no calamity, (leaving me my eyes,) which nature cannot repair. Standing on the bare ground,—my head bathed by the blithe air, and uplifted into infinite space,—all mean egotism vanishes. I become a transparent eye-ball; I see all; the currents of universal being circulate through me; I am part or particle of God."
—Ralph Waldo Emerson

"…in Wildness is the preservation of the World"
—Henry David Thoreau

August 1988. Rain pelted the trailhead in Gorham, New Hampshire. I sat in a friend's car, streams streaking the windshield like tears on glass. "Maybe I should wait for the rain to stop," I thought, "I'm sheltered, safe, removed." But a second thought moved me to open the door.

"Shit," I laughed, as I gathered my backpack. "Wet is my fate. No need to hurry."

Backpack attached, I splashed through a puddle. Cold, stinging droplets hit my face. "It's begun," I said to myself.

The trail was flat but soon inclined with large boulders blocking the path. I climbed and jumped with fifty pounds of gear and Kraft macaroni and cheese jangling on my back, landing with both feet together, leaving behind dual footprints on the muddy trail. Soaked shorts and T-shirt plastered my skin, but carrying extra weight kept me warm.

Adrenaline spiked; I was hyperaware of the rhythm of my steps and sensuous new surroundings.

Wet, cool air.

The scent of pine: pungent. The presence of growth and decay.

The cycles of abundant life and death that civilized culture obsessively attempts to hide.

Teaching at Purdue was still four years away, and I was at the beginning of a 350-mile hike of the northern section of the Appalachian Trail in New Hampshire and Maine. After my failed attempt at graduate school at the University of Maine, I moved back to New Jersey to work as a printer once again in my brother's small printshop, vowing to re-fund and then return to the woods and follow Thoreau, who made three memorable hiking trips to Maine.

In June, two months prior to first steps, James Hansen, head of NASA's Goddard Institute for Space Studies, provided historic testimony before Congress—ppm 351.57 of carbon dioxide, over the threshold and up from 270 ppm at the start of the Industrial Revolution in the mid-1700s—in which he drew three conclusions: the earth is warmer than at any other time in the history of instrumental measurement; there is a high degree of confidence that the greenhouse effect was significantly accelerating warming, and thus warming was not only due to natural cycles but anthropogenic; and computer climate simulations indicate the probability of extreme weather events.

The testimony made some noise, but who was listening? Who had been educated to listen, not only to reports and testimony, which, it must be acknowledged, are largely calculative, but to our own bodies within the earth body, or own minds within larger mind, or own souls within the world soul?

Emerson, in *Nature*, calls for us to listen to Nature, or Spirit, the diverse natural world, and our inner nature. All are teachers; all interwoven, elevating and yet grounding human awareness. Or rather, nature, not necessarily the Bible or any scripture, is the source of revelation through which Spirit speaks. Rafael was my teacher before the hike, and he would be again, but the trail beckoned: there were lessons afoot.

After three days of leaving human relationships and printing ink behind, I made my way into Maine and the most mountainous section of the more than twenty-one hundred miles of trail. I hiked one peak after the next, covering little total ground. Although a mere twenty-eight years old, my knees ached from carrying my weighty pack up and then especially down numerous slopes. It could have been worse. I met a young hiker in those first few days who stopped hiking because he was too sore; he lay in a trail shelter, huddled in a ball like an old tabby cat, barely able to move a paw.

The effort it took to climb mountains gave rewards. I focused physical and mental energy on each step. When I reached a summit the faraway landscape rushed my senses, awareness sling-shotting outward into vast terrain of trees and open sky. After two weeks of alternating between intense focus and expansive vistas, my perception became clear, acute, receptive.

At one point, I was entranced by a small piece of moss along the trail. Sunlight danced upon it, illuminating a bright, jewel-like verdant green. I kneeled, as if receiving a message from the Divine itself—wake up, all is holy—and then turned my head in all directions, hoping to share my discovery. I was the only human present but did not feel alone; everything was alive with presence.

I remained on my knees with a single thought: "My God, I'm losing it over a piece of moss."

The next day, I sauntered along the trail with head down, making sure not to trip over roots and rocks. I looked up and there was an immense creature with full antlers standing ten feet ahead. I had never seen a moose before and was dumbstruck by its long, tree-like legs and huge head and body. And those eyes. I never imagined such large and captivating eyes. We stared like lovers, and I was entranced again, without fear, yet lucky that the moose didn't attack. Perhaps it was more than luck; the danger of the situation never entered my awareness, and I sensed that it never entered the moose's awareness that I was dangerous. I'm not sure how long we stood there—time was no longer a construct of factory timecards or printshop workweeks—but I eventually moved off to the side and proceeded on my way, smiling, and then contemplating my encounter with a wild, other-than-human life form with whom I am somehow kin.

After thirty days, I reached the summit of Mount Katahdin in Baxter State Park, gazed skyward at blackbirds that looked like spirited silhouettes circling in the wind, rested on solid, sun-flooded boulders, and then descended, officially ending the hike. Fellow hikers gave me a ride south to the University of Maine, my old drop-out-of-graduate-school haunts, where I swam in rivers with Mac the Newfoundland, chopped wood, and first read *Walden*.

03

Many have gone on lengthier hikes, ascending death-defying peaks in the far wilder American west and numerous beautiful countries. Still, my month-long hike—with four town stops—took me away from the "civilized" world. Or did it? A lesson from the trip was that there was no getting away. The mountain vistas occasionally included clear cuts off in the distance, and during one town stop I saw a weather report that included an acid rain index.

I also carried a thousand dollars' worth of camping technology on my back and brought along a Walkman and a few tapes for occasional musical interludes. Shutting out the sounds and silence of nature is un-wild-like behavior, but like my moss and moose experiences, dancing on the top of mountains while listening to the bright sounds of Pat Metheny also induced peak moments of freedom and joy.

What, I wondered, did Thoreau encounter, without toys like Walkmans, without Gore-Tex boots, Helly Tech rain jackets, and who-knows-what-tech thermal socks and underwear, and with much more wildness?

On his first trip, he sought out an Indian guide and found Louis Neptune—meeting Indians was part of why he ventured north. Neptune didn't show at the appointed time, so he climbed Mount Katahdin with Maine relatives and a White guide. Few, other than Natives, had attempted the hike, and he was never the same afterward, even though he didn't quite reach the top due to clouds enveloping the summit. Concord had been logged for fuel and parceled for farms. Thoreau wrote in his journal about the constant sound of the axe. Maine was initially filled with loggers, mills, camps, trails, houses, farms, and dams, but he eventually encountered untrammeled wilderness: uncut forests, lakes without cabins, and undammed streams. Then, rocky Mount Kahtadin and awe-filled primitive power. His famous response was a euphoric howl: "What is this Titan that has possession of me? Talk of mysteries!—Think of our life in nature,—daily to be shown matter, to come into contact with it,—rocks, trees, wind on our cheeks! The solid earth! The actual world! The common sense! Contact! Contact! Who are we? Where are we?"

His second trip was led by Joe Aitteon, son of the Penobscot governor, and included his relative and Maine connection, George Thatcher. Thatcher wanted to hunt moose; gun-less Thoreau was hunting Indian ways. Aitteon deftly identified sounds like treefall, taught Indian names, walked noiselessly, and paddled powerfully. But Aitteon shot a moose mom, and then came the butchery, and not fully using the animal due to the difficulty of hauling it out. Thoreau argued for leaving hunting behind in the "Higher Laws" section of *Walden*. He saw it as an activity for youth, not for mature adults, but his views on this trip were somewhat conflicted. He embraced witnessing the event and learning from it, yet, for him, it was too much like sport hunting, too much like "shooting your neighbor's horses," which were ultimately "God's own horses."

More learning ensued at the end of the day at an Indian camp. Thoreau witnessed their world more fully as he listened to Natives speak an unintelligible language to each other, or a "distinct and comparatively aboriginal race" speaking a language "spoken in New England who shall say how long." Thoreau had read everything he could about Native Americans and filled his "Indian Notebooks" with more than five hundred sources, but now he was observing up close. Like his experience near the top of Katahdin, he was once again struck by the limits of his knowledge.

His third trip, in 1857, challenged him still further, as his interactions with Joe Polis, his Penobscot guide, would be more personal and more intense. This time, Edward Hoar, a young friend from Concord, happily joined the hike, but the adventure did not always go well for him. He got lost and had to survive on berries and was forced to hike with raw, wet feet after slogging through swamps. Hoar's experience was another lesson— the Maine woods were not to be taken lightly—but Thoreau's focus was on Polis, a tribal leader who represented his people before the governments of Maine and the US. After losing most of their lands, the Penobscot retained Indian Island, an ancestral home in Maine, and fought to sustain themselves via trade, especially crafts like basket weaving and canoe-making, market hunting, and farming. Many had left, some due to an outbreak of small pox.

Much earlier, in an 1842 journal entry when he was twenty-five, Thoreau called Native Americans "strange spirits, daemons, whose eyes could never meet mine; with another nature, another fate than mine." The vast differences between Natives and him remained fifteen years later, but he would meet Polis eye-to-eye and find common ground and common spirit, if not common fate.

For Polis, guiding Whites was an opportunity to educate, and, after feeling each other out, Thoreau and Polis agreed to share their knowledge with each other. However, at the beginning of the trip, Thoreau likely had an Enlightenment-era bias of superiority, whether conscious or not. Laura Dassow Walls, in her biography of Thoreau, writes that he was not receptive to Polis's creation stories, thinking them superstitious and told with "dumb wonder." He consequently lost a learning opportunity; oral traditions need not be factually true to convey animistic truths of a living earth that would later be confirmed by Gaia theory science.

Polis was honored by his tribe as a teacher and shaman, and he had plenty to teach Thoreau. Thoreau had plenty to teach him from his substantial reading, including botany, but Polis, though he had traveled to Philadelphia and New York and was attentive to a local newspaper, spent his life reading nature.

Polis's multiple skills soon came to the fore. He could carry a hundred-pound canoe on his head and brought only a blanket, axe, gun, and the clothes on his back. He could start a fire with wet wood by gathering dry bark from underneath dead, leaning trees and make tea from available herbs for each day of the week. He never got lost. Thoreau saw a "sharpened and educated sense," as Polis did not recall routes but used refined instinct and perception in the moment. The White man's maps were unneeded, and thus he did not seek them.

Thoreau learned and learned of his ignorance.

Thoreau's and Hoar's many questions were sometimes a bit much for Polis, leading him to respond, "May be your way of talking—may be all right—no Indian way." He was blunt when Thoreau asked him to explain his method for not getting lost: "Oh, I can't tell you—Great difference between me & white man." But his unwillingness to share was not due to enmity; the practice of reading rocks and trees was difficult to put into words.

The trip of many lessons continued: how to carry a canoe—their adventure included portages, and sometimes Thoreau and Hoar hiked while Polis navigated river rapids—how to call to snakes and muskrats and other animals, how to tell the difference between white spruce and black spruce, how to dig up spruce roots and turn them into tough, flexible string for sewing canoes.

Thoreau woke up one night to find a decayed stump five feet from the campfire and the unburned end of burned wood glowing brilliant white. Not surprisingly, Polis had seen it before; Artoosoqu', he remarked. Thoreau, his openness to mystery, myth, and Native ways growing, did not immediately seek a scientific explanation, making an "empty chamber" of an "inhabited house" of "spirits as good as himself." Science could wait while he embraced poetic imagination and direct experience: "Nature must have made a thousand revelations to them which she still keeps secret to us."

Polis revealed more secrets: the medicinal properties of plants, how to paddle a canoe properly, how to write on birch bark with black spruce twig, how to make a candle and pipe out of birch bark. He named stars and easily navigated rough, muddy terrain, and he was confused by their inability to track. But then his tracking led him to kill a moose, no doubt big-eyed and majestic and a spirit as good as himself. For Polis, hunting moose was part of tradition, and he needed money to buy back land and feed his family. For Thoreau, the latter was the "white man's argument," as if his family had no other options. As always and for good reason, Thoreau focused on eternal ethical truths, higher laws, but did not seem to recognize cultural privilege.

They wanted to climb Katahdin—Kataadn, for Natives, meaning "highest land"—but Hoar's feet wouldn't allow it. Polis was saddened. He would have brought home more moose meat if he knew they were going home. At the end of their journey, Polis playfully challenged Thoreau to a race, Thoreau with their gear and Polis with the canoe. The trip covered 325 miles over nearly two weeks; when Thoreau asked if he was glad to be home, Polis responded, "It makes no difference to me where I am."

Polis shared stories of the tribe's history, as well as his belief in education as the means for protecting Penobscot sovereignty and property; he claimed his son was the best student at a White school in Old Town. He also told Thoreau a story of visiting the politician and lawyer Daniel Webster, the perpetrator of Manifest Destiny exploration and exploitation, at his home near Boston; Webster was not open to conversation and raised his hand as if to strike.

Polis was certainly not perfect; Thoreau also took note of mistakes, like leaving matches and his shoes out in the rain. Thoreau also wrote that Polis failed to discern the outlet for a lake, and that he was like an excited fifteen-year-old, rather than a seasoned hunter, when initially shooting at and missing the moose.

Back in Concord, Thoreau tried to make sense of him: Polis navigated the White world, called himself a Protestant, went to church and honored the Sabbath while living in a spacious house, yet led his tribe, tanned animal hides in the front yard, and was completely at home in the woods, displaying "so much intelligence that the white man does not" and increasing his "own capacity, as well as faith." When Thoreau found an intricately woven Indian fishing basket filled with fish after the trip, his deep appreciation was stimulated again, stating its maker was "meditating a small poem," aware that for Indians words were objects, and objects like words; everything spoke, and language was a force that influenced the world and thus must be used with care.

☙

Thoreau knew that he was not braving deep wilderness at his Walden cabin but conducting an experiment in simplicity and self-reliance. He wrote about the grace of the natural world and spiritual transformation because the sanity of the industrialized world would depend upon it. Like Native Americans, he saw nature as a daemonic force of intelligences among differing species, including Natives and himself. We are all part and parcel, after all, we are all kin, and genius is aroused when in sympathy with all things. Oftentimes, this sympathy would make him feel aided by the unseen, allowing him to see what others missed, like arrowheads and rare plants, for which he seemed to have an uncanny gift.

Thoreau's sympathy seemed to take a hit when confronted by bare rock and barefaced wildness near the top of Mount Katahdin, but mostly, the ragged ground jolted him into a new ground of awareness. He was confronted with what we have lost and a reason for why we are lost: the absence of direct contact with the land and deeper reality. Pastoral Concord was of a different, human order, but Katahdin did not undermine his Walden experience, it added another dimension.

Natives, prior to contact with Whites, changed the land without changing, or "civilizing," themselves. They did not even have a word for "wilderness." Reality was a mixing of human hands learning to live in harmony with land while European colonists thought wilderness equaled a fallen world and attempted to save it by dominating it. Thoreau, increasingly influenced by Native ways, reversed the equation: we are fallen and in need of saving. And since we are part and parcel of nature, we are not its lord and master. After his Maine hikes, he placed his experience of nature's balm and calm within the context of harshness and humility. Nature's power must be respected, and so should Native knowledge.

Thoreau called arrowheads "fossil thoughts," and finding them put him on a "trail of mind" that "never failed to set me right." In a sense, he was able to track Natives from arrowheads, or the "subtle spirits that made them." Tilling the land often turned them up; but, for Thoreau, this irony showed how they endure, reminding him of the eternal "winging" through the ages, with each arrowhead "bearing a message from the hand that shot it." Arrowheads, then, were signs that provided lessons on the intertwining of the universal and particular.

Thoreau idolized the Musketaquid leader Tahatawan in his youth, and on a walk with his brother to the former spot of his village, Nashawtuc Hill, he broke into a soliloquy: "How often they have stood on this very spot, at this very hour...and communed with the spirits of their fathers gone before them....Here stood Tahatawan, and there is Tahatawan's arrowhead." He then proceeded to pick up a "perfect arrowhead, as sharp as if just from the hands of the Indian fabricator," amazed at the vital energy and resolve that had crafted it.

Thoreau's views on Natives changed over time. He imagined Tahatawan's strong character, which he wished to emulate, yet he was also uncritically immersed in the all-too-common narrative of savagery. He then compiled more than four thousand pages of research in his "Indian Notebooks," which provided insights but still included the bias of savagery, and then moved to firsthand experience, especially with Polis. Such contact grew his sympathy, often at the expense of his "civilized" brethren, who enacted the narrative in unfair treaties and then unfairly broke them with their "savage" excuse.

Thoreau would go on to defend Natives against prejudice, not just from book learning or from talking to them around Concord, but from personal and profound interactions with Polis. He defended their right to land and advocated for "natural preserves" in which "the bear and the panther, and even some of the hunter race, may still exist" and not be "civilized off of the face of the earth." However, just like he vigorously advocated for abolitionism but not for women's liberation (although he supported the cause), he did not fight for Native liberation; sadly, he seemed to see the Native cause as a lost one, with conquest and assimilation inevitable. Slavery could be remediated; Native sovereignty was too far gone.

Thoreau often equated Natives with the wild, in the good sense, and wanted to learn from them before too much wildness was tamed out from exposure to Whites. In fact, he had a long history, since childhood play with his brother, of imagining himself as Indian, and in their short-lived school they advised students to "think like Indians" while taking walks to Native grounds. Emerson and his friends Bronson Alcott and Ellery Channing thought his sympathy ran so deep that he took on Native qualities. Emerson even once said he was "more like an Indian...than a white man," and recent scholarship suggests that many of his virtues, including heroism, independence, simplicity, self-mastery, and listening to the voices of nature were Indian virtues.

For Thoreau, both nature and Natives were teachers inspiring pursuit of the good. Or, as he succinctly put it, "How near to good is what is wild." Early on, he sought "a more perfect Indian wisdom," which he associated with living sustainably by immersing ourselves within specific places. Such sustainable living included by also ran counter to scientific investigation, which too often divided nature via disciplines rather than perceiving all our relations. Such sustainable living also ran counter to burgeoning techno-industrial capitalism by providing alternative modes of flourishing. Today, such sustainable living runs counter to consumerist habits and climate crisis.

While learning to learn from Native Americans, the ethnographic bias of his time, which saw them as different and inferior, was difficult for him to fully overcome; some journal entries suggest his participation with the bias and others suggest he had overcome it. In many ways, he saw Natives, and Native lifeways, as superior, at the same time he remained somewhat caught up in the biases of his dominant White and male world. A strange mix, to be sure, but also a sign of his times, as well as our own time as Native American struggles remain, along with the historical fallout of systemic racism generally.

Perhaps what Thoreau most discovered from Maine Indian guides is that they were forced to straddle two widely disparate worlds and were flawed like all humans. In his account, he portrays Neptune, although independent, as unreliable and prone to drink. Aitteon, on the other hand, had assimilated into the dominant culture and was more mannered than a good guide. He was also twelve years younger than Thoreau and dealing with problems of youth, just like Thoreau had—but with the added weight of dealing with racism. Add Polis, who acknowledged that a college education would help him manage and keep his land and who hired others to do work he did not want to do, and he encountered complex human beings who deserved respect without being reduced to stereotypes.

Despite his sympathy, no doubt Thoreau's privilege prevented him from fully understanding the lostness of Native Americans. He was more concerned with recovering lost lessons than keeping Natives themselves from vanishing, yet he mourned that vanishing. In a later journal entry, he imagined a turning away from destructive agriculture and a return of Natives and their lifeways. While drawn to westward expansion for its wildness, Thoreau was critical of Manifest Destiny mania and its colonizing deafness to nature's spirits.

This much we can affirm: As a flawed human, Thoreau was still evolving regarding challenging issues of his settler colonialist times, but the more he learned from and about Native Americans, the less lost he became. The same was true for the lostness of the nation at large, which was increasingly embracing materialism at the expense of the spiritual and living well within wild landscapes.

 beta

I did not experience the wilderness and wildness Thoreau encountered. The marked and well-worn trail up Katahdin had iron steps to help hikers maneuver over the rockiest terrain, and during a quick town-stop, I ran into a general store, bought a pint of Ben & Jerry's Coffee Heath Bar Crunch ice cream, and then hiked while shoveling the sugary mixture into my mouth with a plastic spoon. The trail had its dangers—several memorial signs honoring dead hikers were posted, and I fell several times, thanks to a shifting pack—but it was well marked. A typical day of survival included a myriad of early evening chores: find water, filter water, refill water bottles, set up clothes line, hang up wet socks, blow up Therm-a-Rest sleeping pad, set up tent, set up Whisper-Lite stove and cook meal on bare rock surrounded by dense forest. The fake-orange macaroni and cheese tasted like it cost far more than two for a dollar. But when the sun set—after finishing clean-up chores: wash pot with liquid castile soap, unhook fuel bottle, refold stove and tin fire guard—I imagined sharing similar experiences, gazing toward the star-filled night, into infinite space, listening, far enough away from home to discover a deeper sense of home.

My hike was compromised by culture and technology, but we were both bit by "no-see-ums" and awoke to the thrilling voice of loons. I had transformative experiences of expansiveness, timelessness, deep connections and radical otherness, the currents of universal being circulating through me, finding a faith that all is well, or that all could be well. Late in the hike, the woods' magic increasing with each step, I walked early in the morning with a startling but natural clarity—no boundaries between self and other, no filter—and soon after napped on bare rock near a small waterfall and awoke to a deep peace.

I met other transformed souls. I will never forget a conversation with a fifty-year-old vice president of a bank who had been out in the wilderness for more than four months (with periodic town stops). He didn't look like a banker to me—I had trouble envisioning a suit covering his grime and grin—so I asked him what he was going to do once the trip was over. With seriousness and without hesitation, he responded that he was going to start getting rid of stuff because "you just don't need it." Months of carrying everything he needed on his back cured him of his addiction to overconsumption.

I also met unique and complex human beings.

I stopped hiking after navigating the Mahoosic Notch, a half-mile rocky gorge that many consider the most treacherous section of trail.

"Five o'clock. Looks like I'm going to have the trail shelter to myself," I thought. But then an Outward Bound instructor arrived ahead of a group of twelve urban-dwelling teenagers.

"I need adult conversation," she said, sitting down next to me on the wooden floor of the shelter. "One of the kids stole our group lunch, and we had to have an hour-long powwow to talk about trust and the reasons why we're here."

Before we could chat, two army-fatigued, non-English–speaking Italians strolled into camp and attempted to ask for directions. A dazed gentleman, about sixty years old, hobbled in from the Notch, proclaiming that he was the oldest of a church group of six ("two ministers and the rest regular folk"). An American soldier entered, informing us that he was on joint maneuvers with the Italians—a kind of military exchange program— and quickly led them off amid smiling goodbyes. And another Outward Bound group appeared, filled with teenagers out in the woods for the first time.

The hobbled gentleman struggled to prime a camp stove.

"Do you want some help?" I asked.

"I know how to operate it," he replied, still out of breath, "but I could use a match."

He placed the stove inside the shelter, reeking of fuel, and took the match.

"Could you light the stove on the ground, as far away from me as possible?" I chuckled, imagining the shelter ablaze.

He dutifully placed it on the ground and lit the base. Two-foot flames shot straight up, knocking him on his ass.

While I suppressed another laugh, the entire troop of Italian and American soldiers marched through camp with plugged rifles. Then the new Outward Bound gang complained about the outhouse, and an extremely large, long-legged jackrabbit hopped up to the base of camp, causing a minister to scare it away with a camera attached to a foot-long zoom lens.

I wondered if I had been transported inside the pages of freakish fairy tale.

The older gentleman brought me back to reality, cooking food with bluish-white flames shooting up the sides of the pot and circling over the lid. The Outward Bound instructor got her burn-kit ready just in case.

૪

When colonizers first arrived in Maine, northern Indians were entirely hunter-gatherers, with much of the food supply coming from rivers filled with smelt, alewives, sturgeon, and salmon. Like the passenger pigeons that blotted out the sun, one merely needed to dip their hand into the water to find them. In coastal areas, there was seemingly no end of cod and shellfish. But the plenty would end. During Thoreau's third hike, he encountered villages, sawmills, and a store where he had found a house or two eleven years earlier. He also encountered logging and dams that greatly altered the ecosystem.

Scientists question whether a decrease in population after first contact in the 1500s and 1600s, due to the genocide of 90 percent of Indigenous peoples, may have contributed to a decrease in temperatures, called the "little ice age," as there was less human activity. Of course, the cooler climate would not last as colonists denuded the landscape, industrializing everything and increasing temperatures along with population decade by decade, year by year.

Maine is a getaway for many who wish respite from cities and to re-kindle the feeling of dwelling in nature, yet Maine cannot escape the effects of climate crisis: the temperature has increased 3.2 degrees since 1895, extreme-heat days are expected to be two to four times more frequent by 2050, and ocean heat waves in the Gulf of Maine are causing it to lose its sub-Arctic characteristics. Warming has shortened winters and lengthened summers by two weeks, and the seasonal changes have wrought biodiversity ripple effects, including die-off of moose calves from winter ticks, which are no longer dying off due to a lack of early fall snow and cold snaps.

Maine, increasingly "civilized," has changed. The lostness of the eighteenth century has been a stepping-stone to today's lostness, with the memory of my I-Thou moose encounter now paired with the disturbing image of newborns eaten alive by up to a hundred thousand ticks. Still, taking steps on the trail has led many hikers to re-find the compass, and Thoreau's call for land protection in *The Maine Woods* has been actualized via the Katahdin Woods & Waters National Monument, which allows for mixed-use, but not abuse, of the land-base that sustains all species.

Like Thoreau in his lifetime of play as, study of, and encounters with Natives, the Maine woods, and its human inhabitants, are evolving, hopefully in the direction of kinship and respect and learning. But what of the parade of humans who graced the Mahoosic Notch campsite? Did they also deserve respect? Would they also learn and evolve?

What of newfound faith that all is well?

The psychological experience of wildness—expressed as the embrace of life and death and humility before nature's power—would go a long way toward preserving the world, but another question of our time should be a focus of education: How can the world be preserved when the increasingly tamed wilderness reduces the depth and intensity of experience?

Night, and sleep, fell upon the ministers and Outward Bounders, but I lay in my sleeping bag with muscles tired from the day's hike and brain wired from the evening's show. It wasn't a fairy tale; more like an Absurdist drama by Ionesco or Beckett.

The shelter was dark, and I searched for a lesson behind the gathering of this strange group.

"Who are we? Where are we?"

I listened, waiting for God, or moss or moose, or the daemonic in any form, to explain it all to me.

Chapter 9

In the World but Not of It?

"To elude nature, to refuse her friendship and attempt to leap the river of life in the hope of finding God on the other side, is the common error of a perverted mysticality. It is as fatal in result as the opposite error of deliberately arrested development, which, being attuned to the wonderful rhythms of natural life, is content with this increase in sensibility; and, becoming a 'nature mystic,' asks no more."
  — Evelyn Underhill

"I am enormously concerned with just this world, this painful and precious fullness of all that I see, hear, taste. I cannot wish away any part of reality. I can only wish that I heighten this reality."
  — Martin Buber

The process of finding one's voice is filled with twists and turns, and in my case, returns. After my hike, I spent a few days visiting a friend at the University of Maine, and she agreed to drive me to Boston where I could get a bus to New York City and then a train to New Jersey. Sans backpack and on flat ground, I glided like first light flowing across a lake. Spirituality was a state of mind and body. Flushable toilets? Fascinating after shitting in a hole every day.

On the car ride to Boston, we listened to a CD by Kitaro, the ambient music a soundtrack to watching the wooded landscape turn to concrete and steel as if I were viewing a movie. The feeling reminded me of reading Pirsig on trains in Europe: witnessing thoughts, witnessing others like Wim Wenders's angels in *Wings of Desire*.

What is this created world, so troubled yet expressing Spirit?

On the bus ride to New York City, the driver stayed in the fast lane, a foot away from cars, forcing them to change lanes so he could speed. I sat in front, amused by the show, the movie continuing. A woman sitting nearby was in perpetual panic, and her feet lunged at an imaginary brake.

I was soon walking the streets of New York, carrying my backpack and recalling my practice commute a few years earlier, an anomaly among the throng, on my way to Jersey and the printshop.

Printing again. Really?

The shop was a box, and my consciousness, which had grown to include mountain vistas, pushed at the seams.

In our earliest meetings, Rafael described the mystical life as being "in the world but not of it." The phrase disturbed me as it suggested a flight-from-the-world mentality; there was no escaping, nor should there be any desire to escape, existential reality. But Rafael found wisdom in the phrase. He said it described a loving indifference (or healthy non-attachment) to anxiety, worry, and fear that allowed one to productively act in the world. I knew this non-attachment well from my second and third grade religious experiences, and during my better moments on the tennis court when I let go of doubt, embodying the image of the slam or topspin shot, and in Europe and again on the bus trip back to Jersey. I also consciously practiced it when reciting the fifteenth-century Indian mystic Shankara's "He who knows is full of glory, he rides within his body as if within a carriage" while climbing Maine mountains. I focused on spiritual identity rather than achy knees and difficult terrain and so called forth freedom of movement, allowing strength and elasticity to emerge undeterred by the gravity of thought.

The smell of fresh ink replaced the smell of fresh air and pine. The myriad camping chores were transfigured into wiping down the press with chemicals; adjusting ink flow; and straightening crooked text for hospital forms, résumés, and letterhead for lawyers, small businesses, and large corporations. We even printed bright yellow labels for hazardous waste.

Finish a job, start the next.

The hospital forms were endless, but printing résumés and ads for small businesses was rewarding because we were helping the little guy. I occasionally printed materials for a good cause, such as the nonprofit Hunger Project, whose logo I saturated with deep blood red. Most of the time, though, it felt like I supplied the paper for the paper-pushers to push. The woods of Thoreau's time were cut down for heat, the woods of our time for paper. I took numerous breaks outside simply to breathe.

137

A natural non-attachment governed my trail adventures, but when I returned to the cramped and poorly ventilated printshop, it devolved into a dangerous detachment. The energy of Maine vistas, just like the energy of Europe, was gradually denuded, along with the integration of body, brain, and bountiful soul. I soon found myself identifying with free-floating Spirit, instead of Spirit unfolding as matter, life, and mind, as I attempted to escape boredom and chemicals and growing depression. My senses retracted due to the jarring change of scenery, and my body became a mere carriage carrying me through an eight-hour shift instead of invigorating terrain. My emotions dangled, disconnected from a larger energy source and context of meaning. My spiritual and sensuous imagination, which had been so finely tuned that a piece of moss sent me into throes of wonder and awe, was replaced by abstract calculations of the printing trade.

I spent my first few weeks back in New Jersey daydreaming about the woods while ink rooted itself into the crevasses of my hands and under fingernails. But the transition from mountains to the printshop provided another lesson: one's surroundings expand and restrict awareness, and adaptability is both our greatest and worst attribute.

I was fortunate to have work after leaving the trail—it was easy to imagine the unemployed hungering for a job like mine, not to mention the nepotism—but such fortune had little to do with the workings of soul. God knows what those chemicals were, which were also used to clean ink from skin, and if you scratch your nose, you have ink on your nose. I once found a patch of pantone blue in my armpit. Taking a shower always turned into an inventory of where my hands had traveled throughout the day. My brother kindly let me return to the shop, and I was making money, but the job was hard to bear after swimming naked in the lakes of Maine.

Rafael had moved to Corrales, New Mexico, but happened to be visiting in New Jersey. We met, and he offered me a room, food, and chance to study with him again.

I was out the door faster than quick-drying ink on sixty-pound vellum.

This was my first trip to the Southwest, and we drove to his home late at night, the darkness obscuring the landscape. The next day, Rafael told me to walk outside, a smile in his eyes, and I was greeted by a crisp

October morning, the Sandia Mountains, adobe houses, and hundreds of colorful hot-air balloons stretching across the sky like a rainbow. An omen of good things to come?

Rafael was immediately busy editing the *Ometeca* journal and organizing an Ometeca academic conference in Puebla, Mexico. Along with promoting the integration of the sciences and humanities, the institute worked to create dialogue among diverse countries, especially in Latin America.

He was also working with spiritual students; I was now one of them.

ଔ

"Waking up is a long process. We usually just remember the highlights, but waking up is a long process," Rafael said, as we sat on the couch in his adobe home with a fire lightly crackling in the clay fireplace.

"How did you wake up?" I said, realizing that I had never asked before.

Rafael paused, and I started a tape recorder, this time because I wanted to capture his insights. And then I listened.

As a child I would ride my bicycle out into a field, and then sit in the middle and commune. I didn't know what I was doing, but I felt a presence. I didn't know how to say it back then, I was just being "with it." Everything was alive; I remember that very distinctly. But I think I really began waking up around the time of the Cuban revolution. When I was fourteen, after the revolution had broken out, I saw a corpse riddled with bullets lying on the side of the road. I was overcome with a feeling of despair and hopelessness. But at the same time, it was in that moment that I felt an overwhelming call to serve humankind.

After this experience, I ended up working for the revolution for a few months, until I realized that the revolution wasn't what we had idealized. But in the beginning I helped with a census to find the unemployed in the countryside, and this thrust me right in the middle of nature. I used to work on that census twelve to fourteen hours a day, going from farm to farm, and at the end of the day I was dead tired. One night I ended up sleeping in a hut all by myself. The hut had no doors and the windows were just holes. The walls were made out of the bark of palm trees and the roof out of palm leaves. It was a very interesting night because the bed was filled with bed bugs. I had to decide whether I was going to sleep and disregard the bites or get up and not sleep. But I was too tired and went to bed just as the sun set.

Rafael was on a roll now. I knew the signs—the confident cadence, the perfect pace—I'd been here before.

Around midnight I woke up and the thatched ceiling was filled with fireflies. In Cuba we have a firefly that is not intermittent but has two permanent green lights on its head. And so, I woke up to a few thousand of them on the ceiling—it was like Alice in Wonderland—something that you're not quite sure is true because it's so beautiful. I got up and went to the door and there was a tree containing at least ten or twenty thousand fireflies. The whole tree was lit. It was one of those experiences that is hard to believe. I stood there, watching them for hours, totally silent. It's impossible for me to say how beautiful it was. It was incredible. So, I stood there for hours and felt an inexplicable beauty that is full of mystery. I stood there until I got so sleepy that I had to go back to bed. This experience gave me a deep sense of oneness, but I didn't know how to explain it. In those days I did not have the vocabulary to explain it. Even to this day I cannot fully explain it. I always say oneness, or a communion I feel inside me that has neither words nor thoughts.

I ended up spending months traveling with the census, across forests on my way to another farm or hamlet, and every time this sense of mystery would come up, a deep sense of mystery and awe. I specifically remember another time when a student and I traveled to this little hamlet and there was no place to stay. We went to the jail and the guard was kind enough to let us sleep in one of the cells. So, I had experiences with people and with nature, and every time I felt this mystery. In many ways, instead of partaking in the census I was partaking in the lives of people and nature. And this gave me a sense of empathy.

I can't quite explain it. During this whole experience I was more of a listener than a talker. I asked my questions for the census but afterwards I was very quiet and just listened and observed people and everything. It was marvelous.

During another trip I was very thirsty, but I had no water with me. I was in the middle of nowhere. I saw a pond and went over and started drinking from it. Well, for two or three days I got very ill. I couldn't go anywhere so I just lay in a hammock, almost hallucinating with fever. At the end of three days, it disappeared just as suddenly as it came. I thought to myself that I was probably close to death. But the amazing thing I discovered is that it didn't really matter. Perhaps I felt this way because it was my first experience and I had nothing to compare it with, or perhaps I felt this way because death really didn't matter. All I know is that I had no fear afterwards. This experience made me more fully aware that I was part of everything, and so I have never considered it to be a horrible experience. It was a very beautiful experience. I hardly ever talk about it because it's so integrated into my life. All these experiences—these experiences of beauty beyond anything I could imagine—gave me a mystical awareness. All I could do was surrender to them.

When I first came to New York I completely lost my contact with nature because I was in a sea of concrete. But I reconnected spiritually after I attempted suicide. I was in terrible psychological pain from not accepting myself. I was always trying to fulfill images, which were the result of pressure from my family concerning becoming rich and all that nonsense. It also had to do with being an exile, with my parents in Cuba, and having to work two jobs to support both myself and them and then go to school. So, I spent years sleeping two or three hours a night. All that built up and I eventually collapsed. It finally broke my back. It wasn't fun. It was very painful. But I don't regret it because it brought me to where I am. You certainly don't have to attempt suicide to wake up. I would not recommend it to anybody. But after my attempt at suicide, I decided that I would have one job that was my joy to do—play. I found myself by discovering a different kind of connectedness. It's the same connection, the same oneness, but experienced inwardly. And that's how I truly discovered spirituality, at the age of twenty-four.

We are brought up in this society to live up to an image and not be ourselves. I was in college, but I wasn't studying for the joy of it. I was studying just to fulfill a requirement of society. The falsehood of our educational system is that you are studying for

141

grades and not to learn. But after my suicide attempt I dropped all that nonsense and studied for my own enjoyment. And that's when I discovered that I am very creative. I discovered a freedom within myself. I discovered what it means to be fulfilled, without having to explain anything because there is no explanation. It's not logical. It's being content, just because you love what you do. So, I realized that fulfillment was the greatest form of wealth. If money comes, that's fine, but it's not the main source of fulfillment. Ever since I made this realization I have had no regrets, including the mistakes I have made, because I learned a lot from them and so they were worth it. I discovered my higher self in this way. I accepted myself finally. I realized who I am and fully entered the adventure of life.

☙

Rafael and I began taking long evening walks across mesas and amid adobe houses colored and shaped to blend into the surrounding earth, declaring their oneness with the landscape. The Sandia Mountains sat at the horizon, a silent Buddha, Jesus, or Lao Tzu, and I realized that like the mountain, we were witnesses to Spirit's continuous unfolding. After the sunset, we sometimes drove into Albuquerque to a bookstore or cafe. I watched the human activity and realized that Spirit was there too; culture was not other to Spirit or nature, just a different expression. At evening's end we would take the long way home, driving on abandoned highways under expansive night sky. I would gaze upward into the starry night and sense that humans are significant, even though we are a mere ripple in the vast ocean of unfathomable energy that constitutes the universe. We're significant because we are conscious and can bear witness.

Our deeper nature was so obvious, so simple and clear: we are the landscape, we are the Sandia Mountains, we are culture, we are the night sky, we are Spirit expressed. To bear witness to Spirit's glory; that was my job and joy.

The enchanted New Mexican landscape helped me to realize that it is perfectly natural for consciousness to be aware of its own Ground, the mysterious Source of all things. Rafael taught that novice spiritual students tend to think that a mystical awareness is extraordinary rather than simple, clear, ordinary awareness, leading to arduous striving for a fireworks experience of sudden enlightenment. But we usually don't experience a degree of clarity until we drop this pretense of difficulty, the lie that a peaceful awareness is somewhere other than where we are right now.

We once again began studying and meditating together. Rafael even had a meditation room; it was just a small, sparsely decorated room with a bunch of straight-backed chairs, but it was sacred space for silence.

Since first meeting Rafael, I had "practiced the presence," as Goldsmith would say, by consciously recognizing the divinity of everything I encountered. But a deeper peace and clarity grew with each day in New Mexico. Despite questioning being in but not of the world, I felt like I was living a mystical truth: We are all partners in God's dream. Thus, while there was physical distance, there was often no psychological distance between myself and what I encountered; everything was part of the same dream, continually arising and never ending.

Life was perfect.

And not so perfect.

Rafael met with a dentist and his wife for meditation and Infinite Way study, and while they were part of God's dream, I thought them dreamy buffoons. They were nice enough, or too nice in a fake, "aren't I spiritual" kind of way. She wore a mask of Tammy Faye make-up, and he always seemed to be in some far-off realm. I had no way of telling who these people were. He periodically provided free dental care to a nearby Native American tribe, which I greatly respected, but I still wanted to slap him back to earth.

Rafael was more generous in his interpretation. He seemed to be willing to work with anyone who was sincere about spiritual growth. I couldn't help wondering if his stance was secretly, or unconsciously, informed by hope for contributions to the Ometeca Institute. This thought, which I recognized as only a thought but one that might secretly or unconsciously say something about me, was terribly unfair especially since Rafael had given and was continuing to give much to me without asking for anything in return. Still, he wasn't as critical as I would have expected, and I wasn't sure if this was a fault, or him being more enlightened than me, or a strange combination of both.

Rafael also led a weekly Infinite Way study group, including the dentist and his wife, and he tried to persuade me to attend. I refused, fearing a roomful of otherworldly dentists and Tammy Fayes. He eventually convinced me to give it a try, and I was immediately glad I did, but not because of the group. They met after hours at a used bookstore owned by one of the members, and I was able to peruse the shelves.

Rafael soon called the group together, beginning with a guided meditation—the energy of multiple meditators seemed to reverberate within and beyond my body—and then we discussed spiritual passages from Goldsmith. Some of the participants were insightful while others were there to share tales of heartache among a group of sympathetic listeners. Near the end of the gathering a woman spoke with emotion and strength about her adult son, who had recently died in a car accident. She didn't seem to be looking for sympathy, only to share her truth and speak from her heart.

The meeting ended and we mingled outside. The New Mexican night sky was its usual presence, giving the gift of perspective. I gazed upward, receiving, but then turned attention to the group, and then to the woman who had just spoke, who was facing me, smiling, looking into my eyes. Our mutual gaze didn't feel awkward—the meditation and story sharing had made connecting easy—and she stepped forward for an embrace, as if a magnetic force were drawing her to me.

Her hug was like nothing I had ever experienced. There was a depth of release that transcended me and was a true opening to the infinite. In that moment, I was her son, a vehicle for one last physical embrace. The talk of unity during the meeting was just talk, now it was an experienced reality. When she stepped back, I smiled, and she gave me a look of gratitude. We both knew what had happened.

Back in Rafael's home, with him upstairs in the library—he often stayed up all night, a holdover from sleepless New York years when he worked in factories—and myself in a downstairs bedroom, I reflected about the depth of connection experienced through our gaze and hug, which was intimate, alive, open to mystery and the truth of the moment. In contrast, I considered the look of the dentist and his wife, which seemed more like a pose of certainty, a projection of spiritual depth rather than the real thing. The woman's gaze included a more expansive understanding of spiritual and physical reality while the looks of the dentist and his wife felt like they were willfully ignoring physical reality.

The enchanted land of New Mexico was a great place for meeting both types of folks.

A few weeks later, I was walking along a street in Santa Fe when I came across a starry-eyed New Ager sitting on a garbage can. He gave me a glazed-over look and said, "I love you." I was startled at first but then laughed and said, "I love you too." It was oddly amusing to be randomly told that I was loved, but I was also disturbed. He really didn't see me, lost in what Ken Wilber calls an "all pervading, uniform, featureless but divine goo" in which all diversity and multiplicity evaporates. He did not seem to recognize, or cognize, that while I am Spirit, I am also a finite individual expression of Spirit with a very real flesh and blood existence. He was like a floppy, wide-eyed puppy—cute at first but eventually overbearing.

What really troubled me is that I saw myself in him, not in a spiritual sense, but in the scary sense that we were both wandering and seemingly doing nothing.

I loved wandering and seemingly doing nothing, but I began to wonder if my discomfort with the "Infinite Way" was due to the fact I continually avoided getting involved in the messiness of the world. I was twenty-eight years old with a romantic desire to be a novelist, aloof from the difficulties of life while recording the follies of those not wise like me. But, when honest, I had to admit that I was not much of a writer and not so wise. Was I in New Mexico to study, meditate, and grow, or were my mystical and writing pursuits excuses to not get a career? Was I seeking enlightenment, or building up my ego, feeling superior to others while denying my own fears and failures?

I was convinced that I had touched the hem of the transcendent, and even wore its divine robe for a while, but also noticed that I was increasingly detached. My experiences in the printshop led me to ruminate on the difference between a healthy non-attachment and problematic detachment. The former gave perspective and deeper integration with life, losing the weight of the world so we can find it anew, re-finding the compass; the latter degraded into escape from the world, denial of inner life, including our shadow, and projection of enlightenment. In short, another form of lostness, or rather, an especially dangerous form of lostness because I had been equating detachment with finding some degree of spiritual awakening.

I wrote a letter to Preston, who had started graduate school at Purdue, describing the Infinite Way group and the dentist and his wife, while also criticizing Rafael, questioning whether he was projecting a degree of enlightenment with his students supporting the lie. Perhaps being a spiritual teacher massaged his ego, even if his words often seemed to come from a place beyond ego, while we dutifully listened, playing our role. I sealed the envelope, relieved to share doubts—or project doubts like hand grenades—but then felt like Judas when we went to the post office. The mailbox was on his side of the car, so I handed him the letter, wondering if it burned in his hands.

Nothing. He's not so prescient, I thought.

Later, when we were home, I confessed the contents of my letter; Rafael smiled and we talked, like we always did, but he added that I could not hurt him. I went to my room, wondering if he was so enlightened that he couldn't be hurt. Perhaps his spiritual experiences and meditation practice revealed more truth than mine, but he seemed too certain, too sure of himself.

The more I questioned, the more I doubted my own development. I was more grounded than the New Ager on the garbage can, yet I lacked basic life experiences and skills, especially relationships. It had been several years since my failed romance with Jennifer during my Rutgers years, and there had been few romantic encounters since. I wondered if my turn to mysticism had resulted in repression of libido; I knew what Freud would say and didn't like the answer. Rafael was empathetic while also stating that sex was a little dot compared to the depth of relationship, but I wanted to know more of that dot.

I had told myself that relationships were just too messy and imperfect. There were opportunities for girlfriends, but I chose solitude or adventures that I thought stimulated spiritual growth instead. I had watched the relationships of friends, of supposed "soul mates" lying to keep each other happy and didn't want to play that game. But how developed could I possibly be if I hadn't learned to simply love and be loved, and if I had not more fully explored my sexual self?

I also still didn't know why I was here on earth. I knew in my heart that it wasn't to meditate, wander, and work at the printshop. Rafael suggested I read books on science and spirituality, feeling that this integration would be the site of important work in the decades ahead. He was also willing to let me stay with him as long as I liked, despite being Judas, but I began to get antsy after a few months, despite the beauty of the Sandia Mountains and Rafael's offer.

CƷ

My new, more critical view of mysticism turned its attention to Joel Goldsmith. I had always been concerned with the otherworldly spiritual focus of his work, but now I also became concerned with his conception of this-worldly material "supply." Supply, for Goldsmith, is the "added things," such as relationships, money, home, and work, which are supposed to be the fruits of the spiritual life. To receive the fruits, Goldsmith advocated "taking no thought" for the things of this world; or rather, the added things would manifest themselves when materialistic thoughts and desires are transcended. Students were instructed to focus on spiritual identity, leaving their nets like the Apostles, and then to demonstrate a spiritual awareness in their actions, leaving God's infinite creativity and abundance to take care of the rest.

Guess what: if it didn't, it was our problem, not God's. We are just not enlightened enough, not spiritually awake, and not demonstrating the principle of supply—a Catch-22 that leads to feelings of spiritual inadequacy.

I appreciated Goldsmith's emphasis on demonstration, defined as the expression of unity, silence, and peace in the world. But such practice leads to inner riches, or inner supply, not to having the practical realities of life somehow magically met. His views were supported by his experiences as a spiritual healer since clients turned up at his door via word of mouth and by meaningful coincidences when he was in financial trouble. Apparently he developed a healing consciousness via his inner work and spiritual experiences; a practice that made most sense to me, when it worked, as patients having their consciousness raised in his presence and then healing themselves via the mind-body connection.

Goldsmith's healing work led to outward success as employment and money, as well as to world travel, relationships (three marriages), and homes, including many years in Hawaii. I began to worry that, in my case, following a spiritual path led to adventures filled with learning, but also blue-collar work and failure as a writer.

Goldsmith's views on supply also completely ignored economic structures. Were the poor to be blamed for their lack of supply as conservative pundits claimed? Or would it be wiser to consider global capitalism's destruction of subsistence culture and agriculture? Or sweatshops? Or simply limited opportunity, including limited educational opportunities? Goldsmith, democratic in approach, stated that we must overcome the bigotry of the world and express spiritual equality demonstrated as sharing and forgiveness. He advocated for finding voice and vocation, yet the Infinite Way had an inevitable political expression, turning Emersonian self-reliance into the willful ignorance of societal structures that so often limit the enacting of voice and vocation.

I further began to realize, ironically, that attempting to follow Goldsmith's teachings left me less self-reliant in the conservative sense because I assumed that the "added things" would happen without directly addressing the material dimension of life. As a result, I sometimes found myself relying on the supply of my parents or lived in the homes of kind souls such as Rafael. I had never expressed a talent for dealing with financial realities, not only for spiritual reasons but also because I wanted to thumb my nose at the evils of economic systems. Like Thoreau, I was wary of getting and spending, lest it lay waste my powers. But along with existing within a spiritually informed universe and interdependent ecosystem, I existed within an interdependent economic system, no matter how inequitable and destructive. By ignoring it, while hoping some spiritual principle would make it go away, I was ignoring an aspect of living both in and of the world.

I had experienced a giving cosmos, where we receive what we are ready to receive—like the teachings of mentors—because, well, we are ready; when acting in accordance with our highest good, we are seeking and open even if consciously unaware. It was also clear to me that being on a spiritual path leads us to stumble into synchronicities and the uncanny, which may be of great or minor import. Thoreau found arrowheads

and flowers as if drawn to them, and he was also mystified by other occur-
rences, such as when he went to see Nathaniel Hawthorne, a fellow Concord resident, to borrow a music box, and his wife offered it to him before
he could ask. In another instance, with music once again on his mind, he
received a music box from Robert Fuller, Margaret's brother, as a gift for
his tutoring and friendship. He remarked, "I think I may have some Muses
in my pay that I know not of, for certain musical wishes of mine are answered as soon as entertained."

Perhaps Thoreau's musical wishes attuned him to the music of the
spheres or collective unconscious; and the "Muses" is another way of referencing the daemonic. I imagine that Thoreau, like me, hoped that the
intelligence of Spirit unfolding and the cosmos would provide—and they
do. Unity and interdependency are generous principles, which Emerson
called "compensation," but these principles only assure that something will
happen, most likely good things if we are putting good things into the
world. Yet it seemed to me that financial supply was not a guarantee of
spiritual demonstration or else God would be a giant slot machine, dis-
pensing riches to those deemed most worthy.

Rafael may have played into the God as slot machine theory since he
bought a lottery ticket every week for years, hoping to use winnings to
build libraries in Latin America. He never won anything. And Thoreau's
spiritual commitments didn't lead to outer riches. He labored on his writing for years, working numerous jobs, and then died before his writings
bore financial fruit. Still, deeds and consciousness are carried forth, in infinite, invisible, and often tangible ways. This demonstration, I came to
realize, was both spiritual and material supply, open to mystery, leading to
growth.

In my young, White and male life, I was privileged to experience a
measure of inner and outer riches—I never lacked a roof over my head or
food to eat—but I thought the notion of spiritual supply absurd when considering the impoverished conditions of most residents on the planet.
Theirs is a structured impoverishment with the wealth of the so-called first
world historically gained via stolen resources from the so-called third
world, including, as Rafael well knew, the "open veins of Latin America."

I had still other critical concerns related to Goldsmith regarding my
tendency to lapse into detachment.

When the New Ager with fawn-like eyes said he loved me, I gazed back with compassion, flashing a smile, while also laughing since I thought him silly. These responses were born of a healthy non-attachment and perceiving with a degree of clarity. But at times I made others uncomfortable with my gaze as I witnessed them as mere bodies. Instead of putting others, and myself, more in touch with our higher selves, I would stare right through them, dead to the world while wondering who they were. I did both with ease, depending on mood and circumstance, or if my shadow-side was flaring up, the part of me that loved to destroy out of frustration with imperfection, with not being able to transcend the world.

My detachment, which grew along with my inability to be enlightened, to achieve some kind of final liberation, ended up liberating an inclination to lord over others, to think all humans fools, fatally inept, and without redemption. I came to wonder if the true foolishness was that an awareness of Spirit was making me less human, and less engaged in the world rather than more.

Young man Thoreau went through similar challenges, or at least his critics claimed he tended to be aloof. Even Emerson sometimes thought Thoreau's personality to be more sour than sweet, more animal than soulful. Emerson himself was also accused of being detached and aloof, especially by Fuller, whom he met intellectually but not emotionally. Perhaps being a transparent eyeball is not the best approach in interpersonal relations. Or rather, the lesson I was slowly learning the hard way, the lost way, was that transcending was deeply problematic without embrace of everything.

Ultimately, though, I did not wish to be sour or sweet but to find meaningful self-expression; I venture the same was true for Thoreau.

My lostness after graduating from Rutgers led me to Rafael and to explore my spiritual identity, and this journey saved me from spinning over the edge. But in New Mexico, my identification with Spirit and the mystical life started to box me in, just as school and jobs had. Or perhaps doubts and dimness were boxing me in. Either way, I was once again finding it difficult to breathe.

CB

Rafael would sometimes take a "you just don't know yet" attitude with me concerning my criticisms, which I suspected was both false and true. Since he always advised students to be "true to yourself," at least I was voicing where I was. This mantra took on added meaning the day one of his former college students, Susan, invited us to see *Romero*, a movie documenting the life and assassination of Archbishop Oscar Romero of El Salvador.

Susan was attending the University of New Mexico in Albuquerque, enrolled in a master's program in Latin American Studies. Small and feisty with shoulder-length dark hair and abundant energy, she was also a budding poet always up for intellectual debate. Rafael refused her initial invitation to see the film and suggested that he already knew the story. When Susan insisted, he relented, and we were soon driving to the cinema in Rafael's aging copper-colored Mercedes.

Archbishop Romero was influenced by Liberation Theology, an interpretation of Christian faith from the perspective of the poor. Rafael had written academic essays on this movement, praising its integration of scripture, deep religious feeling, social justice, and action on behalf of the disenfranchised as a major step forward for humanity.

The film opened with a suspect election in 1977 that placed a military general in power. The general had the support of El Salvador's wealthy elite, whose land ownership and agricultural policies kept the majority without "supply." The religious, desperate, and lost peasantry tried to make sense of their fate; some suggested it must be God's will. Others gave a more radical interpretation, stating that God must vomit when he witnesses the land-taking and mistreatment by those in power: the cry of the poor and the cry of the earth were linked.

Romero was named archbishop during this combustible time, and the film followed his gradual transformation from a nonconfrontational, bookish priest in favor of modest reform to an outspoken leader supporting revolutionary changes in land use, wages, and human rights. His eyes were progressively opened to the violence and terror inflicted by the army on the Salvadorian people to maintain the current system. His theology called him to act and speak out in protest, but the atrocities continued to grow, including the rape, torture, and murder of those who demanded liberation, or simply to be treated like human beings.

In a sermon before a large congregation, Romero proclaimed that our

151

"faith requires that we immerse ourselves in the world" because "economic injustice is the root cause of our problems, from it stems all the violence…the church must be incarnated in those who fight for freedom." In another moving scene, Romero led the community to retake a church that had been turned into army barracks under the direction of a machine-gun toting American military officer—US foreign policy under Reagan supported the Salvadorean elite, just as it had in Nicaragua during the Iran-Contra scandal.

The film contained graphic images of corpses and the ending scene showed Archbishop Romero being shot in the head while giving mass. Susan and I teared up many times during the movie.

Rafael looked like he was ready to burst.

He stood as text rolled across the screen stating that from 1980 to 1989 more than sixty-thousand Salvadorians were killed. Then he moved swiftly out of the theater, stopping in the lobby to place the contents of his wallet in the collection plate of a religious group protesting the School of the Americas, the training facility in the US where repressive Latin American regimes learned their military tactics.

Rafael's pained expression turned to exasperation as fellow moviegoers passed by the collection plate, calmly discussing the movie while munching on popcorn and sipping Pepsi. He then rushed out of the cinema to the car; Susan and I scrambled to keep up. We were soon on the highway with Rafael driving, me in the front passenger seat, and Susan leaning up the middle from the back, peppering him with questions.

"What's the matter? Why did you run to the car?"

Rafael was unable to speak, as if a cannonball was working its way up his esophagus.

"What's the matter?" Susan asked again, aggressively.

Rafael's hands tightened on the steering wheel and his foot pressed further down on the gas.

"I think you need to back off," I said, but Susan kept at it.

"What's wrong with you?"

"They just don't understand! They just don't understand!" he finally exploded.

Rafael began to wail, tears streaming like rivers, giving voice to an infinite anguish that could not flow quickly enough.

I looked at the speedometer. Headed toward one hundred miles per hour. Susan's chattering fused with the sound of the engine and wind enveloping the car.

"You really need to back off, Susan."

We were on an empty highway that invites such speed, but I imagined us careening off the side of the road: fireball, mangled steel.

"Could you slow down, Rafael?" I asked, in the sweetest voice I could muster, hoping to decelerate tension and car.

For a moment, I thought we might be leaving the planet, without question no longer in or of this world, but Rafael's grief subsided enough for him to decrease our speed and state that he was in complete control of the car. He also explained some of his history in Cuba, especially the man riddled with bullets left by the side of the road. It was a traumatic event and image that had never left him and that churned his insides raw while watching the film.

When we reached home Rafael and Susan went inside to talk.

I remained outside, entranced, again, by the New Mexican starry night, giving thanks to the cosmos for my spiritual teacher, praying he never transcend his attachment to the injustices of this world.

Chapter 10

The Guru as Teacher

"Truly speaking, it is not instruction, but provocation, that I can
receive from another soul. What he announces, I must find true
in me, or wholly reject, and on his word…be he who he may, I
can accept nothing."
—Ralph Waldo Emerson

"That which we are, we teach, not voluntarily but involuntarily."
—Ralph Waldo Emerson

It's the first day in Senior Seminar, the capstone Communication Studies
course at New England College, and I am previewing syllabus readings for
ten students sitting around a large table. There will be two weeks covering
religion.

"I don't like talking about religion," a disgruntled student says.

"Why is that?" I ask.

"I just don't like it," she insists with a frown.

"I'm not asking you to believe anything; I'm asking you to think critically about religious language and faith because religion and faith influence our world, whether we like it or not."

"Well, I don't like it."

The other students grimace.

"I get that, but nonetheless we're going to read about differing interpretations of religion, as well as science, because debates surrounding religion and science define our time. And we're also going to explore the common claim that 'I'm spiritual but not religious' because for many people
spirituality, however they define it, is important to self-knowledge and
finding their place in the world. And that's a main theme of this course—
we're going to explore the ways we live our inner world outwardly, or the
ways that we listen to our inner needs and the needs of the world. If we're
lucky, perhaps the two will come together."

"I thought we were going to write a research paper about our future careers?" she questions, brow furrowed.

"You may write a research paper, or you can work on a project for a business or nonprofit; both can be focused on a future profession. And you will participate in mock interviews with employers, which will help you with your job search. But this class is also my last opportunity to help you to become broadly and deeply educated, so we will explore intrapersonal intelligence by reading some philosophical and theological texts, which you are free to criticize in your reading journals and class discussion. Your final assignment is an education autobiography, in which you will analyze key learning moments of your life, both within and outside of formal schooling. I'm hoping that you will be able to connect the dots, giving you a sense of where you have been, where you are now, and where you might be heading, both in a career *and* in life."

ℤ

Senior Seminar is my dream course, allowing me to explore spiritual themes that have occupied me for three decades—callings and life path—but not all students have ears to hear. I can't blame them. I, too, rejected religious talk in college. And why should they listen to me when other voices, and sociocultural programming, tell a different story? A crucial question, of course, is who or what will they listen to upon graduation. What if, like me at their age, they still don't have much of a clue of who they are and what they want?

The syllabus encourages inner and outer listening by exposing students to Plato's "Allegory of the Cave," Emerson's "Self-Reliance," Thoreau's "Life Without Principle," Jung's process of individuation, Hillman's re-visioning of psychology to include daemons and callings, existentialism via Camus's "Myth of Sisyphus" and Sartre's "Freedom and Responsibility," atheism from an essay by the science writer Nathalie Angier, Einstein's "Cosmic Religious Feeling," personal essays by the nature writer Scott Russell Sanders integrating science, religion, and aesthetics, including "The Way of Things," "Silence," "Beauty," and "Faith and Work," the 1992 and 2017 World Scientists' "Warning to Humanity," and David Orr's address to graduating engineering students at the University of Pennsylvania, in which he challenges them to do their "great work" by designing with the earth and climate crisis in mind.

We also watch documentaries, such as "Happy," which explores the psychology of happiness within differing cultural contexts, and students participate in a "Clearness Committee" group project inspired by the progressive Quaker tradition, helping each other get clarity on possible future life path choices. The career and life planning director at the college also visits the class, details the job search, and sets up mock interviews.

Overall, the course includes readings from lots of White men chosen by a White man who loves and is deeply influenced by the writings of another White man, Thoreau. The academic canon debate has been around for a long time, and what is deemed knowledge has thankfully expanded to include the historically marginalized, adding to many syllabi dynamic and diverse examples of finding your voice and changing the world. Given this history, and the criminality of not exploring questions of our time, we end the course with a current book on eco-social crises such as environmental racism, in which toxic pollution is disproportionately disposed on people of color and the poor, who are considered disposable, or the toxic "culture wars" public sphere, which makes it difficult to have genuine conversations about realities like environmental racism and the pursuit of justice in a climate-disrupted world.

We also explore emerging counter-movements such as intersectional environmentalism, proposed by Leah Thomas, who, while a social-media–savvy student, wrote in her article "Why Every Environmentalist Should Be Anti-Racist" that Eric Garner's desperate "I can't breathe" before dying at the hands of the police may be interpreted more broadly to include people of color and the poor who live with poor air quality and are stricken with asthma. The same system of oppression undermines planetary health and the health of the disenfranchised, and thus forces must be joined, and the good fight must be fought.

Still, I could be more inclusive; after all, one of the reasons I so readily relate to Thoreau is my privileged background. My education and experiences, including nature experiences, reflect an inevitable blinkering; but I am challenged to reflect on that blinkering—and students are challenged to reflect on their blinkering—from reading Socrates's dead, White male exhortations to leave our shadowy one-dimensional caves and step into the multidimensional light, seeing "a thousand times better...because you have seen justice, beauty, and goodness." The same can be said for reading the transcendentalists on higher laws such as unity-in-diversity, which informs the pursuit of beauty and goodness. In Thoreau's writings, one can easily trace his vision of unity to perception of beauty, to wildness and freedom, and then to equality and justice. This trajectory is the thesis of Peter Wirzbicki's *Fighting for the Higher Law*, in which he details the history of Black and White abolitionists, who, inspired by transcendentalist principles, fought to overturn the Fugitive Slave Act of 1850.

If we are to respond to questions of our time, and thus our lostness, we must continually challenge our blinkering. In "The Whiteness of Walden," Rebecca Kneale Gould explores how, for Thoreau, nature is a healing balm where he experiences a "strange liberty," with trees beautiful and hoeing his bean fields a spiritual practice, while for people of color nature may raise quite different associations, with trees reminiscent of lynching and working the fields reminiscent of forced labor. Kneale further contrasts Thoreau's privileged experience of wilderness, which has a long history associated with rugged male Whiteness, with that of Dr. J. Drew Lanham. Dr. Lanham came across a house with the Confederate flag proudly displayed while he was conducting a bird survey in North Carolina, so he wrote, "It's only 9:06 a.m., and I think I might get hanged today." Lanham, a prominent author and wildlife biologist, has experienced the peacefulness and healing balm of nature, but on that day he completely lost his peace due to "traumatic cultural memories" that influence experience and perception.

Spiritual experiences inspired by nature are open to all, in the sense that nature's beauty speaks to the human soul, but the conditions that invite such experience are not equal. Lanham's example makes that disparity clear, but there are many more, including the urban-dwelling Outward Bounders I witnessed on the Appalachian Trail. The wilderness effect is real but so are racial and structural barriers to such experience, so we must reflect on Thoreau's relatively easy access to the balm and calm and feeling part and parcel of nature. We must also acknowledge that while Wirzbicki thankfully recovers the history of Black transcendentalists and activists who were open to learning from White transcendentalists, their relationships were not always characterized by mutual regard.

Kneale highlights Thoreau's statement in *Walden* that the worst kind of slavery is "when you are yourself the slave driver"; in other words, not being free within is worse than not being free without. She argues that his privileged position "shines through" in this sentence "in ways that can make a modern reader squirm." Ruminating on why he would include this line, she concludes that there is no easy resolution, especially given his abolitionist work in which he gave dynamic antislavery speeches and helped runaway slaves via the Underground Railroad. However, Thoreau consistently used exaggeration as a stylistic tool to make his points, or, as Kneale puts it, he consciously deploys "disruptive comparison for the sake of provocation." And she further writes that the "Economy" section provides "a broad critique of the ways in which consumerism, industrialism, and enslavement in the United States are deeply implicated in one another."

Thoreau saw how principles such as freedom, equality, and justice were linked with emerging ecocrisis, so he speaks to our collective lostness, even while we critically assess his legacy. He also wrote that "It is never too late to give up our prejudices" and then castigated old ways of thinking and doing, and the old generally: "I have lived some thirty years on this planet, and I have yet to hear the first syllable of valuable or even earnest advice from my seniors. They have told me nothing." This is clearly Thoreau the exaggerator and provocateur, the humorist, and the contradictory Thoreau, given that he did learn from elders such as Emerson. Thoreau himself needed to overcome his prejudices.

Exploring the Whiteness of *Walden* is a nuanced and complex balancing act. It is fair to be critical of Thoreau but unfair to expect too much; again, he was a flawed human, not an idealized myth. Still, he managed to resist much of the foolishness of the 1800s and anticipate our foolhardy Anthropocene, as well as Capitalocene domination by a particular wealthy class of humans, White and male, via a history of colonialism and subjugation. Thoreau's influence certainly extends beyond White readers, including to Lanham, who has called him a kindred spirit while speaking and writing about him admiringly. So has Gerald Early, who was introduced to Thoreau by his activist sister in the late 1960s: "As I was reading *Walden*, she and her Black friends seemed so Thoreauvian, so engaged in the project of self-improvement, so much simplifying and purifying, so much an escape from prison, so much reinvention and conversion, so much cleansing."

Thoreau's worldwide readership also suggests he has a few cross-cultural things to say that have given him global reach. He is no guru, no all-wise outside-of-time guide to be blindly followed, yet the principles he advocated for have universal resonance and inform diverse lives and life choices. Despite his privilege, we can learn from his many struggles, along with the many struggles of marginalized peoples. Gerald Early writes that he read Thoreau as transforming "sorrow into a form of art" in a way that resonated with the Black experience. Thoreau's ability to transform sorrow into art is also why he speaks to eco-social climate crisis times. After all, lostness also displays universal resonance or is an existential condition of being on this planet, as is education that responds to our lostness.

Syllabi are evolving texts. My choices for Senior Seminar are predisposed toward universal principles, or, as Thoreau wrote in "Life without Principle," we must get our "living by loving" and "see the sun rise or go down every day, so to relate ourselves to a universal fact." Instead of reading gossip in newspapers, he implores us to read the eternal reflected in our genius and higher law. In response to his gold-rush times, he asks why he should not "sink a shaft down to the gold within me, and work that mine."

Applying higher law and universal principles to current calamities, however, often makes me feel like the grim reaper of bad news, both on the state of human nature and the state of the world. Who would have thought that I would read the World Scientists' "Warning to Humanity" in 1992, teach it for twenty-five years, and then start teaching the 2017 updated "Warning to Humanity," which documents the sobering fact that things have gotten worse—in most cases, far worse. Even if climate crisis was not a reality, as deniers claim, we face many other calamities like deforestation and mass extinction (which rising temps exacerbate) and thus are still utterly lost. The warnings are stark and are just two of many studies on climate and biodiversity I could share with students. Such bad news has the potential to wake us up and motivate, or it may not, leading to "might as well give up" depression and inaction.

To motivate students to wake up, while also providing evidence that universal principles may lead lost humans to step out of their one-dimensional cave and into the multi-dimensional light, I also share Project

Drawdown's one hundred solutions to climate crisis, Paul Hawken's claim that more than two million organizations are fighting for eco-social justice, and the Grist website, "a beacon in the smog" that provides an annual "Meet the Fixers" top fifty young folks working on sustainability projects, many of them getting paid while participating in their "great work."

But the bad news can't be ignored, or, I argue, it is immature to do so. Part of the bad news is that we are not enacting those one hundred solutions, at least not fast enough. Climate crisis is not only a complex, wicked problem but a super-wicked one because time is running out, there's no central authority, those seeking to solve the problem are also causing it, and irrational policies disregard the future. Climate is more like an ongoing predicament instead of a problem that can be fully solved, so we may be fighting for what long-time activist Andrew Boyd calls a "better catastrophe," with those one hundred solutions (and no doubt many more), all part of a long, ongoing process.

I was certainly immature as an undergraduate yet heartened by a quotation from James Baldwin: "The world's definitions are one thing and the life one actually lives is quite another...one cannot allow oneself to live according to the world's definitions: one must find a way, perpetually, to be stronger and better than that." Baldwin, a gay Black man born in 1924 in Harlem, had many more reasons than I do to reject the world's definitions, but because his words speak of the universal, they spoke to me, so much so that I wrote it on an index card, cherishing it along with other "secular scriptures."

Not fitting into societal structures or dominant definitions of success is not a sign of immaturity; but not facing the reality of rising CO_2, and not rising to meet interrelated and super-wicked eco-social challenges, most certainly is. Students must be mature enough to not only sit with the disturbing data but also take it in without regress to denial as they imagine a better, less destructive, and more just future. That future is aided by the religious imagination that also displays universal resonance, whether in the mystical core of the world's religions, cosmic religious feeling, or transcendentalism.

I expect resistance to the "religious" readings, especially since some students equate religion with fundamentalism, and fundamentalists invoke a transcendent God and then act from beliefs that deny our not-knowing.

Religious views, whether closed or open-minded, arise from a desire for meaning and thus an escape from our lostness. Humans, I tell students, are religious animals directing our imaginations toward the transcendent in hopes of understanding the world within which we have been thrown. Fundamentalists, desperate for certainty in an uncertain world, are comforted by rigid meanings of God and morality. The religious quest as question mark, inviting new meanings, experiences, and responses, is replaced by the end-of-story period, now and forever, amen. Ironically, such false "knowing" supplies some comfort but only increases our lostness.

The end-of-story period, of course, is why some students resist not only religion but also universals because resonance has too often degraded into rigidity and become another means for the privileged to silence voices of cultural difference and otherness who have plenty to teach. The loss to the fundamentalist here is great. In exchange for cave-like comfort, they live closed to life and life force rather open to mystery and meaning. They forgo an ongoing spiritual path in which transcendent glories are experienced in love, sex, contemplation, including contemplative prayer, meditation, sports, hiking or being immersed in nature, diverse I-Thou encounters, and simply in our daily lives, or rather, when we "simplify, simplify, simplify." Unenlightened religious education is to blame. To deny life is to deny ourselves, and this denial can only be learned.

Christian Armageddon "left-behinders" and Islamist "a hundred virgins in heaven" terrorists, among numerous others, are taught to devalue this world in favor of some heavenly next, rather than be open to reverberating and resonating transcendent Mystery whose center is everywhere and circumference nowhere, beyond-any-category-we-can-fathom, including these words. But words can describe the universal religious impulse: the call to transform self-centered actions into those that serve a free-flowing intelligence in the heavenly here and now. Or, as Thoreau put it, "Men talk about Bible miracles because there are no miracles in their lives."

When crafting the syllabus for Senior Seminar and lost in pedagogical idealism, I imagine the course aiding this transformation and serving this intelligence, yet I know from experience that a discerning resistance is wise for the student. Wise discernment must be learned, however, as students often resist both fundamentalism and genuine spiritual transformation. A spiritual practice might lead students to drop self-deceptions concerning who they think they are, like Socrates's prisoners in the cave, to become better able to perceive higher laws and pursue the good, to be responsive to difference and thus more responsible to others. And, in some cases, to change career pursuits.

Sounds like a lot of weary work. What, exactly, is the pay-off?

And what if the teacher is lost in a web of self-deception, focusing on the spiritual at the expense of the material? Or on the universal at the expense of the particular?

Whatever path students choose post-graduation, I suggest that we are always living a narrative and therefore a faith, answering with our actions whether we will live according to the world's definitions or find a way to be stronger and better.

CB

"We should learn more about practical things in this class, like how to get a mortgage or balance a checkbook or buy stocks," says another disgruntled student.

Thankfully, several classmates look askance.

"I'm sorry but I'm not going to teach the culminating course of your college career as a financial how-to-buy-stuff course."

"But that's what we really need to know before we graduate."

"As you should know by now, I disagree a tad with that statement. And you should also already know how to balance a checkbook and you can ask your parents or a banker how to buy a house and you can consult with a stockbroker or read a book on how to buy stocks. But I like the idea of a practical finance course in the business department, which students could take as an elective."

"What I need is a course on how to pay back student loans," says Elana, who had written in her reading journal that she wants to travel after graduation, despite pressure from parents to get a job immediately. She always took my advice to use assignments to learn about herself and her passions, and she wrote papers that displayed a fine mind and a determined and soulful inner life.

Sometimes students ask questions for information, and sometimes they ask to relieve anxieties by hearing outwardly what they already know within; this felt like one of those moments. I seriously doubted that student loans, or anything, would stop Elana from doing what she was on earth to do.

"Now I'm more sympathetic, and I can give some advice because I know what it is like to pay back loans. You have a six-month grace period after graduation, which goes fast, and then you're supposed to start paying back your loan, but you can defer if you don't have a job or have a job but can't afford to pay it back or if you decide to travel—you just need to fill out some forms. They don't put you in jail if you can't pay."

Some students looked relieved.

"I deferred for a year. The downside, and it's a big downside, is that you are not paying off your loans and the interest accrues. But letting your loans drive your life path too much is also a big downside. You'll need to pay back your loans, and getting a high paying job and paying them off as soon as you can is a good strategy. But you don't have to pay them back right away or in large monthly amounts, and so another strategy is to choose a thirty-year payback plan in the beginning to reduce the payment. Don't get me wrong—debt sucks. Education should be free."

I look at Elana and continue.

"So, you can defer and travel—often traveling, or risking by following your inner promptings, calls forth outer possibilities, like a job that you never imagined for yourself, or one that you did imagine but you only got because you risked. Or you could get a job that includes travel, like teaching English overseas, and that may take you to unforeseen next steps, a path reflecting your individuation process. Or you can look for a job that you know will be your first job, making money to pay back your loan, and then find a job that matters to you, or a calling if you're lucky, and you will be able to start paying back the loan. They automatically take it out of your paycheck—after a while, you don't even think about it. But free education and canceling student debt are on-the-table political issues, and you can work to change the system."

"I still think this course should be more about finances," says the disgruntled student who first spoke.

"I know you do," I say.

☞

In mystic traditions, the guru as spiritual teacher provides guidance along a path of becoming living expressions of universal principles. Chogyam Trungpa, a Tibetan Buddhist spiritual teacher who taught for many years in the West, described the guru-student relationship as a series of stages. In the first stage, students have false expectations of the guru as a saintly figure who will magically transform their lives. They expect "every word, every cough, every movement" to be a gesture of wisdom. But, according to Trungpa, for the student to progress, these expectations must be surrendered, leading, surprisingly, to a deeper surrendering to the presence and energy of the guru and their teachings.

The result is a kind of love affair in which the student is utterly humbled before the grace of the guru. The guru's presence becomes the student's universe, providing a spark that burns away the last vestiges of the isolated ego. Finally, and thankfully, the focus of the student is then directed away from the guru and toward the world, allowing them to see the guru image, or the divine, in everything. The student's openness and love are transferred to life, and each situation becomes a teacher.

Trungpa warned spiritual students about the self-deception that often accompanies these stages, as those who claim to be progressing toward enlightenment often play an ego-driven game, spiritual materialism, in which students model a spiritual self—like the dentist, his wife, and the New Ager on the garbage can, and like myself, for that matter, when too detached—rather than living "the self" as transitory and fluid. The ego-self imitates being spiritual and creates a dense armor that prevents true transformation. Ironically, distorted spiritual techniques lead to the strengthening of egocentricity.

Exploring, and questioning, mysticism led me to research the misdeeds of the guru and the dangers of listening to the authority of the teacher. My favorite example of atrocious behavior comes from Franklin Albert Jones, or Bubba Free John, or Da Free John, or Da Love-Ananda, or Da Avabhasa, or Adi Da (apparently you're supposed to change your name as you become progressively more enlightened). I'll use "Franklin Jones," which will act as a reminder that he's just a guy born in Jamaica, New York, in 1939.

Jones's teachings have been celebrated by prominent spiritual thinkers, including Alan Watts, who wrote in the preface of Jones's autobiography, "He has simply realized that he himself as he is, like a star, like a dolphin, like an iris, is a perfect and authentic manifestation of the eternal energy of the universe, and thus is no longer disposed to be in conflict with himself." But Jones's teaching method of "crazy wisdom" doesn't quite live up to this high praise.

Crazy wisdom, in Jones's hands, demands that students submit to the will of the guru, who, due to their enlightened stature, knows what's best for the student. During one period in his teaching career, he broke down his students' ego attachments by having them participate in "sexual theater," which included switching partners, orgies, and making pornographic movies. Of course, Jones got to have sex with whomever he wanted, whenever he wanted. The result was damaged psyches, emotional abuse, and the permanent breakup of relationships.

Franklin Jones has written numerous books along with his autobiography, and they contain genuine spiritual insight, but his misdeeds supply a message to spiritual students that should have already been obvious: Don't stop thinking.

Jones's behavior suggests that there is no transcending the shadow, which is supposed to be a defining quality of enlightenment. Jones merely detached himself from his shadow-side and let it run wild. The label of "enlightened guru" then elicited the consent of followers, leading everyone to get caught in a crazy, downward spiral of abuse.

Jones, it seems to me, confused a healthy non-attachment, in which we own our emotions and issues and work to transcend them by transforming them, with a damaging detachment, in which we disown emotions and unwanted aspects of ourselves and repress them into our shadows; he did so based on sexual whims influenced by a dangerous mix of power and uncritical allegiance.

A distinction clearly needs to be made between a healthy ego-functioning responsive to both critical rationality and Spirit, and an alienated ego-self that lives a constrained life of fear and anxiety. Freedom interpreted as freedom from ego and ethical restraint, combined with a denied and un-dealt-with shadow-side, inevitably leads to inappropriate behavior, especially when the student has been instructed to rid themselves of their defenses, leading them to accept the wisdom of the teacher in all situations.

Still, I like the idea of "crazy wisdom" because it attempts to incorporate playfulness into the spiritual search. Socrates exposed those who claimed to know as frauds, and crazy wisdom discerns that knowing is often a sham, especially religious belief that clearly demarcates good and evil. We need to lighten up, to walk the middle path beyond good and evil by being open to learning from experience. But in the hands of the guru, crazy wisdom may become play without consequence; a rigid morality is overcome, but so are spiritual principles, conscience, and purpose.

Trungpa's descriptions of devotion to the guru and spiritual materialism should act as warning to the abusive antics of so-called gurus like Jones. They should also act as a warning to his own antics, as his teaching methods earned him the title, "the roaring tiger of crazy wisdom." No student would mistake him for a saintly guru, as he claimed to come from a "long line of eccentric Buddhists," and his eccentricities included teaching while reeking of alcohol, surrounding himself with bodyguards, and dressing in military garb of his own design. Despite stating that the guru is like a spiritual friend, he also argued for hierarchical guru-student relationships because it taught devotion. Such devotion greatly enhanced his sex life—being a guru is a super way to get laid—but he died in 1987 from complications associated with his alcoholism.

Trungpa's accomplishments are many. Along with writing numerous books he also established more than one hundred meditation centers in Europe, Canada, and the US, and he founded the Naropa Institute in Colorado, one of few spiritually and ecologically-based universities. Alan Watts also demonstrated his spiritual awareness through many accomplishments, but he too died from alcohol-related causes. Watts became addicted to vodka because it made him feel less alone; his loneliness is astounding considering that he was a meditation teacher and that his many books and talks point toward transcending the separate self-sense and its attendant alienation.

The irony here is immense, but perhaps the real problem is the tendency for students to expect a teacher to not be human. Watts at least recognized his folly and joked that he was an "authentic fake."

The guru has impressive qualities—knowledge of esoteric religious traditions, insight from spiritual experiences, a degree of compassion and care, and energetic presence—but it's easy to be compassionate and energetic when you're surrounded by followers who believe that you are a divine incarnation of the Absolute. Gurus, again ironically, are prone to spiritual materialism, to the egoic tendency to *act* enlightened rather than *be* enlightened. And things quickly go astray when a group of like-minded searchers get together with a guru who claims that he lives in an ego-less state, especially since the searchers have no idea what an enlightened adept looks like, so someone with plenty of ego invested in being the guru can seem enlightened.

It would be nice if these were just examples of the rousing, yet sometimes foolish, sixties. But a recent guru, Andrew Cohen, the founder of a spiritual community and the thoughtful and provocative spiritual magazine *EnlightenNext*, provoked senior students to finally knock him off his perch due to physical abuse, financial exploitation, and denying students the freedom to leave, which ultimately ended the community and magazine.

It took years for community members to speak up. What causes students to follow with such blind allegiance?

A positive root is the genuine religious desire for meaning, often heightened by intuitive glimpses of unity elicited through meditation with the guru. This desire, though, is easily perverted; surrender is intoxicating, talk of enlightenment is a divine high, and critical questioning spoils the cozy feeling of peace.

There is also the certainty and charisma of the guru, who can dismiss any criticism with "you're just not enlightened enough" or "that's just your ego talking." Everything is justified by the possibility of enlightenment. The core problem with this stance is that problems are not possible within this stance. It's another Catch-22. Enlightenment is perfection, so everything the enlightened guru does or says must be perfection. Another concern, which I first questioned in New Mexico, is intrinsic to the spiritual search: The desire to transcend is a mark of creativity, but this desire is misdirected when it attempts to leave the human behind. Desire for perfection becomes the desire to escape materiality and become superior to others and the world.

Thoreau was deeply influenced by Hinduism and seems to celebrate the guru ideal in a journal entry when he writes that we inspire friendship with fellow humans when we have "contracted friendship with the gods." Such god friendship requires that, leaving our fellows behind, we cease to "sympathize with and be personally related" to be "universally related." Sounds like he is advocating for not being of the world—"We hug the earth—how rare we mount! How rarely, we climb a tree!"—he continues, arguing for transcendence and perspective. But as always, he's also an earth hugger, returning to embrace and being fully in the wild world.

For Thoreau, such "leaving" inspires love, and this love is gifted by practicing the presence, seeing the divine in all things and at all times, or, also in the same entry, "The halo around the shadow is visible both morning and evening." This guru-like claim is much more heartening than his statement in *Walden* equating the mass of men with quiet desperation, providing haloed hope for the shadowy masses, with human potential found in recognizing the miracle of existence. The guru ideal is distorted, however, when the reality of the shadow, in multiple senses and forms, is ignored. Gurus, who claim to be found, are too often lost; by denying that lostness, they cease to learn and live with principle.

Emerson, as the Concord sage, must have had a guru-like allure to Thoreau in early meetings, as well as to other youthful searchers, yet he saw the downsides of being the all-knowing teacher and was pleased to claim that he had no followers. He acknowledged he had truth to share and that he found "intelligent receivers," but he did not wish to "bring men to me, but to themselves": "I delight in driving them from me…This is my boast that I have no school and no followers. I should account it a measure of the impurity of insight, if it did not create independence."

Krishnamurti perceived so much nonsense in the guru-student relationship that he famously declared "no gurus." His teachings were meant to help others become free, but instead he saw students expecting the guru to give them truth instead of them finding it for themselves. Krishnamurti's declaration was shattering because he had been groomed since childhood—for eighteen years—to be a "world teacher" by leaders of the Theosophical Society. But he disbanded the group, claiming he wanted no followers. Thousands of theosophists were ready to prostrate themselves at his feet, but he said "no thanks," choosing instead to give talks in which he constantly turned his listeners back to themselves.

Krishnamurti complained that reporters always asked him how many followers he had, as if the number proved whether what he said was true or false. But the true student, who is open to mystery *and* walks with great critical intelligence, sees the falsity of such inquiries, of all that is "unessential, to unrealities, to shadows." Krishmamurti spoke out in hopes of freeing humans from all fears, "from the fear of religion, from the fear of salvation, from the fear of spirituality, from the fear of love, from the fear of death, from the fear of life itself."

Krishnamurti was not perfect either. Lama Govinda, a Buddhist teacher and the author of *Foundations of Tibetan Mysticism*, stated that Krishnamurti was humorless.

Govinda, it is said, felt a sharp pain in his neck at age eighty-seven, keeled over, and died laughing.

And on it goes.

❣

"I don't see how these readings relate to anything in the world, especially the work world," said still another disgruntled student, an NEC athlete and former star quarterback at his high school.

"Is the work world the world?" I replied, knowing this response was not going to fly.

"We have to get jobs," he insisted.

"Of course you do. The material dimension of life is very important, especially if you have a family. And don't be fooled, I'd love to be rich..."

That got everyone's attention; I assumed because they appreciated my admission and because they all wanted to be rich too.

"...although if I were rich, I would confront the ethical question of what I would do with my money. I would probably build a green-designed house with solar panels, and I like to think I would still live simply and support good causes. There are plenty of folks who follow their souls and become entrepreneurs and make lots of money, and many are philanthropic and support creative innovation, like the development of solar panels, but the readings suggest that solar panels, or any technology, will not solve the climate crisis and other eco-social problems, and you should follow *your* path as best you can. Again, one of the main points of the readings and class discussions is that there is more than one way to live a life. I think that is practical advice that relates to the world, even if I am your parents' worst nightmare for saying so."

Several students laugh. My comments were meant for everyone, but especially for Elana.

"But the readings don't help me professionally."

"You want to be a college football coach, right?"

"I want to be a head coach and make lots of money."

"That's great, and if you make lots of money you should give some of it to NEC because the Communication Studies and liberal arts education you've received, including the readings in this class, will have helped you to reach your goals."

More students laugh, and he smiles, a questioning, endearing smile that I had received many times in our classes together.

"I don't see that."

"The best coaches are smart. They know themselves via intrapersonal communication and they know how to motivate others via interpersonal communication. They understand human psychology, and they know how to read their players; they know that faith, wisely understood, is a key to excellence; they know that there is a religious dimension to sports in the form of zone or flow experiences."

He was thinking, so I asked a question.

"Are pre-game and halftime speeches an important skill for football coaches?"

"Yes, of course."

"Well, public speaking is another skill you've practiced at college, and the best pre-game speeches may have historical or literary or religious references. Your liberal arts education will help you in ways you can't fathom."

"But I don't see all of that in these readings."

"It's the reading, and your education as a whole, that has changed you. I know most of you are sick of writing papers…"

Groans of recognition resounded in Fitch 12, my favorite classroom because its aged walls hold, for me, numerous memories of Senior Seminar conversations like this one.

"…yes, I know, you have senioritis, and you are sick of writing papers, but with each paper, your critical thinking skills have improved. You may not be able to see it, but I can, since I have had most of you in class for several years. And you know I want you to write your papers about something you are passionate about, something that will help you to develop your voice. You can write about the rhetoric of pre-game speeches if you want, or whatever will better prepare you for the professional world. But my goal, my passion, is to prepare you for the professional world *and* life, for living well and contributing to others, and the readings and papers help me to do that. You are more likely to be successful and contribute to others as a football coach, or in any job, if you read and think and are well educated."

I look across the room, smiling because I spoke with force from my depths. No disgruntled responses.

Did I get through to them?

෫

I idealized Rafael when we first met; he was my spiritual teacher and counselor instead of friend. He was also playful although thankfully not a roaring tiger of "crazy wisdom" with ego-whipping sexual theater or drunken meditation sessions.

When I stayed with Rafael in New Mexico, he became more of a friend and I felt free to be more critical. He seemed to be following in Goldsmith's footsteps, including working as a healer, receiving phone calls from people with various ailments, and then rushing off to the meditation room to "take it to God" or to silently witness God within the "patient." Larry Dossey, a medical doctor, has written books on the effects of long-distance prayer and meditation in healing. He argues, from the perspective of the world soul, that mind is a non-local phenomenon and thus individual minds, and bodies, can be influenced by the consciousness of others. Rafael, calling it the "speed of consciousness," remarked that the people who phoned asked for his help. He didn't put out a shingle, and they claimed that they were helped, so he continued to do it. I didn't deny or affirm this practice, but it seemed rife with the potential for self-deception. Once one takes a step down that path, the next thing you know you're trying to channel Ramtha or some other dead New Age guru.

Rafael continued to amaze with his integration of academic pursuits and spiritual practices. If someone had told me about the healing Goldsmithian scholar, I would have thought it a tall tale, but it somehow made sense in the playful and purposeful form of Rafael. He saw spirituality as an aesthetic action of personal growth, creative projects, and service to others. He often stated that service was the highest degree in the mystical life, and this action overrode seeming contradictions, and my fair or unfair criticisms.

Rafael taught the universal principle of spiritual unity resonating as material fulfillment, not as allegiance to him although, at times, I thought he was too beholden to Goldsmith. Early on, after I had just finished at Rutgers, he told a story of Goldsmith coming across a house fire. Someone needed help, so he went into meditation, and someone appeared to save them. The suggestion was that his meditation called forth the rescuer. I thought that was bullshit, and that Goldsmith should have saved the person himself. Rafael countered that he was old and that he did what he could. And so, we debated. The beauty of our relationship is that our debates were a big part of my spiritual education.

When I decided to leave New Mexico, he understood, and while I was there, he tried to help me to express a mystical vision through poetry as he had in several books. His writing advice to not censor myself, or my unconscious, was another lesson I've never forgotten. Being mentored by Rafael often came in moments in which we were just hanging out, thinking and talking together while doing some activity—writing poetry, walking among mesas, or taking day trips.

Rafael would state a whim and off we would go to a historic spot, like Bandelier National Monument, home of Pueblo ancestors, where we imagined living in cave dwellings carved into mountain-side and spiritual ceremonies in underground kivas. Unlike a Socratic cave, these structures no doubt inspired meditative thinking and openness to Mystery. Or, the flip side, Sandia Labs, home of the Manhattan Project and the result of worshiping calculative thinking: the first atomic bombs in the 1940s. The lab website states that the bomb was meant for deterrence, but that purpose misses the danger: meditative ethics evolve slower than new technologies, a problem addressed at Ometeca conferences. Perhaps ethics can catch up, integrating meditative and calculative thinking; Sandia Labs has its hands full with an array of ventures today. It's still involved in nuclear technology but mostly regarding safety, and lab scientists also study wind power and research climate at a facility in Alaska where they collect data on cloud formations and their influence on warming.

Our most profound adventure was to White Sands National Park. White Sands is just that—dune after dune of white sand. It's more than just a lot of sand; it's an enveloping planet of the purest white sand, and the drive in takes you deep into the planet's core. They even plow the road due to wind continually recreating the landscape.

We got out of the car once we found a spot away from other travelers and explored the mounds and swirls like children. The dunes felt other-worldly, inducing silence and stillness and loss of self with ease. We meditated on top of a hill with the sun dropping, streaming light over the horizon, and I again discovered the meaning of spiritual freedom. It was also once again clear why a taste of such divinity leads many to take up the search, sometimes following fallible gurus who lead them astray.

Rafael taught that mysticism was an attitude toward life, and that the teacher should not be put on a pedestal or make decisions for the student because then there is no growth. What can be taught and passed on is the attitude, not specific answers to problems. With the attitude students can listen to themselves and answer their own questions. He also didn't want to be called a mystic because the name led to a deference that was not conducive to teaching and learning. He thought of himself as a person enjoying conscious union with that "thing, that something" that has neither words nor thoughts and that some people have decided to call God.

Our evolving relationship from teacher-student to friendship was most facilitated by anything-goes conversation. I could talk with him about anything, which meant that sex was a frequent topic. We could go from discussing Heisenberg's uncertainty principle in one moment to the sexualized love poems of St. John of the Cross in the next.

Rafael often said he learned a tremendous amount from me, but I was at a loss to what that could be. What I did know was that I always felt valued in his presence and learned from being in his presence. The guru-as-teacher model is flawed, but the sharing of presence, of consciousness, of spiritual and human being-ness, is an ignored aspect of education. It's an aspect that I tried to embody, sometimes successfully and oftentimes not, especially when teaching Senior Seminar.

I felt a sense of responsibility to pass on what I had learned from Rafael by becoming a catalyst for students' growth. I hoped to inspire them to become whole human beings in an age in desperate need of them. Part of that learning was not expecting them to follow a spiritual path. The more I taught, the more letting go became my spiritual, teaching practice although I sometimes conveyed the attitude that "You just don't know yet." Like the religious and agricultural students at Purdue, the students in Senior Seminar already came with world views, which I often thought they held too rigidly, as if, amazingly at twenty-two, they had already figured it all out.

All I could do was challenge them and let go, recalling my own foolishness as a young student, and the many times I have been lost.

Chapter 11

The Bottom Drops Out, Again

"If you bring forth what is within you, what you bring forth will save you. If you do not bring forth what is within you, what you bring forth will destroy you."
—Sayings attributed to Jesus, *Gospel of Thomas* 70

Everything clicked one Saturday night. My brother Jim and I were gambling along with the weekend throng at the Meadowlands Harness Racetrack in northern New Jersey. All types frequented the track: high-end hipsters from Manhattan and a litany of low-enders, including my brother's buddies, a TV repairman, mafia errand runner, and maintenance man for an apartment building. Old betting tickets scattered the floor like the remains of a ticker-tape parade, and the lowest low-enders searched for winning tickets accidently discarded before they were swept away with an oversized broom by a racetrack maintenance man. Most patrons sat behind huge windows, safely removed from the elements while cheering on the action of horse and jockey.

It was 1990, still two years before I taught at Purdue and the first World Scientists' "Warning to Humanity"—ppm 354.39.

A year earlier, the conservative Marshall Institute, whose members included the architects of the Tobacco Institute (which infamously used incomplete and misleading science to blur the connections between smoking and health risks), issued their first report attacking climate science. There would be more, including ad hominem attacks on climatologists and the cherry-picking of one of six climate diagrams to blame warming on solar activity. That's right, they argued the sun is responsible for global warming.

Then, in 1990, the first UN IPCC report concluded that the world was indeed warming, but natural causes were part of the mix. Here's the gamble: it would take a decade of study to have more certainty about the extent of anthropogenic warming, but by that time we would be much farther down the road, and farther away from the opportunity to reverse course. Computer modeling showed that we could be heading for a Celsius increase of 1.5 to 4.5 degrees in global average temperature, or up to a whopping 8 degrees Fahrenheit by the mid-twenty-first century. The report also refuted the claim made by a small group of scientists that solar variation was the main cause.

Two-thirds of scientists polled thought that there was enough evidence to warrant action to lessen the danger. The Marshall Institute argued that disrupting the economy in response to alleged climate disruption was a worse danger.

How to play the odds?

How to play the odds when the stakes are not only all of humanity but all species, the whole planet, the whole shebang?

Like most, I was mostly oblivious to this debate that should not have been a debate even though I had a greater interest in science after study with Rafael. Nor did I seek out a "respectable" career during this time. Instead, after leaving New Mexico I returned to the printshop, then spent a summer visiting Preston at Purdue, then returned to the printshop, then house-sat for four months in an empty home in southern New Hampshire, living a Thoreauvian life of reading, writing, and walking in woods. I lay outside on my thirtieth birthday with a six-pack and watched the moon pass over the night sky.

Thoreau, at thirty, having left Walden Pond to live at the Emerson household while Emerson traveled abroad, embraced family life with Emerson's wife and kids as *Walden* simmered. In response to a Harvard survey on postgraduate activity, he wrote, "I am a Schoolmaster—a Private Tutor, a Surveyor—a Gardener, a Farmer—a Painter, I mean a House Painter, a Carpenter, a Mason, a Day-Laborer, a Pencil-Maker, a Glass-Paper Maker, a Writer, and sometimes a Poetaster."

In a letter to his friend Harrison Blake, he provided some life philosophy: "Do what you love. Know your own bone; gnaw at it, bury it, unearth it, and gnaw it still. Do not be too moral. You may cheat yourself out of much life so. Aim above morality. Be not *simply* good—be good for something."

When I left my Walden-like life in New Hampshire, I once again returned to the printshop, which remained a source of turmoil. I continued to meditate, and the shop supplied funds for adventures and time for writing. Unable to shake writerly aspirations, I hoped to be good for something.

I also had a new plan for making extra money.

Printing is a skill, and the quality of the work is paramount. Type must be bold and clear, colors rich, and logos and lines straight on the page. Customers don't give return business if their letterhead has faded colors and crooked type. Adjusting color and type is easy compared to getting paper stock to run smoothly. The small Ryobi presses we used had an air suction system that was supposed to pick up and shoot each sheet through the press. But different orders use different weights and styles of paper, so we had to continually adjust the amount of suction. Too much, and sheets shoot up into the ink rollers and create one hell of a mess. Too little, and sheets drop down into the conveyor system, gathering ink and oil that eventually transfer to the clean sheets that successfully make it through the press.

I was a damn good printer, so good that I quickly got jobs running and then only made small adjustments throughout the length of a run. The press could turn out five thousand sheets in an hour, and we often had orders between five and fifty thousand. There was quite a bit of time in which I just stood there, listening to the rhythmic sounds of each sheet passing through the rollers—ka-chunk, ka-chunk, ka-chunk. If the rhythm changed, I knew something was wrong. Otherwise, there was nothing much to do, except, on this return, join my brother in his beloved hobby: handicapping horses by studying the charts in the daily *Sports Eye*.

Handicapping charts are filled with statistical information based on the previous six races of each horse in the race. Real gamblers study charts for hours, comparing times, track conditions, jockeys, trainers, post position, probable odds, whether the horses are rising or dropping in class and competition, and most importantly, the trip—did they get stuck on the rail behind a slow horse, getting shuffled out of the race, did they get interfered with, did they make their move too early or too late, did they take too much air on the outside, or did they get plenty of cover and have the perfect trip. Given all these factors, a strong horse can easily finish out of the money and a relatively weaker horse can win. However, the stronger horses are most likely to win. The charts are deceptive, but the clues are there. The novice throws money away on the obvious favorite. The professional, who sees through the deception, can locate a potential pot of gold.

The charts were like a Sherlock Holmes mystery. Only the brightest, most intuitive inductive reasoners could uncover the most salient racing clues. I decided to apply my formal studies, especially in mathematics, to finding the clues and unraveling the mystery of gambling. The work world was a game anyway, I thought, so if I had to live in an over-consumptive, money-driven economic system and a compromised climate system, I might as well play.

I basically figured, why fight it? For a little while, that is, I would embrace the shop and all that came with it, including gambling. After all, I was supremely confident that spending so much time meditating on the Supreme Identity would make me immune to downsides. Plus, the mass of men led lives of quiet desperation due to unfulfilling jobs; I needed something to relieve the boredom.

Finding strong horses was the first step in my handicapping education. The second was learning how and how much to bet. You can bet with caution and still make money by betting win, place, and show, but the desire to make a big score leads to exactas (picking the top two finishers) and trifectas (picking the top three finishers) and especially trifecta wheels. The trick with trifecta wheels is to find two horses that will finish in the top three, and then bet them with every other horse in the race. The permutations and amount of money needed to place the bet can get rather high, but you don't have to worry about the order of finish, and the payoff can be large. I started my gambling career betting win, place, and show, and I eventually worked my way up to larger amounts and trickier bets. I was losing more than winning but told myself that I was learning.

The night things clicked, I won win, place, and show bets the first four races and was up two hundred dollars. A trifecta race was coming up in the sixth race, so I skipped the fifth to review the charts once again for the two horses I planned to wheel. It was the final race from a month-long competition; all the horses were good. The key was comparing racing styles and post positions, and then figuring out the likely trip.

I liked the one horse, Speed Demon; he was a fast starter, and from the first post he wouldn't have to fight to get a shorter trip from the rail.

If he didn't get blocked or shuffled back, he would be close at the end. I also liked Headstrong in the tenth post position. Ordinarily, I would be concerned about such an outside post, but I had watched Headstrong win a couple of races, and he was a closer. No matter what his post, he would drift to the rear, get lots of cover from other horses, and come charging at the end. The race was bound to be fast since there were so many good horses, and many of them would be winded at the finish. I visualized the entire race in my head—a rail sitter and closer were smart picks.

The race unfolded as I had imagined. Speed Demon sat on the rail saving energy, found an opening at the end, and burst through for second. Headstrong disappeared into the back of the pack, but in the last fifty yards of the stretch, a horse soared from the outside, passing numerous tiring ones in a flash. Headstrong rifled home for third. I hadn't even picked the winner of the race but by "wheeling" my horses it didn't matter.

I collected 650 bucks, equal to nearly two weeks of work at the print-shop.

Jim was pretty darn impressed, especially since he taught me everything I knew. My brother, who is five years older, took one course at a community college and wrote a social issue paper on gambling addiction, but that was the extent of his higher education. I was the supposed scholar in the family, and while Jim seemed impressed by my degree from Rutgers, he enjoyed teaching me what he knew: printing and gambling. While he genuinely enjoyed helping his younger brother by hiring me repeatedly, and we both genuinely enjoyed spending time together, my returns allowed him to spend more time gambling instead of printing. Plus, he got to be my boss, which was better than having a degree. He was also happy because he made more money when I was printing, and this time he had another gambling buddy.

Despite Jim's pleasure in my success that night, he was out of cash and wanted to leave. Sweet Success, a horse that I had won money on in the past, was running in race twelve, so I quickly re-scanned the chart, hoping to place a bet before we left. Sweet Success had recently taken a layoff and had only one previous race listed, in which he came in sixth. I knew that weekend Meadowlands bettors—who came to the track for entertainment—would disregard him immediately and bet on the favorite, their favorite jockey, or a favorite number. My favorite thing to do, I thought, flush from being flush, was to take advantage of this stupidity.

The "rule," according to Jim, was that you wait until a horse establishes a racing record after a layoff before you bet them. Or you wait until they are rounding into winning form. But Sweet Success was a special horse, and Saturday-night novice bettors meant the odds would be high. Shoot for a big score, I thought, with no time for a second because Jim was clamoring to go. I took the 650 dollars I had just won and bet half on Sweet Success to win and the other half to place, and then went home and began pacing the floor of my basement apartment where I had lived for several months and that seemed designed to constrict consciousness.

Back, forth, back, forth.

"I can't wait until the morning newspaper to find out the winner," I thought, "gotta call Sportsline."

"Race nine action…" blared a recording. Too soon.

Back, forth, back, forth.

Pacing was a new practice for me. It wasn't meditative like my relatively recent walks in the woods of New Hampshire, but the manic energy of winning and then betting so much money was also new terrain.

I looked down at the blue carpet and then up at the low-hanging ceiling I could touch without jumping. I looked at the small basement windows. I hated small basement windows. I looked at the TV. Darryl Strawberry hit a homer for the Mets.

"You gotta love Darryl, except for the strikeouts."

Back, forth, back, forth. I wrung my hands, as if crushing thoughts in a vice.

"Race eleven action…" Too soon.

"If Sweet Success paid ten dollars to win and five dollars to place—a very conservative estimate—I would win fifteen dollars, 162.5 times."

I got a calculator: $2437.50.

"Race twelve action…"

No mention of Sweet Success.

I was a giddy, adrenaline-pumped nitwit during the past hour. When I heard the Sportsline recording of the stretch run of race twelve, my body drooped like a failed marathon runner, exhausted, empty, as if there was no meaning to anything. In an instant I had lost the 650 bucks I won a few hours earlier. My trifecta wheel bet was so perfect, but I had nothing to show for it. It was as if Sherlock Holmes had solved a mystery, put a dangerous criminal in jail, and then just let him go.

The next day I was back at the printshop telling the story to Jim. Telling the story was part of gambling, part of the "action." The real reason gamblers gamble is that they need action, they need the high, they need the thrill of risk and diversion from dullness.

My brother had been gambling for fifteen years and knew this story all too well.

I swore to myself that I would take a break from gambling. It was fun at first, as if I had been pretending to be someone else at a masquerade ball. By identifying with Spirit, I was free to be anyone I wanted, but expressing Spirit meant ethical discernment; like some "crazy wisdom" gurus, I had begun to reside more in the former than the latter. Another truth is that my return to blue-collar trappings was not just spiritual play; I was blue collar, or had deep roots that had not been transcended, and like the shadow, never could be fully transcended. Old expressions of self were much closer to the surface than I had imagined. They resurfaced when I lived back in New Jersey, by interacting with family, by toiling at the shop.

Those old expressions and the long printing runs and boredom soon brought me back to daily racing charts in the *Sports Eye*. So did the fact that I had tasted the god-like thrill of figuring it out. It was an omnipotent feeling, a transcendent feeling—I craved more. But Sweet Success had put me out of sync. Every time I thought I found a winning horse, I doubted my decision and wondered if I was making the Sweet Success mistake again. He was running the following Saturday, and Jim claimed that now would be the time to bet him. Sweet Success had finished seventh the week before, due to a bad trip, and his odds would be even higher this week. Jim said the third time out after a layoff is often when good horses return to form. I couldn't bring myself to bet him. He won, paying over twenty dollars to win. Jim had placed a bet with his bookie and made a nice score. I had made the Sweet Success mistake again by not betting Sweet Success.

I existed within a netherworld between feeling confident from being close to figuring it out and completely inept from poor decisions. And hour by hour, printing job after monotonous printing job, I descended; gambling was supposed to be mischievous amusement. It was supposed to help me to pass time while making extra cash for my next adventure, but instead

181

I found myself increasingly immersed in a hellish misadventure. I read *Sports Eye* and the sports pages in the New York *Daily News* and in the New York *Post*. I watched Mets baseball on TV. I went to a local bar, the Rail and Ale, for beers with other blue-collar workers. I went to the racetrack. I enjoyed all of it until it became all I seemingly had. Somehow, I willfully ignored Emerson's warning that "a foolish consistency was the hobgoblin of little minds" and that "virtue and vice emit a breath every moment." Instead of making a killing at the track, I was killing the muse a little more each day, with vice victorious over virtue.

When I first arrived back at the shop, Jim and I bet on NFL playoff games. We discussed point spreads and the myriad factors that would affect the games: home field advantage, the team's previous history in the playoffs, the team's history playing each other, injury reports, weather reports, momentum, etc. Still on a non-attached high from solitude in New Hampshire, I wasn't psychologically invested in gambling or who won the games, and my reasoning and intuitions were clear. It seemed obvious which teams would win. I told my brother to put me down for a hundred dollars on two games. He called his bookie, and just like that the bets were in. My teams won, and I repeated the process the next week. By the time the Super Bowl ended, I was up six hundred dollars, which I kept hidden in a Goldsmith book at my apartment as if stowing away stolen supply. But the clarity I experienced when making football bets was nowhere to be found. Too invested, too clouded, too little-minded. I was no longer able to tell the difference between reasoned intuitions and stupid hunches.

The next day, Jim walked into the printshop with a *Sports Eye* for each of us.

"I think I've found one of the best bets of my fifteen years of handicapping," he exclaimed, sounding surprised to hear himself saying it while his eyes gleamed and his bulky, six-foot, six-inch frame looked lighter.

"What?!" I said.

This was quite a comment to hear. My brother didn't just handicap occasionally; he did it every moment he could at work and every evening for hours. He had voluminous records of trainers, jockeys, times, all kept in large plastic containers—an old-schooler, he was slowly transitioning into the computer age. And now he'd found one of the best bets he'd ever seen.

"Jennifer's Dream. Third race off a layoff. He was boxed out the first time back and took lots of air the second. He's even dropping in class. He's a strong horse, but the weekend bettors won't know it. The odds will be high."

I quickly opened my *Sports Eye* to the chart and started looking for reasons. Jennifer's Dream had come in last and second to last in two races since the layoff, but he was clearly not in form and never had a chance anyway due to the trips. His last two races were like warm-ups for this one. All he needed was a good trip.

"I'm in," I said. I already felt stupid for missing out on the Sweet Success win. "Not this time," I thought to myself.

Jim walked in the next day with considerably less animation. We both called Sportsline the previous night. I had bet my entire week's paycheck; I lost my entire week's paycheck.

Jim felt terrible, but there was nothing he could do except tell the story. This time I did take a break from gambling. Losing my paycheck hurt. I was trying to save money so I could leave behind the smelly ink and chemicals to visit Preston and other Purdue friends and perhaps move to Indiana. I also hoped to read books and to write again instead of incessantly calculating racing charts. And there were ignored ethical questions surrounding the racing of horses, who were "God's own"; the forty-hour workweek and gambling had not only changed physical habits but habits of thought. I was only meditating to survive rather than for spiritual growth.

The fun faded with each passing week. Losing my paycheck ripped off the mask. This was my real life, quite in and of the world.

Jim found another bet. Two old mainstays and long-time winners at the track, Excalibur and Kronos, were dropping into a class of inferior competitors. They hadn't raced all that well recently, but they had good post positions and were being driven by the two best jockeys. He suggested an exacta box, Excalibur-Kronos and Kronos-Excalibur. If the morning line held, it would pay around forty dollars either way. A forty-dollar bet— twenty on each exacta—would net about four hundred dollars. I could win back my paycheck. Internally, I said "no"; I was on a break, but the external jackhammered cracks in my resolve. I spent the day at work obsessing over the race, looking for other horses that would ruin it. I went back and forth—bet, don't bet—until I finally re-found my resolve. I didn't trust Jim's judgment anymore. Excalibur won, Kronos came in second, and Jim won $450.

I had been working at the printshop for almost five months and saved a thousand dollars. If I hadn't been gambling, I would have had at least four thousand—a pittance for many, a fortune to me. It was late April, and I hoped to join Preston and others in June for a summer of fun and thinking together. If I saved money in May, then I would leave with at most two thousand dollars—an intolerable amount for time spent at the shop, especially since making money for future freedom was the only reason I was there, the only meaning behind the drudgery.

The next few weeks were miserable. I had put in five months of work and had little to show for it. But my lack of funds was nothing compared to how far I had fallen. What happened to the lessons learned from meditation and intensive study with Rafael, or joyous times frolicking with Mac in the intoxicating Maine woods, or the glories of the Appalachian Trail, or the presence of the Sandia Mountains, or the natural high and clarity of mind I embodied after my recent Thoreauvian life in New Hampshire?

What was this strange allure toward self-destruction? A writ-large question for society. A writ-large question given the gamble of climate crisis.

While in New Hampshire I received a letter from Rafael that basically stated that I didn't fully know who I was, or still didn't fully acknowledge my potential: "Is there one last garment that is veiling who you are, one cloak that hints that 'I am not enough' and haven't earned the right to sing out loud?"

Rafael knew that I tended to fall back into doubting my abilities, but it was easy to exist within spiritual heights amid the mesas of New Mexico, while swimming with Mac and hiking in Maine, and when living in solitude amid autumn colors in New Hampshire; the printshop and New Jersey were once again a different story. It was within my power to change the script, but one of the reasons I kept gambling was because I thought winning was a matter of getting into the right state of mind. I thought I had been in the right state in the past and could get there again. It was both a spiritual challenge and a material one; or, like a Goldsmith healing, the spiritual could influence the material and some magic could happen.

Instead of exiting the shadowy cave to the soul-fired beat of a different drum, I descended deeper, desperate to salvage much-needed cash but also the whole point of returning to the shop. It was one thing to leave behind soulful pursuits temporarily, I told myself, but quite another for there to be no pay-off. Plus, I learned so much gambling knowledge through losing and could use that expertise to finally turn things around.

I decided to bet once more if I found the perfect trifecta race.

I just needed one big score.

One day, in mid-May, I was sure I found it: three horses dropping in class in a short field of eight. Hermes was the clear favorite; in his last race, he had run the fastest mile of the year. I was suspicious of his record time since he had a perfect trip under fast track conditions, but he was clearly in top form and dropping in competition. The other two horses, Search and Destroy and, of all horses, Jennifer's Dream, were also strong and currently in top form. The only question was how to bet.

I could bet Hermes on top, with the other two coming in either second or third, but I decided to box all three horses, which meant six total bets. If my horses finished in the top three, I'd win no matter what the order. The odds on Hermes were going to be even money at best. I was going to have to bet a lot of money to make a lot of money. I bet sixty dollars on each combination, a total of $360, or my previous week's paycheck.

I arrived early evening at the Freehold racetrack, which hosted live racing during the day and Meadowlands simulcasting at night. I had grabbed a table and was again studying the charts, looking for flaws in my planned wager, when a man tapped my shoulder, made a judgmental face, and pointed toward the TV, which was showing canned footage of a waving flag while the national anthem played. He expected me to stand with hand over heart. I shot him a searing look, and did stand, fists clenched, ready to unleash five months of frustration. He gasped, quickly returned to his table, judgment replaced with fear.

I tried to return to the charts, but the sounds of the anthem made me laugh. We were at a track, throwing money away on horses who were forced to run around a track—except the horses were not at this track, they were at another track, on TV, along with footage of a flag. And this guy wanted allegiance to the artificiality, the absurdity, the unreality.

Was this really happening? Was I really here?

It was a moment of questioning, which, if I had stayed with it, could have unraveled both the crazed world I inhabited and the fact that I didn't feel in or of any world. I was once again falling prey to a dangerous detachment.

Freehold filled with patrons just like the Meadowlands but with everyone staring at TVs. The fourth race trifecta began with Hermes bolting to the lead; things were looking good. He could easily take the race wire to wire. But when another horse charged to the lead and slowed the pace considerably, another horse took the lead. When one of my horses, Search and Destroy, took the lead, Hermes got shuffled to the rear of the field. He was locked in at the rail, in seventh place, with nowhere to go. When they got to the stretch run, the slow pace guaranteed that all the horses had leftover energy. The winners were going to be the horses in the lead. Search and Destroy and Jennifer's Dream finished second and third, and a huge longshot won. Hermes was blocked by a wall of horses and came in last. The trifecta paid four thousand dollars.

I shouldn't have been stunned but I was. I drove home, but instead of crying, bursts of cynical laughter kept slipping out of my mouth. And then a large burst emerged from my gut.

"Oh my God," I thought to myself, "I should have thrown Hermes out of the mix."

Another horseracing rule: if there is a big favorite and you can find a reason to throw him out, you throw him the hell out because the odds on the other horses are going to pay big money. Hermes had a perfect trip the week before under the fastest track conditions of the year. His time was inflated. He was good enough to win, but he wasn't as good as everyone thought—that was the clue, that was the professional gambler's edge.

I could have bet a trifecta wheel with Search and Destroy, Jennifer's Dream, and all the other horses for about fifty bucks. If Hermes had finished in the money with the other two, the payoff would have been small. I would have won my fifty dollars back and lost nothing. But if Hermes got a bad trip, like he did, I would have collected four thousand dollars, the exact amount I had hoped to save. It was the perfect bet, and I missed it.

I had to stop gambling. I had to get out of the printshop. I had to do something else with my life. I was not doing what I loved, not gnawing my own bone, not pursuing the good or good for anything, and most certainly not singing out loud.

Jim spent hours, every day, for fifteen years playing a logical gambling system and made a little money or broke even. He made big scores and had big stories, but he also went through dry spells. He enjoyed the action. It was his hobby. Who was I to think I could win? Still, I didn't understand why I had come so close yet couldn't make it work. I started to feel like I was fighting against something larger than poor gambling decisions, larger than the fact that racetracks are designed to take people's money.

Then it hit me: If I had been winning all this time, I might never stop gambling. Is it possible that my daemon, or some unconscious wisdom, was sabotaging me? Or saving me? The feeling that I was at a masquerade was the clue to the mystery I needed to solve.

A mask for Christ's sake: how clichéd. Hadn't I read Jung? How could I forget the feeling of wearing a mask, a false persona, in Fort Lauderdale for spring break when I was falling apart during my final semester at Rutgers?

I had tried to use my math abilities as well as my spirituality to gamble—a contradiction in terms. I thought my spiritual awareness could be applied to activities that went contrary to soul, but soul cannot be put on hold, and thinking that it can is just another form of blinkering.

I also thought that I was somehow immune to the fallibilities of the masses of gamblers, but that arrogance just made me more fallible, more prone to fall, more lost.

Who is this "I," this isolated ego that tries to force a life?

And, just like that, the bottom dropped out again.

Chapter 12

Crisis as Teacher

"In nature every moment is new; the past is swallowed and forgotten; the coming only is sacred. Nothing is secure but life,
transition, the energizing spirit…People wish to be settled; only
as far as they are unsettled is there any hope for them. Life is a
series of surprises."
—Ralph Waldo Emerson

"We do not think about the fact that throughout our lives we
die and resurrect many times. Anytime we have a breakthrough
in conscious awareness, we are born into a greater and deeper
creative state."
—Rafael Catala

The mass of men are suitable for labor, Thoreau wrote, with only a few
desiring an intellectual life, and still fewer seeking a poetic or divine life.
Such elitism turns some readers away from Thoreau even though he labored plenty, respected hard work and local knowledge of neighbors, and
saw the halo around the shadows. It also turned off some of his audience
at lyceum talks, yet he was not speaking only to those in attendance but to
everyone, imploring with good humor for all humanity to embrace a larger
life and destiny. Why humans, whom he compared to a torpid snake,
seemingly refuse to wake up was a source of frustration, especially since he
saw the divine in them. It was also a source of frustration for Margaret
Fuller, who titled one of her Boston bookstore teaching conversations
"Persons Who Never Awake to Life in this World." And it's a source of
frustration for true educators and was a frequent topic of discussion when
I studied with Rafael, who was convinced that most need a crisis, often a
major one, to be humble enough to listen to deeper wells.

After laboring in the printshop, I finally joined Preston in Indiana. I
didn't have much savings but I was saved from gambling by living in a
rental house near the Purdue campus with members of the Icemakers of

the Revolution, a political folk-rock band led by another old Rutgers friend, Stephen. The band formed when I visited the previous summer and was composed of graduate students (Stephen was working on a dissertation on Walt Whitman), a few undergraduates just waking up to an intellectual life, and a young local musician and artist who played a sweet fiddle. I was soon traveling with the group, which played benefit shows across the Midwest for organizations such as Planned Parenthood and Ancient Forest Rescue. We were all hoping to "upset the set-up," as one of the songs bellowed.

My role with the band was hard to measure. To the uninformed eye, I was a mere groupie, but I liked to think I was more: I stuffed my rusted, fake-wood-paneled Mercury Zephyr station wagon with speakers, amps, and guitars and drove to gigs. I whirled and swirled on the dance floor like a dervish, inspiring other free-flowing dancers to join me; provided security when needed, including settling down an acid-tripper who jumped on stage and knocked over microphones at WeedFest in Wisconsin; gave advice at sound checks since I knew the songs so well; and ended up being the band counselor, helping to quell inevitable personality clashes, especially when Stephen, the peace-loving democratic socialist, was perceived as being too dictatorial. I also wrote one song, "Lost at Home," a dirge on ecocrisis and forthcoming calamity.

The band got its unusual name when Shawny, a strong-voiced singer, came back from a refrigerator with a tray of ice. The principal players in the not-yet-formed band were hanging out at Preston's apartment, and the topic under discussion was our hopes for participating in social change. Shawny gave a depressed look, stating that she'd probably end up being the icemaker of the revolution. The comment, after much laughter, became the band's rallying cry supporting the small things that must be done for change to occur. Everyone, even makers of ice, had something to offer.

When I first arrived in Indiana, I found more blue-collar work, this time landscaping in the hot sun, often coming home to the Icemaker lair covered with dirt and sweat, looking like Mad Max—yet the mask was gone. Gambling simulated action, but, like all simulations, it was emotionally and spiritually empty. Now I was again living an intellectual life, questioning, in community, dominant narratives of bigger, better, and more, as well as an activist life.

I was soon teaching Com 114, thanks to my Rutgers diploma, work with the Ometeca Institute, a recommendation from Preston, and perhaps because when the teacher is ready, the job appears. Walking with Jeff under the night sky, I was soon sharing insights from spiritual searching and many crises. As it turned out, the time spent with books and meditation, the struggles and hard times, and the good times spent in solitude exploring inner worlds and in Europe and on the Appalachian Trail and in New Mexico exploring outer worlds—and moments of timelessness—supplied lessons that shaped my pedagogy and the way I treated students.

The beginning of my teaching career coincided not only with the 1992 "Warning to Humanity" but also with the first UN Earth Summit in Rio de Janeiro. Then-president George H. W. Bush had remarked that he would combat the greenhouse effect with the White House effect, and so there was hope. This was a crucial time for a bold response because climate science had not yet been fully politicized, not yet assiduously spun by merchants of doubt who profit from the status quo. The ten-year period from 1979 to 1989 had produced research, growing scientific consensus, testimony before Congress, and McKibben's *The End of Nature*, which shared the data with a broad public. By 1992, the weight of evidence demanded action.

Atmospheric carbon 359.32 ppm, climbing every year.

At Rio, the US, following President Bush's new declaration that the American way of life was not up for negotiation, was a drag on the proceedings. Taking responsible, and thus rational, steps then would have meant a different climate world now. Instead, a framework for creating international treaties to limit greenhouse gases was established, but with no binding agreement, no enforcement. One had to wonder how major a crisis needs to be before those in power are willing to act.

What can one do in response to such inanity, such insanity?

Make some ice.

Along with teaching and traveling with the band, I gave talks on spirituality and environmental ethics for the Purdue Environmental Action student group and the Science and Theology forum at a campus Methodist church. I also attended Heartwood forest activist gatherings, sometimes with students, in southern Indiana.

And, after a couple of flirtations that didn't turn into anything, I partnered up with the fiddle player, exploring the messiness of relationship, in and of the world.

From cultural standards of success, I was an utter failure: seven years to get a college degree, followed by seven years of blue-collar work. I had few possessions other than books and a paltry adjunct salary, yet such thoughts rarely entered my awareness. I was living my version of the divine life: teaching undergraduates and giving passionate talks, activating with the Icemakers, meditating and practicing the presence, pondering the difference between a healthy non-attachment and dangerous detachment, and wondering how many times the bottom needs to drop before I'd attain a degree of enlightenment.

Indiana, of all places, became a spiritual refuge for eight years although it took some time to adapt to a landscape of no mountains, few lakes, and lots of flat land. It was as if God stamped down his foot, but being ever pious, humans still gave praise, labeling it the Bible Belt and planting seeds. I fully attuned with the agricultural land when I once again discovered nature as teacher by spending two years living outside town, twenty minutes from campus.

My friends, Al and Faye, owned seven grassy acres surrounded by cornfields and woods with a midsized main house; large, rickety barn with old, rusted basketball hoop; tiny bunkhouse; and small cottage. The cottage, called the "Caboose" because of its shape and red color, had rattling windows and Virginia creepers poking through cracks in the wall. I thought of Thoreau the first time I saw it and was soon doing landscaping in exchange for rent, saving my adjunct salary for food and books. Like the Walden house, it was an inviting place to read, write, and think. There was no pond, but autumn sunsets threw shoots of orange, red, and purple over an endless horizon of golden-brown corn stalks.

I helped Al put in a brick patio, mowed the lawn with his ancient Gravely tractor, and created plant and flower gardens under Faye's guidance. My specialty, however, was free-standing rock walls made of rocks that farmers had plowed out of their fields and left in the woods. Construction was a Zen practice melding peace of mind with jigsaw-placed rocks, and I ended up building nearly a hundred feet of wall, three and a half feet high. I had plenty of time to do the work when I lost my teaching job for a fall semester due to a decrease in undergraduates and an increase in graduate students, who also taught Com 114.

Al and Faye went away for two months that fall, so it was just the land, the Caboose, one adult cat, four kittens, and me. Before they left, they told me to spend time with the kittens so they didn't become feral, so thus began a ritual: on moonlit nights I would lie on the grass and they would lie on me, one kitten on each leg and two on my chest, two sets of twins, charcoal and orange, purring, all content. The highlight of mornings was a half-mile walk up the gravel lane to get the newspaper and mail. Then I would sit outside in the autumn air with a cup of hot coffee and read the newspaper and mail. Most days were spent building the rock wall, taking six-mile runs amid farmland and sunsets, reading, writing in a journal, and contemplating. I went into town for food supplies or to hang out with friends at pubs and cafes but was mostly living with the land.

In mid-November, I invited a mix of professors, undergraduates, and graduate students, including Aurkene and Inaki, a music-playing grad student couple from the Basque region in Spain, to a bonfire party on my thirty-fourth birthday. Thoreau, a dedicated stock-taker, wrote on his thirty-fourth, "Here I am 34 years old, and yet my life is almost wholly unexpanded…There is such an interval between my ideal and the actual in many instances that I can say I am unborn." He is overly hard on himself here because elsewhere he writes of patience, yet he wished to feel more in sympathy with his daemon and highest good, as he reflected on the frequent ecstasies of his childhood "superior powers."

On that cold, star-filled November night, our highest good was to be warmed by high-flying flames engulfing dry wood, sweet potatoes cooked on red-hot coals, and old folk tunes: Inaki played accordion and Aurkene fiddle, and they suggested we dance as they had growing up. Some guests were inhibited, particularly a young poetry professor, but Aurkene soon had us holding hands, skipping and hopping to the accordion beat, weaving a path like a lively snake until self-created barriers lifted, the superior, childlike lightness lying underneath inhibitions set free. The poetry professor thanked me profusely every time I ran into him after that night. I think he experienced what Walt Whitman meant when he wrote, "I am large. I contain multitudes."

I lived a Thoreauvian truth that fall: economy and supply are more than jobs and money, and everything is enriched when you work and play within the land.

The winter approached, however, and I decided to leave Indiana temporarily. There was a wood-burning stove in the Caboose, but the creepers assured that it wasn't the warmest place in cold weather. I would have had to spend the coldest days with friends in town or in the main house. I also had another reason for leaving: Rafael was back in his condo in New Jersey, and I felt an intuitive need to spend time with him again. After failed attempts at writing a book, I hoped a reunion would inspire a new creative project. On the day of my arrival, I was looking through his bookshelves when Gregory Bateson's *Mind and Nature* caught my eye. Rafael appeared just as I began perusing its pages, so I asked him about the book. He immediately said that we should read it together.

My fall experiences meshed well with Bateson's writings, especially his claim that we are immersed in an evolving communicative system of information exchange. Building the wall by paying attention to the sounds of rocks, allowing the structure to emerge, reflected a nonverbal exchange of harmony. Communing with kittens by inviting them to lie on my legs and torso reflected a nonverbal exchange of comfort and care. And dancing under the vast, starry night reflected a nonverbal exchange of freedom. Verbal habits of the modern world too often led to monologue; nonverbal presence and energy exchange led to dialogue within the world soul.

After four months with Rafael, and some work at the printshop (the shop I seemingly could not escape, the shop that thankfully provided funds whenever I needed them), I returned to the Caboose with seeds for an Ometeca essay firmly planted in mind. But there were unexpected consequences to visiting; I had been away from New Jersey for five years, except for short Christmas visits, and I rarely thought about the past. But living near Rutgers and a few miles from my childhood home caused a flood of memories; there seemed to be a story attached to each place I visited. I tried to resist nostalgia, but Bateson argues that personal stories are intimately connected to larger patterns and that it is worth getting to know those patterns.

I recalled youthful connections with nature while searching under lily pads for turtles and frogs and moments of disconnection during high school and college when I questioned how multiple-choice tests were going to prepare me for anything of importance. But these were mild memories compared to what happened when I took a walk in the park where I fell to the ground ten years earlier, violently crying after my practice commute to New York City.

I found the exact patch of ground, sat down and stared at the barren lilac branches. Long ignored images returned, and my breath shortened. My body remembered everything: the lifeless train trip with seasoned commuters, the imposing physical structure of the giant office building of Ogilvy & Mather, and the following morning in the park, lying face down in the grass. I thought I had left my past behind just because I had physically left home, or that I had meditated it away, but the images still churning in my unconscious held a charge. Why? But then I realized that this crisis marked the moment when I began to risk living the path of soul rather than a proscribed path, a path of less security but more mystery, participating in the pattern that connects, dancing under night sky.

One evening Rafael and I took a walk to the park. We tried to make it to the entrance by crossing a two-lane road filled with commuter traffic, but we were invisible to the drivers. We waited and waited and then simply witnessed the endless stream of blank faces behind steering wheels. After ten minutes, we noticed a small break and dashed to the other side, walked a bit, and then stopped to look at ice that had fused several tree branches. Moonlight shone through the branches, creating a crystallized web of sparkling light. Rafael and I had just finished discussing a chapter in *Mind and Nature* and were struck by the display, as if the earth were instructing us about the aesthetics of patterns that are always present yet hidden to those unaware. Or obscured by long, life-sapping torpid snake commutes.

The Indiana countryside, reading Bateson, and New Jersey memories combined to reveal a clear insight, an insight I already knew but now experienced with power: Living had been a series of disconnections and connections. I recalled all the times I felt hurt, alienated, and lost, as well as the times I experienced the joy of relationship and love, re-finding the compass.

My early life was led by an unconscious desire for this joy and love while in later life, after spiritual study with Rafael, it had become a conscious pursuit although crises ensued whenever I would forget.

CS

My return elicited still deeper revelations during a springtime trip to visit my parents in Upstate New York, where they had retired to a small house on the lake where we had vacationed for the first fifteen years of my life. Every time I visited the Adirondacks I came home to family, as well as the land, lake, and sky that first nurtured my sensitivities. However, when I arrived, my parents and I weren't really communicating. I realized that they were talking with me as they always had, including calling me "Billy," a childhood nickname.

My parents have always loved and supported me even when they didn't understand why I wandered after Rutgers graduation instead of finding a career. But they rarely expressed emotions because they were raised in stoic households. I had never been comfortable with expressing emotion with them either, and now, at least for me, there seemed to be an unspoken block exacerbated by the fact that they were getting older and we had never talked about death. My parents were not old—only in their mid-sixties—but all my grandparents had died in their late fifties or early sixties. I was concerned that they would die without us talking and connecting more deeply. It was an intolerable thought. Here we were, participants within the pattern that connects or world soul, but unable to express it in our family. Stewing for a couple days without my parents knowing that anything was wrong, I felt despair building and tried to figure out how to break free.

I didn't have to figure out a way to break free.

There was a news report on TV about the hungry and homeless, and my dad, who always voted Republican, made an off-handed remark about self-reliance and how "they should get jobs." The remark was nothing new, and they may well have needed to get jobs, but I became overwhelmed with sadness. And then I started to sob.

When I was a huge crier as a kid, with immense gasping and wheezing, my father advised, "Big boys don't cry." This wasn't the worst advice because I cried when things didn't go my way, but, like many men, I turned this silly phrase into a creed and refused to be vulnerable. I did not cry in my teen years, not a drop. I didn't cry again until I lay in the park at age twenty-five, and I hadn't cried since.

"Billy, are you alright?" My father questioned with a mix of surprise and alarm, leaning up from his easy chair.

"I'm okay," I said through tears, sitting across from him on the couch.

Mom hurried into the living room from the kitchen, wearing her well-worn worried look from raising three kids.

"What's wrong?"

"I'm fine," I said, still crying, feeling embarrassed, trying to stop.

They had no idea what my tears were about, and I wasn't completely sure either. Then something switched, and my tears felt incredibly right.

"I'm OK, I'm OK," I reiterated. I got up from the couch, walked outside amid pine trees, and started to wail.

The part of me that would usually stop such a display emerged, but then a deeper part—my still, small voice, or daemon or soul, or non-attached witness, or whatever—emerged and said, "Don't stop, keep going." Every time the sobs started to recede, another wave appeared, and I went with it, knowing that I was not going to stop until empty.

My parents came outside and watched from a distance.

"I'm fine," I said again, "I just need to do this."

At one point my father came over—deep concern written on his face—and wrapped his big arms around me, causing another giant release as distance disappeared.

I sobbed for at least fifteen minutes, if not twenty. I couldn't believe how much I needed to cry. It felt right to be outside, in the natural world that had schooled me in my childhood. I was safe amid the pine trees; it was okay to be vulnerable there.

My sobs finally subsided, and I went back inside and got a hug from Mom. There was a brief silence as we all stared at each other, and then we burst out laughing as I tried to explain what had happened. I told them that every time we visited I wondered if it would be the last time that we would see each other. And they talked about reaching a point in life where you accept the reality of death.

We also talked about my father's, and mother's, conservative morality, which I had once struggled with and then accepted. They grew up in a different time although I couldn't help explaining the difference between Emersonian self-reliance and the current political definition, and that most need help to become self-reliant, help that I was sure Jesus would approve.

After things calmed down with my parents, I went back outside to where I had been sobbing and sat down in a bed of brown pine needles. It was dusk, and the last rays of sunlight scooted along the surface of the lake. There were few thoughts in my head as I took deep, slow breaths.

ଔ

Rafael eventually moved to Florida. He tired of the New Jersey winters and was tired generally after many years of travel to Europe to give classes in mysticism and meditation and after an intensely emotional, memory-filled trip to Cuba after forty years of being in the US. He'd also had several angioplasties to clear clogged arteries. His father died in his fifties from a heart attack, so Rafael's spiritual awareness has not protected him from the physical determinism of his genes. But in Florida he was mostly living a relaxed, and divine, life, working on creative projects, enjoying sunny temperatures, and picking fruit from trees in his backyard.

Our relationship continued to grow over the years. I sought less advice, and he became more open about personal struggles. I've been privileged to see a human side of him that most of his students don't know. Rafael, who suffered greatly due to the stupidity and violence in the world, experienced periods of depression and low energy. He has a deep desire for facilitating spiritual growth, waking up students and the world, but he was sometimes frustrated with the results. I also think he became frustrated with the straitjacket of being a spiritual teacher, especially when students expected him to be something he is not.

Rafael's frustrations seemed to lift, however, after one of his heart operations. I talked to him on the phone while he recovered, and pearls started to flow once again. I took notes due to an intuition that I should.

There is nothing to death. Absolutely nothing. I was ready to go. I wasn't asking God for things or afraid of the unknown, I was just thinking about the nothingness of death. I was so close, but it just didn't matter. I was at the edge of death, but there was nothing to it. It was a beautiful experience. God is not what people think. To realize that you are God—not in the sense of power but like the waves of the sea or gentle nothingness of life and death—makes you conscious. So, I am much more at peace with what people call death, and much more at peace with myself. I added a hundred years of maturity. I didn't have an out-of-body experience; I discovered a deeper awareness. I don't really worry very much about living or dying. No worries whatsoever. I'm ready to go anytime.

I grew up a lot, without major fanfare. Life or death, it just doesn't matter. Either one is okay. Both are beautiful. I feel tremendous contentment with the way I am right now. There are no expectations, only the fun of being alive. It's not that I left the world; in many ways I am closer to it. I just have a deeper sense of peace now. I always had an urgency to do something for humanity, but I don't have that anymore. We will keep growing or we will continue in ignorance. I'm much more at peace with that now. It's not that I plan to stop working. Nothing will stop me from doing my work. But now I do it with peace instead of urgency. The feeling that I had to save the world left me. I didn't push this feeling away, it just left. I will continue to work and the world, well, the world is the best it can be right now, with terrorism and people killing each other all the time. People are so unconscious.

But I just look at it all and say, "how interesting." I'm more of a participant-observer. I'm experiencing the peace that passes understanding. It is such a blessing to come out of my operation with light years of understanding, at peace and enjoying myself. The possibilities of growth are infinite. We always want our personalities to continue after death rather than being aware, but it is not our personality that is having the experience, it is the "I that is all things." I don't know if the personality survives or not. I couldn't know. But it just doesn't matter.

My experience was nothing out of this world. It's so natural. But it is difficult to explain so most times I shut-up. I just watch the students jump up and down—I watch the show. But it is a beautiful experience. I have a deeper dimension of love that is more gentle, more down to earth. I don't care if you are an intellectual or a non-intellectual, I see the beauty in you. In the past I would get frustrated with not being able to explain, but no more. You will either wake up or you won't. I always had to be somewhere saving the world. I suffered dearly with the world. But no more. I don't have to please anyone, and no one has to please me. I don't have to be anywhere, at any time—there is no rush. And I am not disen-chanted with the world. I am more enchanted because I see the world from a different angle, from a place of peace.

I honor all those who are serving the world. But if you are serving and feeling agony, you have to stop and follow your bliss, your waking-up process. You can't help anyone if you are in agony. You can only be a companion with people as they wake up. But when you fall asleep, you need to suffer to wake up. Everyone is afraid to suffer, afraid of pain, but without suffering you won't grow. I'll be your companion, but I'll let you suffer until you wake up. I used to get calls for spiritual healings, but I began telling the callers that I wouldn't pray for a healing, only for the will of God. They might need the suffering to wake up. So, they don't call anymore [*laughs*]. But I can't play games. The world is alright the way it is.

It's fear that causes suffering, which is why I am so thankful for my experience. I don't fear death. I don't fear aging. And now when I go to the hardware store, I'm not afraid of letting one of the employees carry my topsoil out to the car [*laughs*]. Conscious suf-fering is so important. I wish people would realize this truth, be-cause it is literally true, and it leads people to follow their bliss.

I laughed to myself when Rafael used the phrase "follow your bliss" and recalled this popular phrase from Joseph Campbell's PBS interview series with Bill Moyers. Of course, Campbell, the Jungian scholar and my-thologist who was an adviser for *Star Wars*, is famous for his study of the hero's journey, which includes risk, doubt, mentoring, inner listening, cri-ses such as confronting death, and transformation. Back when I looked to Rafael for advice, especially with difficult life decisions, he would suggest that I follow my bliss or "use the force," as if I were Luke Skywalker and he Obi Wan Kenobi or Yoda, making me laugh. But I knew what he meant—the force for Jung was the life force and inner intelligence that guides our process of individuation. And, as Jung intimated, if you refuse to follow your process of individuation, it will often drag you.

Rafael's confrontation with death advanced his process, which is what I found most compelling about his words. My teacher and friend was still growing, still having life-altering spiritual experiences, still caring for the injustices of the world yet less of the world, in the sense of finding more peace.

Still becoming fully human, alive and awake. Still having fun.

My first experience with the death of a loved one was when Casey, our devoted family dog, died after fifteen years. We named him after Casey Stengel, the playful former manager of the New York Yankees and Mets, and he often seemed intent on managing me, especially during younger years when he slept beside my bed with a watchful eye. When he suffered a stroke and Dad took him to the vet, I didn't know he wouldn't be coming home. But I fought back tears, brooding instead over the eternal question of where life goes.

My only other early experience was when Gene, my first mentor, died in the late 1980s. After high school graduation, we went to New York City every year to the US Open Tennis Tournament—I rooted for feisty Jimmy Connors and he for stoic Bjorn Borg—as well as to theater, restaurants, and old, independent, and foreign films. Gene introduced me to the arts, which was significant since my idea of culture was watching reruns of *Happy Days* and *Love Boat*. He did not overtly teach during our social time together unless it came up during conversation, like when we discussed his favorite word, "reverberate" (smart people had favorite words), or when he warned against the use of double negatives (grammar mattered).

Like with Rafael, we had more of a friendship when I got older, and he revealed more of his personal life. And like Rafael, the greatest gift he shared was his consciousness and way of being in the world. But Gene became ill, lost weight and weakened; he told me he once got home from teaching and barely had energy to get out of the car. The last time I saw him we went to see the movie *Hoosiers*. This was before my Indiana days, so the film was my first insight into the farm life and hoops hysteria of the Midwest.

Gene loved basketball, especially the teamwork of the old Boston Celtics, and so the based-on-a-true-story tale of a tiny town's high school beating a larger and more talented school for the state championship was energizing. Chatting in the car afterward, he was in good spirits; the next day he was leaving for his family home in Pennsylvania with plans for extended rest. We pulled up to the front of my apartment, but instead of jumping out of the car, I took his hand in both of mine and looked into his eyes. Gene was shocked—I had never done anything like that before—but he eased into the moment as I told him to please rest and get well.

I didn't know if Gene was seriously ill, but I worried that he might have AIDS. We never spoke about his sexual preference, but I had heard rumors that he was gay. I figured we'd talk about it if it came up in conversation, but it didn't. He was Gene, my witty, caring, and thoughtful former teacher who changed my life, and a friend who continued to open my eyes to culture and beauty. Of course, as a high school teacher Gene couldn't talk about his sexuality because of bigotry and narrow-mindedness. And had he lived in the basketball-loving Bible Belt of Indiana, in Lafayette, near Purdue, where vitriolic, unawakened citizens fought a proposed ordinance to protect the rights of gay citizens from housing discrimination, it would have been even worse.

When I met Rafael, I already knew the value of a mentoring relationship and was ready for further guidance. Both Gene and Rafael integrated anima and animus, leading them to be tremendous teachers because, as Fuller argued and lived, feminine and masculine qualities are fluid, passing into each other, making us more whole.

A week after Gene returned home, I received news that he had died. The cause was listed as pneumonia and collapsed lung. He was in his early fifties.

I was scheduled to take the GRE the next day to complete my graduate school application to the University of Maine. It was my last opportunity to take the test and still meet the deadline, so I arrived at the test site with two number two pencils and a heavy heart. The test was in a large auditorium on the Rutgers campus, and there were hundreds of test-takers. My resistance to testing as measure of intelligence was already at a peak, but Gene's death added even more force to my rebellion. Still, I knew there would be hoops if I was to continue my education, so I convinced myself to jump. I stopped working halfway through the math section, reminded of Gene, and looked around at fellow hoop-jumpers. They were all frenetically focused on filling in tiny ovals, and heaviness turned to absurd lightness, as I realized that I was being directed by academic forces that did not care about my resistance. I further realized that I could rewrite the script. What did the GRE matter in comparison to mourning Gene's death? What did it matter compared to death generally?

The mass of students all engaged in the same act with the same dour faces was disturbing and reminded me of the fleet of commuters that wouldn't let Rafael and me to cross the road to the park. I was witnessing again, as during my sob session but with smiles instead of tears, sweetly non-attached and wondering how much time I had left for the section. I had been committing test suicide by looking around for several minutes without filling in an oval, yet honoring Gene, and death, by taking a moment to reject the grim convention of testing. I decided to further honor Gene by finishing the test with a light heart, free of fear of failure.

Rafael taught that the mystic, dying daily to fears, finds peace by identifying with the "I" that is all things rather than only the personal sense of "I." He had long been on this path and gained a deeper awareness of its nuances after his heart operation, but we all live and die, so we are all on this path.

It's like coming home, home to our deeper identity, to the middle path where the spiritual and material meet.

Study with Rafael led me to realize that religious fundamentalists, who imagine a future home in heaven, degrade this world while existentialists, who brave the absurdity of this world and the feeling of utter homelessness, often ignore spiritual imagination and transcendence. The mystical death in life, however, when so graced, frees our imagination such that we feel at home within the world soul, immersed in patterns and beauty and open to the mystery to come.

Rafael mentioned the middle path of Buddhism early in our work together, and it always appealed but was mostly elusive except when I didn't just *talk* about letting go, but *experienced* deep release. Meditation helped, but usually it took a crisis to be wiped clean, to be and live it.

Death, I was learning, was the ultimate teacher. It undermines the isolated ego by pushing us to embrace impermanence and larger forces; or, as Emerson put it, we must "take our bloated nothingness out of the path of divine circuits." Failing to consult death and confront the essential facts of life often leads to crisis. Too often, death and essential facts are thrust upon us, creating crisis.

For Emerson, it was the death of Ellen, and later his young son Waldo, only five, with his second wife, Lidian. His deep grief over Ellen led him to open her coffin fourteen months after her death, and that act initiated a kind of second birth, in which he more fully embraced the primacy of Spirit and let go of desire for a conventional life. Waldo's death, also deeply grieved, gave further proof that life was ultimately transformation, always about becoming lost and then re-finding the compass. He passed through many moods, bereft of a "beautiful estate" that he struggled to regain, yet calamities, as hard as they are, operate as revolutions in our way of life. We must draw a new circle, with nothing secure but "life, transition, and the energizing spirit."

The death of Thoreau's beloved brother John led to deep depression, which was then exacerbated by Waldo's death since he had cared for and loved the boy. But Thoreau also experienced rebirth by growing out of John's shadow. Embracing John as his muse, Thoreau listened for inspiration, a kind of listening—body, mind, and soul open—that he would practice in nature and use to express his voice in his writing.

Thoreau found solace by seeing death as law, and thus as common as life, rather than mere accident. Nature, always a teacher and symbol for him, does not grieve, as withering flowers or grasses provide soil for new life; "so it is with the human plant." Still, the losses of John and Waldo were hard to accept, to say the least, and finding meaning was a challenge. Faith in nature does not mean that its ways are easy to interpret, even as letting go called forth new inspirations and commitments, allowing him to find the compass once again.

The Indian sage Shantideva, who composed *The Way of the Bodhisattva* more than twelve centuries ago, stated, "By giving up all, sorrow is transcended, and my mind will realize the sorrowless state." This idea sounds like being in but not of the world, but Shantideva continues, "It is best that I now give everything to all beings, in the same way as I shall at death." The second part defines the Bodhisattva vow, in which giving up all and transcending a limited self leads to giving to all, not to transcending the world.

When I yearned for this sorrowless state in my youth, it sounded good, but then, as sorrows continued, it sounded unlikely, and then it didn't even sound good if it meant transcendence without embrace. With plenty of practice, I was convinced of the value of consulting death and finding more perspective, more freedom to be who we are meant to be. How else could Emerson, Thoreau, and Fuller and so many others, risk and learn and give so much? By armoring ourselves from death, we armor ourselves from reasons for being here, now, full of life, on this planet, learning to love and give what we are able to give. And, as Rafael taught, crises often ignite growth, leading us to lose the world as we know it to find it anew at a higher level of awareness.

Mom and Dad, like all good parents, were always giving, but they did more consulting and confronting as they aged. Our emotions softened and the distance lessened; after my sob session, we always hugged when I visited, until Dad died at eighty-eight and Mom at ninety-two. My brother Jim, showing his character, was their main source of comfort and care in their last years. I see in them the possibilities of infinite growth and the human desire to age with grace.

Gene once surprised me by stating that he would be missed after he was gone. We were in the car on our way to another movie, and he just blurted it out. The statement had not an iota of arrogance; it was a fact, clearly articulated from his depths. While in New Mexico, after his death, I remembered this declaration and our last meeting when I held his hand and looked into his eyes. I was walking under desert night sky, and a shooting star marked the moment.

I told myself that it was Gene responding to my intense emotion, caring little if it was a projection. All that mattered was that my connection to Gene had brought me back home to myself, to the cosmos, to the divine life.

How many times must the bottom drop?

As many times as it takes.

Chapter 13

Daemon or Demon?

"For, after all, the one thing that can substantially and truthfully be called rebellion is that which consists in not accepting one's destiny, in rebelling against one's self."
— Jose Ortega y Gasset

"Ecstasy (emotion): a trance or trance-like state in which a person transcends normal consciousness.
Ecstasy (religion): a state of consciousness characterized by expanded spiritual awareness, visions or absolute euphoria.
Ecstasy (philosophy): a term used to mean "outside-of-itself."
Ecstasy: A drug."
— Wikipedia (a bane to professors but there's some good stuff on there)

Student crises can be hard to watch, especially if the student is on the seven-year graduation plan. Josh took my Introduction to Journalism course, failed to hand in anything, and then plopped a portfolio of writings in my mailbox at the end of the semester. I laughed when I saw it. Some naively bold students hand in late work despite deadlines and grade penalties. According to the syllabus, I needn't open the portfolio—Josh had already "earned" an F—but, given my seven-year graduation plan, I did open it and found a fine mind and talented writer.

I hand out an evolutionary timeline in several classes that begins with the "primordial flaring forth" approximately fifteen billion years ago. The timeline, taken from Thomas Berry and Brian Swimme's *The Universe Story*, leads students to realize that humans are latecomers on this planet, and that techno-industrial lifestyles are late and brief in comparison to our history as hunter-gatherers. Thus, while a certain amount of conforming to the pace of the modern world is necessary, the expectations of this world are arbitrary. We have lived quite differently at different times.

Such knowledge is important for perspective, but I also want students to use the timeline to realize something deeper: if they attune to the unique pace that governs their learning and their individuation process, they will know that there is more than one way to live.

I did not see Josh in the following fall semester and wondered if poor grades had forced him to drop out. Then, in the spring, he showed up in my Freedom of Speech course. It turned out that he transferred to another school, known for partying, where his grades were worse. Apparently the classes were even more boring, and professors did not take kindly to late work. He transferred back, a true New England College misfit; if he had a daemon, he didn't know how to listen. Remembering the quality of his writing, I was happily surprised to see him.

One day, seeing him in a hallway, I followed an intuitive thought, emerging from my daemon, and asked if he was interested in writing for the school newspaper.

"You want me?" he sputtered, squinting incredulous eyes.

Tall and rail thin, he looked strung out, and the honesty of his response led to a moment of doubt.

"Yes I do," I said, recovering my initial intuition.

"Why?" he said.

"You're a good writer. You're not good at handing in your work on time, which is a serious problem in journalism, but you're a good writer. We need good writers. Plus, I think it would be good for you."

I saw a glimmer of interest, of life force simmering to the surface.

"I don't know," he demurred, perhaps from the shock of the offer, or perhaps because he was in the habit of resisting most everything.

ೞ

The timeline should awaken students to the evolution of both creative and destructive energy that has produced human beings, human cultures, and the world within which they live. It should awaken them to the blip that is their lives yet connect them to all that has come before, and all that is here now, with our choices to be creative or destructive calling forth our evolutionary future.

How could I understand, and then possibly reach, students like Josh who habitually, addictively, choose to embrace destructive rather than creative impulses?

By turning to the timeline.

In *Wild Hunger*, Bruce Wilshire argues that addictive behavior is a misguided attempt to recover feelings of erotic energy, or ecstasy, which were common for hunter-gatherers living close to nature. This argument raises a troubling question: If we destroy nature, and our source of ecstasy, who are we then? Bateson raised a similar question as he pondered the damage done to the psyche when we destroy our source of mental process and creative thought. Thoreau would respond to both thinkers by stating that we end up leading lives of quiet desperation.

In the modern world, this desperation is expressed as addictions to drugs, alcohol, sex, money, consumerism, gambling (which I knew too well), and, especially for students, electronic gadgetry—anything to experience, at least for a moment, an energy substitute for the ecstasy that defines life within nature. Most troubling of all, we often become so habituated to addictive lifestyles that we are not aware anything is wrong. For Wilshire, the remedy is a return to the body, or a body-self awake to signs of ecstasy deprivation.

In *Nature and Madness*, Paul Shepard furthers this argument. He returns to the Pleistocene epoch when the human genome was formed after millions of years of evolution. For Shepard, our biological heritage holds clues to our deepest psychological needs and traits, formed via predator-prey dynamics. Cooperation among tribal members was needed in the hunt, as was conceptualization, forethought, and planning. Early hunters watched both predator and prey and mimicked their keen sensitivity to their surroundings. Children, learning from animals, trees, rivers, and plants, developed kinship bonds with diverse species. Tribes owned little, wasted little. Ecstasy was habitually aroused, accompanied by an adrenaline and endorphin rush.

Shepard does not deny aggressive traits or examples of brutality and ecological destruction among tribal groups, but he argues that the small social structure of hunter-gatherer life led to mutual dependence manifested as sharing, nonhierarchical gender roles, and communicative skill—early humans attended to the nonverbal cues of nonhuman others, learning from the voices of nature.

The natural world was a school that stimulated creative energies, and the young were schooled through ritual and rites of passage.

My students grow up being schooled by screens and social media.

Shepard can be accused of romanticizing early hunter-gatherers, of ignoring short life spans, infanticide as a form of population control, projection and superstition, and tribalism, which led, and still leads, to conflict and war. His main point is difficult to deny: human traits and needs were formed during our long history as hunter-gatherers. That history began with a chancy game of rewards and pitfalls via the hunt, replete with numerous unexpected encounters. Hunting elicited humility and reverence since the hunters, despite their skills, were ultimately dependent upon animal spirits and the grace of the game. Hunting also demanded risk, which stimulated ecstatic experience, storytelling, and growth within the context of a gifting cosmos

Wilshire and Shepard are this-worldly focused, each warning against the dangers of transcendentalist thinking. Shepard is particularly harsh toward otherworldly spiritual inclinations, since, according to the timeline, agriculture replaced hunter-gatherer life in the Neolithic period approximately twelve thousand years ago, bringing with it transcendent sky-gods worshiped for good growing weather and abundant crops. And as agriculture and belief in sky-gods grew, so did population, the hoarding of food, cities, domestication, disease, toil, violence, hierarchical institutions and social relations, and, ultimately, massive environmental degradation. Humans had less leisure, less time for gaming and game, and fewer experiences of ecstasy. The fusing of the senses with imagination, connecting predator and prey in spiritual give and take, decreased in favor of the abstract imagination with its gods and calculative mode of thought. Our identity shifted along with our imaginative life, and mind was removed from its embeddedness within the natural world.

Many scholars consider this shift necessary for the evolution of the rational or scientific mind—the timeline grinds on. Regardless of one's position on whether it had to happen, or if the shift constitutes progress, it did happen, eventually culminating in Descartes's dictum "I think therefore I am," a caricature of his writings that fully wedded our identity to thought rather than specific places and our conviviality with other species.

The results are everywhere: the glories and depravity of New York

City, factory assembly lines, medical research and science, animal testing, the polluted Wabash River, technological marvels such as computers for would-be-writers and backpacks for hikers, clear cuts, acid rain indexes, the abundance of food in wealthy countries, the abundance of pesticide-riddled food and soil loss, multiple-choice tests and grading, the abundance of addictions and depression, the specter of climate disruption.

And lost students like Josh.

This is a snapshot of the timeline within which I, and all teachers, teach. It's the timeline that has produced a loss of timeless experiences of ecstasy and students afflicted with "nature deficit disorder."

This is the context within which teachers attempt to reach students who have tried, and mostly failed, to adapt to industrial education, an evolutionary latecomer that rarely energizes and arouses the desire to learn. The context within which students search for energy substitutes—drugs, alcohol, shopping, and gizmos—instead of the "high" of creative projects or seeing one's life as a creative project.

The solution, of course, is not to send students out to hunt (although much would be learned if done ethically) or to decry transcendental religions, agriculture, and science and technology. If our evolutionary destiny produced rational thought, with its many triumphs, it is now the destiny of the rational individual to attend to the wisdom of all time periods.

I did not advocate for students like Josh to return to the past, but to learn from the body, the sensuous imagination, and creative energies, all sacred manifestations of Spirit unfolding.

CR

Josh ended up joining the newspaper staff, and floundering. Deadlines were like death sentences and editors like dictators. Josh was not a journalist, or at least not a news journalist. He had to put himself in every piece of writing; otherwise, he was prone to writer's block. Josh took to the community, however—to the other students who were creating something of their own—and he offered to edit or deliver papers or do anything to help until his block lifted. We accepted his limitations, tried to feed his strengths and his creative process, and allowed him to write on any topic he wanted and put himself in the story.

Josh wrote a local travel piece on wandering amid New Hampshire small towns, an amusing theater review in which he described his difficulty in finding the theater and then accidently walking into the dressing room, and a Halloween story on his search for the ghosts of Henniker. But he really blossomed when he tried writing about music. He created his own column, "Audio Aloe," in which he took a "sounds like" approach to CD reviewing, deftly describing instrumentation through metaphor and simile.

Josh also started to come into his own as a student, albeit slowly. He handed in all his work for our Freedom of Speech class late, reducing his grade, but he didn't care about grades. The next semester he took my Feature-Writing Workshop, in which students write longer nonfiction magazine-style pieces using fiction techniques, and he found inspiration in the work of New Journalists Thomas Wolfe and Hunter S. Thompson. His first feature detailed a gonzo-like family trip to Disney World juxtaposing periodic escapes from family to find alcohol, the exhilaration of riding roller coasters with his young niece, and criticisms of Disney as a corporation. His second feature was more controversial: It detailed his celebration of 420, the annual pot-smoking holiday on April 20.

Josh and friends planned out a full day of smoking, in various indoor and outdoor locations, with glazed eyes on the lookout for local police. His feature also included *High Times*–type information on marijuana legalization and the harmlessness of pot, and, briefly at the end, a moment of regret, or ennui, in which he admitted that they were toast by early evening, with nothing to do but sleep it off.

The class loved the honesty of the piece, as did I, but I suggested he add more reflection on the moment of self-questioning. After all, I said, pot smoking can be an addiction, if not chemical than as a habit. And while some drugs can liberate creativity, excessive use inhibits creativity. I mentioned that we might find better, more creative things to do with our time. To illustrate my point, I told a story about American pot smokers I briefly roomed with while traveling in Europe after graduating from Rutgers. They were supposed to be traveling too but got hooked on Amsterdam, stopping for over a month and spending all their time talking about how to get pot, smoking pot, and telling stories of pot experiences.

Josh resisted adding much, but I said what needed to be said, planted another seed, so to speak. Class conversation turned to discussing whether the article should be printed in the newspaper, and the conversation continued with newspaper staff. He wanted to use a pseudonym, and editors rejected it on those grounds.

I did not bring up his drug use again, which editors assumed influenced his psychedelic musings in "Audio Aloe." He was certainly not the first writer to turn to mind-altering substances—Thompson being a prominent example. Remembering my resistance as a young student (and the likelihood that nothing I said would deter him), I tried not to tell him (or other students) what to do. He would have to learn on his own, hopefully by not letting his addiction, if that's what it was, become a personal demon blocking his process of individuation instead of a creative stimulant.

At the end of the semester, Josh said that he felt like he co-taught the course. In a sense, he did—frequent comments on other students' work were perceptive, sometimes better than mine, and classmates respected his views. School-wise, he seemed to be on his way.

Josh was a late bloomer, but something was blooming: a talent, a calling, a sense of destiny?

☙

Destiny is a tricky word, whether applied to students or evolutionary timelines, and I uttered it in class with a thoughtful fear and trembling. Dictators justify themselves with the word, and America's "Manifest Destiny" led to colonization, genocide, and destruction of the land. The guru, acting as if their word is gospel, also makes claims to destiny. A sense of destiny, I tell students—if this phrase has any worthwhile meaning—is a creative tension within ourselves that we feel compelled to play out while remaining self-critical and responsive to the criticisms of others, including criticisms that come from the sense of destiny others feel compelled to live.

The mentor-student relationship is often fraught with a feeling of destiny, as mentor and student seem drawn to each other. Emerson and Thoreau did not initially cross paths in Concord, but the student was ready when they did, with Emerson stirring the daemonic pot by suggesting Thoreau keep a journal, catalyzing his vocation as writer and naturalist. I

211

certainly felt drawn to Rafael, but, as Thoreau quickly learned and as both Rafael and Emerson advocated, we cannot listen only to our teachers, even if they are listening to their withins. I had to listen to my own inner life while taking Rafael's views, his insights and intuitions, into account, until, as he stated by referencing Quintilian, "the teacher is no longer needed."

Despite fear and trembling, I share with students, especially in Senior Seminar, various voices along the timeline who advocate for a sense of destiny, addressing downsides but also the possibility that we are called by larger forces.

For the ancient Greeks, the daemon, knowing more than we consciously know, informs our life paths and is both inner genius and guiding spirit in the intermediate realm between the gods and the mortal. Socrates trusted his daemon, and destiny, all the way to death, drinking hemlock as punishment for corrupting the youth of Athens, an act he denied. But daemonic forces are complex and contain creative and destructive impulses that may take over a life.

In Euripides's *The Bacchae*, Dionysus, the god of wine, ritual, and ecstasy, is angered when King Pentheus orders the masses of Thebes to deny him. So, he razed Pentheus's palace in an earthquake and fire while the women of Thebes, celebrating his power, danced and drank wine in the wild woods, ripping apart cows—and later, Pentheus—with their bare hands. Such Dionysian power represents the daemonic within us, which we might want to attend to by finding a creative outlet, lest being drunk with destiny leads us to devour others and ourselves.

The Stoic philosopher Epictetus, for example, described the daemon as divine guide, with Zeus assigning to each "a director sleepless and not to be deceived." In this sense, we are always in good company, if we are attentive: "So that when you have shut your doors, and darkened your room, remember never to say that you are alone; for you are not alone, but God is within, and your genius is within."

Early Christians, certain of salvation as destiny, were so fearful of destructive impulses that they transfigured "daemon" to "demon," redefining it as an expression of evil contrasted with good clothed in angelic form. The daemonic was cleaved, split into Jekyll and Hyde, leaving our inner life without wholeness. The faithful were instructed to look outward rather than within, listening to church hierarchy, which became the new inter-mediary between the divine and mortal. Humans were called by God to be good, moral, and obedient, but not who we are.

Rainer Maria Rilke, intuitively understanding the false god of out-ward morality and the power of daemonic forces, refused psychoanalysis because he feared that if his demons left him, his angels would flee as well. He knew that inner angels and demons were indivisible and drove his cre-ative process. And it is a process. In *Letters to a Young Poet*, a book Rafael recommended, Rilke advised a young student to be patient with all that is "unsolved in your heart," living the questions themselves because destiny is played out by responding to inner questions rather than finding rigid answers.

Not surprisingly, Emerson and Thoreau wrote often of a sense of des-tiny, as did the transcendentalists generally, who actively explored the question during a time when science and spirit were increasingly at odds.

Emersonian self-reliance boldly defends the destiny of the individual, but always in service to the world soul rather than worldly success. It is only in this service that we discover our deeper nature, which he demands we follow without regret: "No law can be sacred to me but that of my own nature. Good and bad are but names very readily transferable to that or this; the only right is what is after my constitution, the only wrong what is against it." Thoreau confirmed this rousing rhetoric with some of his own: "The greater part of what my neighbors call good I believe in my soul to be bad, and if I repent of anything, it is very likely to be my good behavior. What demon possessed me that I behaved so well.... I hear an irresistible voice, the voice of my destiny, which invites me away from all that."

Teaching such self-reliance taught me that most students struggle to understand where this deep inner direction comes from, as if outer moral-ity does not matter. For Emerson and Thoreau, outer action must reflect the inner for there to be ethics, especially when the inner includes ecstasy.

Exploring ecstasy was central to Emerson's spiritual world view, and he considered such experience as natural as gravity. Thoreau lived it when graced with divine elevation, stating he was often "daily intoxicated, yet no man could call him intemperate." Ecstatic heights were the measure of all things, even though such states are often fleeting; our best guidance comes from listening to ourselves when so imbued. Thus, they provide sound advice, or corrupt the youth advice, for our own good and the good of the polis, yet I would be gravely remiss if I suggested to students that following a sense of destiny is easy.

Emerson followed a sense of destiny when quitting his job as a Unitarian minister and in his subsequent trip to Europe when he had a revelation at the Jardin des Plantes in Paris, a museum of natural history that stirred his soul. Upon returning, he attended to the "strange sympathies" of the natural world and ministered to his call to be a writer, with understanding balanced with the intuitions of reason in his early essay "Nature." Ecstatic inspiration, while providing hope and direction, also tortured him with guilt and drove sleep from his bed. Cultural expectations are not easy to ignore and often still have their sway even as the daemonic calls us to risk.

For Jung, the shadow lurks as destructive impulses, blocking our callings, often via internalized socio-cultural miseducation as to what it means to be a success: obsessing (over material things), repressing (the body, the daemonic), regressing (to childish needs for instant gratification), desiring (certainty and security over risk), displaying unhealthy emotions like envy (toward others who are supposedly successful) and guilt (for not measuring up), and becoming addicted to energy substitutes.

The shadow is our inner genius when it is denied, ignored, frustrated, unheeded, and generally unexpressed. It's the creative process turned inside out and on its head. Franz Kafka commented that a monster is a writer who doesn't write, but it would be foolish to try to rid ourselves of our inner monster; it's a powerful beast that will find other destructive ways of expressing itself, like slaying cows and kings, or a condemning morality that is dismissive of others who are fulfilling their callings. Like the daemonic, the key to dealing with our shadow is to embrace rather than deny its power. Or as Jung put it, "One does not become enlightened by imagining figures of light, but by making the darkness conscious."

The Spanish philosopher Jose Ortega y Gasset, whom I also discovered thanks to Rafael, explored both darkness and light in the pursuit of destiny. For Ortega y Gasset there is often a divide between the person we are and the person we are meant to be. Failing to find an authentic life, our life drama becomes a tragedy, and everyone, and everything, suffers.

214

He further writes that our sense that a destiny is calling us to do a certain thing or live a specific life is produced by the creative tension between inner design and outer circumstance. Thoreau, Emerson, and Fuller, and Archbishop Romero, Rachel Carson, and Ortega y Gasset, for that matter, among many others living a heroic journey (and sometimes dying for it), each followed inner promptings, but outer circumstances called them forth.

Callings, I admit to students, is another tricky word that should be approached with fear and trembling. After all, serial killers claim they are called by inner voices. To have any meaning, I say, this term must be explored within the context of the world soul, or the ethics of relationship, rather than the disconnections of a damaged psyche. But despite misreadings of callings, Rafael convinced me that, at the very least, we are called by our potential. And ever since I began teaching I have made callings a central part of my pedagogy.

In Senior Seminar, I use the timeline to argue that life itself is a calling, in the sense of Thoreau's pursuit of the divine life, Thomas Berry's "great work," and Rafael's advice that our lives are creative projects. By identifying with Spirit Unfolding and the timeline as a whole—involution and evolution, the ultimate creative process—we may find fulfillment by making contributions or making some ice. If we hold onto a specific call too tightly without this larger understanding, identifying as activist, artist, writer, scientist, teacher, parent, or whatever, we will be jostled about like a subway ride during a New York City rush hour. We will go up and down with every disappointment, every problem, every unexpected turn of events.

For Emerson, our collective call is to "lead things from disorder to order," and ecstatic experiences in nature put us in touch with a sense of order, inspiring us to "translate the world" into a mode of living. Still, Emerson explored another side of circumstance, its weight and fate, whether from heredity, family, lack of talent, or many other factors. Or rather, he makes a distinction between destiny and fate, with destiny coming more from within and more in our control and fate more from without and less in our control. We have limits and inevitably work with those limits—we will not all be "poet or prince"—yet limits also have limits: "though Fate is immense," he writes, "so is Power." Power, of course, is expressed as listening to inner genius, or following daemon and a sense of destiny.

For Thoreau, living this power meant becoming less wrong and more right with each expression of his gifts as a writer and close observer of nature. But if we are having trouble discerning a specific call, the persistence of feelings, like Josh's excitement when reading the New Journalists or satisfaction in writing "Audio Aloe," is a good indicator, or at least a step to next steps, with so many more to come. It is also important to note that all are called to character; or, as James Hillman argues, we all have potential for extraordinary character, which is different from a specific job or talent: "character is not what you do, it is the way you do it."

Senior Seminar students are intrigued by daemons, destiny, and callings, but they often reject these ideas, or realities, as a guide to life decisions because they feel like more pressure to follow something, even if it is their withins rather than parents or societal expectations. But Hillman argues that while we may deny our daemons and calls, they never leave us. They flare up as destructive behavior, dissatisfaction, and depression while waiting for us to become mature enough to listen. Jung, again: "People will do anything, no matter how absurd, in order to avoid facing their own souls."

This is a lot to take in for Senior Seminar students, especially with graduation and first jobs looming. I often feel like a youth corrupter though I know that students have heard a materialist story their whole lives and need balance. I am also aware that I provide advice that may be more relevant in their thirties when callings typically take fuller form. Some may have ears to hear because their character and sense of destiny demand it, and the rest may live into a sense of destiny, aided by seeds planted in their unconscious.

I teach on, once again reminding that listening is a choice, but even when we do listen, callings often require gestation periods marked by solitude and contemplation. We seem to be doing nothing, but we are consciously and unconsciously doing preparatory work. Symptoms, like depression, may also be messages, argues Hillman, with dark nights and the voice of soul providing instruction and instigating change, just as the voice and voices of nature speak in the age of climate disruption via symptomatic messages of melting ice, lost shoreline, and more frequent and more powerful storms.

Attuning ourselves to Spirit unfolding, the timeline, and the demands of our historical and particular circumstance—and living the questions—requires inward and outward listening and eventually responding with action. Such is the mark of an educated but always learning soul living within the world soul. That may be asking too much for a graduating senior, but at least I have extended the conversation on future jobs to include meaningful work and callings. While students may not thank me now, they often do later.

∞

Thoreau, like many authors, was not fully appreciated in his own time but made contributions to future generations. Even when we act on our callings, the "fruits" may be a long time coming, sometimes after death. Persistence is key, and Thoreau provides a dynamic example of deep listening and following a sense of destiny, coming to the point that he could write in his journal, "I was born in the most estimable place in the world, and in the nick of time, too."

Before working on *Walden* at Walden Pond and feeling less wrong, Thoreau finished his first book, *A Week on the Concord and Merrimack. A Week* condensed his two-week river trip with his brother John into a seven-day creation story in which they read the symptomatic messages of changing, human-created landscapes of factories and railroads from their handmade boat, the *Musketaquid*. Their boat was named to remind them of Natives, who, like them, were "out of doors and out of time," exploring the holy and profane. *A Week* ended up being an elegy to his brother that explored transcendentalist ideals. It received a few decent reviews but did not sell. Some reviewers could not handle Thoreau's claim that Hindu religious texts were not inferior to the Christian Bible, which they took as blasphemy. As for the Bible itself, "I know of no book that has so few readers," Thoreau harangued, arguing that true disciples would be seeking "the kingdom of heaven" rather than going to church and laying up "treasures on earth."

Thoreau revealed a new world that his current world was not ready for. Even George Ripley, an early transcendentalist and Unitarian minister, was revolted because Thoreau was calling for revolt. Given such sentiment, he had a hard time getting a fair hearing, even if he was just following transcendentalist principles to their radical conclusion. Reaction to the book left him lost, especially regarding a promising literary career. One reviewer called the book "flat," consisting of uninteresting "reveries that could have been written anywhere." Another wrote that it was "interspersed with inexcusable crudities" and "lack of moral discrimination."

Emerson first liked the book and encouraged Thoreau to pay for publication out of his own pocket (after it was rejected by four publishers), but later became critical. *A Week*, along with being an elegy to John, was supposed to fulfill Emerson's promise: he needed a big book to break free from the inevitable shadow of his mentor and to explore identity counter to Emerson's strong influence, which never fully went away even as he went his own way.

Their mentor-student relationship, which began with such ease, was no longer easily lived. Their relationship was breaking; Emerson was not honest with Thoreau until after he went into debt. But because the relationship was rooted in the daemonic and a sense of destiny, it persisted, through this tiff and others, with Thoreau writing in his journal, "I would meet my friend not in the light or shadows of our human life alone—but as daimons…. Ours is a tragedy of more than 5 acts—this is not the fifth act in our tragedy no, no!" It was a powerful remark that suggested they were intertwined souls influenced by reincarnation.

Thoreau also persisted. It took him years to pay off the publisher after receiving 706 unsold copies of *A Week*. He remarked, "I have now a library of nearly 900 volumes over 700 of which I wrote myself." He then turned to *Walden*, in which he used exaggeration for humor and sting, satirizing the getting and spending ways of his fellows and the lucrative standard of industrialization generally, despite his Harvard writing teacher claiming it should be avoided at all costs. Going alone, again, trusting himself, even if it led to failure.

Thoreau did get paid for some of his writing, thanks to Horace Greeley, including a piece on Thomas Carlyle. Greeley advised him to write shorter pieces on other famous men, especially Emerson, because Greeley knew he could sell them. Thoreau declined, returned to *Walden*, which he would refine over nine years before publication, and tried out sections as talks for the lyceum. Those were mostly a hit, his audience entertained by his satire and wit pointing out follies of his time.

Walden was finally published to good reviews. His writing life was not all struggle with success only coming after death, yet *Walden*, while selling better than *A Week*, did not sell well. Bronson Alcott stated that it was a great and lasting book that would find "readers and fame as years passed by."

Much of what Thoreau wrote was either rejected, ignored, criticized, or censored; it was a hard burden to bear that can lead to self-deception—"I am great but misunderstood"—but when one follows eternal verities they should expect to be criticized by transient times. One also imagines Thoreau content, finding fruits of satisfaction from knowing that he was listening to larger forces, doing what he had to do. Emerson wrote of such forces, "It cannot be defeated by my defeats."

Thoreau's example should be inspiring, but most students leave out larger forces such as the daemonic when interpreting who they are and what they are to do with their lives. One reason is that they inevitably follow the larger force of industrial education. Josh, my perceptive, seven-year-graduation-plan student, left high school thinking he was a dunce, without talent or hope, rather than a misfit with nascent abilities and intelligence that demand support and time.

Another reason is the cultural habit of solely identifying with our family story rather than celebrating our roles within the story of the earth and universe. Hillman calls this the "parental fallacy," which he considers a prominent cause of environmental and psychological despair. Students, prisoners of a limited vision, often struggle to leave "the house of the parents" and leap into "the home of the world."

 symbol

Socrates, Rilke, Emerson, Thoreau, Jung, Ortega y Gasset, and Hillman present unique views, yet all articulate an innate drive that resonates across cultures and time periods: a desire—a destiny?—to evolve in the direction of increased wholeness, which the ancient Greeks, so essential to the wisdom of the timeline, called eros.

Plato claimed that eros is a daemon, expressed as an underlying force that binds the universe together. From *The Symposium*: "Human nature was originally one and we were a whole, and the desire and pursuit of the whole is called love." Our innate drive to regain, or remember, our wholeness is the pull of eros, but eros has been reduced to sexual desire for students socialized in techno-industrial cultures. It's a terrible trivialization as well as a telling example of how disconnected humans can be from the ecstatic energy reverberating throughout the cosmos. Ecstatic experience, standing "outside" constricted selves, and connecting to others and everything engenders ethical responsibilities, not do-gooding but pursuit of the good. Socrates did not try to convince students of altruism or duty, but to wake up to eros and see what happens, even if it goes against the State.

Hunter-gatherers expressed eros through participatory consciousness and communication with diverse species, which they saw as articulating presences that provided lessons. Hillman argues, though, that "civilized" culture is also a product of eros and evolution—soul is in the city. Yet the alienating aspects of "civilization," disconnected from the energized love of eros, lead to addictions, denial, and destruction.

Another troubling question: How many are self-medicating or lost in addictions in response to ecstasy deprivation or as a means for denying daemon and destiny? Ortega y Gasset responds bluntly: "Every life is, more or less, a ruin among whose debris we have to discover what the person ought to have been."

During my gambling addiction, I told myself that only the brightest, most intuitive inductive reasoners could uncover the most salient racing clues. I applied my formal education, especially the calculative, logical-mathematical intelligence drilled into my brain through hundreds of multiple-choice tests (the same logical-mathematical intelligence that Wall Streeters use to gamble on the stock market) to finding the clues and unraveling the mystery of horse handicapping.

I had genuine intuitions throughout my misadventure that signaled I was going full speed ahead along the wrong track, but, plunging further into the shadows, I ignored all the warnings, all the stop signs. I was playing a game within a limited materialistic economic system, not exploring purpose and play by living within limitless spiritual systems and larger contexts of meaning, or within an ecosystem and what was happening to this beautiful, degraded planet. I was lost and not listening because I was not guided by larger forces, whether the daemonic or love or world soul, and not responding to our collective lostness by being good for something and making a contribution.

Not living at all, really, so I sifted through the debris.

Gambling became my source of energy and meaning: the god-like feeling of figuring it out, the escape from boredom, the use of calculation and hunches, and the flow of action were all so appealing. But experiencing these qualities within a limited context led to an inevitable crash.

I see my behavior as a refusal to trust the initial seeds of my calling to explore the divine life, to persist by reading, thinking, and writing, going wherever my path took me. But I had no real community—Preston was in Indiana and Rafael in New Mexico—so my commitment to spiritual growth was no longer reflected back to me. I was also disoriented due to the sudden loss of sensuous connections after returning from adventures in New Mexico and New Hampshire, where ecstasy was a daily, lived reality. My call was not strong enough to withstand my shadow-side and the strange allure of self-destruction, an allure with which I had not yet become fully acquainted. I was unschooled in the cousinly connection between creative and destructive impulses, daemon and demon, and thus the difference between listening to the wisdom of soul and doubts that deny potential.

Full speed ahead along the wrong track. Ignoring all the warnings. Plunging further into the shadows. A game within a limited materialistic economic system. An inevitable crash. All are happening writ large due to our climate gamble and lucrative standard context of meaning; all are happening because we are lost and not listening.

There is plenty of debris.

A monster is not only a writer that doesn't write, but anyone who is not whole and thus divided against themselves, or any cultural system that is divided against nature and socializes citizens out of their souls.

Mechanization is not kind to eros. I knew this already from my stints at the factory and from hearing too many stories of assembly-line employees working for thirty, thirty-five, or forty years, sending kids through college, saving for the day they could quit, and then dying a year or two into their retirement. They were finally able to take a deep breath, but it was soon their last. Dad, displaying his inner genius, retired early at fifty-eight and moved with Mom to the energizing yet soothing Adirondacks.

The abstract imagination, and its progeny, is often a killing machine, yet there is an elemental energy to metal, pulleys, and gears. What, after all, is their source? Earth, reconfigured. I befriended my press, like Pirsig and his motorcycle, and it was the secret behind my printing abilities; not quite predator-prey reciprocity, or ecstasy, since the repetitive cycles of the press didn't lead to spiritual experience, but friending provided focus.

Still, there were limits to practicing Zen and the art of printing. I was hardly participating in the rhythmic song of the cosmos but laboring amid the repetitive march of the machine: ka-chunk, ka-chunk, ka-chunk.

Thoreau famously exhorted us to make our lives a "counter-friction to stop the machine," which was a metaphor for the gears of government but also the industrial age generally. He knew that the timeline is a narrative composed of endless narratives, endless ideas and choices of how to live, and that the machine, while bringing benefits, would not express ecstasy and soul and thus would not fulfill human potential.

When Rafael first tried to convince me that I had much potential, I thought, "Why bother?"—the modernist narrative I knew was get job, get married, get things. I rejected this narrative but had no replacement narrative, leaving me, of course, lost, with no awareness of larger forces to which I could attune, find a voice, and change the world.

So, like Rafael, I am patient with lost students, and rebellious students, and try to give them the resources and freedom to choose creative narratives, follow their daemons, and live their own stories. But while we may feel the pull of eros and have a sense of destiny, destiny is not written. Or, as Thoreau argued, part of our destiny is the ability to craft ourselves— our life as an unfolding creative project—and craft our perception, engaging the high art of affecting the quality of the day. We have agency, and should not make the mistake of standing in our own way or blaming circumstance or others for standing in our way and calling it fate. Rather, to the degree that we can, we must overcome the fate of our birth by continually attuning to the daemon that arrived with us at birth.

Fortune is both out of our control and in our hands, although we are often helped by unseen hands, whether our physical mentors who work on our behalf when we are not around—like Emerson did for Thoreau, despite their squabbles—or nonphysical, invisible tutelage that has visible effects.

I met with Josh at a café on campus two years after he graduated. He had worked for his dad, cleaning grimy apartments in the building he owned, traveled to Iceland and Europe, and returned to work for a trailer parts company. He wasn't writing although he had to write something at work dealing with trailer parts, and his boss remarked that he had a talent. No kidding. He also told me that he spent the two years since graduating in self-reflection, taking himself apart and putting himself back together again.

Josh asked to meet because he was considering graduate school. He wanted to be a filmmaker, stating that while he likes writing, he thinks in images. Without my addressing his drug past, he also offered that that part of his life was mostly gone although a cash-rich drug-dealer friend, also interested in film, was planning to buy a camera they could both use. He had a short film planned, which he hoped would get him into school. Most telling of all, there was a maturity in his voice I had not heard before.

Josh, the "dunce" of high school and student of many failures in college, was thinking seriously about graduate school. Still, as he spoke I thought of all the youthful graduates who want to make it in film, or some other glamorous field, but fail. Some are following deep creative impulses, or their ecstasy and bliss, rather than glamor, and reap what they sow and do make it. Others don't, but the trip is worthwhile, taking them to the next step, to where they need to go.

Or perhaps it just wouldn't work out, perhaps his history of poor grades would continue to define him. Perhaps, if his call was genuine, he would need to find another way to express it. Or perhaps he would crash—the machine is unkind and relentless, distractions endless.

I told him that he had my support, that I would help him any way I could: writing a letter of recommendation, being a sounding board, providing advice, if I had any. I basically told him that he should go forth boldly in the direction of his dreams.

Chapter 14

Speaking Out

"The man on whom the soul descends, through whom the soul speaks, alone can teach. Courage, piety, love, wisdom, can teach; and every man can open his door to these angels, and they shall bring him the gift of tongues. But the man who aims to speak as books enable, as synods use, as the fashion guides, and as interest commands, babbles. Let him hush."
—Ralph Waldo Emerson

"The meaning of my existence is that life has addressed a question to me. Or, conversely, I myself am a question which is addressed to the world, and I must communicate my answer, for otherwise I am dependent upon the world's answer."
—Carl Jung

Freedom of speech class, mid-semester. Another high-tech room, another box, another enclosure keeping nature out, but sunlight streams through blinds, and so does the world through critical discussion of presidential lies (Gulf of Tonkin resolution, Watergate, Iran-Contra, WMDs, etc.), media monopolies, junk food news, and citizen-critics who dissent and organize and speak out. I hoped to transform our box into a utopian space where free thought reigns.

"Who do you trust more," I ask, "the president or the press?"

We are discussing Daniel Ellsberg's leak of the Pentagon Papers, the "top secret" report detailing the poor policy decisions that led to and escalated the Vietnam War, to the *New York Times* and other newspapers in 1971.

No one speaks. I wait.

"It depends," a student finally says. "My first thought was that I trust the press, but Fox News is the press, and I don't trust them."

"Yes, good," I say. "The press is not monolithic; there are different levels of quality. Of course, Fox argues that the other networks have a bias and can't be trusted. What do the rest of you think?"

We will be exploring media bias soon, including that bias is inevitable, but that there are better and worse biases, some based in facts, some not. Right now, I just want to get them talking instead of me pontificating. No one speaks. I wait—that usually works, if I wait long enough, but still, no one speaks.

"Who one trusts is a provocative question," I think to myself, my brain firing for ideas of where to go next.

"Have any of you heard of Julian Assange or Chelsea Manning or Edward Snowden? They have been persecuted for releasing top secret government information. Their cases are similar to the Pentagon Papers."

Nothing.

"Do any of you keep up with the news?"

Such an "okay, Boomer" thing to say, adding to our generational divide instead of crossing it, but I can't help myself.

Several shake their heads from side to side. A few are looking down. Ashamed, I assume, but then I notice they're texting.

"Who are these students? What do they want?"

ೞ

I am constantly working to figure out my students, especially as I age and they stay in the same age group, and find myself doing *The Breakfast Club*-type musings. (Have they seen *The Breakfast Club*?)

NEC's top high school students come because they love the small town, small classes, personal relationships, natural environment, and, thankfully, the liberal arts. Or they simply grew up nearby and want to stay close to home.

The students with learning differences—ADD, ADHD, degrees of autism—come because they get lots of support. Some are lacking in a particular intelligence and may not make it at the college level and leave. Others work hard, acknowledge their weaknesses, and do quite well, finding the intelligences they do possess and improving the rest.

We also get lots of athletes who are not good enough to play sports for a Division I school but want to keep playing the game they love. Most are strong students, transcending the jock stereotype, and many come from distant places. Coaches are invested in their athletic and academic lives.

We get a few spoiled kids who did poorly in high school because when you are pampered and have material things, why care about school? Their grades have left them with few options, and their parents think a small school will be good for them—plus they want them out of the house. Unbeknownst to them, NEC is their chance not only to leave the house but also to leap into the home of the world.

We get nontraditional students, including some returning from military service, who, continuing in the tradition of NEC's founding, find a welcoming college with professors happy to have adults with life experience in their classroom. One of the best pieces I received in the Feature-Writing Workshop was from a student who had returned from service in Iraq. He joined the National Guard in hopes of saving money for college, and the next thing he knew he was in basic training and then shipped overseas, where he watched buddies blown to bits. The kicker was that although he was now in college, he could be sent back.

Increasingly, we get students from urban areas—New York, Boston, Baltimore—who bring city lives and unique experiences to small-town New Hampshire. They embrace the respite from noise and traffic, and often see the stars for the first time, but sometimes lament that there is not enough to do. We get our share of international students who also come with the gift of unique perspectives and who deal with the challenges of unfamiliar terrain.

Of course, we get plenty of magnificent misfits, who often cross my so-called categories.

All, except perhaps some nontraditionals, are addicted.

When I was at Rutgers with Preston in the eighties, we would rent a VCR and VHS tapes—few owned either—and then invite friends for an all-night movie gathering with Dunkin' Donuts coffee and munchkins. We enjoyed new gizmos, including video games like Pac Man and Popeye, but the pace of new technologies increased in the nineties, and now there is no comparison between my college years and today's iPads and iPhones. Students embrace the flood of toys and stay inside dorm rooms texting, tweeting, TikToking, Instagramming, and Snapchatting across the globe, or across the hall, which they interpret as freedom, and freedom of speech, rather than another box. They are certain that social media, and technology generally, is their friend.

But a reductionistic *Breakfast Club* understanding of my students doesn't help much when I am struggling in the classroom, trying to engage student souls with subject matter I think is interesting. Is it the material? Is it the delivery? Is it me?

What do they want?

Students want freedom; that much I do know. Freedom to frolic, freedom from the tiresome rigidity of school, freedom as self-transcendence—they unknowingly know the pull of eros as they turn to alcohol or drugs or toys to overcome puny, anxious selves, forgetting rather than embracing the world. What should they embrace? When they don't speak in class, I wonder if they are tired of hearing bad news—you can't trust government, you can't trust media, you can't trust corporations with the protective rights of citizens who plunder the planet for profit.

Perhaps they simply don't know what to do in response. Perhaps cynicism is their default position, silence their repose, new gizmos an escape, because they do not yet have rational reasons to fight cynicism, or a spiritual place in the world, a place to take a stand, to fight for their right to a vibrant and meaningful life path. Yet the timeline provides numerous examples of freedom-inspiring events and freedom-loving thinkers who found their voice and fought to change the world.

⚬

In 1492 Columbus and crew sailed the ocean blue, murdering Indigenous peoples and stealing their wealth, and in 1619 the first African slave ship landed on the American mainland, further institutionalizing racism in the "new world"; but in my Freedom of Speech class, we initially focus on a different culture-transforming event: Johannes Gutenberg's invention of the printing press in 1439 and the eventual shift of our epistemology, or the medium of communication that tells us what we know, from orality to the printed word. The western Enlightenment project, instrumental rationality, and modern notions of freedom were not far behind.

In Neil Postman's *Building a Bridge to the 18th Century,* a course text, he argues that orality is marked by storytelling, ritual, and community, and print by introspection, reflection, and individuality. Our imaginative life changed, for good and ill. The good: democratic processes—citizens were able to freely disseminate information, fostering a nation. The ill: mind became even more dissociated from nature, fostering science and technology but also eco-crises galore.

But the good is so good.

Kant, writing in 1784, argued that enlightenment was the ability to use one's reason without direction from another. "*Sapere Aude!*" he proclaimed, "Dare to know!" All that is required for such enlightenment is freedom, but the masses, being masses, fell prey to restrictions at every turn, especially from clergy and religious incompetence. But those who throw off the yoke find a vocation for thinking for themselves. How I would have loved to use my press to print Kantian exhortations on freedom and rationality. Yet enlightenment also includes the spiritual, or the enlightenment of the East and esoteric West, which is why I love the transcendentalists, my historical mentors, who fought for both spiritual and societal freedom.

Transcendentalist writings are not the main course texts of Freedom of Speech, but they do direct core themes of the class: ideals of freedom are empty if not turned into action; freedom of speech is one thing, speech guided by conscience quite another; and freedom is found within nature, not from working against it, and thus all species have a right to a healthy planet, free from forces destroying our collective home.

Transcendentalism is considered the first intellectual movement in the US. Its heyday was a brief decade between the mid-1830s and 1840s, with Boston, and then Concord, home of the first Revolutionary War battle and prior home to native Algonquians, a core influence. Or more precisely, Emerson's home, where early transcendentalists gathered to meet. Scholar Lawrence Buell argued that transcendentalism was more like "an outpouring of radiant energy" than "an organized enterprise." That energy was rooted in philosophical idealism, but they did not discuss ideas detached from the world. Instead, they gathered because they were dissatisfied with philosophy, religion, and literature regarding how they influenced social and political life. Their transcendentalist vision, extolling self-reliance, intuition, and a fuller rationality (or logos) in pursuit of freedom led to radical activities in the abolitionist movement, the women's move-ment, Native American rights, elementary education, journalism, labor, and at Brook Farm, a short-lived eco-socialist commune.

Emerson's essays and lecturing were often directed at reforming the church and religious education, making them responsive to the active soul and to the tension between following conscience or commerce. He also got involved in the abolitionist movement, or rather, he was eventually dragged into it by Lidian and other members of the Concord Female Anti-Slavery Society. At first, he was more sympathetic observer or aloof phi-losopher than advocate. Despite despising slavery, he mostly stayed on the sidelines because his constitution skewed towards intellectual discussion and moral persuasion. In contrast, Concord women, including middle and lower classes, felt the pull of sympathy based on shared concern for justice, leading them to organize and petition and act.

Emerson seemed to be hesitant to join any crowd. Perhaps he feared do-gooder-ism (what we would call virtue signaling today), the mistake of acting without sufficient reflection, or his heartfelt belief that outer change is not lasting without inner change and thus it must be led by the self-reliant. Perhaps he was hesitant because he tended to be in but not of the world and was sometimes too detached. But further outrage in response to the Trail of Tears, with southern Cherokee forced to relocate beyond the Mississippi River, led Lidian to urge him to speak out.

Make no mistake, Emerson, a man of the people, traveled extensively for many years to give public lectures, and he advocated for the reform of everything, stating we must "revise the whole of our social structure, the state, the school, religion, marriage, trade, science, and explore their foun-dations in our nature." For him, social evils were structural, and thus struc-tures needed to be changed, not just single issues, but he leaned toward education over direct action.

Thoreau's activism was similar but different. He wrote and gave lec-tures, but his radicalism was mainly expressed in the way he lived, in what he did each day. He also displayed radical freedom in what he refused to do.

In "Life without Principle," Thoreau assailed bustling businessmen and suggested that most jobs are like throwing a rock over a wall and then throwing it back again. We would be insulted if this rock-throwing were our actual job, he claimed, but most are "no more worthily employed," or worse, they find employment cutting down the forest, "making it bald before its time." He was not against jobs, or logging, but he was against destruction. He thought an awakened community would be as well, if only the bustling would stop long enough for citizens to reflect on what truly matters. Meaning is what we crave, and we could have it if we lived a life of simplicity, without the clutter of extraneous needs. In Thoreau's hands—hands that built cabins, hoed bean fields, engineered pencils, and surveyed land—the call for simplicity was a radical act.

Thoreau's activist heart is fully expressed in "Civil Disobedience," but students initially read it only as a treatise against big government. But this seminal essay criticizes life without principle, as well as life without conscience, which ends up being no life at all. For Thoreau, to be free, we must first and foremost be subjects of individual conscience rather than governments, or any majority for that matter. Respecting the collective good and the higher good within ourselves, we must separate the diabolic from the divine, doing what we must in many moments of daily decision-making rather than what laws or social convention tell us to do.

The arguments in "Civil Disobedience" have their roots in Thoreau's refusal to pay a poll tax for six years, a protest of the government's support of slavery and war with Mexico, but also, it is important to note, a protest of the removal of Native Americans from their land. He spent a night in jail, which would have been more, but, to his chagrin, his aunt bailed him out. The result was his well-known claim unknown by most students: jail is the true place for a just citizen in an unjust society.

To Thoreau, the only way to freely serve the State is with conscience. Politicians, legislators, lawyers, ministers, and office-holders tend to serve with their heads only, so they are poor ethical decision-makers. They patronize virtue instead of living virtuously, sold to institutions that make them rich, beholden to free trade instead of true freedom. On the other hand, Thoreau greatly respected the courage of soldiers, who served with their bodies, but argued that they often march counter to head, heart, and ethical sense. True heroes and patriots, then, serve their conscience—their inner genius—expressed outwardly in the pursuit of justice. Such citizens are friends of the State but treated as enemies. Thoreau understood that the machinery of government can't be perfect, that there is a degree of injustice in its workings, but if this imperfection makes us an agent of injustice against another, conscience demands that we make ourselves a "counter-friction to stop the machine."

Thoreau wrote "Civil Disobedience" in 1849, but I ask students, Does any of this sound familiar? The freedom to follow conscience as a radical act? Politicians and others in power privileging profit over principle? The inner demand to counter the machine of the powers-that-be?

Thoreau's activism became more radicalized as he encountered and confronted the machinery of slavery. When Thomas Sims, a young runaway with an unknown birthday, was sent back to Georgia under the 1850 Fugitive Slave Act on April 12, 1851, a week before celebrating the freedom fought for in the battles of Lexington and Concord on April 19, 1775, he was horrified by the hypocrisy, referencing Jesus: "inasmuch as ye did it unto the least of these his brethren ye did it unto him. Do you think *he* would have stayed here in liberty and let the black man go in slavery in his stead?" Emerson, too, had reached his limit, appalled, and thus called by conscience to speak out two weeks later: "The last year has forced us all into politics." He also mirrored Thoreau's strong rhetoric in "Civil Disobedience": "An immoral law makes it a man's duty to break it, at every hazard."

When twenty-year-old Anthony Burns was captured and tried in Boston in 1854 in accord with the Fugitive Slave Act, Thoreau wrote in his journal that it was Massachusetts on trial: "every moment that she hesitates to set this man free—she is convicted." Inspired by Frederick Douglass and Wendell Phillips, a transcendentalist pastor and abolitionist orator, he soon gave a fiery address, "Slavery in Massachusetts," before a crowd of two thousand, one of the largest antislavery gatherings, in Boston in July 4th heat in which he appealed to higher law and called for secession from the union. He had lived for months with a feeling of "vast infinite loss," unsure what it was, and then realized: "At last it occurred to me that what I had lost was a country." Running with this theme, he said, "The remembrance of my country spoils my walk. My thoughts are murder to the State, and involuntarily go plotting against her." He ended on a hopeful note: the white water lily is rooted in the "slime and muck of the earth," and thus a lotus may yet bloom, despite the "sloth and vice of men, the decay of humanity."

Thoreau had become a radical abolitionist. His address ran in newspapers, one with the headline "Words that Burn." Emerson also continued to speak out against slavery, stating "we must get rid of slavery, or we must get rid of freedom," while no longer just calling for education and persuasion but collective direct action; we cannot practice self-reliance if we are not free. But Thoreau's burning words signified a break from Emerson in the public's eye. The defender of nature and proponent of simple living had joined Douglass and others in declaring that the Declaration of Independence was a lie.

Walden was finally going to the printers in 1854, yet his ethical vision was being trampled and discarded. How could he write of freedom in nature, of beauty and justice as part of the framework of the cosmos, when so many were enslaved? This question haunted him on the eve of his biggest triumph. The annexation of Texas and further march of Manifest Destiny stirred the pot by adding more slave states in the South and West. Thoreau, stewing on the unethical illogic of slavery, stoked a rage not yet fully formulated while he and his family continued to help runaway slaves escape as part of Underground Railroad.

And then, John Brown.

Most students have never heard of him; I, too, did not learn about Brown, or Douglass, or the Concord Female Anti-Slavery Society, or Sims and Burns, or Thoreau for that matter, in my formal education. Or, if I did, their lives and deeds did not stick, likely because they are typically taught as names and dates to be regurgitated on tests rather than catalysts driving larger narratives of freedom and rights, narratives we are living today and will always be living. It's impossible to predict what will stick with students, but I am convinced that more will stick if they are provoked to listen to conscience by exploring controversial callings that illustrate the tension between daemon and demon. There is no better illustration than Brown.

Brown and his followers murdered five proslavery householders in Kansas. They dragged them out of their homes in retaliation for the overthrow of Lawrence, where the presses of two abolitionist newspapers were destroyed and the "Free State Hotel" was burnt down. He was further angered when he heard that Charles Sumner, an abolitionist senator, was nearly beaten to death on the Senate floor by a southern congress person.

Brown then traveled east, including to Concord, dined at the Thoreau home, and then gave a speech at a town meeting to raise funds for the abolitionist movement. Thoreau was initially suspicious of what Brown would do with the money and gave little, yet was won over by his passion, even though Brown had turned to violence in response to violence.

After Brown's imprisonment due to his failed raid on the federal arsenal at Harper's Ferry, Thoreau simmered. Then, two days after hearing the news of Brown's capture, he was ready to explode and passed the word among fellow townsfolk that he would speak. Friends and some family begged for silence. He replied to one friend, Sanborn the schoolmaster, who had been involved in Brown's plot but now feared for his life: "I did not send for you for advice but to announce that I am to speak."

Brown was on trial for treason. Newspapers denounced him, and Thoreau was the first to stand up in public to defend him. The church was filled, and Thoreau read "A Plea for Captain John Brown" before a curious but doubtful audience, with "no oratory, as if it burned him." Young Edward Emerson, Ralph's son, said Thoreau sounded as if he were speaking about his own brother and summarized the reaction: "Many of those who came to scoff remained to pray."

Word spread, thanks to Emerson, who as a defender of Brown lent his authority as a nationally known figure to the cause. When Douglass, scheduled to speak in Boston, was implicated in the plot by a letter found on Brown, a warrant was issued for his arrest, and he was forced to flee to Canada. Thoreau stepped in before a crowd of twenty-five hundred: "The reason why Frederick Douglass is not here is the reason why I am," he began, the audience rapt and applauding for an hour and a half. An abridged "Plea" was printed in newspapers across America; he hoped to get it published as a pamphlet, but no publisher would touch it. Thoreau felt lost, again, while waiting for Brown's death by hanging; nature was not its usual comfort, the soul of a nation at stake: "So great a wrong...overshadowed all beauty in the world."

Thoreau planned a memorial service on the day of Brown's execution; not all in Concord were happy about it; not all were in favor of Brown. Thoreau later helped Francis Jackson Merriam, a Harper's Ferry plotter and financial supporter, and the most wanted man in America, to escape to Canada although Merriam's identity was supposedly unknown to Thoreau. It's hard to imagine that he did not know, with Thoreau putting himself at great risk, potentially jailed and hanged himself for aiding a fugitive. Along with his family, Thoreau also helped take care of John Brown's children, another act of defiance against the government.

Brown was a man of action against physical institutions, schooled in liberty by what Thoreau termed the "great university of the West," taking "many degrees" and commencing the "practice of Humanity." Spurred by Brown, Thoreau's position on violence and nonviolence evolved, and he refused to judge "any tactics that are effective of good, whether one wields the quill or sword." Thoreau most certainly entered difficult terrain here, but, for him, any castigation of Brown must also consider the crimes of a country so lost that it institutionalized the violent enslavement of four million fellow Americans. While turning ideas into actions marked the transcendentalist call to conscience, Thoreau also provides another lesson to students: words, and speaking out, turn actions into ideas that can drive a wedge into institutions. In the growing response to slavery, he wrote, "The North is suddenly all Transcendental," giving him hope in the power of words and ideals and speaking the truth: the government was on the wrong side, maintaining slavery and killing "the liberators of the slave."

Brown's turn to violence alienated many, but Thoreau, having none of it, called the government a brute force, and worse, "a demoniacal force!" while questioning what citizens were willing to do. Thomas Jefferson wrote that "Rebellion to tyrants is obedience to God." Brown justified his actions as God's will, or a response to the fact that slavery could not possibly be God's will, so action was needed; caution equaled cowardice. Thoreau agreed, stating, "The man this country was about to hang appeared the greatest and best in it."

In a later essay, "The Last Days of John Brown," Thoreau argued that Brown, a transcendentalist above all, revered higher law over law and embodied principle and conscience. But, in a compliment to himself, he stated only the noble perceive the noble: "How can a man behold the light who has no answering inner light?" And if anti-Brown citizens were Christians, they were neither citizen nor Christian, having no genius for listening to inner light or being a free man: "They seem to have known nothing about living or dying for a principle."

For Thoreau, John Brown's most profound lesson was living and dying for a principle. The public now had an example of it, if inner light is not completely dimmed.

In a provocative move, Thoreau then turned to liberal arts education, stating that for the Romans only free men were worthy of such education while slaves learned trades and professions. Working from this premise, he argued that only the liberally educated are truly free and thus able to revolt: "In a slaveholding country like this, there can be no such thing as a *liberal* education tolerated by the State." A liberal arts education, in other words, is dangerous to those in power, as those contented under tyrannies "have received only a *servile* education."

Brown, as martyr, revealed the States' character: it could admit its failures and culpability, or it could choose violence. It chose violence. For Thoreau, government was not only a brute but human force, so appeal to protect the rights of dissenters was possible.

Slavery infected everything and caused Thoreau to continue to ponder the worth of *Walden* and love of nature in the face of the baseness of man; despite his support of Brown's violence, or his refusal to rule it out in response to violence, being one with Spirit and part and parcel of nature led him to further ponder the possibilities of an ethic of least harm whether toward moose, snake, or man. "We must ask ourselves weekly," he wrote, "Is our life innocent enough? Do we live inhumanely—toward man or beast—in thought or act?" Thoreau even advocated for thinking like a bream and writing from such thinking since the bream is "another image of God...a provoking mystery."

Freedom, for Thoreau, included the rights of humans and nature, with the freedom to be (or exist), to dwell in habitat (you need habitat to exist), and to become (by interacting within our habitat) all having universal resonance. Such resonance provided him with hope, as it should today, but his spiritual pondering also led to a question: What should we do when an ethic of least harm is not universally held, or not held by those in power? Thoreau lived questions we still ask and that I ask students: What are the limits to freedom? Is violence ever an appropriate response to violence, including the violence of rising greenhouse gases that will likely displace millions?

The Civil War loomed, and Thoreau wondered how he could do

more: "I do not wish to kill or to be killed, but I can foresee circumstances in which both of these things would be by me unavoidable." The commons were also increasingly being lost—he bemoaned no trespassing signs and having to pay for berries he used to pick for free. The financial panic of 1857 led to mass unemployment, so he questioned an economic system that distains simple living. The Trans-Atlantic telegraph arrived in 1858; it was a great invention but for what purpose? What would it do to the quality of our speech, our communications?

Would it be an "improved means to an unimproved end"?

That's another question that has reverberated throughout the decades to the digital age, along with "How can acknowledging our lostness lead us to listen to the call of conscience, and thus be better arbiters of what it means to be free?"

೦੪

Reading Thoreau, and about his life and times, discloses that our consciousness must be raised before we can raise the consciousness, and conscience, of others. The freedom to inquire, to dare to know, integrated with a degree of spiritual maturity, should lead us to recognize common home and humanity, including with adversaries. We need to recognize our own alienation and desire to lash out in violence. Yet, while we are called to respond to historical circumstances that cause conflict, and violence, the most fitting response is not always clear.

How am I supposed to teach these ideas to students, who have different interpretations of freedom, especially in pandemic and "culture wars" times, where we cannot agree on wearing masks or getting a vaccine?

Martin Luther King, who was influenced by Thoreau, stated he just wanted to do God's will. But King had moments of doubt, illustrated by his "kitchen table experience" when he appealed to God, with deep humility, to give him strength. He was considering leaving the struggle for liberation due to threats on his life, but God's presence descended, and his inner voice granted him peace with his calling. King, despite the threats and hatred he confronted daily, resisted the desire to humiliate others in retaliation because he understood that the true enemy was the bondage of ignorance.

Archbishop Oscar Romero also turned to civil disobedience fueled by conscience and described his allegiance to God's will. In one of the few amusing scenes in *Romero*, he asks a friend what he should do, and the advice he receives is to do what God wants. Romero's reply is honest and simple: "What is that?" For liberation theologians, interpreting God's will begins with considering the poor and asking basic questions such as, "Would not God like the people to have clean water?" Such questions allow them to see with God's eyes and to unite with God and the poor so that they'll be conscious agents of God's will. The focus on the salvation of the individual soul is expanded to include the liberation of a community of souls from economic, political, cultural, religious, and environmental oppression.

God's will, mystically, is the principle of unity expressed uniquely within the individual will—if all life is one, we must serve the all. A deep surrendering to something larger puts us in touch with this creative force and silences fears that block listening and action. Mahatma Gandhi, also influenced by Thoreau, actively listened via *satyagraha*, translated as "truth," "love," or "soul force." Satyagraha draws from the ancient Indian higher law of *ahimsa*, or doing no harm, as the core of nonviolent living. In Gandhi's activism, satyagraha is a tremendous force for the simple reason that following conscience inspires others to do the same. It breaks down ego-barriers and the illusion of separateness—a root cause of social and environmental violence—and potentially creates a wave of grassroots transformation. Or as Gandhi put it, "Things undreamt of are daily being seen, the impossible is ever becoming possible."

When my students seem despondent from too much bad news, I remind them of the record of nonviolent, and sometimes violent, resistance bringing down oppressive dictatorships and changing governments, and enlightenment rationality in service of freedom bringing progressive change generally, with citizens speaking out because their conscience demands it.

We discuss the 1848 Declaration of Sentiments, principally penned by Elizabeth Cady Stanton, which declared that "all men and women are created equal"; the hundred signees—sixty-eight women and thirty-two men, including Frederick Douglass—were called to use every instrument within their power to do the great work of fighting for equality, including the right to education and fulfill potential, despite enduring ridicule. And we discuss Douglass's 1852 speech, "What to the Slave Is the 4th of July?," a stirring example of enlightenment rationality taking on unfulfilled ideals of a nation.

We discuss the spirituality of Thoreau and Gandhi and Romero and King, but also King's "Letter from a Birmingham Jail," which, along with proving Thoreau's point that jail is the true place for the just in an unjust society, is another stirring example of enlightenment rationality and passionate rhetoric in which King takes on the wrong-headed arguments of fellow clergy wary of civil rights and protest.

We discuss Malcolm X's more virulent rhetoric, change by any means necessary, and claim that nonviolence is fine, if it works; Thoreau, despite influencing Gandhi and King, was often more rhetorically aligned with Malcolm X.

We discuss Ellsberg's call to conscience in releasing the Pentagon Papers, a free press bringing down Nixon, and the digital resistance of Assange and Manning and Snowden. Heroes or traitors? Or more complex than that simple dichotomy?

And, for good measure, we explore Katharine Hepburn's refusal to wear a dress, Billie Holiday singing "Strange Fruit," and Muhammad Ali's resistance to the draft—and the Arab spring, partially spurred by organizing via social media; Ai Weiwei using Twitter to flip the bird in China; and Occupy Wall Street in the students' own backyard.

And Majora Carter's TED talks, in which she speaks out against environmental racism and for transforming urban wastelands into parks that support healthy living, as well as David Orr's call for an amendment to the Constitution providing rights to nature and future generations for breathable air, clean water, and green space.

And, via the documentary *Disruption*, the People's Climate March in New York City in 2014, at which point atmospheric carbon registered 401.20 ppm, the first reading over 400.

And Black Lives Matter and Extinction Rebellion and another key number: according to Erica Chenoweth, a scholar of civil disobedience, every nonviolent movement in the twentieth century with at least 3.5 percent of the population involved met with political success, which is quite a different measure of success compared to the lucrative standard.

I also can't resist mentioning Jesus's declaration that "what I have done, you will do also," along with Emerson's claim in "Self-Reliance" that "In every work of genius we recognize our own rejected thoughts," to argue that the call to enlightened rationality and conscience and spiritual maturity should not be displaced onto heroic others.

What, I ask, will you do?

Silence.

☙

The transcendentalists dared to know via rationality integrated with religious feeling and ethical action; in other words, they practiced logos. When I traveled with the Icemakers of the Revolution, who expressed freedom via creative protest, the religious feeling part was mostly absent; its neglect was wrongheaded since the band hoped to be a catalyst for creating citizens of conscience. There was an implicit spirituality in the group's social justice message but a lack of embraced spirituality in the band itself. The fun was undeniable, and raising awareness and support for good causes was laudable before it imploded after a three-year run.

The band encountered all kinds of alternative political and social groups on the road, and there was often a split between those who were anti-spiritual, mostly leftist organizations, and those who were somewhat goofy-spiritual, such as the Rainbow Family, who gather each year for back-to-nature living in national forests. The former appealed to urban-focused critical rationality and the latter to earth-focused spiritual intuition, each at the expense of the other. The band leaned far more toward the critical rationality leftists, so a favorite memory is when a group of Rainbows, who loved dancing to the music, convinced band members to participate in a post-concert hand-holding sharing circle. Everyone but me was uncomfortable, and discussing its silliness became a major pastime as we traveled to future gigs.

To me, urban-focused critical rationality leftists and Earth-focused spiritual folks both had valuable views to share, yet each expressed a limited vision. But they did hold one view in common: for the most part, they disregard a transcendent dimension, and thus, to my chagrin, the transcendentalists.

239

Groups like the Rainbows deny the transcendent because the Earth is often seen as ultimate reality; there's no need to imagine other dimensions when you can practice the sensuous imagination. But this denial leads them to romanticize hunter-gatherer life and *regress* to a pre-rational past, and thus to poor interpretations of both rational and spiritual progress. I am sure that living close to the land opened them to genuine insights, but they often rejected rationality as a block to feeling, which, ironically, is a poor use of rationality. The youthful Rainbows we met embraced childlike play and innocence. They willfully forgot that pre-rational children must grow up to embrace rationality, and then, with still greater maturity, transrational contemplation and spiritual experience.

Most leftists deny a transcendent dimension because they find such talk pure imagination and anti-rational. The notion of God's will would be laughable if not for all the wars fought in God's name. Many won't entertain a mystical interpretation of God's will since they deny the worth of spirituality of any sort—the proverbial baby thrown out with the bathwater. Such attitudes *repress* possibilities for learning from transrational spiritual experience and pre-rational immersion in nature. Leftists perceive the downsides of instrumental forms of rationality treating nature as standing reserve, yet rationality is often considered the only way to receive knowledge.

The critical rationality leftists were often highly educated and held advanced degrees, but many had cut themselves off from listening to the voices of nature and the voice of Spirit. And repression, along with regression, ultimately leads to poorly articulated solutions to eco-social problems and insufficient activism because we are not expressing our full capacities; we don't fully understand who we are or our predicament in an age of climate crisis.

The timeline provides a history of predicaments: mind and nature were not fully differentiated for hunter-gatherers, leading to both good and ill; mind and nature were fully differentiated with the birth of agriculture and then science and technology, again leading to both good and ill. And now, with the freedom to learn from past ages, we may take the good and rid ourselves of the ill, differentiating *and* integrating mind and nature, embracing wisdom from pre-rational attunement to the body and nature, critical rationality that both learns from and rejects traditions, and trans-rational spiritual experience.

Differentiating and integrating mind and nature is, for me at least, the core of a liberal arts education in pursuit of the true, good, and beautiful. My informal education with Rafael led me to emphasize the spiritual and to claim that genuine religious feelings are essential for rational social activism. To see with God's eyes or from the perspective of Spirit unfolding—which are just other ways of saying sympathy with intelligence—lessens ego, enlarges compassion, increases clarity of vision. Seeing from this perspective assures that whatever the activism, it is not merely a projection of a limited self-image, including the image of the peace activist or protestor. Rational inquiry reveals numerous atrocities in the name of God's will that perpetuate cycles of violence but only because these atrocities were in the name of ego and limited self-image, and thus limited understanding.

Students seem to intuit the potential downsides of ego-activism. They wisely argue for nonviolence and marching for the right reasons so that protest does not alienate those who would otherwise be sympathetic. They love the loving rhetoric of King and are more skeptical of the more virulent rhetoric of Malcolm X. Unaware that King's love was revolutionary, turn-over-the-boat love (not only for civil rights but for economic justice), they are willing to rock the boat but not turn it over.

Students, the Rainbows, leftists, and the Icemakers might learn from transcendentalist love merging spiritual and sensuous and rational inquiry, embodying larger selves while practicing democratic action. Spiritually-minded folks who envision a transcendent dimension expressed in and as the world, with subtlety, grace, and humility, are not just sitting on their butts or kneeling in piety, prostrating themselves in the dirt; they're out kickin' butt.

The Icemakers made their mark. They sang the praises of small changes and small steps, and they challenged Herbert Marcuse's claim that one-dimensional capitalist culture contains *all* change by selling revolution in advertisements and on T-shirts—think of all the kids with Che Guevara on their chest. The dominant culture, when seen in three dimensions (thanks to critical analyses like Marcuse's), yields fissures for marginalized voices to speak out, for freedom of speech, but not just any speech—*quality* speech. It's fun to stand up to the man, but a spiritually-informed view in pursuit of the true, good, and beautiful is necessary for lasting change.

Living our ethics can be hard, but better to be active with the activists rather than sleeping with the sleepers, I tell students, referencing a Billy Bragg lyric. Mentioning Bragg, whom students also haven't heard of, allows me to start a conversation on the power of music as protest. But the point is this: There's lots of noise out there, but sonorous voices may get through, especially those of conscience beholden to larger forces, including the fourth dimension of the cosmos, of space and time, and the fifth dimension of transcendent mystery.

Sapere Aude. Satyagraha.

ᘓ

Perhaps students tend to be silent when I ask who they trust more, government or the press, because it's a bit of a false dichotomy. A better question is who or what can we trust at all, and on what grounds.

So many are speaking out: Who do we listen to?

Long before the internet and "fake news" and "alternate facts," Thoreau wrote, "Shams and delusions are esteemed for the highest truths, while reality is fabulous." Not much has changed, yet the internet has changed everything. Anyone can propagate shams and delusions, and Facebook makes such fakery part of their business model. Post-truth used to mean postmodernists wisely deconstructing claims for absolute Truth; now it seems to mean that everything is up for grabs because everything can be manipulated to suit one's preferred, and profitable, version of reality. One might think that "the true" would be easiest to teach—just focus on facts—but students live not only in the age of climate crisis but also in an age of spin spawned by Edward Bernays in the early twentieth century.

Bernays, whom I teach in several classes, started the profession of public relations in the 1920s. He used it to "engineer consent" among the masses, whether for consumption or candidates or, most famously, for American Tobacco Company. Thoreau questioned the habits of the masses, but Bernays manipulated them, using a variety of PR strategies and tactics—front groups, stunts, symbols and images, so-called expert opinion, an easily influenced press, and Freudian group psychology—to bias responses in his favor, or the favor of his corporate clients. Fast-forward to climate denialism: Exxon's own scientists knew that global warming was a serious threat as early as 1977, yet this mega-corporation, becoming ExxonMobil, spent the ensuing decades spewing disinformation that undermined the transition from fossil fuels.

Bernays's fingerprints are all over ExxonMobil's lies in the service of profit over people and planet, or the intentional propagation of our lostness via propaganda, making the public more pliable. One trick was not in his bag because it did not exist: social media, which, like all new communicative technologies, has the power to teach but also to falsify, distort, and corrupt, or to proliferate shams and delusions, as illustrated by the Cambridge Analytica scandal, which I also explore with students.

What of my bias? "Deniers" would consider *Disruption* global warming propaganda expressing a one-sided, "alarmist" point of view, but the talking heads in the film have impressive credentials, including Naomi Oreskes, a historian of science, who argues that climate research is old and well-established. The fundamental understanding of carbon dioxide as a greenhouse gas dates to the 1824 musings of French mathematician Joseph Fourier and Irish scientist John Tyndall's 1859 experiments on the properties of gases, just before the publication of Darwin's *On the Origin of Species* and a mere three years before Thoreau's death. They dared to know, and others followed in their footsteps. In 1895, the Swedish scientist Svante Arrehenius studied the effect that doubling CO_2 would have on global climate, and in 1958 Charles Keeling measured atmospheric CO_2 at the Mauna Loa Observatory in Hawaii and established the Keeling Curve, which records the continual uptick of CO_2 ppm.

In 2004, Oreskes was the first to find overwhelming consensus among peer-reviewed scientific papers that warming is happening and significantly anthropogenic, which has grown to 99 percent. In other words, some claims are supported by the weight of evidence, and credentials matter; I have a bias toward such weight and things that matter.

I often highlight my bias by telling students why I am teaching their class. My degrees are one reason, sure, but the main reason is I am older and have been researching and thinking about our course topics for decades. I am there to share what I have learned and to keep learning along with them. I also start some classes with the oft-quoted section from the preface of Walt Whitman's *Leaves of Grass*, beginning, "This is what you shall do; Love the earth and sun and the animals," and then continuing with a lively list, but I focus student attention on "re-examine all you have been told at school or church or in any book, dismiss whatever insults your own soul, and your very flesh shall be a great poem." My message: Respect my experience and credentials, and listen to evidence, but find out for yourself what is true.

Whitman along with Joe Polis, John Brown, and Emerson, probably had the most influence on Thoreau; he carried *Leaves* around for weeks, saying it had done him more good than any other reading for a long time. He and two others met Whitman in New York; the meeting was short, but Thoreau remarked that Whitman was a great fellow who spoke more truth than any other American, no doubt in his passion for sensuous and spiritual freedom.

Despite my practice of letting go, I hope to have a Whitman-like influence on students. My advice has long been to not label yourself, especially liberal or conservative or any political persuasion; be free by practicing logos, take issues one by one, and then see what happens. Create your own list, I say, and transform yourself into a great poem, having "the richest fluency not only in its words but in the silent lines of its lips and face and between the lashes of your eyes and in every motion and joint of your body."

In the meantime, I soldier on.

Late in my Purdue adjunct career, an agriculture major, castigating Rachel Carson, gave a speech on the benefits of pesticides. His facts seemed accurate—increased food production and lower prices in a hungry world—although he did not mention that regenerative agriculture, which builds soil and draws down carbon, has not been broadly implemented, and regenerative benefits defy calculation: interdependency, resiliency within specific places, and the ability to respond to change. Also, during the Q&A I asked if reduced costs came at a human and environmental cost, and if the distribution of food, rather than the amount, was a root problem. I also stated, matter-of-factly and with a smile, that if Carson could hear his speech she would be spinning in her grave, as my bias says that Carson is a logos-wielding eco-hero.

I later looked over his citations, which were one-sided even though I had required a diversity of sources. Researching diverse sources is an internet-easy fix, but evaluating the quality of sources has become increasingly difficult. Seemingly sound attacks on Carson, another speaking out exemplar discussed in class, are readily available online, and thus I am not sure if I should blame my student for what he did not know.

When I googled James Hansen's 1989 testimony before Congress, the first link was not a transcript of the testimony but a blog by a global warming denialist claiming that Hansen spun the facts to get funding for NASA and line his pockets. I often tell students that they need a bullshit detector that recognizes logical fallacies to counter our lostness and re-find the compass, and this claim is false equivalency bullshit: We live in moneyed economy where people get paid for doing both good work and being merchants of doubt, yet there is obviously a world of difference between working for the common good and working for your own good, or corporate good, or the good of an ideology. While the easy appeal to authority is a logical fallacy, Hansen has impressive credentials and data on his side.

Such unpacking can be a lot for students to wade through, but Orwellian illogic and obfuscation are only partly to blame; Postman argues that Huxleyian distraction is often worse. In *Brave New World*, citizens are not manipulated by Big Brother but sedated by the pacifying drug "soma" and other amusements, willfully giving up freedom to habits of overconsumption and endless entertainment. For Postman, the problem, as he presciently saw it in 1985, is not the banning of books or information, but that no one would want to read a book, happily lost in a sea of irrelevant information in the age of television, or, fast-forwarding, a visually arresting, always available social media age of click-bait, carried wherever we go via cell phones.

Orwell or Huxley, pick your poison; both dystopian visions are available, if you hurry to buy, buy, buy.

Thoreau argued that we should not "underrate the value of a fact," as "it will one day flower into a truth." For blossoming to happen, we must not only be a scientist, but a scientist-poet like him, midwifing truths through sympathy with intelligence, an act he equated with Native wisdom learned from living and listening within intersubjective nature. His science was infused with wonder and morality, so he was particularly critical of Samuel George Morton, a physician and scientist of his time who

245

filled the skulls of Indigenous peoples with lead shot in a terrible attempt to quantify intelligence and promote racist theories. Thoreau wrote, "Of all the ways invented to come at a knowledge of a living man, this seems to me the worst…There is nothing out of which the spirit has more completely departed, and in which it has left fewer significant traces."

Thoreau thought that the gulf between science and spirituality may be bridged, so good science, as wonderful as it is, is not enough. New technologies, even when they serve sustainability, are also not enough. Once calculation becomes our dominant epistemology, our value system is off, and we accept what we should not accept. Buber wrote that some degree of I-It relationship is inevitable—we are not perfect and the earth supplies resources—but what would it be like to live in an I-Thou dominant world, a world where love—eros, agape, philia—was not a platitude but lived reality?

There is so much for students to consider, so much to fight for, if they step out of the cave and perceive the dystopian spin machine.

Thoreau's vision at the end of *Walden*, in which he implores readers to "go confidently in the direction of your dreams," was once co-opted by a Merrill Lynch commercial imploring consumers to buy into financial systems and a materialist dream. And his phrase in "Civil Disobedience" that "government is best which governs least" is often championed by libertarians. It's more out-of-context logical fallacy spin, this time in the form of an invalid analogy: Less government when government upholds slavery is one thing; it does not follow that Thoreau would argue for least government in the age of climate disruption when the so-called free market threatens all that he loved. If Thoreau was alive during Carson's time, or today, one can imagine what spinmeisters would say about his continual call for simple living, or speaking out against tyrannical government or any tyranny that degrades true liberty. And one can imagine his response, that government is best that protects the commons, the ecosystem upon which we all depend, as there is no freedom without acknowledging that we all live downstream.

Such logical fallacies often lead to irony: In Oreskes and Conway's *The Collapse of Western Civilization: A View from the Future*, a science-fiction essay based in current fact, antiregulation right wingers who delay a governmental response to climate crisis pave the way to the inevitable: a huge expansion of government as the crisis is not addressed and continues to worsen. But internet trolls, immune to irony, continually attack good science and logic and Oreskes, who does not enjoy being a lightning rod, but states, "the whole purpose of a lightning rod is to keep people safe."

My bullshit detector is informed not only by logical fallacies and pursuit of what is scientifically true but also by ongoing and endless pursuit of the good and beautiful. At the end of the "Divinity School Address," Emerson made this challenge: "I look for the new Teacher" who "shall show that the Ought, that Duty, is one thing with Science, with Beauty, and with Joy." Emerson goes big here, in tone and with his capitals to emphasize the universal resonance of pursuing the true but within the larger context of the good and beautiful.

To Thoreau, we are slaves of institutions when we surrender our "unalienable rights of reason and conscience," and we are most free when embracing wildness, especially when sauntering in the woods. To saunter is to intentionally lose the world of our personal worries, returning to our place within nature and finding that the depths of conscience emerge from apprehension of divine unity. Sauntering is spiritual, then, because we often need to lose ourselves to find ourselves embedded within a wider world, and radical because such finding engenders responsibility, the call to listen beyond the human and act.

Carson, while not espousing transcendentalist spirituality, does marry her science to the pursuit of the good and beautiful via experience of wonder. After all, DDT silences the spring voices of songbirds. Definitely and defiantly a voice of conscience, she was the most acclaimed science writer of her time before dying in 1964 from cancer.

Most of my students have also never heard of Carson, yet her influence in the fifties, sixties, and beyond was substantial. Three of her books on the sea were bestsellers prior to the publication of *Silent Spring*, and her writings serialized in the *New Yorker* helped her reach a broad audience. She challenged biases against trusting a woman scientist and financially supported herself, her mother, her sister and her two children, and an adopted grandnephew by working for the government as an aquatic biologist and editor. She carved out time to write in evenings and some weekends.

Carson, who kept a copy of *Walden* at her bedside, had plans for four more books, and, further anticipating the Anthropocene, was increasingly interested in atmospheric science and climate. Despite serious illness and family responsibilities, her daemon was operative until the end.

While recovering from radiation treatment and in pain, she gave her last speech, "The Pollution of our Environment," for a symposium of medical experts because she was committed to educating a potentially influential audience about the dangers of pollution in all its forms, from pesticide runoff to nuclear waste. She ended her speech stating, "I look forward to the day when we, also, can accept the facts of our true relationship to our environment. I believe that only in that atmosphere of intellectual freedom can we solve the problems before us now."

Carson knew that when intellectual freedom and pursuit of truth are under attack, so too are the good and beautiful. Thus, in the social media age of spin, and an age in which we don't vote on what corporations do to the planet when they serve profits over living beings, students especially need mentors to guide them along the middle path of facts and conscience, logic and logos, matter and spirit, becoming less lost and thus better arbiters of what it means to be free. If we look for someone to trust in the process of trusting ourselves, our heart vibrating to that "iron string," it wouldn't hurt to ask, What would Thoreau, or Whitman, or Carson do?

Or Anthony Burns. After he was returned to his "master" due to the Fugitive Slave Act, he was bought and brought back to Massachusetts by a Boston abolitionist and then educated at Oberlin College in Ohio. The astounding fact that Burns made it to college is worth sharing with students, who often take their education for granted. Burns went on to become a Baptist minister serving escaped slaves in Canada. He found his voice and changed the world.

Or Brister Freeman, a Concord slave I knew little about until I read Elise Lemire's *Black Walden*. Concord is revered as a birthplace of freedom due to minutemen who faced down the British, yet from its beginnings in 1635, it was a slave town, built on the backs of slaves who did the hardest work. Lemire writes that the percentage of slaves did not exceed 2–3 percent, yet the White town majority supported the institution until the 1800s.

Freeman, who died five years after Thoreau was born, was largely forgotten, yet Thoreau writes in *Walden* of his later life, after he was enlisted in the war by his "master." He then enlisted himself, taking the name "Freeman." But, after the war and as a free man, his only option for a place to live with his wife was near Walden Pond since it was the worst land for growing crops. In the section "Former Inhabitants and Winter Visitors," Thoreau honors Freeman and the other slaves who lived near the pond before him. Freeman fought for his right to own land, knowing that ownership gave him other rights, including the ability to bequeath his property to others.

Or John Lewis, a descendant of slaves born into a Georgia sharecropping family in 1940. Lewis marched with Martin Luther King and later became a congressperson known for conscience and continuing to fight for civil rights; he was arrested forty-five times in acts of civil disobedience, or what he called "good trouble." Or Greta Thunberg and youthful Sunshine Movement activists, who understand what too many adults in power do not: that I-It instrumental rationality and lucrative standard economics are killing the planet and thus killing the freedoms of future generations. Or anyone who has lived or is living a more encompassing logos, listening to inner genius and genius of place.

And then risk the same for yourself.

The climate stakes are high—BP spent a hundred million on PR to "contain" the 2010 Deepwater Horizon Gulf of Mexico oil spill—and much depends on whether students, the next generation of activists, are ready to turn the boat over. The Icemakers were right about at least one thing: revolution is needed.

The epigram to *Disruption* is from Frederick Douglass: "Power concedes nothing without a demand. It never has and it never will."

"What will you do?" I ask students.

Or a better question: "What gets in the way?"

CB

Silence. They look bored.

It's early April, the worst time of the spring semester. One month to go and everyone is a bit worn out, including me. It's been a long semester—are fifteen weeks of class too much? Most students are doing well; others are behind in their work, in counseling, disappearing.

While we've covered inspirational examples of social change, we've also covered several heroic figures who paid the ultimate price for freedom: Gandhi, King, and Romero, all assassinated because of their ethical response to violence. Malcolm X, whose more virulent call for freedom made the public more receptive to King's nonviolence—also killed. And we cover the Haitian radio broadcaster Jean Dominique, who spoke out against the Haitian dictator Jean-Claude Duvalier, nicknamed "Baby Doc." Dominique—inspirational, but shot and killed by an assassin. All of this is a downer when you are trying to wake students up to be active with the activists.

I stare at blank faces.

"What do you want?" I finally ask.

One student asks what I mean.

"What do you want most here at the college?"

Now I've done it. I've unintentionally unleashed complaints, a staple at every college I have been to. At Rutgers University, students complained about bureaucracy and not getting into classes, calling it the "RU Screw."

"I want hot water," says a student who has barely peeped all semester, "our dorm sometimes runs out of hot water."

I try to look sympathetic while imagining a hundred students waking up and taking thirty-minute hot showers, as if their tuition gives them the right to ignore social and ecological constraints.

But they are just getting started.

"I'm sick of getting parking tickets from Campus Safety. I'm not going to park a mile from my dorm. I paid for my parking decal, and I should be able to park where I want."

I continue to try to look sympathetic, but I'm saddened by the resistance to walking and the general entitlement. At some colleges first-year students are not even allowed to have cars.

"The food at Gilmore has no right being called food, and they are not even open past seven."

Ah, food complaints. Another staple at every college I have been to and often an *ad populum* logical fallacy with perception and taste buds shaped by snowballing opinion. I eat at the dining hall and always enjoy my meal.

"So, you don't like the food," I finally say, "but you want access to more of it after seven."

The class laughs but I'm riled up.

"You need to stop complaining, and stop texting, and get off your asses and do something!"

Another student, a thoughtful senior I've had in other classes, speaks. "Everyone loves the small classes and professors here, but small-town life in Henniker can be boring. We want more of a social life."

"What, specifically, would you want if you could have it?"

"All we want is some good music and a place to dance," she says.

"Doesn't the Student Entertainment Committee bring bands to campus?"

"No one likes the bands they bring. We just want a good DJ at the campus pub."

"What's stopping you from getting it? I'm sick of students complaining about there being nothing to do. This is a beautiful place to study—that's the number one reason why you are here—and there are events all the time, and you could get out of your rooms and explore the natural surroundings, but I understand that you also want more of a social life. What's stopping you?"

Students are talking now. Both to me and in little conversations. All are eager to share their version of a good time. An idea is thrown out to have an event with bands playing outdoors. Soon it grows into bands and DJs and cookout and water slides and dunk tank and tie-dye T-shirts and live artists and raft-building contest for the river and beer tent and a freedom of speech tent where students can vent concerns and hopefully begin to organize to alleviate inevitable campus problems. The vent tent, we'll call it.

And the name of the event? After much brainstorming: Pilgrim Palooza, named after our sometimes criticized school nickname.

I offer extra credit to those who want to work on putting it together, and for the rest of the semester, we start class with updates from students on what still needs to be done and who is doing what. A student, not me, stands in front of the class and organizes. I sit in the back, happier than I have been all semester. It's not world-transforming activism; other professors are doing service learning in the community and taking students on study-away trips, but they are changing their world. It's a start. At least they are learning that they can do things.

The last two weeks approach, which I've saved for "Speaking Out" speeches. Students are instructed to deliver a short, three- to four-minute speech on what pisses them off. Passion is expected—I want them to let loose, speaking on something of substance they feel needs to be said and heard—but I emphasize that they should also practice logos and ethos. You have freedom of speech, I say, time to use it.

I am taking a big risk here. Who knows what they will say? A senior and the main student organizer of Pilgrim Palooza offers to go first.

She walks to the front of the class, looking pissed, and begins detailing her summer job in a Maine mill, a mill filled with kind but also sexist men. Anger rises as she talks of verbal abuse, which she dismisses with "no one is going to put me down or tell me what I am." The speech ends up being a Whitman-like song of herself, of her pluck at the mill, but also of accomplishments on the women's field hockey team, which reached the playoffs every year she was involved.

Her voice is powerful and eye contact intense. No fear.

The tone has been set.

Another student railing against taxes says that if corporations can get away with paying no taxes, then she will be damned if she is going pay.

A male student passionately argues against abortion. Most female students look alarmed, and he softens a bit but argues that he knows too many girls who have treated abortion as a form of birth control. His passion returns as he concludes, "It's just wrong."

Another student, a cross hanging around his neck, defends the Catholic Church. His voice cracks as he admits priestly sins, but then he argues, pleadingly, that the church has consistently worked for the public good in areas of education and social justice. As editor-in-chief of the school newspaper, he also rails against the person or persons who have put the most recent edition in the trash due to a controversial article criticizing Student Senate. He vows to check security tape.

An atheist takes on religion, mostly the fundamentalist variety, and provides excellent arguments from that position, happily confident that stating what pisses him off will piss others off. I am happy to add his voice to the mix. Some students challenge him, but all appreciate his boldness, with one stating, "You've got balls." We all cracked up.

252

Two students tell stories, with plenty of venom, of being unfairly harassed and arrested by the police. One gets so agitated that he just stops his speech, throws his hands up, and sits down while shaking his head. Another student, whose father is a police officer, defends the good work of law enforcement, which leads to robust discussion.

A nontraditional student gives a lengthy but engaging speech on numerous things that piss him off—he's lived longer, so he has a longer list—including drivers who don't stop for pedestrians and the income gap between rich and poor, which, he soulfully states, is hurting too many people, wherever you are on the political spectrum.

A student from New York City shares her experiences growing up with a single mom while watching gentrification ravage her neighborhood, making it impossible for many longtime residents to remain due to high costs. She speaks with plenty of passion but also logos and ethos, imploring fellow classmates to imagine what it is like to lose your home.

A political science major chastises fellow students for so often stating that they don't like politics and reminds us that politics influences everything, including who we get to marry, the roads we drive on, and if we go to war. He implored classmates to educate themselves, get involved, and vote.

A student who told me she might be too nervous to speak energetically criticizes spoiled students who drive around campus with expensive cars bought by their parents while she must work to buy and maintain a beat-up used car.

A soft-spoken student, who is shaking and admits he is incredibly nervous, speaks from his heart about his beloved uncle who died from smoking. He emotionally asks for everyone to think about his uncle before getting addicted. He receives big applause from his classmates for the content but also in support of his courage.

And another student who has not spoken much all semester does a speech inspired by her general education class (titled No Oceans, No Us) on climate change, coral reefs, and ocean acidification. She champions her hero of speaking out, Sylvia Earle, whose Mission Blue organization fights for "Hope Spots," or vital ocean ecosystems that need protection.

Not all can get into the spirit of the assignment. One student calls me out for assigning books that can't be sold back to the bookstore. I joke that they should save all books and handouts from class, put them in a box with my name on it, and then, after they graduate, periodically take them out, reread them, and think of me fondly. Another complains that tanning salons are too expensive, making it hard to keep her year-round tan. But during several speeches we laugh or are moved until tears form in the corner of our eyes.

Pilgrim Palooza goes off, with lots of hitches, on the last day of the semester before exams. Some bands and DJs don't show up, so students gladly improvise by playing their own music over the speakers. The beer tent and raft building don't happen—not enough time to get the proper approval for the beer, and the water is too cold for rafting—but the T-shirts and water slide are popular. The dunk tank, which is frigid, is especially popular when a good-natured member of Campus Safety awaits his fate on the platform.

Palooza was scheduled for six hours, and we had good attendance until two-thirds of the way through when a speed-metal band started to play and drove some away. My students hung out for the final hours, and then cleaned up, exhausted but smiling.

⅓

I love speaking out students and organizing students and activist students, especially since our epistemology has shifted again in the digital age; not only do I not know who my students are, I don't know who any of us are. Our destiny is still being written, for good and ill.

I have a better sense of what we are losing in our "improved means to unimproved ends" digital world. Emails and texts and Snapchats are handy but have largely replaced handwritten letters and Thoreauvian journaling, speeding things up at the cost of reflection, artful writing, and intrapersonal intelligence generally. The nineteenth century was an age of conversation supported by clubs, salons, front porches, parlors, and table talk. Today, unmediated interpersonal contact wanes, even when we're in the same room, and thus so does skill. There is no more telling image of how attention has shifted, or been captured, colonized, and siloed, than students sitting together in social settings on campus but lost in their isolated phone worlds. Solitude has also taken a hit as we respond to app notifications like Pavlovian dogs; as solitude goes, so does silence and still-ness, our daily life filled with busyness and distraction at the expense of moments of timelessness.

What we are losing is life lived deliberately, which is to say a life where we pay attention to the more-than-human communicative world, communing with and listening to everything.

For Thoreau, reading nature puts us on the right track whether as spiritual searchers, scientists, or activists. As he wrote in an 1857 journal entry, observing a field mouse's tracks in the snow, so delicate that "they suggest an airy lightness in the body that impressed them," makes us more literate, more refined, more deliberative in our thinking. He continues, "So it was so many years before Gutenberg invented printing with his types, and so it will be so many thousands of years after his types are forgotten, perchance."

Of course, along with the necessity of reading nature, there are nu-merous upsides to the invention of print media. Thoreau even designed an innovative machine to finely grind plumbago for pencils, which was then used for mass print technology, directly benefitting him in the form of affordable books, both for reading and his own writings. And there are also upsides to digital communication, including working from home, less time in cars, and potentially more time for sauntering and listening and learning, assuming we don't use that extra time interacting with a device after endless Zoom meetings. Who has time for sauntering, which stimu-lates re-finding the compass, is one question; even more concerning is Who, especially among the young, desires it, recognizing the importance of timelessness to soulful sanity?

Postman, following Marshall McLuhan, argues that the medium re-mains the message, and thus how we get our information influences us more than the information itself; or rather, both the means and ends may be unimproved. This is a difficult question to get students to consider since they are thoroughly seduced by the technology as savior but also the tech-nology as neutral narrative, with them in complete control of how their "pretty tools" are used. Postman alerted us to danger: people adore tech-nologies that distract and inhibit their ability to think. After all, Huxleyian citizens thought they were free, so they were more easily controlled.

The future is daunting, yet we make it far more daunting when we are unable, or unwilling, to have logos-based dialogue on technological dominance and epistemological shifts, or scientific consensus on what we have lost, are currently losing, and likely to further lose. Or, as David Orr puts it, "most everything will be negatively affected by higher temperatures: Ecologies collapse, forests burn, metals expand, concrete runways buckle, rivers dry up, cooling towers fail, and people curse, kill, and terrorize more easily."

Given our climate crisis and culture wars, we desperately need liberal arts education to advocate for genuine freedom: free *quality* speech, press, and protest, a free society marked by the freedom to fulfill potential, materially and spiritually, and free inquiry into our collective lostness that prevents us from realizing that potential.

Whether climate crisis brings out our best or worst is another key question of our time and thus a key question for education: how students respond in classroom speech is both training for and a precursor to the difficult conversations foisted upon their generation. They will need bullshit detectors and the ability to reach basic agreements about the wicked problems we face. When climate refugees seek higher ground, we will need to respond by dwelling within the higher ground of the true, good, and beautiful, where disagreements still emerge but listening is possible and thus collective action is possible.

Employers like smart people, I tell students, but along with being prepared for the world of work, they are being prepared for the messy and challenging and engaging world, a disrupted and fragmented world, and an increasingly tamed world in need of their offerings.

Students are most assuredly lost, yet despite techno-addictions and despondency due to untrustworthy powers-that-be and being overwhelmed by heroic acts they feel they can't match and questions of what they want and will do, some are finding freedom by transcending myopic high school and college selves. Some are becoming media savvy and politically and ecologically literate, discovering how to think critically within an earth context. Some are reading the books and essays they are asked to read, frolicking within the pages, learning to become jazzed by learning.

Some are becoming, bit by bit and class by class, engaged citizens who are enlarging their identities while dipping toes in various forms of spiritual exploration. Some are trusting themselves and their process of individuation while remaining open to mystery.

Some are transcending cynicism, learning to do, to act, despite their despair and the despair of the world. Or rather, some feel addressed by the despair of others and are ready to answer.

And one of the students who looked like he was texting in class said he was researching Daniel Ellsberg.

Hmm.

Chapter 15

Calling Forth the Future

"The fact that I am here certainly shows me that the soul had a need of an organ here. Shall I not assume the post?"
—Ralph Waldo Emerson

"What is the use of a house if you haven't got a tolerable planet to put it on?"
—Henry David Thoreau

"I used to think the top environmental problems facing the world were global warming, environmental degradation and eco-system collapse, and that we scientists could fix those problems with enough science. But I was wrong. The real problem is not those three items, but greed, selfishness and apathy. And for that we need a spiritual and cultural transformation."
—Gus Speth, Dean of Forestry at Yale, speaking
to a group of religious leaders

In 1999, when I applied to graduate school at the University of Montana, I expected to be accepted. I was thirty-nine, with lots of nontraditional learning experiences that can't be put on a vitae, but also plenty of vitae-worthy accomplishments: teaching at Purdue for seven years; speaking on spirituality and environmental ethics for student and community groups; academic papers delivered at Ometeca conferences in Mexico, Costa Rica, Venezuela, and the US; work as an editor for the *Ometeca* journal; and two essays published in the journal and one in an anthology on Rafael's theory of sciencepoetry.

I also finally had a book published, *The Path of My Soul: Journey to the Center of Self*, a cheesy title, to be sure, but the small, Goldsmithian press wanted "soul" in the title, as *Chicken Soup* books were bestsellers. The title was accurate, though; I wrote in the introduction of an epiphany when I realized my career would be the path of soul. The book is mostly spiritual reflections taken from my journals—years of journal writing bore unexpected fruit—placed in three sections in which the inner unfolded into the outer: solitude, relationship, and the world.

I imagined myself sitting next to Oprah, doling out spiritual wisdom, a bestseller, a book tour. *Why not?* I thought. The author of books like *Don't Sweat the Small Stuff* was on *Oprah*, sharing obvious advice.

It sold five hundred copies, mostly to family and friends. I once again took stock of my life.

I wrote a published book and so accomplished a life goal, but hardly anyone bought it. I had found a calling to teach and taught my Com 114 class fifty times but lost my enthusiasm for the course. I had lived the divine life, lived simply and joyfully, but still had no savings. I decided it was time to leave Purdue one morning on my two mile walk to campus—along Main Street past the Brew Pub and court house, across the bridge and murky Wabash River, past McDonald's and undergraduate bars—my energy draining with each step. My habit body had led me to walk the same path too many times.

But then I wasn't accepted to the University of Montana; they placed me instead on a waiting list. I was visiting with Rafael when I heard the news, and he casually commented that maybe it was a sign, a message from larger forces; maybe I was not destined to go to graduate school right now. I recoiled. I had visited the University of Montana in the summertime four years earlier, finding the river, the mountains, and an Environmental Studies department with an activist and writing emphasis. If I ever decided to try school again, I had found the right place.

"A message my ass," I thought to myself. "Outer signs are relevant when they match inner signs, or because of what they stimulate within. That's the path of soul."

I was ready for a change. I rationally and intuitively felt I had found the right graduate program. I wasn't going to passively accept their decision or wait for the good graces of an academic committee; I was going to create, not reality—too mysterious, too unknowable—but a path informed by a sense of destiny, or what I felt called to do.

Emerson argued that engaging a path of character and calling activates spiritual law, in which what we need for growth is attracted to us, but the road is often bumpy. It is easy to get caught up looking for outer signs and messages, when the message is always to turn within, to intuitions and interrogating intuitions, and then to take next steps, knowing that the process of individuation continues. Still, those steps may be informed by the mystery of synchronicities. Jung wrote that coincidences are thinkable as pure chance, but the greater their number and correspondence, the more they become meaningful arrangements between psyche and world operating outside of causal logic and linear time. The body functions when we are not aware of it, and so does the world soul and collective unconscious, expressing a timeless sympathy among all things.

A timeless sympathy and the possibility of synchronicities, however, do not mean that everything happens for a predetermined reason—it happened, so it had to happen—like many of my students believe. "Everything happens for a reason" is their most common statement of truth, of how they think the world works, but this claim neglects the fact that we make choices. There is a world of difference between choosing rigid belief—whether religious or scientific or "everything happens for a reason"—and remaining open to mystery by exploring multiple responses to the world and particular circumstance. Sure, reasons and lessons can be drawn from everything that happens—I am happy that students have figured that out—but there is quite a difference between passing the salt at the dinner table and Martin Luther King responding to world-historical events. Even if one has a sense of destiny as strong as King's, everything does not happen for a reason. Although forces and circumstance may coalesce, he knew he may not get to the promised land.

We must remember the lessons of chaos.

Emerson argued for spiritual laws and a circular correspondence among events, but also emphasized that the universe is fluid and volatile, stating that only when people are unsettled is there any hope for them.

Thoreau argued for simple living and sympathy with intelligence guided by principle and conscience but also recognized the darkness and primitive power of nature, and that what is most wild is most free.

Bateson argued for the recognition of order and pattern as well as the role of randomness in evolution. Novelty and creativity demand disruption.

Volatility, wild freedom, and randomness temper the desire for the cosmos to offer us gifts via pleasing synchronicities. The path of soul may be guided by meaningful coincidence, but it is also stimulated by more grounded fates, like being pushed into new terrain when challenged by others, or by losing the world such that we once again find it and ourselves anew.

Black Elk, the Oglala Sioux holy man, had a world-shattering dream in the Badlands at age nine, which seemed to speak of ancient wisdom. Where did it come from? How should it be interpreted?

To be found, we need to be awake to larger forces, within and without, but we also need to question larger forces, remaining open to learning and new possibilities and new life paths. Wise discernment is a learned skill, and based on that skill we often must fight for what is right for us.

I sent an email to the department chairperson citing academic accomplishments, asking if accepted students had taught college, or published essays and a book. It worked; I was immediately accepted although now it was too late to receive a teaching assistantship. I was going to have to go into debt, something I had vowed to avoid, equating loans with loss of freedom.

The chairperson stated that I wasn't initially accepted because they didn't have anyone on faculty suited to be my adviser, as I had proposed a thesis titled "An Ecology of Love," exploring agape, eros, and philia in relation to eco-spiritual ethics. I should have known better than to propose that thesis: even progressive academic programs often don't know what to do with spiritually-minded students.

∞

I arrived in Missoula for graduate school in early August and was greeted by regional forest fires that caused intense debates about human expansion and the role of fire. In mid-August, a Hell's Angels gathering led to a riot between police and citizens protesting the excessive police presence used to contain the Angels. In late August, I attended the Festival of the Book, an annual event celebrating writers, writing, and place. My apartment was a two-mile walk to campus along the Clark Fork River, a clean river thanks to the Clark Fork Coalition, a nonprofit group founded and led by a former Environmental Studies student.

Home.

I whispered to the river that I was never leaving.

Still, the semester began awkwardly; it was strange sitting in a desk rather than leading the class, especially since I was the oldest student in the program, older than some of my professors. Yet fellow students, mostly in their mid-twenties, treated me like a friend, especially in our frequent visits to the Old Post Pub. Age didn't matter; what mattered was that most were in the program because they were called to make a difference in the world.

By November I was more comfortable being a student. I even had "Happy Birthday" sung to me in two afternoon classes on my fortieth, and then again at night by the band and crowd at the pub. My classmates enjoyed celebrating my advanced age, and I wasn't going to stop the party.

Turning forty can stimulate reflection on the wasted years of a materialistic lifestyle, resulting in a mid-life crisis and search for spiritual meaning. Instead, I, again, took stock—student loan debt, no life partner, no house, no job, plenty of spiritual meaning, and still happy. But my mood shifted in December when I prepared to write three final papers for my classes. The last time I was faced with writing for a grade was fifteen years earlier during my breakdown in the park. And, unbelievably, my body *still* remembered as resistance and anxiety resurfaced. I had given grades for the last seven years; how could I be so childish and pathetic?

I told a friend of my resistance to performing for grades, and she suggested counseling for what must be an unexamined traumatic school experience troubling my unconscious. I had doubts about this interpretation but made an appointment at the university health center and requested a counselor with spiritual interests. I soon met Kerry, a counselor who was also a practicing Buddhist and former nontraditional student. She concentrated on getting me through the last weeks of the semester, leaving questions about trauma and repression for calmer days. I was grateful to have an empathetic person to talk with, especially since I had spent most of the last decade being the one people talked to, being the "spiritual guy" at Purdue, always available for conversations and advice.

My anxiety subsided, I wrote the papers, and Kerry and I began the lengthier process of exploring my history with school and grading. We soon realized that instead of repressing a single traumatic event, my entire educational life was filled with traumas big and small, from trying to escape

262

second grade by running home at recess, to high school and college follies, to being forced to give the waste-of-time Com 114 final exam at Purdue, to my current resistance. My anxiety was not childish; rather, it was a natural reaction against being treated like a child. Or, I wondered, a reaction from my daemon. Kerry worked with students damaged by academia all the time, uncovering evidence for what should be termed "educational abuse" and thus support for grading being relegated to the prehistory of education. Like canings in Thoreau's day, grading should be refused in the pursuit of the true, good, and beautiful.

Can any academic imagine Socrates giving grades? Or any genuine spiritual teacher? It's one thing to have rigor and discipline; performing for a carrot while being threatened with a stick is quite another.

Our focus turned toward my spiritual life outside of school. I thought I had already dealt with the mistakes of my search, especially a tendency for detachment, but wondered if I had developed a self-image that restricted my life choices. I laughed at my lack of possessions and rejoiced in my contemplative life, but when I was honest, I desired a home, meaningful work, and lasting relationship. My most recent relationship ended in tears after two years. We cried together because we loved each other, yet still felt we hadn't found the right person. We cried because we were accepting that we would be friends instead of lovers. We cried because we now had to keep looking.

We pored through the particulars of our break-up, including the issue of spirituality. I once complained that she was not spiritual enough, and she countered that I was not human enough.

Ouch.

During my crisis at Rutgers at age twenty-five, and the contemplation of suicide, I was heartened by Albert Camus's claim that realizing we cannot live in this world is of no great moment; what matters is where we go from there. I also first read "The Myth of Sisyphus" at Rutgers, in which Camus imagined Sisyphus happy despite his meaningless toil of pushing a rock up a hill and affirmed the human ability to determine our own fate. We can say yes to life despite the absurd nature of existence and certain death. Rebellion against meaninglessness gives life meaning, so suicide is not an ethical option. For Camus, struggle toward the heights is worthwhile. But as I got older, met Rafael, and experienced toil at the factory and printshop, I sought to live, move, and have my being in the heights, consistently and with strength. Camus's vision of humanity was too limiting and all too human.

Camus's existential response to life denies our nothingness via a self-image that embraces absurdity, struggle, and rebellion. My initial spiritual response was to embrace our nothingness, our emptiness of self-image, in pursuit of enlightenment. But now with Kerry I was exploring whether I was being led by a spiritual self-image rather than choosing and creating a full life. Was my quest for spiritual enlightenment partially an ego-driven desire to be better than everyone else, or to have power over others? Was it a way of protecting myself from being hurt in school, relationships, and daily life, and thus simply another form of armoring? In some ways, was I still the huge crier from my childhood, fearful of a harsh world? Had my spiritual search been an overreaction to being over-sensitive?

Kerry praised my willingness to examine my life choices honestly. It wasn't easy to do so. Even though my meditation practice had made me spiritually happy and mostly fulfilled, sitting in a classroom at age forty, with no relationship, money, or home, once again made me wonder if I had made mistakes. When I had mucked around in childhood memories with Rafael, I was looking for signs of a daemon, but now I was looking for roots of problems, probably once again over-interpreting, foisting regrets. A bit much, I thought after some sessions. But counseling, another part of my education, was needed.

Another reason why I came?

Or rather, we give reasons for everything that happens. Counseling, which happened only after being willing to leave Purdue and being put in challenging situations, provided especially rich lessons.

In one session I laughed with the realization that I was going through a "reverse" mid-life crisis. I had sought spiritual meaning, and found it, but perhaps I had done so at the expense of the material. I sometimes warned students about mid-life crises. I suggested that they may want to find their passion in life now rather than suffer later, waking up in mid-life in an age of climate crisis with too many kids, too many polluting SUVs, and too little meaning. I never would have thought that I'd wake up in midlife to therapy, exploring concerns over too much meaning and too little cash. Kerry simply said that she had one wish for me: that I allow myself to be vulnerable.

Was vulnerability the key to a more enlightened life? To a deeper acceptance, stillness, and love, living everything that comes our way?

My self-questioning was aided by a philosophy of ecology seminar that, to my deep pleasure, was focused on Thoreau. The professor was rigorous, willing to learn from students, and open to spirituality. She was also passionate about *Walden* and led the class in a thorough reading of Thoreau's work and life. I had not returned to Thoreau in years, other than quick reminders of quotations, like when I dressed up as Thoreau for the favorite-dead-radical party back in Indiana. This was my first time reading *Walden* critically with others in an academic setting.

I was enthralled, like I had been thirteen years earlier in Maine. Many in the class shared my enthusiasm, but a few thought little of Thoreau's caustic remarks concerning industrialization and fellow citizens. They were especially critical when they learned that his Walden cabin was a mere two miles from Concord, and that he sometimes made visits home to his parents' house for meals. Thoreau was suddenly a phony, dependent on others rather than living deep in the woods and practicing true self-reliance.

One member of class, a local high school English teacher, was particularly dismissive, arguing that the mass of men led productive lives rather than lives of quiet desperation, and that Thoreau was merely an angry slacker. I was dumbfounded and disturbed that this man might be teaching *Walden* to students. I imagined sitting in his classroom as a teenager, finally engaged with a text that stirred my heart, and then having my teacher stomp on it. I suggested that he was making a gross misreading by failing to appreciate the honest humanity and critical humor of Thoreau, as well as the spiritual vision that perceived, with prescience and conscience, the transformation of the planet at the hands of the industrial machine.

Thoreau was also no slacker. He read and wrote voluminous amounts and worked numerous jobs while defending simple living. It seemed to me that the high school teacher, who probably did not live simply or pursue the divine life, was defensive and preferred to attack the myth of Thoreau rather than engage the relevance of his ideas and actions. But I had another reason for defending him. I was defending myself. During our study, I discovered a startling similarity between our lives.

We both learned plenty from but were critical of formal schooling, learned more from a spiritual mentor, and heeded a call to teach and write.

We both worked on a journal with our mentor (the *Dial* for him, *Ometeca* for me), lived at times with our mentor, worked with our family (his father's pencil business and teaching with John, the factory with my father and my brother's printshop), discovered a deep sense of place in nature, particularly by water (Lake Vanare at my parent's house for me), and experienced solitude by living in a tiny house (the Caboose in Indiana for me).

We both have transcendentalist world views, experimented with consciousness and perception, had life transforming eco-religious experiences in Maine, had difficulty getting published but eventually published books based on our journals, chose inner riches over financial wealth, and worked a variety of jobs to make a basic living. We both are activist by nature but doing little activism other than teaching, writing, speaking, and making spiritual life choices counter to the materialist mainstream.

We also both went through spiritual crises and dark nights during our early to mid-twenties. For Thoreau, it was losing out on Ellen, his first love, not finding initial success as a writer, and his brother John's death. For me, it was losing out on my first love, deadening work in a factory, and struggling to find purpose—or some semblance of who I was and what I had to offer—before and after graduation from Rutgers.

At age twenty-eight, after intense learning with our mentors, Thoreau was building a cabin at Walden Pond, and I was walking the Appalachian Trail, both finding ourselves in the right places, at the right times, emerging from dark nights ready for more growth and next steps in pursuit of the divine life.

Oh, and I also once considered work as a surveyor after an aptitude test listed it as the job for which I was best suited, due to math skills and desire to be outside rather than in an office, which sounded like death to my young self.

Sure, there are a few differences. Thoreau's writings have a major influence on the environmental movement and the course of human thought and action while I was hoping to find a teaching job that paid more than twelve thousand dollars a year and published a book read by a mere five hundred. Of course, Thoreau ended up having to buy back most of the copies of his first book. So, the comparisons amused. They also seemed apt, recharging my commitments.

Most importantly, I became acquainted with Thoreau the human being, who accidentally set fire to the woods by trying to cook a meal in an old tree stump, causing townsfolk to call him "woods burner" for years afterward; who danced and sang songs, cared for children, loved swimming, boating, and ice skating, explored the night and night sky, played often with kittens, and played his flute in the parlor for family and friends but also on the river for fishes; who wrote often of love and beauty as keys to knowing more, and, despite caustic comments on the masses, stated that a "lover of Nature is preeminently a lover of man"; and who experienced double consciousness, aware that mystical moments and devotion to higher laws is mixed with frequent mundaneness, yet we are inspired to express what is real in our ideals and actions.

I also became acquainted with Thoreau the lost, who didn't always fit in with classmates and had a youthful identity crisis; who struggled with unrequited love after his marriage proposal to Ellen was rejected, leading him to write in his journal, "There is no remedy to love but to love more," yet he did not ever find romantic love; who had a long search for vocation, filling him with self-doubt, before landing at Walden Pond; who was so distraught at John's early death that he contracted a sympathetic case of lockjaw for two days and stopped writing in his journal for five weeks; who was turned down for numerous teaching jobs and had *A Week on the Concord and Merrimack* rejected by publishers and mocked by reviewers when it was published; and who suffered symptoms of tuberculosis as early as 1841 and lived with it for twenty years.

Counseling helped me to confront my humanness, and therefore my lostness—I will always be grateful to Kerry, who is following her calling as a counselor. I realized that by coming to Montana I was already making practical life changes to teach again, to find a career in a calling, hopefully teaching classes on Emerson and Thoreau someday. Despite the foolishness of gambling away paychecks and so much other folly, I had made no mistakes in my past worthy of lasting regrets because I had consistently reflected on my choices, true to who I was at that moment. I also had not laid waste my powers by getting and spending, choosing material possessions over vibrant living and learning.

In the "Economy" section of *Walden*, Thoreau wrote, "The cost of a thing is the amount of what I will call life which is required to be exchanged for it, immediately or in the long run," which is often paraphrased as "The price of anything is the amount of life you exchange for it." This Thoreauvian dictum flips the lucrative standard on its head, embracing the spiritual first and foremost, but also the material in the form of the actual earth. Yet, as we both knew well, economy and exchange remains.

Midlife concerns also suddenly seemed quaint in comparison to Thoreau's death from tuberculosis at the age of forty-four. *Walden* had been published eight years earlier but with little acclaim. In the last months before his death, a new edition of *Walden* was proposed; he was finally becoming known as a significant writer.

When he was sick at home, an outpouring of care from townsfolk softened him, and he had some regret for his "oafishness." His very being had often challenged others; his presence was a call to which most could not (or did not want to) respond. But while interpersonal intelligence was not always his strength, he went from town oddity to respected voice, and displayed kinship with outcasts, willing to converse with and learn from most everyone—children, farmers, wood choppers, shopkeepers, Natives, Irish railroad workers, hunters, fishermen, former slaves—and, always, with the outdoors, expressing biophilia with woodland animals and plant life.

Thoreau was endlessly curious and well versed in many fields of knowledge and actual fields, the physical earth; he had so much yet to offer. In his last few years, he continued to advocate for the Concord commons, for both preservation and mixed use, or what we would call ecology integrity. His whole life was a response to expanding techno-industrial capitalism and many losses to the commons generally, with his anger stoked by the loss of huckleberry fields to private property. He turned his anger into writings and resistance and regenerative solutions, and he advocated for appropriate technologies and public parks. In his bedridden last days, a neighbor, presenting his park proposal to the Concord Farmers' Club, created first steps that others would follow to today's protected land and water.

Laura Dassow Walls writes that his anger at what had been lost led him to be committed to the cultural commons; he spoke for and organized the Lyceum, spoke at town meetings, and supported public schools and the library. He was also committed to the political commons, fighting for conscience as the engine of democracy and for making ourselves a counter-friction if necessary.

Despite his illness, he also continued to work on his Kalendar project mapping the seasons. He needed the help of his friends Ellery Channing and Horace Mann, who brought him specimens and continued his practice of measuring the height of the Concord River. With the help of his sister, Sophia, he revised numerous essays, including "The Allegash and East Branch" section of *The Maine Woods*, which he had delayed returning to out of concern about Joe Polis's reaction to his account of their time together. *The Maine Woods* was not published until 1864, after death, while Polis was fighting for the Union, where he lost an arm.

The scholar Kristen Case argues that Thoreau's illness challenges the myth of him as rugged individualist; rather, this myth, to the degree that it was true, needs to be balanced by the Thoreau who was lost and vulnerable, having lived for so many years with symptoms of tuberculosis. Thoreau was most assuredly a hearty outdoorsman, but, in his last year, he was too weak to hold a quill pen without help from friends and family. It was this vulnerability, along with spiritual experiences, that led him to embrace the infinite extent of our relations, including those living lives of quiet desperation. For Case, such vulnerability leads to empathy and an ethic of care, which then leads to resistance and the fight for justice. Civil disobedience does not merely come from "masculinist stoicism" but from solidarity with others who are also lost and searching.

Thoreau the vulnerable is not how we typically think of him, but it should be along with numerous other interpretations of his complex and full but sadly short life. Death is the ultimate teacher because it is the ultimate vulnerability, and at the end, he did not seem to fear it. His sister wrote of his "childlike trust...as if he were being translated rather than dying in the ordinary way of most mortals." Preferring not to have his senses dulled, Thoreau refused pain-relieving opiates, and when a well-wisher at his bedside inquired "how the opposite shore may appear to you," he responded, "One world at a time."

The Concord church filled for his memorial, and three hundred children followed his coffin to the town graveyard; Sophia Hawthorne, Nathaniel's wife, said there went "Concord in one man." His grave was later moved to "Author's Ridge" to be placed with Emerson, the Alcotts, and the Hawthornes.

Even to Emerson, he sometimes seemed to lack ambition. Their friendship, marked by tenderness, would sometimes return to criticism. When Emerson returned from a trip and did not contact him, Thoreau felt rebuffed. But Thoreau soon found out Emerson was ill, which made him worry about his death and vow to never doubt their bond. When Emerson recovered, they once again walked together, challenging and enjoying each other. He knew that Thoreau, whose deepest purpose was to live well, had a different kind of ambition and that no one stayed truer to themselves.

Emerson wrote that wisdom is "living the greatest number of good hours"; by that measure, few, if any, were as consistently wise as Thoreau. Bronson Alcott once called Thoreau "The independent of independents...indeed, the sole signer of the Declaration of Independence, and a Revolution in himself." Emerson, in his eulogy, said, "The country knows not yet, or in the least part, how great a son it has lost."

Emerson often visited Thoreau at his bedside and continued to promote and read him after his death. In reading Thoreau's journals, Emerson stated that he found a voice stronger than his own: "He has muscle, and ventures on and performs feats which I am forced to decline." Many years later, when Concord townsfolk wanted to name a street after Emerson, he convinced them to name it "Thoreau" instead. At age seventy-five, with failing memory, he asked Lidian, "What was the name of my best friend?" "Henry Thoreau," she replied. "Oh, yes," he repeated, "Henry Thoreau."

Before death, Thoreau planted four hundred pines on the site of his Walden Pond bean-field.

On his deathbed, his Aunt Louisa asked him if he had made peace with God. "I did not know that we had ever quarreled," he replied.

His last words were reported by his friend Ellery Channing to be "Moose" and "Indian," but his sister, who was at his bedside, reported that he said, "Now comes good sailing."

Thoreau did not want to find at the end of his life that he had not lived. Neither do I. And neither should my students.

୧୨

Thoreau's time on this planet provides many lessons but especially this one: out of our lostness arises new possibilities, new responsibilities, new actions and realities, and endless learning and growth.

A lesson on auto-repeat.

I am pretty grounded these days, at age sixty-three, despite being divorced with three kids in the age of climate crisis. Yep, the bottom dropped out again. When I first met my wife, she laughed because my possessions mostly amounted to twenty-six boxes of books, but she looked askance when I mentioned my qualities were like Thoreau's. Wise woman. Louisa May Alcott, who revered both Emerson and Thoreau, wrote that he was married to "swallow and aster, lake and pine." And Thoreau, a bit smitten after taking a long walk with a young woman and nature lover who also resolved to live free, reminded himself, "All nature is my bride."

My beautiful, now ex-wife and our struggles taught me much. Relationship as teacher: I discovered, and continue to discover, that despite being more grounded, I still have much to learn about myself and being a worthy partner, especially to someone whose worth and intelligence are beyond compare.

When we first separated, crisis was just pain—no learning—but with vulnerability thrust upon me, and impermanence, always the reality, all I could do, when pain finally ebbed, was listen, learn, and let go. Moving out was the hardest thing I have ever done, but I found a secluded small house only a couple miles from my ex and the kids, and the amenities of town, up a hill and surrounded by woods with trails out back. It's rustic, to say the least—I will be fixing it up for years—but I'm grateful for being close to family, and for thirteen years of good and hard times, of learning from being in and of the world.

My ex-wife is a longtime nonprofit activist, including for Greenpeace. She scaled a building to hang a banner, worked on the *Rainbow Warrior*, the ship used in campaigns against whaling and the dumping of nuclear waste, and has been in jail—the only place for a just woman in an unjust, nature-destroying society. No wonder I fell in love, and still love her intellect, heart, and current activism managing the local farmers market and co-parenting children with grace. All that matters now is working together to take care of our kids, who will hopefully take after their mother. Oh, and I will have teenagers throughout my sixties, Spirit willing. Talk about a cosmic surprise, which I am happily playing out.

I ended up teaching at New England College for twenty years, climbing the ladder thanks to a third master's degree, a "terminal" MFA in creative writing. My whisper to the Clark Fork River didn't end up being true, but I got to teach close to the Contoocook and I live near the Connecticut.

Sometimes I wonder if I was destined to teach and learn near rivers.

I teach Thoreau in three courses I designed—Senior Seminar, The Voice of Nature, and Finding Your Voice, Changing the World—although not all students are as enthralled as I upon first reading *Walden*. I advise them to read for the quotations that leap off the page like verdant jewels. Of course, students take their own steps, just as I did in my own stumbling education, and they receive what they are ready to receive while marching to their particular drummer.

Over time, I have taught *Walden* less and "Walking" more, Thoreau's last essay before his death. "Walking" explores the art of sauntering, which, along with being spiritual and radical, is a healing tonic. Thoreau, his humor caustic yet often missed, remarked that he was surprised that fellow townsfolk who busied themselves with business, forgetting what their legs are for, had not committed suicide long ago.

In The Voice of Nature, we go for a walk on wooded trails near the Contoocook River, as sanity depends on such daily practices (not lengthy wilderness excursions, despite their lessons). Assignments include writing a reflection paper on a weeklong spiritual practice, whether walking meditation, contemplative prayer, turning off social media, or eating lower on the food chain, and a nature narrative, in which students tell a personal story of connection to nature, in whatever form it takes. A student from Boston wrote of his tiny patch of green that made up his front yard, where he would just sit. He protected it by continually cleaning up the refuse from passersby. A student from New York City wrote about coming to New England College and seeing the stars for the first time, and feeling lost, in the good sense of being overwhelmed and inspired to re-find the compass.

I also have students write a field note, in which they are asked to research a species after finding a spot in nature that speaks to them, and then just sit and listen to the unique song of a nonhuman other via close observation, awakened senses, feelings, imagination, and intuition. Such songs speak of the wildness that remains, and, in listening, something precious is preserved: worldly material relations but also soul and world soul.

Finding Your Voice, Changing the World is part of our liberal arts general education requirement, or opportunity, as I call it, to take a seminar on the natural world and what it means to be human. It's mostly for first-year students and is listed in the schedule of courses with shortened, caveman syntax: "Find Voice, Change World." Students find a place on campus for solitude and write a "my own personal Walden" reflection paper, and give several speaking out speeches on topics such as what they love and how they would change the world.

The first time I taught the course, students participated in robust conversation; the second time, it was hard to get them to talk. Was it them? Was it me? The challenges of teaching never end, including the challenges of teaching *Walden*. Only a few really get into the text; some complain it is too hard to decipher and makes them feel stupid. I admit that *Walden* can be a slog for new readers, given his many references to books and happenings of his time. But I also state that struggling with texts is part of college and will lead them to improve their reading and thinking skills. For many first year students, putting effort into reading, unless bribed with a grade, does not appeal.

Perhaps, with thinkers like Thoreau, you need to teach to the few, challenging those who are ready and taking what you can get from the rest, knowing that his call to "simplify, simplify, simplify" will cause cognitive dissonance among those socialized by bigger, better, and more. Or maybe they are just busy with school, extracurricular activities, jobs, and personal struggles, like I was as an undergraduate.

Or perhaps I need to follow Rebecca Kneale Gould's lead, who has begun to teach sections of *Walden* alongside his abolitionist writings and current texts by Black authors such as J. Drew Lanham. Gould's course is more inclusive while opening the door to dynamic discussion on Thoreau's privilege, his political commitments, and the way he speaks to current environmental racism.

Another possibility: perhaps student brains have been so addled by addiction to social media that they don't have the attention span required for deep and difficult reading.

Thom Hartmann, the author and progressive radio host, argues that ADD and ADHD, or just the difficulty for an ever-larger percentage of youth to focus, is not the problem we think it is. When our long, brain-developing history as hunter-gatherers changed with the shift to agriculture, life became less novel, more predictable. Fast-forward to industrial times and industrial education, and student brains, which still need stimulation, are deadened by rote learning. No wonder many students don't want to read, especially a difficult and challenging text such as *Walden*—it's too much effort, too boring—as their brains are still wired for stimulation. I get it, but I am not completely buying it.

We need the ecstasy of nature, as Thoreau modeled, but, as he also modeled, reading and contemplation stimulate our inner lives and conjure the daemonic. There is also the ecstasy, or collective energy, of sharing insights with others in a classroom setting, whether indoors or outdoors. But to share, you need to do some work and come to class with an offering, a gift. I ask for that gift, appealing to conscience, trying to draw forth devotion to their highest good. I also tell students that if they having trouble focusing, then get off social media and get outside. Research shows that techno-addictions exacerbate ADD. Research also shows that nature, while less wild, stimulates soft fascination, or wonder, peace, and focus.

Our hunter-gatherer brains and needs are thankfully still with us but too often ignored by education. Still, a pastoral sense of place rather than a nomadic existence and the reflective, critical thought inspired by books also provide stimulation. Reading, for Emerson, was a spiritual practice that inspired self-culture, and Thoreau wrote a section of *Walden* on reading in which he argued that it was a noble exercise, elevating mind and spirit, and that we need to exercise, training like an athlete. Neither read just to read, or to pass a test, but for spiritual insights they could live.

I explain all this to students, asking them to read for those jewels, or the "lusters," as Emerson called them, finding moments of insight that speak to them. With encouragement and direction, they do, but, sadly, reading for tests and grades has robbed many of the joy of the printed word. It would help considerably if they were seekers on a spiritual path and not only sloggers on a lucrative standard job path; their eyes would be on the lookout for lusters without any external promptings.

Or perhaps it's me: sometimes I feel like I have lost some of the spiritual clarity and energy I had while living in New Mexico with Rafael; that I am too in and of the world and have less presence in front of the class—too much will, not enough grace. I strive to integrate the spiritual and the material in the present moment but fail. Other times, laughing at the absurdity of human striving, I let go and some magic happens, with unplanned insights coming from not just me, or students, but collective intelligence, as if we have tapped into something larger. I am assuming that questioning and struggle and moments of magic will continue.

The education researcher Angela Duckworth has studied why students do well in school, stating that it is not IQ or social circumstance but grit defined as passion and perseverance. An interesting finding, but researchers can't figure out why most students lack grit. I respect the research, but it makes me laugh, as if students' lack of passion and perseverance is a mystery, as if industrial education's false rewards and disregard for inner life is not a problem, as if techno-industrial capitalist–planned obsolescence rewards of material stuff is not a problem, as if the anthropocentric narratives of bigger, better, and more, sold to the young by incessant advertising, with their unfulfilling rewards, is not a problem.

Why persevere to fit into a screwed-up world of ecocrisis, neo-Nazis, and inept and untrustworthy politicians, among numerous other dysfunctions? Many students are misfits and struggle in school with little passion for obvious reasons: to the degree they retain soulful predilections, outer rewards often seem empty of meaning, or they have simply been socialized out of their souls. Much needs to change if more students are to demonstrate grit, find their voice, and change the world. A good place to start is within specific places. If they are rooted to the natural world and local culture—embracing their Concord—they'll have a place to stand and something to fight for.

Thoreau, if read closely and carefully, offers guidance that students need, and he offers a pedagogy of listening for educators.

In *Walden*, Thoreau wrote, "There are a thousand hacking at the branches of evil to one who is hacking at the roots," which can be linked to his response to Emerson's assertion that Harvard taught all branches of knowledge: "Yes, indeed, all of the branches and none of the roots." It may be a stretch to compare the failure to hack at the roots of evil with the failure to teach the roots of knowledge, or it may not. Evil does not just mean behaving badly, but a moral badness, or, to use Thoreau's language, life without principle or conscience. The question, then, is whether compartmentalized education can create principled students of conscience, and if not, how might we hack at the roots of such education and increase our capacity to listen to and respond to the evils of our time, including, of course, the specter of climate emergency.

In *Seeing New Worlds: Henry David Thoreau and Nineteenth-Century Natural Science*, Laura Dassow Walls writes that the scientific method was established and institutionalized during Thoreau's lifetime, but the sciences and humanities were not yet fully divorced into differing cultures. The divorce decried by C. P. Snow would eventually emerge—specialization led to astonishing discoveries and techno-industrial productivity—but the unity of disciplines exploring the unity of cosmos and earth was increasingly lost.

That loss of unity is a root cause for why we are so lost, and why evil, as moral badness, is structured into so many of our institutions.

The tradition of the liberal arts college, with a mission of creating deeply educated, whole human beings, is supposed to be the solution. But, as Thoreau argued, the Harvard of his time did not participate in this mission, and the Harvard of today does not fully participate either, nor does any market-model university, although Harvard and other universities have divested from funding fossil fuels, largely due to many years of student voices rising in protest. Now that is an example of wholeness and grit. And there are many examples of universities and colleges responding to climate crisis, whether in programs, courses, infrastructure, science and data collection, or technological innovation, but a hard truth remains: industrial civilization supported by industrial education is grounded in extraction and extinction, or even more bluntly, destruction and death.

Thoreau wrote in his journal, "How important is a constant intercourse with nature and the contemplation of natural phenomenon to the preservation of Moral & intellectual health. The discipline of the schools or of business—can never impart such serenity to the mind." This criticism demands that we ask: What would a deep education look like, addressing the questions of our time, and thus the evils of our time that inhibit our ability to answer and act?

For Thoreau, the roots of knowledge, or a more complete knowing within the context of our not-knowing, emerges from listening inwardly and outwardly and living in sympathy with intelligence. To begin, we must "simplify." We must practice listening when walking, or sauntering, and contemplate the voice and voices of nature; when stimulated by logos within the context of world soul, welcoming paradox and contradiction as fuel for critical thinking; when engaged in the science of the naturalist, integrating the poetic imagination with close observation; and when in dialogue with others, following Emerson's advice: "Let me never fall into the vulgar mistake of dreaming that I am persecuted whenever I am contradicted."

All these listening practices support self-culture, or cultivation of the soul, and we begin wherever we are. When he was a mere twenty-one, his schoolteacher sister Helen asked for his advice on student reading and writing in philosophy, and he responded: "Set one up in a window, to note what passes in the street...or let her gaze in the fire, or into a corner where there is a spider's web, and philosophize, moralize, theorize, or whatnot. What their hands find to putter about, or their minds to think about, that let them write about." Young Thoreau had plenty more to learn himself, but his rootedness in both Spirit and Concord led him to claim that the seeds of "heroic ardor" within emerge when stirred with the soil without, inspiring "voice or pen, to bear fruit of a divine flavor."

If I had my way, colleges and universities would practice a pedagogy of listening by creating experiential, transdisciplinary courses on the rivers that flow near campuses. The history of the Contoocook, for example, could be explored, along with its economics (there used to be logging mills along its banks; what, I wonder, is there now and why?). And the ecology of the river (what is the water quality?) and the politics of cleaning it up or keeping it clean. And the literature of rivers, and writing inspired by rivers (students could create field notes, poems, stories). And its botany, the trees and plant life, and their ecopsychological gifts to the psyche and power to evoke philosophical reflection.

And the theological, the spiritual, call of the river.

I imagine Purdue students exploring the history and present of the

Wabash River. What would it say? So much connection to place. So much learning connected to the actual world.

I have long ago lost touch with Purdue connections, but a quick internet scan shows the school has made a commitment to sustainability, like most universities. There's an Engineers for a Sustainable World club and Student Farm club, and Wabash Riverfest activities, including conservation exhibits from numerous river activist groups. However, I also found a student newspaper article stating that while the Wabash is cleaner than it has been in many years, sewage still flows into the river when it rains, and swimming and fishing remain strongly discouraged due to pathogens such as E. coli.

At New England College, which keeps chugging along thanks to successful online graduate programs, fundraising for new buildings, and that mentoring heartbeat, we have River Day when classes are canceled and there's outdoor play and study of the river (I wish there was more); a Sustainability Task Force made up of a small group of professors, staff, and students working on sustainability solutions; and a sustainability major as part of Environmental Studies. A new general education liberal arts seminar exploring our bioregion is also offered in some summers, The Power of Place, team taught by several professors from different disciplines, the arts to the sciences.

This is mostly good news, but "sustainability" has become a catch-all word, spun to support status quo systems rather than signaling radical structural change. I also don't think this good news is due to fully overcoming the Cartesian rift between mind and nature; more likely it's a rational, enlightened self-interest response—what we do to the land, water, and air, we do to ourselves. The emphasis on sustainability is a key step because it reflects an awareness of connections. More steps are needed, beyond Cartesian bias by perceiving shared cosmos, shared planet, shared DNA as well as shared sentience, shared breath, shared stories, and shared communicative systems to which we must attend via deep listening.

છ

A major reason for studying the transcendentalists is that they lived through and confronted problems emerging from the shift from agrarian-ism to industrialization, or the beginning of the Anthropocene, the age of humans and their machines putting the screws to the planet. Thoreau, la-menting the failure of education to go to the roots of knowledge, also wit-nessed the roots of today's crises.

All came together in his sorrow: an increasingly debased nature and loss of the commons, slavery, mistreatment and murder of Indians, the fur industry and trafficking of animal pelts and parts, townsfolk cutting down woodlots for train fuel and railroad ties at the same time sparks from trains set fire to the woods, and the Bellerica Dam changing whole ecosystems that sustain wild fish. "How do you expect the birds to sing when their groves are cut down?" he asked. Or "Who hears the fishes when they cry?" These are questions of animal sentience that might seem sentimental and anthropomorphic but are increasingly confirmed by current research.

Thoreau, as always, saw what others did not see, yet Thoreau the sci-entist and engineer was fascinated by machinery, taking tours of factories, including a locomotive factory, wanting to explore every part, wishing he could make one himself, and remarking that such learning should be part of education. He was also fascinated by the telegraph, but for his own rea-sons: he once witnessed the wind playing the wires, turning it into a giant Aeolian harp. Messages sent by telegraph paled in comparison to the vi-brating sound, which reminded him of higher communications. There were no bounds to his attentiveness and desire to learn.

Emerson also praised invention and machinery because they showed the potential of the human mind and displayed hope and progress. The train also served him well since he was a traveling lyceum speaker. Humans and their machines could be a thing of wonder; they both saw possibility, but this marriage was destructive. Thoreau would question whether we ride on trains or if trains ride upon us, and Emerson feared that the mech-anization of man outpaces the humanization of the machine.

The need for scientific advancement was clear to both men; after all, average life expectancy in the mid-1800s was approximately forty years due to factors such as infant mortality and tuberculosis. But despite supposed advancements—traveling, grinding, weaving, forging, planting, tilling, along with "new shoes, gloves, glasses, and gimlets" and making "every square acre of land give an account of itself at your breakfast table," as

Emerson put it—they also perceived that we were still in crisis, still lost, because of unquenchable thirst for new technologies.

Prescient, those two.

Near the end of his life, Thoreau surveyed twenty-two miles of the Concord River. He was trying to figure out the effect of a dam used to power a Lowell textile mill on flooding, which threatened fertilized farm-land. Farmers had called on Thoreau, the only one from town who could take on such a grand task. He studied the river as a human-natural system, reading it using math talents along with his talent for close observation, data coming alive, but the problem turned out to be more complex than a dam. Farmers were at fault for the loss of wetlands and denuded hillsides, and the more the plains flooded, the more they cut down hillsides, making it worse, changing the Concord landscape. Thoreau did not figure it all out but saw the damage, leading to his forceful arguments for public parks and land that would become part of his legacy.

Of course, I-It attitudes were not confined to war on the natural world. As Thoreau's health worsened in 1861, Confederate troops fired on Fort Sumter in South Carolina, and Union soldiers surrendered less than thirty-six hours later. In 1862, the year of his death, starved Dakota Sioux living on a Minnesota reservation didn't receive promised aid from the government and killed five White settlers. The ensuing conflict left many dead, and the governor vowed to exterminate or drive Natives out of the state. Treaties, which were already not being honored, were nullified, and thirty-eight Dakota Sioux were killed in a mass hanging, the largest in US history. Chief Little Crow fled west and was killed by a White set-tler while picking berries with his son. His head and arms were displayed at the Minnesota Historical Society until 1971.

That this history is so little known is no surprise given other little-known history: During Thoreau's lifetime, the US government began tak-ing Native American children from their tribal communities, forcing them into Indian boarding schools. The children, forbidden to speak their In-digenous languages, had their names changed and their hair cut. The main curriculum? Erasing the children's cultural identity and traditional ecolog-ical knowledge (TEK), which we now need in response to climate crisis. The devastating irony here is immense: forcible re-education created eco-social problems and suppressed solutions. Such "teaching" went on for more than 150 years. Each school also had a graveyard for burying kids who died from abuse and disease. The number of dead is still being tallied.

There is still more irony, as is often the case when utterly lost: Indigenous peoples removed from their land and cultural traditions are now facing removal again as climate refugees. Daniel R. Wildcat writes that while Indigenous peoples are least responsible for "global burning," they are most vulnerable to its effects, especially those living in Arctic regions, the Great Lakes region, and the Southwest US. Alaskan Natives, for example, are already having their land and lifeways drastically affected by melting ice. Those lifeways—like stories, ceremonies, rituals, behaviors, and actions that perceive nature first and foremost as relationships rather than resources—reflect the place and community-based education we desperately need.

As Thoreau surmised, Indigenous peoples have much to teach about long-term sustainability because they have humility to listen to the land and learn through trial and error. They also provided warnings long before current scientists, such as Hopi prophecies about what happens when we in our arrogance fail to listen: life out of balance.

The human family has so much yet to learn. So much growth awaits.

In March 2024, atmospheric CO_2 peaked at 425 ppm, 75 ppm over 350 ppm (the "safe" threshold), 50 percent higher than preindustrial levels, and higher than any time in the last 3.6 million years. That number doesn't include other greenhouse gases such as methane, which is also rising.

In terms of traditional ecological knowledge, what do the numbers indicate? How about a world governed by separation rather than interbeing and dead rather than alive, inspirited matter; a world governed by the loss of love as a larger force and thus a lack of love for place and others, including other-than-humans; and, more irony, a world governed too much by numbers even as we need to learn from them. We are too stuck in our heads when we need to reside in our hearts, or, as Rafael taught, to be truly educated we must filter our heads through our hearts because the heart is where different modes of thinking and experiencing come together to create whole human beings.

TEK also reveals that ecocrisis is not just about heartless half-humans treating nature solely as a standing reserve to serve our rapacious wants, but also about the social effects of that avarice. In *Collapse*, the anthropologist Jared Diamond details that long history, with numerous earlier cultures paying the price for assuming resources are inexhaustible. In Thoreau's time, the example of Brister Freeman and other formerly enslaved people link the social and ecological; the Walden woods are a Black heritage site, or, as Elise Lemire puts it, "the history of slavery and its aftermath reveals that at least some of our nation's cherished green spaces began as black spaces." Many townsfolk feared the Walden woods for that reason; Thoreau, who did not flee racism like Freeman but instead capitalist stupidity and other forms of conformity, felt at home amid land that held former outcasts.

Today, climate disruption is the most wicked eco-social challenge because we have lost the Holocene, the 10,000-year period of climate stability. We are currently approaching 1.5 degrees Celsius above preindustrial temperatures with no realistic end, and no return, in sight. Even if we stopped emitting greenhouse gases immediately we are likely committed to decades of heating. We are not close to stopping, and so rising waters will not stop, nor will refugees fleeing coastal areas and flooded cities, which may lead to more violence and perhaps wars over resources. The loss of biodiversity, the very fabric that weaves together the possibilities of life, will accelerate. In Australia in 2020, an estimated three billion animals were killed or displaced during out-of-control bushfires across an estimated fifty million acres of land. What are we to do with such numbers, which glaze over the mind because they are too incomprehensible, too overwhelming? Those living in the mostly poor and Black neighborhoods in New Orleans during Hurricane Katrina know the ecological and social are not separate; some residents were forced to rooftops, others to the Super Dome, the first time most had been inside due to high ticket prices.

Gregory Bateson, like many early ecological thinkers, made dire predictions concerning the future. In 1967 he estimated that within ten to thirty years ecosystem instability would reach major proportions; he cited the risks of the population explosion, nuclear warfare, and the increased concentration of carbon dioxide in the atmosphere. That we are still here despite the Exxon Valdez and BP oil spills, the Bhopal chemical spill, the Chernobyl and Fukushima nuclear disasters, and on and on, does not lessen the worth of his vision. His championing of systems thinking anticipated the challenges we face, including climate crisis. Precise prediction is impossible, but endless expansion and extraction have made societal collapse, broadly defined by Diamond as drastic decline in population and complexity, more and more likely. Despite new technologies that aid sustainability, this is our reality because technology as savior, intertwined with faith in linear progress and unlimited growth, keep us from embracing TEK and Thoreauvian, voluntary, "less is more" simplicity lifeways.

Mark Z. Jacobson, a professor of civil and environmental engineering and director of the atmosphere/energy program at Stanford University, argues that current wind, water, and solar technology could solve climate crisis if we just had the political will. In other words, technology can save us, and he and his team have plans for countries and cities that can do so. Jacobson is one of the best and brightest that the university has to offer. His heart is in the right place, and he provides hope, but as he well knows, the lack of political will is not a minor problem. It's the roadblock that has stopped climate action for decades. The faith that technology, all by itself, can save us is another roadblock since it leads us to believe that we are not lost, that we don't need to change systems or ourselves. This belief is not only self-deception but also death for many humans and many, many nonhumans.

Renewable energy holds promise as part of a solution, but global economic activity still runs on fossil fuels. Fossil fuels are necessary to mine the ores and metals needed to produce wind turbines and solar panels, and we have reached peak oil, and are approaching peak everything, including ores and metals. New technologies are on the way to make mining less destructive and to reuse existing metals—that is, with faith, the planet, and the lucrative standard, may be saved if we can just get the tech right—but throw in the basic math of exponentials along with tipping points, and systems, both ecological and human, can go downhill quickly.

Collapse would mean severe contraction and powering down. Bateson argues we have a "snowball's chance in hell" of avoiding bleak possibilities unless we address a root cause of ecocrisis: we are living a mistaken epistemology, and mistaken narratives, that we learned and continue to learn in school.

Just like individual crisis leads to growth, our collective lostness is pushing us to search and evolve. There is the argument that collective crisis is leading to a positive tipping point: a great awakening in which the baseline awareness of a significant portion of humanity rises to a higher level of soulful connections, with world citizens consciously immersed within the larger intelligence of the world soul.

In *Dark Night, Early Dawn*, Christopher M. Bache, a professor of religion, ruminates that our sense of separateness, or "species-ego," has been breaking down for some time due to numerous factors, including the fight for rights brought to the fore during Thoreau's time and played out via numerous grassroots movements; quantum theory challenging the Newtonian world view; and a global economy producing unprecedented global communications systems. That's right, to Bache, TV, the internet, and social media have aided the breakdown of the isolated ego, and isolation generally, and contributed to more global thinking. Perhaps my students intuitively know the potential of the global mind, of thinking together in a grand social media classroom. If so, this potential needs focus from deep reading and time in nature. Otherwise, our wired world degrades into students, and citizens, isolated in their rooms sending selfies, watching porn, and distracted from the actual world, leading to more, rather than less, separateness.

Still, for Bache, these factors, along with ecocrisis, are pushing us to have a "dark night of the species-soul," as techno-industrial capitalist structures are not sustainable. Something must give. Our individual dark nights, while painful and often lengthy, lead to transformation, to an awakening of a new sense of identity and new awareness; our collective dark night may do the same.

We are feeling the heat, internally and externally.

Bache argues that the internal goes deep into the collective unconscious where our suffering but also new realizations are held, as if stirred in a caldron, ready to bubble up into the lives of those prepared for new learning from confronting external challenges to psyche and planet. He then focuses on individual transformation as a catalyst for collective evolution, or, as Jung put it: "Does the individual know that he (or she) is that makeweight that tips the scales?"

In a sense, this is the enlightened guru argument, in which the consciousness of one shines a path for the many, except that many have the potential for and are already actualizing a more enlightened awareness. Whether this awareness also streams into the collective unconscious, making new realizations available to everyone (but especially those ready to listen to and be re-formed by the fire of soul) is open to debate. From the perspective of a great awakening, however, a leap in consciousness has been gestating on multiple levels for some time—conscious, unconscious, collective unconscious, as well as transcendent dimensions—and running through them all is eros or Spirit unfolding, regardless of whether we have been aware.

Better to be aware or to consider the possibility. Ken Wilber, in *The Religion of Tomorrow*, plays out this possibility, writing that, based on research and historical example, a 10 percent change in consciousness among the collective population leads to significant material change. But this change does not happen through magic, or magical thinking, but from new forms of thinking becoming dominant, like ecological thinking, systems thinking, and meditative thinking in sympathy with larger intelligence. Colleges and universities can be on the forefront of this shift; rather, this they must do. Exploring relational forms of thinking intertwined with principled actions must be core to both their mission and structure to assure that mission statements don't become empty ideals.

In Thoreau's time, with enlightenment rationality becoming the leading edge of consciousness, and crises like slavery stirring our souls, values like freedom, rights, and equality emerged as a force for change, taking us to the modern world. In the 1960s, the fight for civil rights, women's rights, and clean air, water, and soil stirred the soul, and enlightenment rationality evolved to include postmodern pluralistic values. As diverse voices were being heard and diverse movements were being formed, dominant narratives were deconstructed, including magical thinking and fundamentalist religious views. According to Wilber, our next developmental stage is characterized by integrating modern science with postmodern pluralism. That next developmental stage would integrate techno-logic with logos (marked by I-Thou science and global care and concern), insights from our hunter-gatherer past, and wisdom traditions that point toward evolving spiritual principles that have universal resonance. In other words, transcending the worst aspects and including the best aspects of a variety of views may lead to a new vantage point: The first time in human history in which a significant percentage of people perceive and integrate partial truths, leading to more depth of consciousness and less deep-seated conflict.

Picture this: a common humanity on a common home, guided by non-mythic-magic forms of spirituality that honor all sentient beings, that implements rational and regenerative solutions to eco-social problems—solutions that are already available and which go well beyond switching to renewable energy.

Sounds good, and sounds like the transcendentalists were pushing the leading edge of consciousness back in the mid-1800s. Of course, there is the argument that crisis is pushing us to evolve gradually, in fits and starts, with some meandering yet learning in steps. There is also a third argument: We are being pushed to awaken, but after the collapse of civilization as we know it. Only a whopper of a crisis will wake us up, making us vulnerable enough to listen and act, and climate disruption will oblige, with downward spiral tipping points building upon each other: melting ice releasing trapped CO_2 and methane, the carbon storage capacity of the Amazon lost to clear-cutting and fire, and the weakening of ocean currents that keep temperatures more mild. The cumulative result will be the heating of, well, everything.

◌

Great awakening, steps, collapse, or a complex combination of all three: We explore these possibilities in class, but, most importantly, I share with students that there is no shortage of world citizens participating in the great work of our time. Whether they would like join is the core question of my teaching, and liberal arts pedagogy generally.

Thomas Berry argued that we have moved from "suicide to homicide to genocide to ecocide to geocide"—a depressing assessment for students to consider—and the psychotherapist Gary Greenberg writes that long-term grief, which has been codified as a mental disorder by the American Psychiatric Association, has its roots in too many crises and too little done in response, thanks to culture-wars politics. When Congress does respond with monetary relief, the programs are often saddled with graft. As a result, more and more people feel lost, including Trump supporters who long for the so-called "great" America they grew up in, where you didn't need advanced technical knowledge to fix things and talked to your neighbor rather than texting. Tragically, that longing is often intertwined with fundamentalist religion, I-It attitudes toward marginalized others, and climate denialism, which only makes us more lost.

For Greenberg, living in community is the best response to our grief while Berry states that we are fortunate to live at a crucial moment when we can consciously celebrate the community of life and life force, listening inwardly and outwardly, playing a creative role in the evolutionary epic. The timeline, after all, is a history of lost humans learning what they need to learn. Our lostness has brought us right here, right now, to the breath of Spirit, to the newness of fresh revelations.

Humans crossed a line long ago, and we have paid and will continue to pay a stiff price for our arrogance. Still, a growing awareness of our roles in the earth and universe story could lead us to avert full collapse, a softer landing afterward, or, someday, a flourishing Anthropocene although most likely with far fewer souls. We face this tragic opportunity with every fraction of a degree of warming. Whatever happens, the questions of our time beckon us to find the compass together, and such great work demands rational and imaginative and spiritual inquiry in support of a pedagogy of listening.

In *Biomimicry*, Jeanine Benyus argues that we should mimic nature's intelligence, or rather, nature as model, measure, and mentor. Nature as model leads to science and technology that takes inspiration from natural designs, such as a solar cell inspired by a leaf. Nature as measure causes us to ask whether new innovations are well adapted for the flourishing of life. Nature as mentor changes our primary relationship with the earth from a storehouse of resources to a source of learning. There are many benefits from this tripartite—changing how we make materials, store information, harness energy, heal ourselves, conduct business, and grow food—and all begin with perceiving and listening to nature's patterns.

In *The Nature of Design*, David Orr argues that everything will need to be redesigned with the earth in mind. Ecological design is a listening challenge, as well as opportunity. Design principles must be propagated skillfully, but once they are put into place in buildings, transportation, landscaping, and infrastructure generally, they will speak to us. The natural

287

world communicates but so do our created environments, and working with this understanding is especially important in populous cities. If the majority of world citizens are not exposed to places that elicit deep listening and make us feel connected or alive or peaceful, we must question if we are living lives of quiet desperation.

In *What We Think about When We Try Not to Think about Global Warming*, a book I have studied with students, Per Espen Stoknes, a psychologist, economist, and entrepreneur who integrates science with the humanities, asks that we re-imagine climate as living air, and "a grand subject, to which we are subjected." We exist within the air like fish immersed in water, yet, because it is invisible, except when we experience it as floating clouds or sunsets or wind, we take it for granted. We spew the byproducts of industrial life into what gives us life. The air is historically and rightly correlated with breath and spirit. It overflows with information of beauty and pattern and voices that should make us think twice before despoiling it. And it overflows with information of disruption and chaos and symptoms that convey messages of what happens when we do despoil it. But, most often, we fail to listen.

In *Braiding Sweetgrass* and her many essays, Robin Wall Kimmerer, an enrolled member of the Citizen Potawatomi Nation and professor of environmental biology, argues that scientific ecological knowledge, or SEK, must learn from TEK, with everyone learning from plants. Plants are the oldest teachers, making "food and medicine out of light and air," uniting "earth and sky" and healing the land, and exemplifying "the virtues of generosity, providing us with all that we need to live." Plants give and give, providing inspiration for a gift economy marked by reciprocity among all our kin, yet students can identify corporate logos more than plant species. Education, if we are humble enough to listen, may focus on regaining lost practical knowledge held by the plants themselves.

For Kimmerer, mosses may hold the most compelling lessons during the climate crisis because they were the first species to green the earth. They have endured, covering our mistakes at Chernobyl and old, rusted, useless cars manufactured in Detroit, which polluted the air even when functioning. Mosses make minimal demands and provide maximum gifts: They build soil, purify water, store carbon. Creative, adaptive, and resilient through periods of extinction, they signal that small is beautiful and abundance "emanates from self-restraint, from enoughness." They are models of humility and contentment because they fit into their niche rather than arrogantly attempting to dominate and control. They also slow our heartbeats, if we attend to them and learn. If we don't, Kimmerer writes, "the laws of nature will bring us to our knees." Maybe then we will see mosses as a measure of success.

Benyus, Orr, Stoknes, and Kimmerer, like Thoreau, give educators the deep listening practices we need most to transform our awareness and souls in response to climate crisis. Attending to the voice of Spirit, the voices of nature, and inner voice engenders us to better listen to science and warnings and the eco-social suffering of the world. Such listening leads to living with less, not continued participation with the narratives of bigger, better, and more. Such listening leads us to redesign infrastructure and the way we live. Such listening leads us to make ourselves a counter-friction to stop the machine. Such listening leads us to educate students not to become another gear, another pulley of business as usual.

Students need a radical education because to be radical means to go to the roots: to the roots of moral blindness and badness, to the roots of structures and thinking and habits that are killing the planet and us, to the roots of our lostness. Orr wrote that one can hear the creation groan during commencement ceremonies when another supposedly educated, yet ecologically illiterate, graduate enters the "real world" that is disconnected from what is real: our participation with and immersion within a biosphere. Rachel Carson gave a commencement address in 1962, just before the serialization of *Silent Spring* in the *New Yorker*. She was gravely ill and aware she would not see much of the future. In her speech, she passionately called forth a better future by imploring graduates to "face realities instead of taking refuge in ignorance and evasion of truth." She told the students that "yours is a grave and sobering responsibility" but also a "shining opportunity," as humankind is being challenged like never before "to prove its maturity and its mastery—not of nature, but of itself."

Some are listening, thanks to wise education that engages key questions of our time with seriousness but also an unburdened, light heart. The world has already changed, deeply—Bill McKibben's 2011 book on warming, *Eaarth*, argues that we are changing the planet so much that it needs to be renamed. When we embrace purpose despite dire predictions, or rather, when we embrace purpose emerging from identifying with the play of Spirit, with humans destined to be creative and have fun, we will express our full capacities by thinking and acting our way to soulful and genuinely sustainable living.

Educators must help students to become mature enough to listen to bad news and to accept that we are headed toward a drastically changed world. They would do well also to affirm positive possibilities so that we don't fall prey to negative self-fulfilling prophecies. Thoreau wrote, "In the long run we find what we expect; we shall be fortunate, then, if we expect great things." A statement filled with portent, to say the least, that should guide our life-choices.

After all, Thoreau's caustic criticisms of industrialization come from the vantage point of ecstasies, joy, and love, from insights and inspirations when experiencing the heights and higher laws.

ভ

I remain inspired by the teacher as psychopomp, guiding students to new worlds, but I am most moved by, and try to practice, the teacher as bodhisattva, embracing this world the way it is from an enlightened, joyful perspective while committed to service as an expression of awareness, of who we are. Or, as Buddhist monk Thich Nhat Hanh says, the bodhisattva listens to the suffering of the world and then responds with compassion. And, by the way, I tell students that they may work to change the world to find their voice. No sense waiting around. Engagement stimulates the process of individuation.

Many are engaging as best they can. The priority of most students postgraduation, understandably, is to find a job, knowing that the economic system into which they were born values their labor but rarely their soul work. Thoreau's struggles postgraduation were also centered on this tension. Most of his surveying was for good causes. He had high standards, was known for his craft, and expressed his character in his work, but when he needed to pay back his publisher for unsold copies of *A Week*, he surveyed woodlands cut down and turned into housing lots. Plagued by guilt, he wrote that he saw "the prince of darkness with his surveyor."

Thoreau's essay "Life without Principle" was originally delivered as a lyceum speech titled "What Shall It Profit?" The title refers to Mark 8:36: "For what shall it profit a man, if he shall gain the whole world, and lose his own soul?" When we lose soul, all is lost until we rediscover its messages in quiet moments. While Thoreau was hardly beholden to the lucrative standard, making money was a concern for all transcendentalists due to a national financial crisis. It was also a concern because pursuing an intellectual and writing life, and a divine life sticking to ideals, often did not bear financial fruits. But despite lamenting his work for new housing lots, surveying often provided him with satisfaction; after one week-long job of hard outdoor labor, he wrote that he came home each day "more susceptible than usual to the finest influences, as music and poetry."

Thoreau spent a lifetime devoted to finding pleasure and soul in work, and productivity and soul in leisure. His profession, he wrote in an 1851 journal entry, was to "always to be on the alert to find God in nature," and his "everyday business" was to "extract honey from the flower of the world." I do not pretend that these are easy ideals for students to follow. Thoreau wanted his Walden experiment, and the principles it represented, to be imitated in our own ways, for the sake of our souls, for wildness, for the whole planet. Despite the moral evil of their loans, I challenge students to find a career in a calling, or at least meaningful work so that they can make a contribution while making a living and living simply. This challenge really does not come from me; it comes from their raised consciousness, and perhaps collective unconscious and their own gestating unconscious, and from the daemonic lived as self-reliance.

At the end of Senior Seminar, I ask students to send me emails from time to time, updating me on what they are doing.

Southie continues to do well in sales. He appreciates his education more as it becomes more removed; he is gritty and smart and likely will always make a good living within the machine because that is what is most available to us. In one email, he amusingly reminded me that we disagreed on just about everything ideologically, yet I remain his favorite teacher. He wrote, "divisive as this world may be, civility should always triumph" before thanking me for shaping his thinking.

Anna seems to be thriving, at least from information gleaned from Facebook posts, which include big smiles, a loving marriage, amazing travel, and deep, spiritual connection to nature's diverse beauty and her own heart. Elana did, of course, end up traveling. She spent a year in China teaching English to children, among other adventures, including time in Maine teaching troubled youth and work in various locales teaching kids outdoor climbing skills. She has also struggled—I sense the bottom dropped out—but emerged doing work that she loves for a nonprofit that provides healing nature experiences that quell loneliness, depression, and anxiety. She is called to be herself and teaches by being herself.

Josh didn't get accepted to film school—I thought perhaps due to his grades—but it turns out that he did not submit the applications on time (some habits die hard). We lost touch for a while and that's okay, or part of the mystery of teaching and learning and life path. He resurfaced via email after losing his job as a photography production manager due to a pandemic slowdown. Instead of being depressed, he said getting laid off was a blessing in disguise. He started training for a new career in customer relationship management (CRM) software like Salesforce and said the pandemic gave him time to think straight. He hopes his new skills will place him with a company where he'll work with leadership, and then move into leadership roles. He ultimately wants to scale up a business or be a CEO someday. These are his dreams, and he should continue to go in their direction.

As always, Josh showed off his good mind. He said that technology is a double-edged sword, but we'd have no problem wielding it well if we educated people properly. We need to teach computer and media literacy in grade school and teach good research skills before college, he argued; people were not prepared for the internet and social media and it's "turning them into monsters." He also made me laugh by adding that I shouldn't worry, he's not selling out. He plans to work at a nonprofit or an ethical company that makes a positive difference: "Even if the American empire topples down around me, I'm not going to let it stop me from having a good life and being a good person."

The student who wanted to become a college football coach and questioned the value of the liberal arts, got a job as a high school football head coach and then received an opportunity to teach an English class. He sent me an email asking if I would write a letter explaining how our courses, like Freedom of Speech and Senior Seminar, would benefit him in the classroom. I wrote the letter about the courses, and the value of his liberal arts education generally, laughing to myself; I had told him several times that his education would help him in ways he could not fathom. Most importantly, from Facebook posts it is clear he is a deeply respected member of his community. He is not just teaching football, but principles and virtues his players will carry with them throughout their lives.

Recent editors-in-chief of the school newspaper quickly found work in radio and for a media group designing newspapers. The newspaper designer changed jobs and took a communications position with the Humane Society, fulfilling a long-held heart desire that she explored in her Senior Seminar "clearness committee." Another got a master's degree, worked for a nonprofit, had two children, is fighting for all kinds of good causes in her town and beyond. She now works as a communication director for the New Hampshire State Senate. Another began her postgraduate life by serving and bartending, then got a job running a small healing herbs business for an entrepreneur, and then worked at an elementary school while also working with community members to create two online publications, one on international issues and the other on women's issues. She had a caring heart when she arrived as a first-year student and said that she learned to think at college. She is using her writing, editing, and organizational skills practiced at the school paper.

One student, bright and a bit older with strong interpersonal skills, struggled to find his way. He had multiple DUI charges and spent time in jail, only to rise and rebuild his life through the 12 Steps of AA. He now spends his free time sponsoring other men, teaching them how to lead spiritual, other-oriented lives, and helping them get sober. Our teacher-student relationship was more like a friendship and he generously credits our classes together for introducing him to differing forms of spirituality. Today, he is committed to growing through Buddhism and Taoism, which has taught him to strip away conditioning and meet all beings with acceptance, loving-kindness and equanimity. He is also in a committed, loving relationship and sounds fulfilled and happy.

Another student got a paid internship at the UN and said that our classes together prepared her for the conversations she was participating in and the special projects she was working on. This especially pleased me, as if her good work proved the value of the liberal arts. But then I realized that some would criticize this interpretation, stating that the problem with liberal arts colleges is they prepare everyone as if they are going to get a job at the UN, which is impractical and disconnected to the actual economic world.

Thinking this way is the problem. Still, I was equally pleased when I received, not an email, but a handwritten letter from a student stating that the readings from Senior Seminar had led her to take risks. She had thought that the best she could do was middle management at Walmart but decided to get more education to become a wilderness firefighter. The benefits of a liberal arts education may be expressed at the UN, as a wilderness firefighter, in all jobs, and we need more forest firefighters in a climate-compromised world.

Another student was consistently critical of the "religious" readings in Senior Seminar and felt he didn't need a clearness committee—he knew he wanted a career in marketing and got a marketing job in Boston just before class ended. I was happy for him and asked him to share his interview process with classmates so they might learn. While critical of religion, he was turned on by the philosophical readings and the questions raised by the class. Who can say how soul may emerge someday, even if he does not like the word, in marketing or another materialistic profession.

My former students are just getting started in various careers, and some have struggled to find decent jobs. A magnificent misfit who never thought he would make it through college and thought he would struggle to get a job, got a lucrative one with the oil industry and returned to campus to thank me. This student once challenged me in class, insisting that I would accept a free GMC Hummer if offered. He found it inconceivable when I said I wouldn't want it but would consider taking it to sell and then use the money for a far more environmentally-friendly car.

I did not outwardly judge his career choice; my job, my calling, is to do what I can to help students be "less wrong" and then let go by letting them learn what they need to learn. Their degree, of course, opens more possibilities for them in the present, yet what he did not have ears to hear is that a Hummer-filled future would likely take down our economic system and civilization (to which he desperately wanted to conform) and drastically redirect all our possibilities. Whatever students end up doing, they have paid for, and been blessed with, the opportunity to be broadly and deeply educated. They embraced that opportunity to various degrees;

hopefully, they have become jazzed by learning such that they keep seeking new understandings, pursuing the true and good.

Knowing this possibility, and that they will vote and may be more mindful as consumers and more thoughtful in their human and other-than-human relationships, heartens me as an educator. The millennial generation, and now Gen Z, are addicted to phones and constant conversing, too often diverted from their still small voice, but they also know the power of digital communication. They are a diverse lot open to diversity, to equality, rights, and freedom, and they are increasingly ecologically aware.

Knowing that a few really get it—not many, but some—feeling the joy of being alive from discovering silence and stillness, and devoting their energy to fostering the beautiful, will truly sustain us because they will add to that 10 percent needed to raise collective consciousness, and that 3.5 percent needed for nonviolent protest to change structures and policies, with their commitment to conscience teaching others.

Who knows, however, where we are all heading, what a climate-disrupted world will bring: Will we create a circular economy governed by ethics of compassion and care, finally moving beyond fossil fuels and creating meaningful work in renewable energy? Will we focus on degrowth and energy efficiency lest a so-called green economy leads to more of the same one-dimensional techno-industrial madness, or bigger, better, and more in a greenwashed guise? Will the global economy crash altogether, leading to local economies of much smaller scale based in practical skills, like plants-as-teacher gardening and simple living on this alive planet? After all, sustainability solutions should not be measured by saving civilization as we know it, but by saving as much diverse life as possible and restoring the land and our souls.

Who knows if education, transforming to meet the challenges of our time, will teach students to restore and re-story, and if spiritual intelligence and listening will be incorporated in our educational vision.

ೞ

Emerson wrote of hope and faith, stating that "the believer beholds not only his heaven to be possible, but already to begin to exist." We may be "incompetent to solve the times," he admitted, after many years of speaking out against slavery, but that raises the question "How shall we live?" Transformation eventually occurs when we are "raised above ourselves by the power of principles." In a powerful and principled exhortation that is even more powerful during a climate crisis, he argues we must begin now: "One of the illusions is that the present hour is not the critical decisive hour. Write it on your heart that every day is the best day of the year. No man has learned anything rightly until he knows that every day is Doomsday."

Thoreau, of course, also knew the value of the present moment, wisely enjoining us to expect great things. He further knew that neither optimism nor pessimism is the final word because new worlds will be called forth through us. The good news is that despite and because of our lostness, there is plenty of room for new insights, for the unexpected, for being open to mystery.

In *Walden Warming: Climate Change Comes to Thoreau's Woods*, Richard B. Primack documents changes to the land, pond, and New England bioregion. At first blush, the uninformed might welcome warmer winters, earlier springs with blooming wildflowers, and longer summers, but animals and plants are not suited to these changes: wetlands will likely dry up, non-native insects may move in, and forests will be undermined. We are not only losing Arctic ice, but also ice in rivers and lakes and ponds; Thoreau's many depth measurements have helped current scientists study the changes around Concord. In his time, ice receded from Walden Pond around April 1; today it lasts until March 17, but even then it is not safe to skate on. Ice two feet thick has given way to a danger sign forbidding skating.

The Walden woods communicate to us what is being lost and what is already lost. And what is happening at Walden is happening writ large and in larger ways, including increasingly more violent storms and out-of-control wildfires thanks to violent and out-of-control lucrative standard economic systems. Disaster capitalism hit new heights of absurdity during the Covid-19 pandemic as billionaires became multibillionaires and sent phallic vanity rockets into space. A warmer earth also means a higher probability of future pandemics as increasingly uninhabitable habitat causes wild animals to flee and interact with humans. What shall it profit, indeed.

None of these changes would please Thoreau, despite mostly seeing them coming. We have certainly failed him by doing pretty much the opposite of what he advised. Our actions (and inaction) are nothing less than tragic, but they also prove his relevancy. He became especially relevant during our pandemic pause, when staying put and living well within specific places were obvious virtues. Thoreau, as a model of self-reliance, mattered more than ever as we navigated enforced solitude amid our collective time-out. In an article for *Fast Company*, the authors argue that he is also a good model during the "Great Resignation," as more people question the value of poorly paid work and explore alternative modes of living. An article for *Recruiter.com* finds lessons in his commitments, including changing course by staying true to ourselves and refusing to "associate adulthood with unquestioned allegiance to professional misery."

Thoreau's appeal to principles and practices that display universal resonance has much to offer us, especially in times of crisis. His writings also have global reach; there have been numerous translations of *Walden*, and he has inspired radical environmentalism and radical personal change. He's become the "patron-saint" of tiny houses and simple living. He's inspired films and novels and music. He's been referenced in TV shows, memes, and cartoons, and he was the subject of a "Final Jeopardy" answer. Ironically, his face and words have appeared on a variety of merchandise: T-shirts, mugs, blankets, bags, hats, and even shower curtains.

Thoreau has long had broad popular appeal, but he has also been put into boxes—hermit, fraud, misanthrope—as a means to disparage him. Rebecca Solnit calls this our "Thoreau problem," arguing that he transcended boxy dualities such as nature and culture, solitude and society, consciousness and conscience. Thoreau easily bridged these divides, being and doing as natural expressions of embracing all of life, including its darkness and downsides. So, despite attempts to keep him at bay, thoroughly human and imperfect Thoreau has worked his way into our collective consciousness. A key reason we have failed him, and fail to get out of our boxes, is because industrial education has failed us. Spirit and nature and specific places that schooled him have largely been absent from our schools, and subsequently, from our experiences.

Thoreau shows the way through that lostness, embracing living on the edge as a catalyst for self-culture and societal transformation, listening to "something more" such that we may become something more.

Such spiritual maturity means being comfortable with doubts, with contradiction, paradox, and uncertainty, at home on the earth but also within the unknown. In the Anthropocene, being willing to live within and embrace not-knowing is a necessary skill. But from the perspective of Socrates and the daemonic, there may be a remembering, a recollection of purpose and why we are here. Being lost is an invitation to memory, and thus perhaps we need to invite being lost.

Getting lost to be found is a spiritual practice marked by an intentional embrace of risk and the faith that obstacles will lead us to grow down into our daemons. Too many students never embrace the unknown, and thus they do not know, do not learn, do not grow. Roaming, wandering, and risking activate larger forces and a sense of destiny; being lost may be the only way to find a better way.

Spiritual maturity may also mean losing the self, including the daemonic, to discover a deeper and wider identity, the Supreme Identity, one-in-many, many-in-one, in moments of just this, just that, just life force expressed always and never-endingly, unity and diversity knowing each other intimately. In such inspired moments we realize that we are never actually lost, never without Source and resources, never anywhere but home. In such moments we transcend faith and growing down, going beyond will to the grace of effortless effort, to being and doing what we must be and do. Such moments are moments yet resonate as a larger life.

Spiritual maturity is key to leaving the cave of denial, including denial of climate crisis, as one-in-many and many-in-one becomes a baseline reverberating reality waking us up to primordial interbeing, I-Thou interrelationship, and ecological interdependency, and thus the cosmic karma of stupidly fouling our own nest. But when spirituality veers off course into fundamentalist fervor or blind faith in gurus or New Age certainty, in which we attempt to ascend without embrace, we remain asleep. When we reject questioning and adopt rigid beliefs, whether that climate crisis is fake news, or that it is real but of no consequence because God will save us, or that a spiritual new age is imminent no matter what we do to matter, it's just more slumbering.

Losing ego-selves may recall purpose. Going further into grace reawakens play. Thoreau experienced both but also double consciousness.

Thus, spiritual maturity further means accepting humanness and being vulnerable. But double consciousness and struggle along the path of purpose and play is one thing; the sixth great period of species extirpation is quite another. We are losing without knowing what we are losing, and there is no greater lostness. Lost habitat, lost Indigenous peoples, lost languages, lost voices, human and nonhuman, lead to an impoverished mind, heart, soul, and spirit. In wildness is the preservation of the world because wildness anchors us in the reality of vibrant and diverse nature, and in our own wild nature. The tamer we are, the more lost to who we are and may become in and of this world.

There are so many horrible ways to be lost: war and PTSD, drugs and addiction, technology and distraction, but there is nothing worse than being lost at home, whether within the specific places we dwell or the whole planet. We have lost, or are out of touch with, our ecological unconscious, our long history of hunter-gatherer immersion within the land and memory of the land. We are lost to Spirit unfolding as matter, life, and mind, and memory of the daemonic.

When the bottom drops out, much becomes possible. When losing the world, figuratively and literally, what is necessary and vital may reappear. Losing and gaining are intimately related, sorrow and beauty too, and thus there is a beautiful melancholy to lostness, and to accepting that there are things we can't have. Some things are just plain out of reach, and for good reason. Spiritually, having it all is to be empty of the need to have it all. Some humility is in order to more fully live in sympathy with intelligence.

Living in sympathy is not easy, but we will never find a degree of clarity until we embrace both halves of the equation: moments of sweet solitude and inspiration and the callings that emerge from them *and* the existential and quotidian. My stumbling life experiences have taught me that our range of responses should be spiritually informed, including the possibility of personal predisposition, and that we are all destined to be human, to engage the purpose and play of life, and then, as we mature, to discover why we're here on earth, or what contributions we can make with humor and gratitude, stumbling more lightly.

The highest we can attain as educators and lifelong students inspired by Thoreau is to be productively lost such that we may continually re-find the compass and embrace the infinite extent of our relations. Exploding stars gave birth to a solar system, placed us here, intertwined with and beholden to every earthly expression. Rebirth is a matter of survival, and possibly flourishing in turbulent times; to call forth a better future, we must teach the spirituality of being lost and learn to read inner nature and the language that all things speak.

Notes

Chapter 1: Voice

p. 4: The Emerson epigram, "Good as is discourse, silence is better, and shames it," is from the essay "Circles" in *The Portable Emerson*, edited by Carl Bode (234). Emerson also writes in this essay that "every end is a beginning" (228).

p. 9: The William James quotation on suicide is from a letter to a friend during a time when he was deeply depressed. It can be found in *William James: His Life and Thought* (46).

p. 9: The 1992 "Warning to Humanity" is available on the Union of Concerned Scientists' website and other online sources, as well as in *Life Stories: World-Renowned Scientists Reflect on their Lives and the Future of Life on Earth*. *Life Stories* shares the personal paths of famous scientists to their specific branches of science and their call to share what they have learned. Many of today's climatologists, including Michael Mann and Katherine Hayhoe, are called to use their voice to teach the public. Hayhoe, a progressive Christian, has made science communication an art form in her "Global Weirding" videos, along with her public speaking and writings.

p. 10: The Emerson quotation on learning to "detect and watch that gleam of light which flashes across his own mind from within" is from his essay "Self-Reliance," which can be found online and in several anthologies. My 1986 *The Portable Emerson*, edited by Carl Bove, is thoroughly marked up (the quotation can be found on page 139).

p. 12: My early teaching style had no real design; I just wanted to break down hierarchal barriers and make our collective classroom space vibrant and participatory. I came to learn that feminist pedagogy has long advocated for the deconstruction of power differentials in teacher-student relationships in favor of a more democratic approach. An excellent book displaying examples of such pedagogy is bell hooks's *Teaching to Transgress: Education as the Practice of Freedom*; I sometimes re-read the first chapters for inspiration prior to starting a new semester. Learning along with students is inevitable although I have had colleagues who are quite talented at lecturing. I also have colleagues who feel they cannot experiment with giving up authority; in other words, student biases, which are culturally constructed and learned at early ages, make it easier for a male to play with their authority in the classroom.

pp. 14-15: The Emerson quotations from "Self-Reliance" on a "foolish consistency" being the "hobgoblin of little minds" and "virtue and vice" emitting "a breath every moment" can be found in *The Portable Emerson* (145–46). Hobgoblin is not a word one hears much these days, and it literally means a mischievous sprite. To Emerson, we are harassed by habits to follow the crowd. The psychoanalyst Wilhelm Reich furthered this argument, stating that social structures become part of our unconscious, which we then play out via our bodies habitual responses to authority. See Ramsey

Eric Ramsey's *The Long Path to Nearness* for insights on Reich and "habit bodies," and how to widen our "a-whereness" and increase our capacity for virtuous action.

p. 15: Thoreau's advice to confront the essential facts of life is from the "Where I Lived, and What I Lived For" section of *Walden* (*The Portable Thoreau*, 343); Thomas Merton's advice to consult death is referenced in Gregg Levoy's *Callings: Finding and Following an Authentic Life* (31). Levoy's text and Stephen Cope's *The Great Work of Your Life: A Guide for the Journey to Your True Calling* are the best books on callings I have found. A book I do not like is Rick Warren's 30 million-plus bestseller *The Purpose Driven Life: What on Earth Am I Here For?*, which argues for a Christ-modeled life but with no regard for the earth. Warren is also known for asking then-presidential candidate John McCain to define "rich," and then laughing his ass off when McCain responded $5 million. Hardly Christ-like. Excellent progressive Christian takes on callings and finding your voice are *Listening Hearts: Discerning Call in Community* (by Suzanne G. Farnham et al.), *Insight and Action: How to Discover and Support a Life of Integrity and Commitment to Change* (by Fran Peavey et al.), and Parker Palmer's *Let Your Life Speak: Listening for the Voice of Vocation*. The latter two are rooted in the Quaker tradition and include guidance for "clearness committee" group exercises designed to help one get clear on questions of voice, vocation, and difficult life decisions.

Chapter 2: The Bottom Drops Out

p. 17: The Jung epigram on people being "confined within too narrow a spiritual horizon" is from his autobiography *Memories, Dreams, Reflections* (140). I went to a workshop conducted by a Jungian counselor during my Purdue years, and she said all of Jung's ideas are in this book. I read it right after that recommendation and was not disappointed.

p. 17: The Thoreau epigram, "What does education often do? It makes a straight-cut ditch of a free, meandering brook," can be found in *The Heart of Thoreau's Journals*, edited by Odell Shepard (39), as well as *Uncommon Learning: Thoreau on Education*, edited by Martin Bickman (39).

pp. 17-18: The material on Thoreau's youthful struggles associated with growing up and being educated in the changing times of the mid-1800s are from Richard Lebeaux's *Young Man Thoreau* (9–27). See also Walter Harding's *The Days of Henry Thoreau* (17–31) and Lawrence Buell's introduction to *The American Transcendentalists: Essential Writings* (xi–xxviii).

p. 24: Data on the yearly rise of atmospheric CO_2 parts per million can be found on the NOAA (National Oceanic and Atmospheric Administration) website, as well as the Scripps Institution of Oceanography at UC San Diego website. Charles Keeling, from Scripps, was the first to measure atmospheric CO_2 at the Mauna Loa observatory in Hawaii in 1958, and he established the Keeling Curve that records yearly increases of CO_2. James Hansen, the former head of the NASA Goddard Institute for Space Studies, stated that CO_2 needs to level off at 350 ppm "if humanity wishes to preserve a planet similar to that on which civilization developed and to which life on Earth is adapted," which can be found on the 350.org website.

A good quick history of recording atmospheric CO_2 can be found in *Washington Post* science journalist Chris Mooney's article "30 years ago scientists warned Congress on global warming. What they said sounds eerily familiar." In discussing a 1979 report by the US National Academy of Sciences, led by the atmospheric physicist Jule Charney of the Massachusetts Institute of Technology, Mooney writes, "That group famously assessed that if carbon dioxide levels in the atmosphere were to double, the 'most probable global warming' would amount to 3 degrees Celsius, with a range between 1.5 degrees and 4.5 degrees, a number quite similar to modern estimates."

Mooney is the co-author of *Unscientific America: How Scientific Illiteracy Threatens Our Future* and author of *The Republican War on Science*, which address the importance of science communication to a broad public and the forces that undermine this communication.

Chapter 3: When the Student Is Ready

p. 27: The Emerson epigram on the reality, influence, and gifts of the daemon is from his essay "Plato; or the Philosopher" (*The Portable Emerson*, 309). The Thoreau epigram on the great strain of trying to conform outwardly while living our "own life inwardly" is from *Letters to a Spiritual Seeker*, edited by Bradley P. Dean (62). The letters, sent to Harrison G. O. Blake, show Thoreau as a friend but also passing on the gift of mentoring provided to him by Emerson and others.

p. 28: Krishnamurti's books, which are all transcribed talks and answers to questions, can get repetitive. All are good though. *Think on These Things* is a favorite since it was the first one I encountered, and he doesn't hold back:

> Life is really very beautiful, it is not this ugly thing that we have made of it; and you can appreciate its richness, its depth, its extraordinary loveliness only when you revolt against everything—against organized religion, against tradition, against the present rotten society—so that you as a human being find out for yourself what is true. Not to imitate but to discover—that is education, is it not?

A documentary on Krishnamurti's life, *With a Silent Mind*, states that he traveled for sixty-five years and gave talks to more people than anyone in modern history. Many talks were given in Ojai, California, the home of the Krishnamurti Education Center and where he put down roots. All his talks—and criticisms of the modern world and education—are centered in silence and stillness and living simply and free, so I think Krishnamurti would have seen Thoreau as a kindred spirit, and vice-versa.

After graduation from Rutgers, as I struggled to fulfill societal expectations, I was also heartened from reading portions of Eric Fromm's *The Sane Society*, in which he questioned the sanity of the society into which we are supposed to find our place, as well as Abraham Maslow's *Toward a Psychology of Being*, in which he stated that despair was a healthy response when trying to fit into a despairing situation. I found both titles at a used bookstore near campus, along with *Think on These Things*, after knocking over a pile of books on the floor and having a cover photo of Krishnamurti staring me in the face. I like to think that I found what I needed to find because I was open to mystery and engaging my process of individuation, even if I did not know it at the time.

p. 31: The material on Thoreau meeting Emerson can be found in Richard Lebeaux's *Young Man Thoreau* and Jeffrey S. Cramer's *Solid Seasons: The Friendship of Henry David Thoreau and Ralph Waldo Emerson*. Both men greatly valued friendship, and each other, despite their tiffs. Cramer writes that their relationship influenced the history of American thought and letters, which is quite a measure of the profundity of their meetings of mind and soul (xi). "Sympathy" was undoubtedly one of Thoreau's favorite words, and he wrote that friendship is an "unspeakable joy and blessing that results to two or more individuals who from constitution sympathize" (xiii).

pp. 31–32: Emerson wrote on nature's uses, including "service to the soul," in the "Commodity" chapter of "Nature" (10–12). My favorite copy of "Nature" is paired with Thoreau's "Walking" in John Elder's anthology *Nature/Walking*. Elder's valuable introduction states that Emerson's "Nature" "reveals an abstract, idealizing impulse that can jar a modern reader." I have taught "Nature" to students, and they are jarred by his focus on Spirit more than nature, or Spirit as nature. In many ways, Emerson argues for a spiritual anthropocentrism; in other words, nature is deeply valued but mostly as a vehicle for human enlightenment.

p. 32: For the history of New England, see environmental historian William Cronon's *Changes in the Land: Indians, Colonists, and the Ecology of New England* (3, 20–25, 36–37). Cronon is also the editor of *Uncommon Ground: Rethinking the Human Place in Nature*, which includes his influential essay, "The Trouble with Wilderness; or, Getting Back to the Wrong Nature." Cronon argues that Thoreau's dictum, "In Wildness is the preservation of the World," has been poorly interpreted to assume that only wilderness contains wildness, leading us to idealize it at the expense of where we live.

pp. 32-33: A description of Thoreau walking nineteen miles to hear Emerson speak in Boston, and the Emerson quotation on beauty, can be found in Laura Dassow Walls's 2017 biography *Thoreau: A Life*, the latest and greatest history of Thoreau's life and commitments (89).

p. 33: Robert Pirsig's 1974 *Zen and the Art of Motorcycle Maintenance* is one of the books I most frequently recommend to undergraduates, for an obvious reason: it takes readers on a ride of philosophical and spiritual inquiry.

p. 36: Herbert Marcuse's *One-Dimensional Man* was an influential text informing the revolutionary spirit of the 1960s. Other excellent books by Marcuse include *The Aesthetic Dimension*, *An Essay on Liberation*, and *Counter-Revolution and Revolt*.

p. 40: Emerson and Thoreau's views on "double consciousness" can be found in Barry Andrews's *Transcendentalism and the Cultivation of the Soul* (30).

p. 40: The Thoreau quotations on the expansion of his being and the expansive night sky are from Kevin Dann's biography *Expect Great Things: The Life and Search of Henry David Thoreau* (2, 24). I read Dann's biography after reading numerous other

Thoreau biographies and wondered if he would have anything original to add. He does, especially by viewing Thoreau's life through the prism of the daemonic.

pp. 40–41: *In The Varieties of Religious Experience,* William James articulated four characteristics of religious experience: ineffability, or that such experiences are beyond words and thoughts and thus cannot be fully described in words (although we try); noetic quality, which suggests that while such experiences are transrational they still provide knowledge, typically an intuitive insight of unity; transiency, or that such states of consciousness are usually not sustained for long although the effects are typically long lasting; and passivity, which means that while we can meditate or do other spiritual practices to prepare the way for religious experiences, they come unbidden, or as grace, when the will is in abeyance. He also added that most religious experience occur outdoors (380–81).

The spiritual philosopher Ken Wilber has catalogued transrational or religious experience via four levels: psychic/nature mysticism, in which one identifies with nature; subtle/deity mysticism, in which one identifies with their higher self; causal/formless mysticism, in which one identifies with the unmanifest Source of all form; and nondual/nondual mysticism, in which one identifies with both emptiness and form, or the transcendent and immanent, experiencing them as not-two, or, as Thoreau put it: "I caught two fishes as it were with one hook." Wilber explores transrational experience, along with pre-rational and rational experience and knowing, in numerous books. The most accessible is *A Brief History of Everything* (202–40) although *Integral Spirituality* is a more evolved articulation of his thought, integrating postmodern criticisms of totalistic knowledge claims into his theory of individual and sociocultural development. His still more recent tome, *The Religion of Tomorrow,* fully explicates the varieties of religious experience, along with their shadow-sides.

p. 41: The first Joel Goldsmith book I read was *The Thunder of Silence,* which argues that to be enlightened one must move beyond the pairs of opposites, such as good/evil or sickness/health, as "There is just God, just spiritual Being, perfection" (91). While there is wisdom to recognizing the perfection of "God is," or that everything is God, we are also finite, imperfect expressions of God. Goldsmith highlights the former, arguing that spiritual healing may occur when we dwell in the presence of "God is," taking no thought of the pairs of opposites.

p. 43: The Krishnamurti quotation on unity versus fear can be found in Ken Wilber's *Grace and Grit: Spirituality and Healing in the Life and Death of Treya Killam Wilber* (99). This personal book intersperses spiritual wisdom with his wife Treya's cancer diagnosis and eventual death. Wilber is fully aware that the mind-body connection may influence health, but he's critical of the New Age notion that we can create our own reality and think our way to health, or that the experience of "God is" will heal cancer.

Grace and Grit includes excerpts from Treya's journal on her search for vocation, which Wilber explicates via the daemonic: "We came to describe her search for her 'work' as her search for her 'daemon'—the Greek word that in classical mythology refers to 'a god within,' one's inner deity or guiding spirit, also known as a genii or jinn, the tutelary deity or genius of a person, one's daemon or genii is also said to be synonymous with one's fate or fortune." Wilber goes on to write that our daemon is our "own Higher Self" and that Treya would come to express her higher self via art, just as he had in his writings (58).

p. 43: Emerson and Thoreau's views on friendship, as well as details on their friendship/mentor-student relationship, can be found in Cramer's *Solid Seasons* and in Harmon Smith's *My Friend, My Friend: The Story of Thoreau's Relationship with Emerson*.

Chapter 4: The River Knows

p. 45: The Thoreau epigram on rivers, and nature generally, as educators that surpass "any hired teachers or preachers" is from *Uncommon Learning: Henry David Thoreau on Education*, a book of quotations edited by Martin Bickman (46).

p. 45: Purdue's founding as a land grant university can be found on the Purdue University website.

p. 47: The quotation from Gregory Bateson on Lake Erie is from *Steps to an Ecology of Mind* (484). Bateson argues that we exist within cycles of nature and culture expressed as mental process, or as a constant communicative exchange of information, yet we act as if these cycles of communication somehow don't apply to us. I discovered Bateson when perusing the bookshelves at Rafael's home; he walked around the corner, saw that I was holding *Mind and Nature*, another Bateson title, and said we should read it together, so we did.

p. 48: The quotations from Senators Chaffee and Gore on the specter of global warming in 1986 are from *Washington Post* science journalist Chris Mooney's article, "30 years ago scientists warned Congress on global warming. What they said sounds eerily familiar."

p. 49: Thoreau's well-known *Walden* quotations are from *The Portable Thoreau* edited by Carl Bode. Bode, the original editor of this anthology, does a Freudian analysis of Thoreau in an epilogue, arguing that his unconscious was marked by an Oedipus complex that "aborted his emotional life but richly informed his writing" (690). Rejected by Ellen Sewall in his early twenties despite her fondness for him, Thoreau "failed" in romantic love and had a propensity for older women, including Emerson's wife, but Freudian psychology is often reductionistic, accounting for behavior via the libido. I don't discount the possibility that sexual frustration and Oedipal fantasies were influential in Thoreau's psyche, but a strict Freudian analysis does not fully explain Thoreau; rather, it is in danger of explaining him away. It's better to analyze Thoreau from the perspective of transpersonal psychology, which provides a more expansive context and criteria for psychological analysis that explores the importance of religious experiences to our development. Thoreau's main psychological influence was his quest for spiritual freedom. This quest for freedom—by listening to inner genius, the natural world, and Nature/Spirit—is what makes him such an influential figure. Thoreau's life is complex and resoundingly unique, but his process of individuation and struggles have universal appeal. A newer edition of *The Portable Thoreau*, with Jeffrey S. Cramer as the new editor, has a more straightforward introduction on Thoreau's life and work.

pp. 50-51: My nonverbal experiences with Mac the Newfoundland are not surprising for anyone who spends time with animals. There are also numerous books on interspecies communication and various animal "whisperers," and some Communication Studies scholars have explored such experiences. I particularly like Emily Plec's 2013 anthology, *Perspectives on Human-Animal Communication: Internatural Communication*. The term *internatural* suggests that humans are also nature, only a different species, and provides a counterpoint to the study of intercultural communication. There are also more and more books coming out on communicating with plants, and they support Bateson's insight that we live within a larger communicative system of information exchange. Indigenous peoples have long affirmed and lived by this idea. Hopefully, a shift in awareness is occurring as we practice deep listening within the context of the "wood wide web." See my 2021 book, *An Ecology of Communication: Response and Responsibility in an Age of Ecocrisis*, for a thorough treatment of communication within a more-than-human world. I include a chapter on Thoreau and another on interspecies communication.

p. 51: Thoreau's phrase "the language which all things and events speak," is from the "Sounds" section of *Walden* (363). My essay, "The Language that All Things Speak: Thoreau and the Voice of Nature," was published in the 2014 anthology *Voice and the Environment*.

p. 51. The characteristics of and influences on transcendentalism can be found in *The American Transcendentalists: Essential Writings*, edited by Lawrence Buell, and Barry M. Andrews's *Transcendentalism and the Cultivation of the Soul*. I initially learned from Robert D. Richardson's *Henry Thoreau: A Life of the Mind* (71–76) and *Emerson: The Mind on Fire*. The latter book includes a telling story. A guest at the Emerson home, John Albee, wrote the following of Thoreau, who was also visiting: "He was much at home with Emerson: and as he remained through the afternoon and evening, and I left him still at the fireside, he appeared to me to belong in some way to the household." Albee also recalled that Emerson continually deferred to Thoreau, "and seemed to anticipate his views, preparing himself obviously for a quiet laugh at Thoreau's negative and biting criticisms, especially in regard to education and educational institutions" (281).

pp. 51–52: Thoreau's school and work background is detailed in Robert D. Richardson's *Henry Thoreau: A Life of the Mind* (5–42). Other excellent biographies include Walter Harding's *The Days of Henry Thoreau* and David M. Robinson's *Natural Life: Thoreau's Worldly Transcendentalism*, along with the biographies by Laura Dassow Walls and Kevin Dann.

pp. 51–52: The details on Thoreau at Harvard and the short-lived Thoreau brothers' school and educational practices are from Laura Dassow Walls's *Henry David Thoreau: A Life* (57–81, 99–102).

pp. 53–54: Henry's boat trip with his brother John and return to teaching is described in Walls's *Henry David Thoreau: A Life* (106–10, 124). The quotation on the river, and water generally, reflecting heaven, quieting negative passions, and preserving equipoise, was taken from *Thoreau on Water: Reflecting Heaven*, edited by Robert Lawrence France (13–14).

p. 55: Thoreau's reference to the "profound secret" of the daemonic, although not using the word "daemon," is from Dann's *Expect Great Things* (45).

p. 55: The myth of Thoreau the hermit, along with other mistaken understandings about Thoreau, is specifically explored in Robert Sullivan's *The Thoreau You Don't Know*. Laura Dassow Walls, and any good biographer, also counters this myth. However, as Lawrence Buell points out in *Henry David Thoreau: Thinking Disobediently*, Thoreau called himself a hermit when at Walden Pond, while adding that he was not a hermit by disposition (30). Thoreau's good friend Ellery Channing said his Walden house, which is what Thoreau called it rather than a cabin, was like a hermitage. Thoreau was not a hermit in the sense of complete isolation; rather, staying at his tiny Walden house was more like a writer's retreat that included lots of solitude but also visitors, walks with friends, and trips to town. Also, he was not alone without fellow humans, but living in community with diverse nature. He was most certainly not a hermit when he left Walden Pond to live at the Emerson household before living again at his family home.

p. 55: The quotation on the three chairs, "one for solitude, two for friendship, and three for society," is from the "Visitors" section of *Walden* (*The Portable Thoreau*, 390).

p. 56: The quotation about our ability to "elevate our lives by conscious endeavor" is from the "Where I Lived, and What I Lived For" section of *Walden* (*The Portable Thoreau*, 343).

p. 56: The quotations, "When my hoe tinkled against the stones, that music echoed to the woods and the sky, and was an accompaniment to my labor which yielded an instant and immeasurable crop" and "...it was no longer beans that I hoed, nor I that hoed the beans," are from the "The Bean Field" section of *Walden* (*The Portable Thoreau*, 408).

p. 57: The quotation on Thoreau's predilection toward a "higher, or as it is named, spiritual life," and another toward a "primitive rank and savage one" is from the "Higher Laws" section of *Walden* (*The Portable Thoreau*, 457). I have always found the "Higher Laws" section to be the most provocative and revealing as it argues for the reality of a transcendent dimension. Thoreau even writes that "nature is hard to be overcome, but she must be overcome" (465). However, nature must be overcome such that we recognize nature as expressed Spirit, leading us to value nature more, not to devalue it. He also became increasingly more grounded as he turned to science in the last decade of his life, seeing Spirit in nature while also arguing for a more biocentric perspective that countered Emerson's focus on using nature for spiritual reasons. In many ways, he grew out of Emerson's spiritual anthropocentrism in "Nature," bringing his mysticism down to a sensuous earth where all species have voice and inherent value.

p. 57: The quotation, "The highest we can attain to is not Knowledge but Sympathy with Intelligence" is from "Walking" in John Elder's *Nature/Walking* (113). I have used this slim volume in class to get at the core of Emerson and Thoreau's thought.

p. 57: The phrase on being part "vegetable mould myself" is from the "Solitude" section of *Walden* (*The Portable Thoreau*, 389).

p. 57: The quotations on comparing Walden Pond to earth's eye and on having "caught two fishes as it were with one hook" are from the "The Ponds" section of *Walden* (*The Portable Thoreau*, 424).

pp. 58–59: The material on Thoreau, Tahatawan, and the history of Concord and Native Americans is from Walls's *Henry David Thoreau: A Life* (3–6, 13–17).

p. 60: Emerson's quotations "Who looks upon a river in a meditative hour, and is not reminded of the flux of all things?" and "Nature always speaks of Spirit" are from the essay "Nature" (23, 53).

p. 60: The quotation on rippling rivers reflecting the spiritual journey, restoring and uplifting as we embrace "new water every instant," is from Thoreau's *A Week on the Concord and Merrimack Rivers* and cited in the introduction to *Reflecting Heaven: Thoreau on Water*, edited by Robert Lawrence France (xxi). This slim volume of quotations also includes an excellent foreword by the novelist and essayist David James Duncan. Duncan's books, including *The River Why*, *River Teeth*, and *The Brothers K*, are highly recommended. Duncan thanks Thoreau for helping us to understand that "wildness is Earth being Earth," and for "driving home the fact that wildness is the Great Tapestry itself, that it is what allows natural selection to select, what allows biodiversity to diversify…" (xiii.).

pp. 61–62: Information about The Feast of the Hunter's Moon in Lafayette, Indiana, can be found online on the Tippecanoe County Historical Association website or the Feast of the Hunter's Moon website. The Feast is still going strong, and the fifty-seventh event was in October 2024.

Chapter 5: Open to Mystery

p. 63: The Charles A. Eastman (Ohiyesa) epigram on the Great Mystery and proper worship is from *The Soul of an Indian: An Interpretation* (4, 18). The back cover states that Eastman (1858–1939) was a mixed-blood Sioux who was educated in Indian ways until age fifteen. He later earned a science degree from Dartmouth College in 1887 and a medical degree from Boston University three years later. He became a physician at Pine Ridge and witnessed events that led to the Wounded Knee massacre. Such an amazing, and soulful, life and pursuit of education holds many lessons.

p. 63: The oft-quoted Einstein epigram on experiencing mystery is from the essay "The World as I See It" and is available online. This quotation reminds me of a well-known quotation from William James in *The Varieties of Religious Experience*:

> [O]ur normal waking consciousness, rational consciousness, is but one special type of consciousness, whilst all about it, parted from it by the filmiest of screens, there lie potential forms of consciousness entirely different. We may go through life without suspecting their existence, but apply the requisite stimulus and at a touch

they are there in all their completeness...No account of the universe in its totality can be final which leaves these other forms of consciousness quite disregarded.

Both deserve to be oft-quoted, as they reveal a deeper religious impulse and more encompassing logos.

Along with "Cosmic Religious Feeling," another essay by Einstein that got me thinking as an undergraduate is "Why Socialism?" published in 1949 and found online, in which he writes that the "worst evil of capitalism" is the "crippling of the individual," and "our whole education system suffers from this evil." He further writes that an "exaggerated competitive attitude is inculcated into the student, who is trained to worship acquisitive success as a preparation for his future career." "Why Socialism" can also be found in *Ideas and Opinions*, 151–58.

p. 65: Along with recommending Jack Weatherford's *Indian Givers*, *Black Elk Speaks* (Black Elk's life as told to John G. Neihardt), Charles Eastman's (Ohiyesa) *The Soul of the Indian*, and Leslie Marmon Silko's novel *Ceremony*, I am also fond of two more novels on Native American life and experience: James Welch's *Fools Crow* and N. Scott Momaday's *The Ancient Child*. All three novels explore the search for identity and listening to the voices of nature, particularly via animals, in relation to finding individual voice. The scholar Donal Carbaugh's excellent essay, "'Just Listen': 'Listening' and Landscape among the Blackfeet," explores such listening addressed to the land. I have taught *Ceremony* and "Just Listen" in an interpersonal communication course to explore more-than-human relationships.

p. 65: The material from Calvin O. Schrag's *The Resources of Rationality* is from page 22. Along with *Resources*, Schrag has written numerous books, including *God as Otherwise than Being*, in which he explores agape love in relation to the "gift event," like when a mentor gives to a student without expecting a return gift, yet the gift moves in the form of learning and future gifts to others. A lengthy interview with Schrag by Ramsey Eric Ramsey and David James Miller in *Experiences between Philosophy and Communication* (edited by Ramsey and Miller) reveals key aspects of his thought and has been most useful to me.

p. 66: Thoreau's remarks on true philosophers as lovers of wisdom who live according to the dictates of this love is from the "Economy" section of *Walden* (270).

pp. 66–67: The thesis of Pierre Hadot's *Philosophy as a Way of Life* is also explored in his book *What Is Ancient Philosophy?* Hadot's quotation, "Professors did not merely teach, but played the role of genuine directors of conscience who cared for their students' spiritual problems," is from *What is Ancient Philosophy?* (156).

p. 68: The mission of the Ometeca Institute to create dialogue among scientists and humanists is influenced by C. P. Snow's 1959 *The Two Cultures*, in which he states that academics from differing fields had "almost ceased to communicate at all" (2). However, the Ometeca Institute was also devoted to creating dialogue among scholars from differing countries, particularly the US and Latin American countries, along with a holistic vision of education. This vision was expressed in Rafael Catala's *Sciencepoetry*, a book of poems with an introduction that articulated a theory of knowledge integration.

p. 68: Emerson's quotation, "The reason why the world lacks unity, and is broken in heaps, is because man is disunited with himself," is from "Nature" (64).

pp. 71-72: Wendell Berry is the author of numerous books on agriculture, culture, and sustainability, among other themes, as well as poems and novels. His 1977 classic, *The Unsettling of America: Culture and Agriculture*, explores farming as a spiritual discipline, or exercise, and includes the influential essay "The Ecological Crisis as a Crisis of Agriculture." Wes Jackson's 1980 classic, *The New Roots of Agriculture*, details the damage done by high-tech forms of conventional agriculture, including erosion and loss of soil from tillage. Jackson has also written other excellent books on agriculture, culture, and sustainability, including *Consulting the Genius of the Place: An Ecological Approach to a New Agriculture*. Jackson's wisdom is featured in a film I have shown to undergraduates, *Y.E.R.T*, or *Your Environmental Road Trip*, in which three recent college graduates travel the US (in a hybrid) in search of sustainability solutions.

p. 72: Wendell Berry's essay "Whose Head is the Farmer Using? Whose Head is Using the Farmer" can be found in *Meeting the Expectations of the Land: Essays in Sustainable Agriculture and Stewardship*, edited by Berry, Jackson, and Bruce Colman.

p. 72: The Wendell Berry quotation "We had better respect the possibility of a larger, unseen pattern that can be damaged or destroyed and, with it, the smaller patterns" is from *Home Economics* (4). He explores the genius of the place and listening to this genius in the spirit of dialogue in *What Are People For?* (209).

p. 74: Thoreau's scientific practice is explored in Daniel B. Botkin's *No Man's Garden: Thoreau and a New Vision of Civilization and Nature*. Botkin uses the example of Thoreau measuring the depths of Walden Pond to show his early and adept practice. Using a compass, sounding line, and weight, Thoreau made more than one hundred measurements, which he translated into a map. Botkin writes that his curiosity concerning his quantitative measurements led him to formulate hypotheses about other ponds that required further measurements and hypotheses (65–67). The quotation on the bravery of science is from *No Man's Garden* (75). The quotations on his killing of the box turtle and the man of science studying nature as if dead language is from *The Heart of Thoreau's Journals*, edited by Odell Shepard (112, 135).

p. 74: The Emerson material on the "advantages" gained from studying natural history is from Robert A. Gross's *The Transcendentalists and Their World* (243). Gross provides a detailed historical accounting of the changing economics of Concord, Massachusetts, in the early 1800s and its influence on the transcendentalists.

p. 75: Emerson's comments on Thoreau's observatory powers, becoming a "log among the logs," is from his eulogy for Henry, which can be found in *The Portable Emerson* in the section simply titled "Thoreau." Emerson was a bit critical in the eulogy, stating that Thoreau was "rarely tender" and did not "feel himself unless in opposition," which I imagine was both true and false, depending on the interpersonal situation. For example, he does not mention Henry's kindness to his own kids. But most of the eulogy is filled with high praise and honest assessment, including "He chose to be rich by making his wants few, and supplying them himself" (575–76).

pp. 75-76: The negative reaction to Thoreau's talk was taken from The Thoreau Society Facebook group daily postings. Most posts are quotations from his journals, but some are bits of history from historian Richard Smith, like on his lyceum speeches. Smith dresses like and embodies Thoreau while giving walking tours at Walden Pond—a tour worth taking. The positive reaction is from Laura Dassow Walls's *Henry David Thoreau: A Life* (282).

p. 76: Material on Thoreau as both scientist and poet, including his reading of Darwin, dealings with Louis Agassiz, and talk and essay "The Succession of Forest Trees," is from Walls's *Henry David Thoreau: A Life* (458–60, 471–72). The quotation on killing for science as not being the proper "means for acquiring true knowledge" is from page 345. The quotations "Do you think I should shoot you if I wanted to study you?" is from page 374.

p. 76: The quotation on Natives being "damned, because his enemies were his historians" is from Walls's *Henry David Thoreau: A Life* (420).

pp. 76-77: Thoreau's quotation on the muskrat, "he is a different kind of man, that is all," can be found in Walls's *Henry David Thoreau: A Life* (305). The quotation on someone shooting the summer ducks he cared for, lamenting that they considered it more important to "taste the flavor of them dead than I should enjoy the beauty of them alive," is also from Walls (433).

p. 77: The quotations on the subjectivity of the scientist, who should watch "the moods of his mind as the astronomer watches the aspect of the heavens," and being "incessantly wary" of exchanging the microscope for "views as wide as heaven's cope," are from Kevin Dann's *Expect Great Things* (196).

p. 77: Discussion of the use of Thoreau's journals to map climate change can be found in Alison Flood's *Guardian* article "Scientists use Thoreau's journal notes to track climate change: Researchers use Walden author's tables of flowering dates in 1840s Massachusetts to show temperature has risen 2.4C" (May 12, 2012).

p. 77: The quotation "Perhaps the facts most astounding and most real are never communicated by man to man" is from the "Higher Laws" section of *Walden*.

p. 77: Richard B. Primack calls Thoreau a climate scientist in *Walden Warming: Climate Change Comes to Thoreau's Woods* (30). Robert Sattelmeyer explores Thoreau's many scientific accomplishments, including his studies on wildflowers, seed dispersion, and rivers systems, in "The Evolutions of Thoreau's Science" from *Thoreau in an Age of Science: Uses and Abuses of an Icon* (36–40). Sattelmeyer approvingly cites Primack's book but does mention that calling Thoreau a climate scientist is "perhaps pardonable hyperbole," as he was not "clairvoyantly recording" data to study climate.

p. 78: The Emerson quotation "Beware when the Great God lets lose a thinker on the planet" is from his essay "Circles" in *The Portable Emerson* (232).

p. 78: The question of population has often popped up in class discussion during my many years of teaching, and if we are to practice logos, we must consider what Tom

Athanasiou, in *Divided Planet*, calls the "ecology of rich and poor," in which socioeconomic inequities are the core issue. High population density places such as Holland and Japan, for example, do not come to mind when we think of overpopulation, but poorer countries such as India do (81). We must further consider the fact that when women have social, political, and economic equality, population goes down without draconian restrictions on the number of kids parents can have. Paul Hawken's *Project Drawdown* book and website ranks the education of girls and family planning as a top solution for combating rising CO_2. Blaming overpopulation for all our eco-ills is a poor argument in which the poor get blamed, given "first world" overconsumption and energy use. Having said that, population remains a serious concern as we have tripled our numbers since the 1960s and are headed toward 10 billion by 2050.

pp. 79–80: The Martin Heidegger quotations on calculative and meditative thinking in *Discourse on Thinking* are from his "Memorial Address" in 1955 (43–57). He also had strong words to share on technology: "The power concealed in modern technology determines the relation of man to that which exists. It rules the whole Earth" (50). Heidegger, of course, wrote these words after the dropping of atomic bombs on Hiroshima and Nagasaki. He saw the "taming of atomic energy" as a "crude start," in which technology would increasingly control our lives, leading to "radical changes" (51). One wonders what Heidegger would have thought of the internet, social media, and climate crisis, as his writings anticipated a completely changed world.

An excellent book that draws on Heidegger's views on meditative and calculative thinking to explore the limits of science is Ramsey Eric Ramsey and Linda Weiner's *Leaving Us to Wonder: An Essay on the Questions Science Can't Ask*. Ramsey and Wiener explicate the dangers of scientism while extolling the necessity of philosophical questioning and pursuit of the good.

p. 80: Heidegger's comments on the problem of perceiving and treating nature only as a standing reserve of resources are from *The Question Concerning Technology and Other Essays*.

p. 83: An excellent anthology of Vine Deloria Jr.'s work is *Spirit and Reason: The Vine Deloria Jr. Reader*. I have taught an essay from this volume in my The Voice of Nature course, "If You Think about It, You Will See That It Is True," which defends the so-called prescientific yet systematic and philosophical inquiries into the workings of the natural world by Indigenous peoples. This essay suggests some universal views and experiences among different Native American tribes, including a moral universe of aliveness, relationship, and responsibility. On the other hand, Shepard Krech, in *The Ecological Indian: Myth and History*, questions the ecological morality of Native Americans, arguing that historical evidence reveals many misdeeds, including overexploited buffalo herds, cutting too many trees, and the inappropriate use of fire. Thus, the myth of the ecological Indian is just that—a myth. From my readings, the myth of the pure Indian doing no harm to animals or to the land was propagated most famously by the media in the 1970s; the Keep America Beautiful advertising campaign showed a heroic-looking and then teary-eyed Native American on horseback viewing the litter and pollution of industrial society. The ad reflects one end of a spectrum, and Krech's account reflects the other. Both go too far in opposite directions, with the complexity and principles of Native life articulated by Deloria (not always fully actualized) being lost. But there is growing interest in traditional ecological knowledge (TEK) in our climate crisis times and for obvious good reasons. Excellent resources on TEK include Fikret Berkes's *Sacred Ecology* and Robin Wall Kimmerer's wonderful *Braiding Sweetgrass* and *Gathering Moss*, which articulate grammars of animism, aesthetics, and spirit integrated with science and Native knowing. Kimmerer, like Thoreau, integrates the sciences and humanities in her writings and thus models a holistic vision of education. See my online article in About Place Journal for a special issue on the more-than-human world: "Robin Wall Kimmerer and Deep Listening: Practicing an Ecology of Communication."

pp. 83–84: Information on Tecumseh, the Prophet, and Battle of Tippecanoe can be found on the Tippecanoe County Historical Association website. An excellent biography is Allan W. Eckert's *A Sorrow in our Hearts: The Life of Tecumseh.*

Chapter 6: World Soul

p. 85: The Emerson epigram on living in the "lap of immense intelligence" is from his essay "Self-Reliance" in *The Portable Emerson* (150). The Thoreau epigram on the inability of science to tell how and whence "light comes into the soul" is from his journals and discussed in Laura Dassow Walls's *Henry David Thoreau: A Life* (309). Walls has written extensively on Thoreau's embrace and criticism of science, including in *Seeing New Worlds: Henry David Thoreau and Nineteenth-Century Natural Science.*

pp. 85–86: The insights from James Hillman are from *The Soul's Code: In Search of Character and Calling.* I am also fond of *We've Had a Hundred Years of Psychotherapy and the World is Getting Worse*, written as a correspondence with the journalist Michael Ventura. Hillman, like Erich Fromm and Abraham Maslow, is critical of mainstream psychology when it helps people fit into a damaged world, or a quiet desperation world, that they should not be fitting into, a sentiment conveyed often by Thoreau. Books on ecopsychology also frequently make this claim, including Theodore Roszak's *The Voice of the Earth.* A more academic work by Hillman is *Re-Visioning Psychology.*

p. 87: An excellent book on Emerson's views on the Over-Soul connected to reason and understanding is Richard Geldard's *The Spiritual Teachings of Ralph Waldo Emerson.*

p. 87: The material and quotations on Emerson's grief and transformation after the death of his first wife, Ellen, are from Barry Andrew's *Emerson as Spiritual Guide: A Companion to Emerson's Essays for Personal Reflection and Group Discussion* (1–3).

p. 87: The Emerson quotation on commerce transferring the "devotion of men from the soul to the material in which it works" is from Barry Andrews's *American Sage: The Spiritual Teachings of Ralph Waldo Emerson* (3).

p. 88: The Emerson quotation "The difficulty is that we do not make a world of our own but fall into institutions already made..." is from Barry Andrews's *American Sage:*

The Spiritual Teachings of Ralph Waldo Emerson (23–24). Andrews explores the risk involved in Emerson giving up his minister's post on page 26. It is worth noting, however, that Emerson had the good fortune of eventually receiving monies from Ellen's estate after her death, which he used to buy a house in Concord and take in relatives (46).

p. 89: Ken Wilber's articulation of spiritual methodology similar to scientific methodology can be found in *The Eye of Spirit: An Integral Vision for a World Gone Slightly Mad* (12–13).

p. 90: Emerson's arguments on self-culture as an "educating of the eye" are explored in Barry Andrews's *American Sage: The Spiritual Teachings of Ralph Waldo Emerson* (42).

pp. 90-91: Material on Emerson and other transcendentalists seeking to reform the Unitarian church of their time, and Emerson's call for "first, soul, and second, soul, and evermore, soul," can be found in John A. Buehrens's *Conflagration: How the Transcendentalists Sparked the American Struggle for Racial, Gender, and Social Justice* (1–11). Further material on the conflict about the direction of the church and Thoreau's decision to no longer attend can be found in Walls's *Henry David Thoreau: A Life* (48–49).

Chapter 7: Magnificent Misfits

p. 95: The Emerson epigram on leaving institutions and addressing individuals is from his lecture "Education." This lecture can be found online: archive.vcu.edu/english/engweb/transcendentalism/authors/emerson/essays/education.html. The Thoreau epigram on making education a pleasant thing and learning with students can be found in *Uncommon Learning: Thoreau on Education*, edited by Martin Bickman (29). The Margaret Fuller epigram on giving the soul free course is from "The Great Lawsuit," which can be found in the anthology *The American Transcendentalists: Essential Writings*, edited by Lawrence Buell (317).

pp. 96-97: Howard Gardner explores multiple intelligence theory in several books. I have taught from *Intelligence Reframed*; chapters 3 and 4 define the differing intelligences. During my years teaching at Purdue, when I met with students in the woodsy café, I would often suggest multiple intelligence theory when a student was struggling to find a social issue speech topic. I knew it would be good not only for them but also for the class, especially engineering and agriculture majors who excelled at logical-mathematical intelligence and were successful test takers because of it but were lacking in other intelligences.

pp. 97-98: Thomas Berry and Brian Swimme's *The Universe Story* includes a timeline of key approximate dates of evolution taken from Nigel Calder's *Timescale*, which I often share with students. Berry's *The Dream of the Earth*, *The Great Work*, and *Evening Thoughts* are also excellent. I was fortunate to hear an elderly Berry speak on "Education for the 21st Century" at an outdoor ecopsychology conference organized by Prescott College in Northern Arizona, where he argued that education must be tied to the unfolding universe and earth story, as the university often has no universe in it, no connection to cosmos or place. Berry's kind and compassionate presence matched his wise words. He passed away in 2009, leaving behind many gifts in the form of teaching, mentoring, writing, and just being in the world.

Thoreau anticipated Berry's critical concerns in an October 15, 1859, journal entry (see *Uncommon Learning: Henry David Thoreau on Education*, 45–46): "We boast of our system of education, but why stop at schoolmasters and schoolhouses? We are all schoolmasters, and our schoolhouse is the universe. To attend chiefly to the desk or schoolhouse while we neglect the scenery in which it is placed is absurd."

p. 103: Material on the mentor-student relationship between Emerson and Thoreau is from Harmon Smith's *My Friend, My Friend*. The Emerson quotations recalling his excursion with his "good river god" Thoreau, the stars saying, "Here we are," their "ineffable beams" stopping human conversation, is from Jeffrey S. Cramer's *Solid Seasons* (23–24). When I read this quotation on the influence of the night sky, I immediately thought of my nighttime walk with Jeff at Purdue, as well as Thomas Berry's argument that not being able to see the night sky due to light pollution is a soul loss.

Cramer took the title of his book from Thoreau's comment in the "Former Inhabitants; and Winter Visitors" section of *Walden*, where he writes that he had "solid seasons, long to be remembered, at his house in the village, and who looked in upon me from time to time...." He is referencing his visits to see Emerson in the village and Emerson's occasional visits to the pond to converse with him.

pp. 103–104: Material on Emerson's education, family, and speaking are from Robert D. Richardson's *The Mind on Fire*. His relationship with Mary Moody Emerson is explored on pages 23–28.

p. 104: The mission of *The Dial* can be found in Kevin Dann's *Expect Great Things* (66–67).

pp. 104-105: The Fuller quotations are from "The Great Lawsuit," which can be found in *The American Transcendentalists: Essential Writings*, edited by Lawrence Buell (307, 309).

p. 105: Fuller's mystical experience is described in "Recollection of Mystical Experiences" from *The American Transcendentalists: Essential Writings*, edited by Lawrence Buell (158–61).

pp. 105–106: Biographical material on Margaret Fuller comes from the introduction to *The Portable Margaret Fuller*, edited by Mary Keller. A more recent biography of Fuller is Megan Marshall's *Margaret Fuller: A New American Life*. The Barry Andrews's quotation on Fuller being the most well-read woman in America is from *Transcendentalism and the Cultivation of the Soul*. Andrews also explores Fuller's teaching "conversations" (86–87) and Elizabeth Peabody's educational reform views (123).

p. 105: Material on Fuller being influenced by the daemonic, along with the quotation on destiny and doing "holy work" by making "the earth part of heaven," is from Dann's *Expect Great Things* (69).

p. 106: Fuller's advice to Thoreau, "Nature is not yours until you have been more hers," is from Laura Dassow Walls's *Henry David Thoreau: A Life* (292). Walls also discusses their literary relationship on pages 117–18. Thoreau was a writer of place and thus needed to be rooted in Concord, and the woods, to be himself and write.

p. 107: Aunt Mary Moody Emerson's claim that women were "frivolous, almost without exception" can be found in Walls's *Henry David Thoreau: A Life* (321).

p. 107: Thoreau revealed some of his attitudes toward women after attending two speeches. Elizabeth Oakes Smith wrote a ten-part series on women's rights in the *New York Tribune* in 1850 and soon became the first woman to speak on the lyceum circuit. Thoreau stated that the most important fact about the speech is that she spoke. In his journal, he was more critical: the pocket in which she carried her lecture reeked of perfume, and he saw contradiction in a champion of rights expecting a "ladies' man" (Walls, *Henry David Thoreau: A Life*, 320–21). Nine years later, Caroline Dall, a transcendentalist and feminist writer, would speak on "Lives of Noted Women"; Emerson stated that Thoreau was not coming because he thought that women had nothing worth saying, yet he did attend, enjoyed the lecture, and invited Dall to stay an extra day at the Thoreau home, where they had engaging conversations. Dall would later write that Thoreau's tongue was "hardly fit for ordinary use," as it was more like a "severing blade." Thoreau's attendance at Dall's lyceum talk and their talk afterwards is described in Walls's *Henry David Thoreau: A Life* (440) and Cramer's *Solid Seasons* (88–89). Dall's quotations on Thoreau are from *Solid Seasons*.

Walls further explores Thoreau's interactions with women in *Henry David Thoreau: A Life*, which were no doubt complicated by his failures in love. Thoreau loved men and women, he wrote, as philia or friendship love, as if there were a "third sex." He also loved keen intellect and expression of higher laws as poetic friendship. The women he loved, as friends or sisters (including his own sisters), were married or older, except for Ellen Sewall, whom he fell for in his early twenties.

Did his lifetime focus on the spiritual, and on exploration of the material via nature study, at least partially stem from an asexual life? Is this why he wrote "nature must be overcome" in the "Higher Laws" section of *Walden*; in other words, not only overcoming nature to focus on Spirit as nature, as transcendentalist do, but also overcoming his animal nature, his desiring, sexual nature? Hard to say. But overcoming as transcending, rather than repression, may be experienced as sublimation, transmuting sexual energy into creative energy. He was not ashamed of his body, or bodies, but sexual relationships just did not happen for him and could not have easily happened with a man, if desired, due to Victorian times. He did have a bit of a prudish reaction to the more sexual and sensuous lines in Walt Whitman's *Leaves of Grass*, yet he was no prude and argued that we should be artists of the body, builders of the temple.

Emerson, in a deleted section of his eulogy, claimed he was nearest to "the old monks in their ascetic religion," yet perhaps this was deleted for good reason as he was so much more than a monk. He was so vibrant in his love for the natural world and celebration of life and so involved in the workings of his beloved Concord. A magnificent misfit, to be sure, pouring his energy into being free, but no monk.

"Intercourse of the sexes," he told a friend, was, he could only dream, "incredibly beautiful" and "an inexpressible delirium of joy." But sexual love was not to be, so he sublimated, not living in dreams, but finding joy, and miracle, in experiencing intimacy by looking "through each other's eyes for a moment" (Walls 239–41).

As for Emerson, he sometimes came up short in his relations with women, especially a lack of emotion in interactions with Fuller and Lidian. His equanimity had its benefits but was frustrating to the women in his life when taken too far. He did write that superior men were as rare as superior women, and, if given the right to vote, women would not vote any worse than men. It was a backward compliment but also a statement of equality, which he backed up when he added, "If women feel wronged, they are wronged." Emerson's comments on women are from Cramer's *Solid Seasons* (90). More on Emerson's lack of expressed emotions, especially in his interactions with Fuller and Lidian, can be found in Robert A. Gross's *The Transcendentalists and Their World* and Megan Marshall's *Margaret Fuller: A New American Life*. Emerson's relationship with Fuller was complex, with Fuller wanting more than Emerson was able to give, yet they met intellectually and soulfully. His evolution on women's rights is explored in Barry Andrews's *American Sage: The Spiritual Teachings of Ralph Waldo Emerson* (138–40).

p. 107: Thoreau and Emerson's praise of Fuller's "The Great Lawsuit" is explored in Cramer's *Solid Seasons* (88–90).

p. 108: The essay "The American Scholar" can be found in *The Portable Emerson*. Barry Andrews explores "The American Scholar" speech and Emerson's views on holistic education in *American Sage: The Spiritual Teachings of Ralph Waldo Emerson* (53–54).

p. 108: Material on Thoreau not attending Emerson's "The American Scholar" address at Harvard can be found in Cramer's *Solid Seasons* (7).

pp. 108–109: The "Divinity School Address" is also in *The Portable Emerson*.

p. 109: Material on Thoreau giving Emerson his own ethics can be found in the chapter on Thoreau in Robert D. Richardson Jr.'s *Emerson: The Mind on Fire* (280–85).

p. 109: Discussion of Thoreau's not measuring up to Emerson's ideals in "The Poet" can be found in Walls's *Henry David Thoreau: A Life* (170).

pp. 109–110: Material, including the quotations, on Thoreau's "failed" attempt at a literary career in New York City and rebound by building a cabin on Emerson's land at Walden Pond, is described in Walls's *Henry David Thoreau: A Life* (163, 188–92).

p. 111: The Thoreau quotation, "I know of few radicals as yet who are radical enough," can be found in Walls's *Henry David Thoreau: A Life*. Emerson tended toward middle ground, arguing that extremism/extreme measures are "all in vain" (168).

p. 112: John Taylor Gatto's 2003 article, "Against School," is from *Harper's* magazine. I share this piece with Senior Seminar students, and they relate, especially with Gatto's assertion that both high school students and teachers are often bored.

p. 112: The Thoreau quotation "What does education often do? It makes a straight-cut ditch of a free, meandering brook," can be found in *The Heart of Thoreau's Journals*, edited by Odell Shepard (39), as well as in *Uncommon Learning: Thoreau on Education*, edited by Martin Bickman (39). I also used this quotation as an epigram for chapter 2, but it is worth repeating here.

p. 113: The Thoreau quotations on love are from Dann's *Expect Great Things* (87).

p. 113: The Thoreau quotation "A man is rich in proportion to the number of things he can afford to let alone" is from the "Where I Lived, and What I Lived For" section of *Walden*.

p. 113: Lawrence Buell reflects on the American Dream and Thoreau's "antimaterialist counterdream" in *Henry David Thoreau: Thinking Disobediently* (29).

p. 113: Thoreau's question, "Why should we be in such desperate haste to succeed, and in such desperate enterprises?" is from the conclusion to *Walden*.

p. 114: Emerson's "rules of life" are explored in Barry Andrews's *American Sage: The Spiritual Teachings of Ralph Waldo Emerson* (155–56). The quotations "All education is to accustom him to trust himself" to become a "self-searching soul, brave to assist or resist a world" and "only humble or docile before the source of the wisdom he has discovered within him" are also from *American Sage* (180).

pp. 114-115: Thoreau's famous quotations on going in the "direction of our dreams" and meeting with "success unexpected in common hours" are from the conclusion of *Walden* (*The Portable Thoreau*, 562). The quotations on life, destiny, and wanting his neighbors' "original thoughts" are from an October 18, 1859, journal entry that can be found online at walden.org in "The Journal of Henry David Thoreau."

p. 115: The Thoreau quotation on each person finding their own way and not following him or their mother, father, or neighbor is from the "Economy" section of *Walden* (*The Portable Thoreau*, 562). Of course, the same goes for following the teacher. In an undated journal entry (around October 31, 1850), he writes, "How vain it is to teach youth, or anybody, truths! They can only learn them after their own fashion, and when they get ready." This quotation can be found in *Uncommon Learning: Thoreau on Education*, edited by Martin Bickman (38).

Chapter 8: Nature as Teacher

Note: This chapter includes previously published material from my 2021 book, *An Ecology of Communication: Response and Responsibility in an Age of Ecocrisis*, specifically parts of my trail story and some content on Thoreau's Maine hikes. The story and Maine content are crucial to both projects although editing and many additions are included here.

p. 121: The Emerson epigram on being a "transparent eyeball" is from "Nature" (8). The Thoreau epigram on wildness is from "Walking" (95). These well-known quotations deserve to be well-known, as well as reinterpreted and lived. In *The Abstract Wild*, Jack Turner argues that many have misinterpreted Thoreau's "In Wildness is the preservation of the World," thinking he wrote "wilderness" instead of "wildness." Wilderness is a place, wildness is a quality, and for humans, an endangered experience because wilderness areas are often too small. They are also increasingly tamed, remade into recreational areas, and even then we spend too little time in them. Also, for Turner "the World" is not just human society but an ordered cosmos, which we come more in contact with through experiences of wildness, feeling ourselves part and parcel of nature and larger patterns. Being free to experience wildness, and thus less tamed by civilization's biases, increases meditative thinking on these patterns and our place within them, preserving the World.

The ecopsychologist Robert Greenway, while providing plenty of evidence for nature as teacher and wilderness as a healing balm in his essays "The Wilderness Effect and Ecopsychology" and "Healing by Wilderness Experience," also argues that we can't all turn to wilderness for therapy because our numbers would destroy the wilderness that is left. Instead, we need to generate similar healing experiences from spiritual practices like meditation and yoga, and getting outside wherever we live, hopefully sauntering like Thoreau and finding wildness as best we can within human-created environs. All of this makes a strong case for designing urban spaces, where more than 50 percent of the world's population live (expected to reach 70 percent by 2050), with nature in mind, if we are to preserve the world and thus our sanity and freedom.

pp. 124–128: Thoreau's three hiking trips to Maine and learning about Native American ways from Joe Aitteon and especially Joe Polis are catalogued in *The Maine Woods* and in Laura Dassow Walls's *Henry David Thoreau: A Life* (218–19, 334–41, 407–22). Walls reports that despite all of Thoreau's learning, he could write, when in a foul mood from illness and a hapless winter, that the Indian was "passing away" despite efforts to "Christianize and educate them," and that the white man represents a "history of improvement," the "red man a history of fixed habits" and "stagnation." By spring, after reading a dictionary of the Abenaki language, hearing a Native American speak, and finding an intricate fish basket, his exuberance for all things Indian returned, leading him to claim they have a "more practical and vital science" (427-428).

p. 124: Thoreau's famous euphoric howl, "What is this Titan that has possession of me? Talk of mysteries!—Think of our life in nature,—daily to be shown matter, to come into contact with it,—rocks, trees, wind on our cheeks! The solid earth! The actual world! The common sense! Contact! Contact! Who are we? Where are we?" can be found in *The Maine Woods*, edited and annotated by Jeffrey S. Cramer (64). More biographical information and insights on Thoreau's Mt. Katahdin experience can be found in Robert D. Richardson's *Thoreau: The Life of the Mind* and Laura Dassow Walls's *Henry David Thoreau: A Life.*

p. 125: The quotations on Aitteon killing a moose, which Thoreau equates with "God's own horses," and later listening to Native language at an Indian camp are from Walls's *Henry David Thoreau: A Life* (334–37, 339).

p. 125: The Thoreau quotation on Native Americans as "strange spirits, daemons, whose eyes could never meet mine; with another nature, another fate than mine" is from his journal on March 18, 1842, and can be found online at walden.org.

p. 126: Polis's remarks in response to the many questions of Thoreau and Hoar, "May be your way of talking—may be all right—no Indian way" and "Oh I can't tell you— Great difference between me & white man," are from Walls's *Henry David Thoreau: A Life* (411).

p. 127: Thoreau's remarks on not needing scientific explanation, making an "empty chamber" of an "inhabited house" of "spirits as good as himself" and nature making "a thousand revelations" to Natives that "she still keeps secret to us" are from *The Maine Woods*, edited by Jeffery S. Cramer (168–69).

p. 127: Thoreau's disagreement with Polis about the killing of a moose, including Thoreau claiming that Polis's reasons were the "white man's argument," is from Walls's *Henry David Thoreau: A Life* (416). Polis's remark, "It makes no difference to me where I am," at the end of their hike is from *The Maine Woods*, edited by Jeffery S. Cramer (276). The material on Polis being threatened by Daniel Webster can also be found in *The Maine Woods* (235).

p. 128: The quotations on Natives displaying "so much intelligence that the white man does not," increasing his "own capacity, as well as faith" and the intricately woven Indian fishing basket filled with fish after the trip, its maker "meditating a small poem," are from Walls's *Henry David Thoreau: A Life* (419, 428).

p. 128: The material on Maine's changing landscape is from William Cronon' s *Changes to the Land* (39).

p. 128: Thoreau's uncanny gift for finding arrowheads is explored in Kevin Dann's *Expect Great Things* (39).

p. 129: The quotation on Thoreau calling arrowheads "fossil thoughts" and them putting him on a "trail of mind" that "never failed to set me right" is from a March 28, 1859, journal entry and can be found online at walden.org.

p. 129: Thoreau's idolizing of Tahatawan in his youth is explored in Dann's *Expect Great Things* (38, 44–45).

pp. 129-130: The Thoreau quotation advocating for "natural preserves" in which "the bear and the panther, and even some of the hunter race, may still exist" and not be "civilized off of the face of the earth" can be found in Walls's *Henry David Thoreau: A Life* (341).

p. 130: The material on Thoreau imagining himself as Native and learning and living and teaching their virtues comes from Brent Ranalli's "Henry David Thoreau's Life- long Indian Play," as does the Emerson quotation on Thoreau being more Indian than white (145). Ranalli wisely brings up the critical charge of Thoreau appropriat- ing Indian ways although appropriation is a modern construct. Still, this is a serious concern, as Philip J. Deloria, in *Playing Indian*, argues that such play was part and parcel of settler colonialism and genocide. For the most part, however, imaginative play for Thoreau was a means for learning. The material on Thoreau's struggle to overcome the ethnographic bias of his time and in many ways doing so is from John J. Kucich's "Thoreau's Indian Problem: Savagism, Indigeneity, and the Politics of Place." These insightful essays are from *Thoreau in an Age of Crisis: Uses and Abuses of* *an American Icon.* Kucich has also written provocative and informative essays on Thoreau and Native Americans in *Thoreau beyond Borders: New International Essays on America's Most Famous Nature Writer,* "An Imperfect Indian Wisdom," and *Henry David Thoreau in Crisis,* "Native America." The material on Thoreau seeking "a more perfect Indian wisdom" that runs counter to techno-industrial capitalism and materialism generally is from "Native America" (200–201).

p. 130: The Thoreau quotation, "How near to good is what is wild," is from "Walking" in John Elder's anthology *Nature/Walking* (97).

p. 131: The material on Thoreau's Maine Indian guides, Neptune, Aitteon, and Polis, who were forced to straddle two worlds, is from Michael Stoneham's article, "Remeasuring Thoreau: The Maine Woods and Thoreau's Evolving Appreciation of the Racial Other," in *The Concord Saunterer: A Journal of Thoreau Studies* (68–88).

p. 131: Thoreau's concern with recovering lost Native American lessons rather than keeping Natives themselves from vanishing—and then the counterview in his late journal entry imagining a turning away from destructive agriculture and a return of Natives and their lifeways—is explored in John Kucich's "Thoreau's Indian Problem: Savagism, Indigeneity, and the Politics of Place" in *Thoreau in an Age of Crisis: Uses and Abuses of an American Icon* (128, 141). Kucich also explores Thoreau's views on Manifest Destiny in this essay.

p. 134: The material on the genocidal murder of 90 percent of Indigenous peoples possibly contributing to a decrease in temperatures, called the "little ice age" because there was less human activity, is from Mark Trahant's "How Colonization of the Americas Killed 90% of Their Peoples—and Changed the Climate" in *Yes!* magazine.

p. 134: Maine's changing climate is documented on the climatecouncil.maine.gov website.

Chapter 9: In the World but Not of It?
p. 136: The Evelyn Underhill epigram on the dangers of a perverted mysticism, in which we focus on God instead of nature or nature instead of God, is from *Practical Mysticism* (90), which was another used bookstore find that was important to me before meeting Rafael and attempting to live a spiritual life. Underhill is best known for her seminal and much longer book, *Mysticism: The Preeminent Study in the Nature and Development of Spiritual Consciousness.* The Martin Buber epigram on heightening reality rather than wanting to escape it is from *Pointing the Way* (28). Buber's writings were also influential in early years; I was especially intrigued by his turn away from mysticism toward dialogue and a more grounded existence.

p. 137: The Shankara quotation, "He who knows is full of glory, he rides within his body as if within a carriage," is from the *Crest Jewel of Discrimination* (122). Shankara is an advocate of Vedanta, which, in some ways, is like Joel Goldsmith's Christian mysticism, but instead of focusing attention on "God is," Shankara states that liberation occurs when we realize that "Brahman is" or "I am Brahman." Despite its spiritual wisdom, Vedanta has been criticized for being world-denying although Vedanta does not argue that the earth or body are not real, but that the reality of Brahman is not revealed by sense knowledge. Whether or not Vedanta is world-denying, those who try to live an awakened life based on its principles may mistakenly take a world-denying path, thinking they are enlightened when they are not. In other words, the One obscures the many, rather than seeing the One in the many and the many in the One.

John Welwood coined the phrase "spiritual bypassing" to describe transcendence without embrace, especially regarding personal inadequacies. In other words, instead of dealing with our emotional issues, or demons, if you will, we attempt to use spiritual practices such as meditation to bypass them. Welwood calls this "premature transcendence" and, not surprisingly, it does not work. The phrase "In the world but not of it" may suggest spiritual bypassing, or, in a more positive interpretation, transcending the debilitating, quiet desperation aspects of the world so that we may more fully embrace it. As always, wise discernment is imperative. I needed to be lost before discerning more wisely. Welwood's insights on the spiritual path can be found in *Toward a Psychology of Awakening: Buddhism, Psychotherapy, and the Path of Personal and Spiritual Transformation.*

p. 147: Goldsmith discusses "supply" in numerous books, but it is the focus of *Invisible Supply: Finding the Gifts of the Spirit Within.*

pp. 148-149: The material on Thoreau's musical wishes being answered, suggesting synchronicities, is explored in Kevin Dann's *Expect Great Things* (119).

p. 149: The phrase "open veins of Latin America" comes from a book of that title by Eduardo Galeano, which Rafael recommended to me. I eventually found my way to Galeano's *Memory of Fire* trilogy, which details in short, journalistic, yet story-like chapters the inequitable history of US and Latin American relations. Despite advocating for Goldsmithian supply, Rafael knew well the forces that lead to the lack of supply for the poor, stating in one of our early meetings that every time you eat a banana it is like eating the bloody toe of a Latin American. When I poll my students on the phrase "banana republic," they immediately think of the trendy clothing store, not realizing that it is a derogatory phrase suggesting a backward and underdeveloped country. They also don't know the history of the United Fruit company, which, with the backing of the US government, controlled millions of acres of Latin American land and exploited the poor, or that in 1954 the US government orchestrated the overthrow of democratically elected President Arbenz in Guatemala, who created policy to take back that land.

Rafael also introduced me to Paulo Freire's influential *Pedagogy of the Oppressed,* which argues that education must be liberatory, enabling the marginalized and oppressed to overcome their oppression. As such, Freire is critical of "banking" forms of education, in which teachers treats students as blank slates upon whom they make deposits of information: "If men are searchers and their ontological vocation is humanization, sooner or later they may perceive the contradiction in which banking education seeks to maintain them and then engage themselves in the struggle for liberation" (61–62).

p. 150: Emerson's comments on Thoreau sometimes being more sour than sweet is from Jeffrey S. Cramer's *Solid Seasons* (99–100).

pp. 151–152: A collection of Archbishop Oscar Romero's quotations can be found in *The Violence of Love*, edited by James R. Brockman. There are several excellent books on liberation theology, beginning with Gustavo Gutierrez's seminal *A Theology of Liberation*. Philip Berryman provides a good overview in *Liberation Theology: The Essential Facts about the Revolutionary Movement in Latin America and Beyond*, and Leonardo Boff links liberation theology with earth ethics in *Cry of the Earth, Cry of the Poor*. I am also fond of Dorothee Soelle's *The Silent Cry: Mysticism and Resistance*, where she argues that we are all mystics, as mystical experience and awareness is a human attribute. A good anthology on mysticism and resistance is *Mysticism and Social Transformation*, edited by Janet K. Ruffing. All these books argue that a genuine religious or mystical sensibility leads to love in action.

Rafael also introduced me to Ernesto Cardenal's *Cosmic Canticle*, an epic narrative poem that integrates science, religion, Latin American history, and politics. Cardenal is most definitely a science-poet, and, like Thomas Berry, in his hands the birth of the universe becomes a grand story.

Chapter 10: The Guru as Teacher

p. 154: The Emerson epigram "Truly speaking, it is not instruction, but provocation, that I can receive from another soul. What he announces, I must find true in me, or wholly reject, and on his word …be he who he may, I can accept nothing" is from his "Divinity School Address" in *The Portable Emerson* (76–77). The second Emerson epigram, "That which we are, we teach, not voluntarily but involuntarily," is from "The Over-Soul," also from *The Portable Emerson* (221). Emerson deeply believed in the power of education to transform, but he was often deeply critical of formal education. For example, in his essay "New England Reformers," from *The Political Emerson* edited by David M. Robinson, he writes, "We are students of words: we are shut up in schools, and colleges, and recitation-rooms, for ten or fifteen years, and come out at last with a bag of wind, a memory of words, and do not know a thing" (75).

p. 156: Leah Thomas's June 8, 2020, article "Why Every Environmentalist Should Be Anti-Racist" is from *Vogue* online.

pp. 156-157: Plato's "The Allegory of the Cave," which, of course, details Socrates's dialogue with Glaucon, can be found in Frances MacDonald Cornford's translation of *The Republic of Plato* (227–35).

p. 157: Peter Wirzbicki's *Fighting for the Higher Law: Black and White Transcendentalists against Slavery* details the contributions of Black transcendentalists, including Jeremiah Burke Sanderson, Alexander Crummell, and William Cooper Neill. A key educational question is why these historical figures, and the history of Black transcendentalism generally, is so little known. Of course, my Senior Seminar syllabus can be criticized for not doing enough to honor such lost historical figures, despite focusing on higher law and universal principles. On the other hand, Wirzbicki's book came out in 2021, and I am just learning about this history myself. Eventually the information filters down into my teaching and revised syllabi as the class explores questions of our time together.

pp. 157-158: Rebecca Kneale Gould's "The Whiteness of Walden" is from *Thoreau in an Age of Crisis: Uses and Abuses of an American Icon*. The J. Drew Lanham quotation "It's only 9:06 A.M. and I think I might get hanged today" is from page 165. This quotation comes from Lanham's *The Homeplace: Memoirs of a Colored Man's Love of Nature*. The analysis of Thoreau's statement that the worst kind of slavery is "when you are yourself the slave driver," along with her commentary on his intentionally provocative style and eco-social connections, are from pages 170–71.

p. 158: Thoreau's criticism of his elders, including the claim that they have told him nothing and therefore have taught him nothing, is from the "Economy" section of *Walden* (*The Portable Thoreau*, 264).

p. 158: Jason W. Moore argues that "Capitalocene" is superior to "Anthropocene" as a term that accurately describes our crisis-filled age in the anthology *Anthropocene or Capitalocene?: Nature, History, and the Crisis of Capitalism*. He writes, "The Anthropocene sounds the alarm—and what an alarm it is! But it cannot explain how these alarming changes came about" (5).

p. 158: J. Drew Lanham calls Thoreau a kindred spirit in "A Letter to Hank," which appears in the Fall 2021 *Thoreau Society Bulletin*. Lanham was also a keynote speaker at the 2022 Thoreau Society Gathering, an annual conference on all things Thoreau, which also includes sessions on Emerson and Fuller. Gerald Early writes admiringly of Thoreau in "*Walden* and the Black Quest for Nature," which appears in *Now Comes Good Sailing: Writers Reflect on Henry David Thoreau* (37).

pp. 158-159: Gerald Early's identification with Thoreau's ability to transform "sorrow to a form of art" is from "*Walden* and the Black Quest for Nature" (38). Early also writes that *Walden*'s message to him was like that of Booker T. Washington's: for Black people to "create their own kind of civilized life with their own effort and to civilize the world through their effort" (39). Of course, this idea is another way to express transcendentalist self-culture and Emersonian self-reliance. Early further extolls Thoreau's support of John Brown, opposition to the rise of industrial capitalism, and linking of spirituality and activism, which endeared him to Black radicals. He concludes, "I think Walden profited me more than any other book I had read in my young life because of the time, the place, the circumstances, and my particular need for what I thought and hoped that it said" (39).

p. 160: Andrew Boyd writes about fighting for a "better catastrophe" in his highly informative and provocative *I Want a Better Catastrophe: Navigating the Climate Crisis with Grief, Hope, and Gallows Humor*. Boyd's book includes interviews and encounters with seven leading thinkers on climate, as well as the claim that we are facing a complex super-wicked crisis characterized by time running out, no central authority, those seeking to solve the problem also causing it, and irrational policies disregarding the future (116–17). Citing John Michael Greer, he also makes an important distinction between a solvable problem and an ongoing predicament that requires endless ethical response, with climate crisis being the latter (28–29).

p. 160: I can't recall where I first found the James Baldwin quotation "The world's definitions are one thing and the life one actually lives is quite another…one cannot allow oneself to live according to the world's definitions: one must find a way, perpetually, to be stronger and better than that," but it can be found on page 77 of *The Evidence of Things Not Seen* (first published in 1985, reissued in 2023, with a foreword by Stacey Abrams).

I still have the quotation on an index card, along with other "secular scripture" quotations that helped me get through my undergraduate years. I was also greatly influenced by Richard Wright's *Native Son* and Ralph Ellison's *Invisible Man*, which I read in literature courses.

p. 161: The Thoreau quotation "Men talk about Bible miracles because there are no miracles in their lives" can be found in Kevin Dann's *Expect Great Things* (171).

p. 164: Chogyam Trungpa's descriptions of the guru-student relationship are from his chapter "The Guru" in *Cutting through Spiritual Materialism* (31–50).

pp. 164–166: The misdeeds of Trungpa and Adi Da are detailed in Georg Feuerstein's *Holy Madness*. Adi Da tells his own story in his autobiography, *The Knee of Listening*. A provocative book on the power abuses and problematic teachings of gurus generally is Joel Kramer and Diana Alstead's *The Guru Papers*.

p. 166: Alan Watts's alcoholism is detailed in Monica Furlong's *Zen Effects: The Life of Alan Watts*. I am a fan of Watts, especially his books *The Supreme Identity* and *Nature, Man and Woman*, and these days many of his talks can be found on YouTube, but Furlong's biography supplies balance, showing the man himself and thus his humanness and failings.

p. 167: Andrew Cohen's many misdeeds are catalogued in Andre van der Braak's *Enlightenment Blues* and William Yenner's *American Guru*, as well as in numerous online sources. Despite his misdeeds, Cohen's spiritual community produced *EnlightenNext*, an insightful magazine filled with provocative interviews and profiles on spiritual leaders and what Cohen calls "evolutionary enlightenment." Ironically, Cohen missed out on a key element of evolutionary enlightenment: if we are individually and collectively evolving, rethinking the authority of the spiritual teacher is crucial to taking next steps.

p. 168: The Thoreau quotations on transcending via "friendship with the gods," being "universally related," and perceiving the "halo around the shadow" can be found in Kevin Dann's *Expect Great Things* (171, 190).

p. 168: The Emerson quotation on not wanting to "bring men to me, but to themselves" and having no school or followers is from Barry Andrews's *American Sage: The Spiritual Teachings of Ralph Waldo Emerson* (18).

pp. 168-169: The material on Krishnamurti is from Pupul Jayakar's *J. Krishnamurti: A Biography* (81). Krishnamurti also states "no gurus" in *Think on These Things*, arguing that we learn from life: "everything teaches you—a dead leaf, a bird in flight, a smell, a tear, the rich and the poor, those who are crying, the smile of a woman, the haughtiness of a man. You learn from everything, therefore there is no guide, no philosopher, no guru. Life itself is your teacher, and you are in a state of constant learning" (14).

p. 169: Lama Govinda's claim that Krishnamurti was humorless can be found in the philosopher Renee Weber's *Dialogues with Scientists and Sages: The Search for Unity* (67). I discovered this book of interviews with respected spiritual leaders and scientists, including the physicist David Bohm, in the mid-1980s when attending Rutgers, and it had a great influence on me because it showed that the religious and scientific searches for a deeper understanding of reality were similar.

p. 171: Larry Dossey's books on non-local mind and long-distance healing include *One Mind: How Our Individual Mind Is Part of a Greater Consciousness and Why It Matters*. While I read books of this type with a "I don't affirm or deny" attitude, I appreciate that Dossey has a science and medical background and remain open to mystery. I have a fascination with Psi phenomenon, once again not affirming or denying but exploring, particularly the books of the biologist Rupert Sheldrake, who argues for a larger mind along with what he calls morphogenetic fields that influence evolution. The theologian Jeffrey J. Kripal's books are also interesting, such as *The Flip: Epiphanies of Mind and the Future of Knowledge*, in which he documents changes of perspective due to Psi or religious experiences, including from scientists. Psi phenomena are being studied at the University of Virginia's Department of Perceptual Studies and by the Institute of Noetic Sciences (IONS) under the leadership of Dean Radin, a scientist who also writes good books on Psi and religious phenomenon, including *Supernormal* and *Real Magic*. My own book, *An Ecology of Communication: Response and Responsibility in an Age of Ecocrisis*, explores Psi and religious experiences as communicative while attempting to discern unfit interpretations. Whatever one thinks of such phenomenon, there is a long history of possible examples, and perhaps we should listen to Werner Heisenberg: "Not only is the Universe stranger than we think, it is stranger than we can think. What we observe is not nature itself, but nature exposed to our method of questioning. The reality we can put into words is never reality itself" (from *Across the Frontiers*).

Chapter 11: The Bottom Drops Out, Again

p. 175: The epigram "If you bring forth what is within you, what you bring forth will save you. If you do not bring forth what is within you, what you bring forth will destroy you" is attributed to Jesus in *The Gospel of Thomas*.

pp. 175–176: The history of climate science and denialism is detailed in Naomi Oreskes and Eric Conway's *Merchants of Doubt*. Another excellent article on climate science denialism is Chris Mooney's "Some Like It Hot" in *Mother Jones* magazine.

p. 176: Thoreau's response to a Harvard survey on graduate activity and advice to Harrison Blake can be found in Kevin Dann's *Expect Great Things* (140–41).

Chapter 12: Crisis as Teacher

p. 188: The Emerson epigram is from his essay "Circles" (239) The epigram from Rafael Catala is from *Mysticism of Now* (175), which came out before Eckhart Tolles's bestseller *The Power of Now*. The basic message is the same, although Rafael writes from the perspective of Christian mysticism and liberation theology and is more grounded in action or service. Tolle is a fan of Joel Goldsmith, as well as Emerson and Krishnamurti. For Rafael, the mysticism, and power, of "now" is expressed when the ego finds its rightful place and Silence speaks:

> Silence is the absence of the controlling ego. In silence, the selfish sense of self is transformed into what it really is: the avenue of expression of Consciousness, the Christ. The ego deals with daily life in order to help in the awareness and expression of Being, but the ego is not the master of consciousness, it is its servant. Therefore, a fully functioning ego does not worry about defending our image and appearance before the world. It spends its time expressing the substance of our Being. Here is where Silence speaks. (120)

p. 188: Thoreau's comments on the masses of men being like a torpid snake are from the "Economy" section of *Walden*. The material on turning off some of his audience at lyceum talks, yet speaking to everyone, imploring with good humor for all humanity to embrace a larger life and destiny, can be found in Kevin Dann's *Expect Great Things* (135). The title of Fuller's teaching conversation, "Persons Who Never Awake to Life in This World," can be found in Maria Popova's *Figuring* (136). Popova writes the excellent online resource "The Marginalian" (themarginalian.org).

p. 190: George H. W. Bush's failure to act on climate science at the 1992 Rio Earth Summit is detailed in Scott Waldman and Benjamin Hulac's "This Is When the GOP Turned Away from Climate Policy" in *E&E News*.

p. 192: The material on Thoreau's thirty-fourth birthday is from Kevin Dann's *Expect Great Things* (192).

pp. 193–194: Bateson's *Mind and Nature* is a bit easier to decipher than *Steps to an Ecology of Mind*. Both have tremendous insights and should have more influence; in my view, he was ahead of his time, integrating science with the humanities, and we still have not caught up. Of course, Thoreau was ahead of his time as well, and we most certainly have not caught up.

p. 199: I took the Jung quotation, "If you do not follow your process of individuation, it will drag you," from *Mysticism of Now* (174).

p. 202: The Emerson quotation on taking our "bloated nothingness out of the path of divine circuits" is from his essay "Spiritual Laws" (204).

pp. 202–203: Emerson and Thoreau's lostness and learning from facing the death of loved ones are explored in Robert D. Richardson's *Three Roads Back: How Emerson, Thoreau, and William James Responded to the Greatest Losses of Their Lives*.

p. 203: The Emerson quotations on losing a "beautiful estate" and then drawing a new circle with nothing secure but "life, transition, and the energizing spirit" are from

Barry Andrews's *American Sage: The Spiritual Teaching of Ralph Waldo Emerson* (88–89, 98). The original sources are his essays "Experience" and "Circles," with both partially being responses to his son Waldo's death.

p. 203: The Thoreau quotation on death and grief, with withering flowers or grasses providing soil for new life, "so it is with the human plant," and material on faith in nature and the difficulty of interpretation can be found in Dann's *Expect Great Things* (80).

p. 203: The quotation from Shantideva on the bodhisattva vow and path is from the anthology *Dharma Rain: Sources of Buddhist Environmentalism*, edited by Stephanie Kaza and Kenneth Kraft (33–34). Another excellent resource on Shantideva and the bodhisattva vow is Pema Chodron's *No Time to Lose: A Timely Guide to the Way of the Boddhisattva*. Kaza's *The Attentive Heart: Conversations with Trees* is an excellent book on listening to the voice and voices of nature from both a Buddhist and scientific perspective. It has been re-released as *Conversations with Trees: An Intimate Ecology*.

Chapter 13: Daemon or Demon?
p. 205: The Jose Ortega y Gasset epigram on rebellion and destiny is from *The Revolt of the Masses* (116). The epigram from Wikipedia includes all the senses of 'ecstasy' explored in the chapter, so I couldn't resist using it.

p. 207: Bruce Wilshire, a philosopher and the author of *Wild Hunger*, is also the author of *The Moral Collapse of the University*, a 1990 text in which he argues that professionalism, research, and careerism have taken precedence over teaching in large universities. He also wrote *The Primal Roots of American Philosophy*, in which he argues that American philosophy has been greatly influenced by Native American thought, as well as by Emerson and Thoreau.

pp. 207–208: The material from Paul Shepard comes from *Nature and Madness* (24–24) and *Coming Home to the Pleistocene* (51–65, 154–55). Many environmental thinkers, especially those influenced by the eco-philosophy deep ecology, see the birth of agriculture twelve thousand years ago as the beginning of our ecological problems. A popular author, Daniel Quinn, makes this argument in his novel *Ishmael*, in which a gorilla becomes the guru as teacher, calling the turn to agriculture "taker" culture, in contrast to "leaver" hunter-gatherer life. I have used this book in the classroom, as have others, and students take to the narrative and arguments. On the other hand, Ken Wilber argues that the birth of agriculture marks a step forward toward a fuller rationality, a fuller expression of Spirit unfolding, even if mind and nature were conceptually separated, or dissociated, so that this unfolding could occur. Wilber further argues that this rift needs to be healed, or that nature and culture needs to be in a dialogic, rather than monologic, relationship if we are to evolve to a post-carbon age of sustainability (see *Sex, Ecology, Spirituality: The Spirit of Evolution*). Gregory Bateson, of course, forcefully makes that argument in his books from the late 1960s and early to late 1970s.

p. 212: I first read Euripides's *The Bacchae* in a greening of religion graduate course at the University of Montana. In the age of climate crisis, everything must be greened:

religion, economics, agriculture, law, and, of course, education, among other institutions. Thomas Berry makes this argument in his 1999 *The Great Work*. He writes, "As now functioning, the university prepares students for their role in extending human domination over the natural world, not for intimate presence to the natural world" (73).

p. 212: The Epictetus quotation on the daemon as genius and guide, with Zeus assigning to each "a director sleepless and not to be deceived," is from Barry Andrews's *American Sage: The Spiritual Teachings of Ralph Waldo Emerson* (79).

p. 212: The transformation of the ancient Greek daemon (or daimon) to demon in Christianity is described in Patrick Harpur's *Daimonic Reality*, as well as in online sources.

p. 213: Emerson's quotation, "No law can be sacred to me but that of my own nature. Good and bad are but names very readily transferable to that or this; the only right is what is after my constitution, the only wrong what is against it," is from "Self-Reliance" in *The Portable Emerson* (141–42).

p. 213: The Thoreau quotation "The greater part of what my neighbors call good I believe in my soul to be bad, and if I repent of anything, it is very likely to be my good behavior. What demon possessed me that I behaved so well" is from the "Economy" section of *Walden* (*The Portable Thoreau*, 266).

p. 213: Thoreau's statement that he was often "daily intoxicated, yet no man could call him intemperate" is from Barry Andrews's *Transcendentalism and the Cultivation of the Soul* (37).

p. 214: Emerson's revelation at the Jardin des Plantes in Paris is explored in Richard D. Richardson's *Three Roads Back: How Emerson, Thoreau, and William James Responded to the Greatest Losses of Their Lives* (11–12). His turn to "strange sympathies" in nature and invisible inspiration when making life decisions, which suggests the daemonic, is explored in Kevin Dann's *Expect Great Things* (23–24).

p. 214: The Jung quotation "One does not become enlightened by imagining figures of light, but by making the darkness conscious," is from *Psychology and Alchemy* (99). This popular quotation is easy to find online. Jung equated the daemon with the unconscious, or a mythic aspect of the more scientifically termed "unconscious," which allows for personification and thus dialogue with its wisdom. Jung, via a dream and active imagination, had conversations with a daemonic image that he called Philemon and who he claimed represented "a force which was not myself," "superior insight," and "what the Indians called a guru" (see *Memories, Dreams, Reflections* 182–83, 336–37). Jung also saw the daemonic in nature, so the daemon can be experienced as inner genius or teacher, a seemingly outer guiding spirit, or as spirits within nature and the world soul. In each case, some insight or degree of wisdom may be imparted, if we are open to mystery and judiciously listen.

Personally, I am fond of the phrase "inner teacher." In *The Spirit of Shamanism*, Roger Walsh, a professor of psychiatry, philosophy, and anthropology, writes,

Inner teachers may also arise spontaneously and have powerful, indeed life-changing, effects. Some people who have literally changed the course of history have been directed by inner teachers. The philosopher Socrates, the political leader Gandhi, and the psychologist Carl Jung all reported that they learned from and were directed by inner guides who arose unbidden from the depths of the psyche. (132)

Walsh is also the author of *Essential Spirituality: The Seven Central Practices to Awakening Heart and Mind*, which is a good introduction to various spiritual traditions and practices.

pp. 214-215: Jose Ortega y Gasset's views on destiny are from the essay "In Search of Goethe from Within," found in *The Dehumanization of Art and Other Essays on Art, Culture, and Literature.* This is a profound essay that supported and influenced my convictions on inner listening and callings. He writes, "Life is essentially a drama, because it is a desperate struggle—with things and even our character—to succeed in being in fact that which we are in design" (141). That design is our "I" in relation to the dramatic dynamism of the world and includes soul, body, mind, character, conscience, and circumstance, or the specific places within which we dwell. The more that we stay true to this design, to this unfolding "I," the more we live our vocation and embody an authentic life, and the more we live our destiny.

p. 215: Emerson's quotation on leading things from "disorder into order" and being inspired to "translate the world" is from his essay "The Method of Nature" (Boston: Samuel G. Simpkins, 1841, pg. 15; also available at archive.vcu.edu/english/engweb/transcendentalism/authors/emerson/essays/method.html). His quotation "though Fate is immense, so is Power" can be found in Barry Andrews's *American Sage: The Spiritual Teachings of Ralph Waldo Emerson* (146). The original source is Emerson's essay "Fate." Andrews makes the point about limits having limits.

p. 216: James Hillman's views on character are from *The Soul's Code.* For me, his inclusion of character saves his argument about the soul and callings; otherwise, only those with special talents and abilities are called by daemonic forces.

p. 216: Jung's "People will do anything, no matter how absurd, in order to avoid facing their own souls" is the first line from the previously cited well-known quotation: "One does not become enlightened by imagining figures of light, but by making the darkness conscious" from *Psychology and Alchemy* (99).

p. 216: Hillman's views on symptoms can be found in *Re-Visioning Psychology* and are applied to climate disruption by Per Espen Stoknes in *What We Think about When We Try Not to Think about Global Warming* (190–201).

p. 217: Thoreau's journal entry, "I was born in the most estimable place in the world, and in the nick of time, too," can be found in Dann's *Expect Great Things* (24).

pp. 217–218: Thoreau's experiences writing *A Week on the Concord and Merrimack* and the critical reaction to its publication, including from Emerson, are described in Walls's *Henry David Thoreau: A Life* (254–57).

p. 218: Critical reviews of *A Week* can be found in Dann's *Expect Great Things* (142).

p. 218: Thoreau's journal entry "I would meet my friend not in the light or shadows of our human life alone—but as daimons.... Ours is a tragedy of more than 5 acts—this is not the fifth act in our tragedy no, no," can be found in Dann's *Expect Great Things* (349).

p. 219: Emerson's quotation on the daemonic, "It cannot be defeated by my defeats," can be found in Dann's *Expect Great Things* (9).

P. 219: As a longtime educator, I find it hard not to like, and be a bit amused by, Hillman's descriptions in *The Soul's Code* of the difficulty students have in leaving "the house of the parents" and leaping into "the home of the world." On the other hand, I am a parent now, and I like to think I will have some good advice for my kids while respecting and supporting their inner genius and the wisdom of their path.

pp. 219-220: Plato's claim that eros is a daemon is explored in Rollo May's *Love and Will* in the chapter "Love and the Daimonic" (122–53). May writes that "the daimonic will never take a rational 'no' for an answer. In this respect the daimonic is the enemy of technology. It will accept no clock time or 9 to 5 schedules or assembly lines to which we surrender ourselves as robots" (127). In the chapter "The Daimonic in Dialogue," he further writes, "The more I come to terms with my daimonic tendencies, the more I will find myself conceiving and living by a universal structure of reality. This movement toward the logos is transpersonal. Thus, we move from an impersonal to a personal to a transpersonal dimension of consciousness" (177).

p. 220: The Ortega y Gasset quotation, "Every life is, more or less, a ruin among whose debris we have to discover what the person ought to have been," is from "In Search of Goethe from Within" in *The Dehumanization of Art* (143–44).

pp. 222–223: Thoreau's views on fate and not making the mistake of standing in our own way or blaming others or circumstance for standing in our way are explored in Dann's *Expect Great Things* (79).

Chapter 14: Speaking Out

Note: This chapter includes some previously published material from my 2021 book, *An Ecology of Communication: Response and Responsibility in an Age of Ecocrisis*, including Thoreau on John Brown and civil disobedience, the brief story and commentary on the Purdue student giving a pro-pesticide speech while castigating Rachel Carson, Walt Whitman's advice to "dismiss whatever insults your soul," and the question of whom students should trust. The material is crucial to both projects although editing and additions are included here.

p. 224: The Emerson epigram on the person "on whom the soul descends…alone can teach" is from his 1838 "Harvard Divinity School Address" in *The Portable Emerson* (81). The Carl Jung epigram on being a question "addressed to the world" is from *Memories, Dreams, Reflections* (318).

p. 224: An excellent documentary on Daniel Ellsberg and the Pentagon Papers is *The Most Dangerous Man in America*, which I have shown in class.

pp. 227-228: The significance of the invention of the Guttenberg printing press in 1439, shifting our epistemology from orality to the printed word, is explored in Neil

Postman's *Building a Bridge to the 21st Century*. Postman also explores the epistemological shift from print to electronic media, arguing that we live in age of too much information, misinformation, and disinformation and not enough knowledge, or information in a context, as well as wisdom, or knowledge applied to specific problems. In another book, *Technopoly*, he argues that the timeline shows that we have shifted from technology as tool (pre-seventeenth century) to technocracy, in which tools begin to infiltrate all aspects of our socio-cultural life-world (the Enlightenment period), and now to technopoly, or technological dominance, in which we have become the tools of our technology. Students mostly reject this argument because they feel in control, but I counter that dismissing Postman without some meditative thinking, soul searching, and honest self-reflection is a mistake. I also reference Nicholas Carr's *The Atlantic* essay "Is Google Making Us Stupid?," in which he discusses his own techno-addictions and increasing loss of focus. A fine book on how our techno-addictions continue to change us and what we have lost in the process is Michael Harris's *The End of Absence: Reclaiming What We Have Lost in a World of Constant Communication*. A fine film on how distraction is designed into social media is *The Social Dilemma*, which I often recommend to students.

p. 228: Kant's famous declaration "*sapere aude*," or dare to know, is from his 1784 essay "Answering the Question: What is Enlightenment?" Michel Foucault ruminates on Kant's arguments in his 1978 essay "What is Enlightenment?"

pp. 228-229: The material on the spiritual activism of the transcendentalists is from Robert D. Richardson's *Emerson: The Mind on Fire* and John A. Buehrens's *Conflagration: How the Transcendentalists Sparked the American Struggle for Racial, Gender, and Social Justice*. Lawrence Buell's statement that transcendentalism was more like "an outpouring of radiant energy" than "an organized enterprise" is from his introduction in *The American Transcendentalists: Essential Writings* (xi, xxvii). Buell also writes that transcendentalism was "anticipated by Jesus' insistence that 'the Kingdom of God is within you' and by the inner 'daemon' that helped keep Socrates from going astray" (xxiv).

It is also interesting to note that the term "transcendentalism" was coined by a critic of Emerson's essay "Nature," not by the group that would eventually move their meetings from Boston to Emerson's house. The founding original group was called "Hedge's Club," named after Unitarian minister Frederick Henry Hedge since they met when he was available. Buell writes there was a nucleus of approximately fifty to seventy-five transcendentalists, including women and different generations. They met for approximately four years, but members stayed in touch afterward. Emerson wrote an essay called "The Transcendentalist" but did not call himself a transcendentalist, while Thoreau was more receptive to the term.

p. 229: Emerson being dragged into the Abolitionist movement by his wife Lidian and other members of the Concord Female Anti-Slavery Society and being hesitant to join any crowd is described in Robert A. Gross's *The Transcendentalists and Their World* (522–23). Despite becoming virulently antislavery in writings and speeches, Emerson was not above ideas of superiority in his book *English Traits*. Nell Irvin

Painter does a thorough analysis of his over-the-top racial bias toward Anglo-Saxon heritage in *The History of White People*. This bias certainly says something about Emerson, but it says even more about race theory during his time.

p. 229: The Emerson quotation on the reform of everything—we must "revise the whole of our social structure, the state, the school, religion, marriage, trade, science, and explore their foundations in our nature"—can be found in Barry Andrews's *American Sage: The Spiritual Teachings of Ralph Waldo Emerson* (64). The quotation is from Emerson's speech and essay "Man the Reformer."

pp. 229-230: The Thoreau quotations from "Life without Principle" can be found in *The Portable Thoreau*, edited by Carl Bode. Thoreau writes of doing work that yields "real profit, though but little money" and then defends himself against the charge of idleness: "If a man walk in the woods for love of them half of each day, he is in danger of being regarded as a loafer; but if he spends his whole day as a speculator, shearing off those woods and making earth bald before her time, he is esteemed an industrious and enterprising citizen. As if a town had no interest in its forests but to cut them down!" (633).

pp. 230–231: Thoreau's "Civil Disobedience" can be found in *The Portable Thoreau*. Thoreau's declaration that we must make our lives a "counter-friction to stop the machine" is directed toward the machinery of government that leads to injustice, not government as a whole although he is clearly in favor of less government, fewer rules and regulations, and more freedom for the individual (121). However, these beliefs must be read in the context of his time; I am sure that he would be in favor of government regulation that frees us from the dominance of the oil industry, and in support of clean energy in response to climate crisis, among other regulations that increase social justice and the freedom to have breathable air, fertile soil, and drinkable water, along with nature's "services" generally.

pp. 231-232: Thoreau and Emerson's responses to Thomas Sims being sent back to Georgia to his "owner" due to the 1850 Fugitive Slave Act is described in Kevin Dann's *Expect Great Things* (186) and Walls's *Henry David Thoreau: A Life* (317). Barry Andrews also describes Emerson's evolution in response to slavery as he became increasingly radicalized in *American Sage: The Spiritual Teachings of Ralph Waldo Emerson* (126–32).

pp. 231-232: Thoreau's "Slavery in Massachusetts" speech in response to the jailing of Anthony Burns is detailed in Walls's *Henry David Thoreau: A Life* (345–47).

pp. 232–233: The material on Thoreau's increased radicalism and support of the antislavery movement and John Brown, including his speech "A Plea for Captain John Brown," can be found in Walls's *Henry David Thoreau: A Life* (445–55).

pp. 233–235: Thoreau's defense of John Brown and the evolution of his views on violence and nonviolence are explored in Sandra Harbert Petrulionis's "Between 'That Farthest Western Way' and 'The University of the West'" from *Thoreau beyond Borders: New International Essays on America's Most Famous Nature Writer*. Petrulionis argues that Thoreau must have known that he was helping Francis Jackson Merriam, a Harper's Ferry plotter and financial supporter and the most wanted man in America, to escape to Canada. The quotations on Brown learning in the "great university of the West," taking "many degrees" and commencing the "practice of Humanity" and Thoreau's refusal to judge "any tactics that are effective of good, whether one wields the quill or sword" are also from this essay (208). The quotations "The North is suddenly all Transcendental" and "The man this country was about to hang appeared the greatest and best in it" are from Thoreau's essay, "The Last Days of John Brown," which can be found in *The Portable Thoreau* (676–82).

pp. 221–22: The quotations on living and dying for a principle and the connection between freedom and a liberal arts education are from Thoreau's "The Last Days of John Brown," which can be found in *The Portable Thoreau* (676–82).

p. 235: The Thoreau quotations on living an ethic of least harm and "thinking like a bream" are from Walls's *Henry David Thoreau: A Life* (348, 435). Aldo Leopold would write his influential "Thinking Like a Mountain" section in *A Sand County Almanac* in 1949, which details his changed perspective after shooting a mother wolf and seeing "a fierce green fire die in her eyes" (138).

p. 235: Thoreau's admission "I do not wish to kill or to be killed, but I can foresee circumstances in which both of these things would be by me unavoidable" can be found in Walls' *Henry David Thoreau: A Life* (451).

p. 236: Dr. Martin Luther King Jr.'s "kitchen table experience" is described in Anthony Lewis's *Make No Law: The Sullivan Case and the First Amendment.* I use chapters from this text in my Freedom of Speech course because it provides a history of law cases that shows how the US came to its current understanding of freedom of speech and freedom of the press, and thus a history of the Common Law.

pp. 236–237: The film *Romero*, starring Raul Julia, came out in 1989. I have an old VHS copy, but it can be found on streaming services. There is also a documentary on his life, *Monsenor: The Last Journey of Oscar Romero*, which includes actual footage.

p. 237: Gandhi's essay, "Nonviolence—The Greatest Force," can be found in an anthology on the practice of nonviolent resistance, *Peace is the Way*, edited by Walter Wink. Other essays in this volume also explore Gandhi's influence, including Richard Deats's "The Global Spread of Active Nonviolence," which chronicles the successes of nonviolent civil disobedience in numerous countries. There is also a chapter on "Soul Force" in Louis Fischer's *Gandhi: His Life and His Message*, and Gandhi explains that satyagraha is not passive resistance in *The Penguin Gandhi Reader*. More recently, Erica Chenoweth, a scholar of civil disobedience, argues from her research that every nonviolent movement in the twentieth century with at least 3.5 percent of the population involved met with political success, yet Peter Gelderloos has written books critical of the claim that nonviolence always works and argues that it may aid state repression.

I was first introduced to the practice of satyagraha from the Philip Glass's opera of the same name. I had a tape with liner notes that included highlights from three of his operas—*Satyagraha*, *Akhnaten* (the first Egyptian king who believed in monotheism), and *Einstein at the Beach*—that I listened to on a Walkman while walking amid the mesas of New Mexico. The music and mesas were a powerful combination that led to an expansive and joyful awareness.

p. 238: Erica Chenoweth's research on civil disobedience can be found in *Civil Resistance: What Everyone Needs to Know*. However, in Andreas Malm's *How to Blow Up a Pipeline*, he argues that the nonviolent movements explored by Chenoweth were supported by the threat of violence and strategic violence against property, but she ignores these details in her analysis. The title of Malm's book makes it sound like an instruction manual, but it is a nuanced exploration of social movement strategies and tactics.

pp. 239–241: My views on the mistake of rejecting a transcendent dimension when seeking to understand what we can know of reality, and the necessity of integrating the enlightenment of the East with the enlightenment of the West, are influenced by the books of Ken Wilber. Wilber is concerned with the "pre-trans fallacy," in which the pre-rational (go back to nature and the senses) and rational (the interdependency of ecological systems science) are mistaken for transrational spiritual experience. The result is much confusion and regression, including a romantic celebration of early cultures as spiritually advanced, web-of-life systems science being taken as a new eco-spiritual paradigm, and the lack of a genuine model of development due to the relativizing of value. To Wilber, there are many negative results of these regressions, with the most extreme being a doom-and-gloom environmentalism that tends toward eco-fascism. In other words, if the ecological golden age was in the past, the *only* solution to ecocrisis is to de-industrialize the world back to beginnings of human emergence. Of course, along with the problem of mistaking pre-rational and rational modes of knowing with the transrational, there is the problem of disregarding insights from transrational experience altogether, with rationality being the only way to know. *Sex, Ecology, Spirituality* explores these arguments in depth.

p. 242: The Billy Bragg lyric is from his song "Waiting for the Great Leap Forward," which is on the 1988 album *Workers Playtime*, a favorite during my Icemaker years in the early 1990s.

pp. 242-243: The Thoreau quotation, "Shams and delusions are esteemed for the highest truths, while reality is fabulous," can be found in Kevin Dann's *Expect Great Things* (96). I explore Edward Bernays's impact in several classes but especially in two courses, Advertising: History and Criticism and Principles of Public Relations. In the latter course we read Larry Tye's *The Father of Spin: Edward L. Bernays and the Birth of Public Relations*, which I highly recommend for all citizens. ExxonMobil's longtime knowledge of climate change and their disinformation campaign is detailed in Bill McKibben's *New Yorker* article "What ExxonMobil Knew About Climate Change." James Gustave Speth documents that the US government also knew but did nothing in *They Knew: The US Federal Government's Fifty-Year Role in Causing the Climate Crisis*.

p. 243: Naomi Oreskes is featured in the documentary *Disruption*, which can be found on YouTube, but she also has two excellent books on climate with Eric M. Conway, *Merchants of Doubt*, which was made into a documentary, and *The Collapse of Western*

Civilization: A View from the Future, which mixes scientific facts and analysis with a fictional story of what may happen in the coming century due to global warming. All are excellent resources that I have used in the classroom. The brief history of climate science, from Joseph Fourier to Charles Keeling and his Keeling Curve, is documented in *Disruption*.

pp. 245–246: Thoreau's quotation on Samuel George Morton's racist practice of filling the skulls of Natives with lead shot to measure intelligence ("Of all the ways invented to come at a knowledge of a living man, this seems to me the worst…. There is nothing out of which the spirit has more completely departed, and in which it has left fewer significant traces") can be found in Dann's *Expect Great Things* (220–21).

p. 247: The quotation on Naomi Oreskes being a lightning rod alerting us to climate dangers is from Justin Gillis's *New York Times* article "Naomi Oreskes: A Lightning Rod in a Changing Climate."

p. 247: Emerson's "Divinity School Address" quotation on seeking the "new Teacher" can be found in Dann's *Expect Great Things* (98).

pp. 247-248: I explore Rachel Carson's call to science and conscience and the logical fallacy and disinformation response by the chemical industry and conservative "think tanks" in "A Fitting Responsiveness: Communicating Our Way into the Future," the epilogue of *An Ecology of Communication: Response and Responsibility in an Age of Ecocrisis*, with much research coming from Oreskes and Conway's *Merchants of Doubt*. Carson's life and work are also explored in Maria Popova's *Figuring* and the anthology *Courage for the Earth*, edited by Peter Matthiessen.

p. 248: Rachel Carson's last speech, "The Pollution of Our Environment," can be found in *Lost Woods: The Discovered Writings of Rachel Carson*, edited by Linda Lear.

pp. 248-249: The material on Brister Freeman is from Elise Lemire's introduction to *Black Walden: Slavery and Its Aftermath in Concord, Massachusetts* (1–14). Biographical information on Anthony Burns can be found online.

p. 250: The assassination of Haitian radio broadcaster Jean Dominique is detailed in the documentary, *The Agronomist*, which I have shown to students. It's a powerful example of living with principle and conscience.

p. 255: Thoreau's 1857 journal entry on field mouse footprints in the snow, so delicate that "they suggest an airy lightness in the body that impressed them," in comparison to typography of the Gutenberg press, is from Kristen Case's "Following Thoreau" in *Now Comes Good Sailing* (151–52).

p. 255: The material on Thoreau's design of an innovative machine to finely ground plumbago for pencils, which were then used for mass print technology, directly benefiting him in the form of affordable books, both for reading and his own writings, is from Laura Dassow Walls's "Technology" in *Henry David Thoreau in Context* (166).

p. 256: The quotation from the environmental educator and writer David Orr, "Most everything will be negatively affected by higher temperatures: Ecologies collapse, forests burn, metals expand, concrete runways buckle, rivers dry up, cooling towers fail, and people curse, kill, and terrorize more easily," is from *Dangerous Years: Climate Change, the Long Emergency, and the Way Forward* (25). Along with his many excellent books, Orr also speaks frequently, including with a stellar slide show on sustainable buildings that I have had the good fortune of seeing twice. Orr is known for spearheading the construction of an innovative green Environmental Studies building at Oberlin College, and the call to green college campuses generally.

Sustainable buildings and greened infrastructure teach students by their presence. They see what is possible when leaders lead and people care. If you have been in meetings with administrators, you know that cost is a major consideration, but, over the long haul, greened buildings and infrastructure save money. Campus infrastructure devoted to sustainability would also mix scientists and humanists; in other words, the damaging divorce between the "two cultures" structured into campus life by separating scientists and humanists into separate buildings leads to less dialogue and less learning among faculty, and that loss of communication leads to the loss of a holistic vision of education in response to ecocrisis.

Chapter 15: Calling Forth the Future
p. 258: The Emerson epigram "The fact that I am here certainly shows me that the soul had a need of an organ here. Shall I not assume the post?" is from his essay "Spiritual Laws" in *The Portable Emerson*, edited by Carl Bode (206). The Thoreau epigram "What is the use of a house if you haven't got a tolerable planet to put it on?" is from a letter to his friend Harrison Blake (see *Letters to a Spiritual Seeker*, edited by Bradley P. Dean). The Gus Speth epigram comes from a speech he gave to a group of religious leaders and can be found online. Speth is the former Dean of the Yale School of Forestry and Environmental Studies and is also the author of *The Bridge at the End of the World: Capitalism, the Environment, and Crossing the Bridge from Crisis to Sustainability*, which I once used in Senior Seminar.
p. 258: Many of the writings from my book *The Path of My Soul: Journey to the Center of Self* come from journal entries in my twenties. When I look at them after all these years, I inevitably see a much younger self; still, I hit on universal aspects of staying true to a larger sense of self, or Emersonian self-reliance and the cultivation of soul.
p. 260: My source for Jung on synchronicities is *Memories, Dreams, Reflections*, including the glossary of terms. An excellent overview of his thought is June Singer's *Boundaries of the Soul*, which includes a chapter on the process of individuation.
p. 260: Ramsey Eric Ramsey explores our range of responses, like passing the salt versus being called to act by world-historical events, in *The Long Path to Nearness: A Contribution to a Corporeal Philosophy of Communication and the Groundwork of an Ethics of Relief*.
p. 261: While I was initially put on the waiting list when I applied to the University of Montana, I loved the Environmental Studies graduate program and received an excellent education. The professors were both accomplished and committed to educating for a sustainable present and future and provided many experiential learning opportunities for students. One was the PEAS organic farm, which provides hands-on participation in local agriculture while also creating community; farm produce goes

to the Missoula Food Bank. Such programs are spiritual acts even if not labeled as such.

After I graduated and moved on to earn another graduate degree in the Communication Studies department at the University of Montana, the Environmental Studies department hired Daniel Spencer, who has expertise in theology and restoration ecology, among other areas. I was fortunate to take his Greening of Religion course, which explored the world's religions and the spiritual dimension of life in relation to environmental ethics. Students in the Environmental Studies program are following a calling to learn and make a difference, and thus are implicitly, if not explicitly, responding to a religious impulse.

The Communication Studies graduate program had excellent courses in environmental rhetoric taught by Steve Schwarze, who wrote on the rhetoric of the coal industry and was active with the International Environmental Communication Association (IECA) before passing away from colon cancer in his early fifties. Steve's death was a great loss for the field of environmental communication, and a great loss generally—he integrated a discerning intellect with plenty of heart. He was also generous with me, chairing my master's thesis and introducing me to the IECA, which holds conferences every two years. His influential paper "Environmental Melodrama" is worth reading.

pp. 267–268: Robert Sullivan's *The Thoreau You Don't Know* focuses on Thoreau the human being, but I have cited many excellent biographies and interpretations of his life and writings, and all reveal his humanness and struggles while countering mistaken myths. In *Young Man Thoreau*, Lebeaux analyzes Thoreau's early years via Eriksonian psychology, arguing that he went through a crucial period of intense vulnerability, or an identity crisis, that resulted in a radical change in perspective, with his life and writings reflecting an unwavering search for meaning. On the other hand, some interpretations of Thoreau are unkind. In *Dark Thoreau*, a deeply critical review of Thoreau's life and writings, Richard Bridgeman runs with the theme of Thoreau's aloofness, stating that "the uncertain, lonely young man enlarged his own isolation into a trope of independence" (80). For me, this book cherry-picks passages to support a thesis rather than looking at Thoreau's life and work as a whole.

A scathing look at Thoreau is "Pond Scum," a 2015 *New Yorker* piece by Kathryn Schulz, which, if one has read Thoreau well, can be easily countered. Schulz makes some interesting points that make one think, like criticizing his ascetic practices laid out in the "Economy" section of *Walden* and thus an adherence to an ideal purity that leaves out the rest of humanity, but even this point can be countered. Thoreau was experimenting—the Walden experiment—exploring not only what one needs to survive but also how to live mindfully and well. Did he go too far, make mistakes? Perhaps. Again, Thoreau was a human being, not a myth. But Thoreau's writings are part of the canon of great literature, and frequently taught because he remains relevant, especially in the age of climate crisis. His ascetic experimenting, for example, resonates deeply with today's world, where we live in cultures of overconsumption with little distinction between wants and needs. In *Thoreau's Religion*, Alda Balthrop-

Lewis calls Thoreau a political ascetic as his renunciations are motivated by the instinct that "our everyday choices make up our politics" (14).

Another Schulz criticism is directed at Thoreau's contradictory arguments throughout his writings, defending civilization in one moment, arguing against it in another, or extolling vegetarianism and then describing an impulse to devour a woodchuck. Any close reader of Thoreau notices these contradictions, but instead of reading him as making poor arguments, I have always found his contradictions stimulating. For me, the contradiction was the point—I don't think Thoreau was unintentionally being contradictory, I do think Thoreau was being true to himself, to his thought and experience in particular moments, while also putting forth principles, or higher laws, that have universal resonance.

Many authors wrote response pieces questioning and countering Schulz's interpretations, including Jeffrey S. Cramer, as well as Jedediah Purdy in the *Atlantic* magazine. The Schulz article and many response pieces can be found online.

p. 267: Thoreau on love and the claim that a "lover of Nature is preeminently a lover man" can be found in Kevin Dann's *Expect Great Things* (219–20).

p. 267: Thoreau the lost, especially in his response to his brother John's death, is explored in Richard D. Richardson's short book, *Three Roads Back: How Emerson, Thoreau, and William James Responded to the Greatest Losses of Their Lives.*

pp. 268–270: The material on Thoreau's last days, including the quotations, can be found in Laura Dassow Walls's *Henry David Thoreau: A Life* (494–500). Thoreau's perfect comment about God on his deathbed, "I did not know that we had ever quarreled," is also in Robert D. Richardson's *Henry Thoreau: A Life of the Mind*, which chronicles the many authors and ideas that influenced him. As Richardson well knew, Thoreau also lived a life of Spirit, as indicated by his deathbed remark.

pp. 268-269: Laura Dassow Walls explores Thoreau's commitment to the Concord natural commons, as well as the cultural and political commons, in "Counter Frictions: Thoreau and the Integral Commons" from *Thoreau beyond Borders: International Essays on America's Most Famous Nature Writer.*

p. 269: Kristen Case's argument that Thoreau's vulnerability led him to more fully experience the "infinite extent of our relations," especially when needing help from friends and family to continue his Kalendar project when sick at home with tuberculosis, is from "Thoreau's Vulnerable Resistance" in *Thoreau in an Age of Crisis: Uses and Abuses of an American Icon* (255). Case also found an example of Thoreau being depressed and potentially suicidal in an 1857 journal entry where he states, "To how many—perhaps to most—life is barely tolerable & if not for the fear of death or of dying, what a multitude would immediately commit suicide." That's a strong sentiment, but he follows it up with how we can be "lifted above ourselves" via a strain of music and "all meanness & trivialness disappears" (256). It should be no surprise that Thoreau would get depressed, or even contemplate suicide, like all lost humans, but this extreme example of double consciousness moves from deep existential despair to spiritual exaltation.

p. 270: Emerson's quotation on wisdom being "living the greatest number of good hours" is from his essay "Experience" (275). Bronson Alcott's calling Thoreau "The independent of independents...indeed, the sole signer of the Declaration of Independence, and a Revolution in himself" can be found in Walls' *Henry David Thoreau: A Life* (307). Emerson's praise, "The country knows not yet, or in the least part, how great a son it has lost," is at the end of his eulogy for Thoreau. The last line reads, "His soul was made for the noblest society; he had in a short life exhausted the capabilities of this world; wherever there is knowledge, wherever there is virtue, wherever there is beauty, he will find a home" (593).

p. 270: Emerson's commitment to Thoreau after his death, including his praise and promotion of his writing, naming a street after him, and being reminded by Lidian that Thoreau was his best friend when his memory was failing, is described in Jeffrey S. Cramer's *Solid Seasons: The Friendship of Henry David Thoreau and Ralph Waldo Emerson* (100–102).

p. 271: The quotations on Thoreau being "married" to nature can be found in Walls's *Henry David Thoreau: A Life* (402, 462). See the note in the "Magnificent Misfits" chapter on Thoreau's failure to woo Ellen Sewell in his early twenties and his seemingly asexual life.

p. 271: Having three kids, of course, is not considered sustainable behavior. Bill McKibben even wrote a book, *Maybe One*, in which he explored the eco-social dilemma of having kids and made an argument for smaller families. More recently, Ezra Klein, in a 2022 *New York Times* article "Your Kids Are Not Doomed," also explored this dilemma, including the fact that more and more prospective parents, and thus more and more students, are deciding not to have kids in climate crisis times. Klein argues, via interviews with climate journalists and activists who are parents, that having kids is an act of hope; despite the scientific warnings and bad news, which he has long reported on, there is still time for us to change course and some signs that we are doing so, such as the cheaper cost of renewables. He also argues that humans have always had children in crisis times—history is filled with crises, such as war and famine and pandemics—although climate is the most encompassing crisis we have faced, affecting the whole planet, not just particular civilizations.

Klein sums up his views this way:

> I don't just prefer a world of net-zero emissions to a world of net-zero children. I think those worlds are in conflict. We face a problem of politics, not a physics problem. The green future has to be a welcoming one, even a thrilling one. If people cannot see themselves in it, they will fight to stop it. If the cost of caring about climate is to forgo having a family, that cost will be too high. A climate movement that embraces sacrifice as its answer or even as its temperament might do more harm than good. It may accidentally sacrifice the political appeal needed to make the net-zero emissions world real.

Klein hits on the long-debated "sacrifice" question here and the need to have a positive vision of possibilities that include joy. In contrast, the growing Deep Adaptation movement spearheaded by the scholar Jem Bendell—see his book *Breaking Together: A Freedom-Loving Response to Collapse*—argues that societal collapse is inevitable and already happening. After grieving, we may find joy in working together and making necessary sacrifices that focus on vital needs.

The Danish architect Bjarke Ingels also addresses sacrifice in his TED talks, where he calls for "hedonistic sustainability" in the form of buildings and infrastructure that decrease carbon and increase pleasure. I have shown these videos with his compelling examples to students, but we also read Duane Elgin's arguments for "voluntary simplicity," in which we do more with less, including finding more joy with simpler and more focused living—again, vital needs rather than manufactured wants. It's a sentiment that mirrors Thoreau's vision of economy.

For my ex-wife, Meghan (who, once again, was a Greenpeace activist), having children is an act of hope, and she thinks people who care about the climate are the best people to raise children because they will raise them to care generally and to be kind, loving people. She even stated that she "prefers to see a couple with those values having six children rather than a couple that doesn't have those values having one." For me, neither hope nor despair was a factor when considering having a family; rather, I was in love and we wanted kids. I also knew we would raise our kids to be critical thinkers. Still, there is much privilege in being so-called first world inhabitants of this planet when making such decisions, and all decisions on warming will affect rich and poor—but not equally.

p. 272: I am not the only one who has had some struggles teaching Thoreau. William Howarth, a former president of The Thoreau Society and a longtime professor at Princeton University, taught *Walden* for decades to Ivy League students. He writes in "Reading Thoreau at 200" that most are indifferent, or worse, hostile: "Those bound for Wall Street often yawn or snicker at his call to simplify, to refuse, to resist. Perhaps a third of them react with irritation, shading into hatred. How dare he question the point of property, the meaning of wealth?" This reaction says a lot about the power of the narratives of bigger, better, and more, and the industrial education that supports those narratives. Howarth finds satisfaction, however, from teaching to the few who get Thoreau, and therefore get our existential predicament. His article can be found on the American Scholar website (theamericanscholar.org/reading-thoreau-at-200/).

p. 274: Thom Hartmann's views on ADD/ADHD can be found at www.thomhartmann.com.

p. 274: Research on how time spent in nature increases focus and well-being, including for those dealing with ADD/ADHD, can be found in MJ Raleigh's "Restorative Environments and Human Well-Being: How We Treat the Earth is How We Treat Ourselves." This article appears in *Ometeca* v. 14/15, a double issue from 2020 on "Educating for Ecological Sustainability."

p. 275: Moments of classroom magic are explored in Christopher Bache's *Dark Night, Early Dawn: Steps to a Deep Ecology of Mind*. Bache, a professor of theology with interests in transpersonal psychology, writes personally of collective classroom experience in which he and students are open to the Sacred Mind, or a larger intelligence: "When I first learned to enter these moments many years ago, I discovered a small door in the back of my mind. This door would sometimes open and through it slips of paper would be passed to me. I found that if I took the risk and used these gifts, something magical would happen" (188). I know this experience, and it happens more often when I am open to mystery, to purpose, but mostly to play. Of course, as with anything, there is the potential for self-deception, in which we think we are opening doors, saying what students need to hear, but are going on tangents and droning on. You don't want to be one of those professors. Bache has also authored *The Living Classroom: Teaching and Collective Consciousness*.

p. 275: Angela Duckworth's research on grit and student success are presented in her popular 2013 TED talk.

pp. 275-276: The Thoreau quotation "There are a thousand hacking at the branches of evil to one who is hacking at the roots," is from the "Economy" section of *Walden*. Thoreau's response to Emerson's assertion that Harvard taught all branches of knowledge, "Yes, indeed, all of the branches and none of the roots," can be found in Walter Harding's *The Days of Henry Thoreau: A Biography* (51).

p. 276: While industrial civilization supported by industrial education is grounded in extraction and extinction, climate crisis is most certainly being addressed in higher education. Universities are often of two minds: preparing students to enter status quo systems while also challenging those systems. I argue for more challenging; the question is what more can, and must, be done, especially regarding the spirituality of being lost.

Some positive examples include the Harvard Divinity School, which has a focus on religion and ecology, as does the Yale Divinity School. Yale Climate Connections is also a fantastic resource for climate news. Harvard introduced the Thich Nhat Hanh Center for Mindfulness and Public Health in 2023, thanks to a $26 million donation. While at a 2023 International Environmental Communication Association (IECA) conference, I learned about a year-long and team-taught climate action and leadership course at San Jose University that includes science, policy, emotional intelligence in the form of climate grief, and steps toward action, including doing what you are good at in community with others. Along with the University of Montana's excellent Environmental Studies department and PEAS farm, they also have a climate change studies minor. Unity Environmental University in Maine (formerly Unity College) and Prescott College have long had sustainability and experiential learning at the core of their mission (as do other colleges and universities). New England College added a course titled "Will Climate Change My Life?" It's an inviting question, but a more accurate but too long title might be "How Climate Crisis Is Already Changing and Will Further Change My Life."

There is also AASHE, the Association for the Advancement of Sustainability in Higher Education, which includes a sustainability tracking, assessment, and rating system (STARS), and the Presidents' Climate Leadership Commitment, which includes a pledge to accelerate climate action. As of 2023, there are 482 member colleges and universities. Bryan Alexander's 2023 *Universities on Fire: Higher Education in Climate Crisis* attempts to predict how climate crisis will transform colleges and universities in the ensuing decades. The use of fire in the title has three meanings: the planet heating up, including wildfires; other climate threats, including sea-level rise; and the fire of student activism but also activism from professors and staff (and hopefully administration), or what I have called "the fire of soul."

p. 276: The Thoreau quotation, "How important is a constant intercourse with nature and the contemplation of natural phenomenon to the preservation of Moral & intellectual health. The discipline of the schools or of business—can never impart such serenity to the mind," is from a May 6, 1851, journal entry and can be found at walden.org.

p. 277: Emerson's advice "Let me never fall into the vulgar mistake of dreaming that I am persecuted whenever I am contradicted" is from a November 8, 1838, journal entry and can be found online. This advice, while written nearly two centuries ago, is especially salient in our culture wars and cancel-culture times. However, as explored in the "Speaking Out" chapter, we also live in an age of spin that is vulgar in its denial of climate science; in other words, there is a big difference between contradiction that makes us think and misinformation/disinformation that contradicts the facts while claiming to be "alternative facts."

p. 277: Thoreau's teaching advice to his sister Helen can be found in *Dann's Expect Great Things* (48–49).

p. 279: The quotations, "How do you expect the birds to sing when their groves are cut down?" and "Who hears the fishes when they cry?" can be found in Walls's *Henry David Thoreau: A Life* (237, 254). While these questions of more-than-human sentience may seem anthropomorphic, they are increasingly proven by current researchers, including in Jonathan Balcombe's *What a Fish Knows* and Monica Gagliano's *Thus Spoke the Plant*, among many others.

p. 279: Thoreau's witnessing of the wind playing the telegraph wires, turning it into a giant Aeolian harp, is described in Dann's *Expect Great Things* (198).

p. 279: Emerson's list of technological advancements and his questioning of our thirst for more are from Barry Andrews's *American Sage: The Spiritual Teachings of Ralph Waldo Emerson* (167). The quotations are originally from Emerson's essay "Work and Days." The information on the approximate life span in the mid-1800s is also from *American Sage* (175).

p. 280: Thoreau's surveying of twenty-two miles of the Concord River to figure out the effect of a dam on flooding is described in Walls's *Henry David Thoreau: A Life* (441–44). See also Robert Thorson's *The Boatman: Henry David Thoreau's River Years*.

P, 280: The description of starved Dakota Sioux living on a Minnesota reservation but not receiving promised aid from the government and then killing five white settlers, leading to thirty-eight Native Americans killed in the largest mass hanging in US history, and the murder of Little Crow, a Dakota Sioux chief, whose head and arms were displayed at the Minnesota Historical Society until 1971, are described in Walls's *Henry David Thoreau: A Life* (487–89). A 2022 Department of Interior investigative report commissioned by Deb Haaland, the first Native American secretary of the interior, provides more little-known history of Native mistreatment and death: the US government's removal of Native children from their tribal communities and forcing them into boarding schools. They each had a graveyard for kids who died from abuse and disease. A Native American secretary and the report were long overdue.

p. 281: Daniel R. Wildcat's views on "global burning" and TEK as a response are from *Red Alert! Saving the Planet with Indigenous Knowledge*. Wildcat writes, "Education was only one, albeit the most potent, representative of the final removal attempt waged by every social institution that American society could bring to bear on who we were as indigenous peoples" (3).

p. 282: The example of Brister Freeman and the quotation on the Walden woods as a Black heritage site ("the history of slavery and its aftermath reveals that at least some of our nation's cherished green spaces began as black spaces") are from Elise Lemire's *Black Walden: Slavery and Its Aftermath in Concord, Massachusetts* (11–12).

p. 282: My comments on refugees of Hurricane Katrina being taken to the Super Dome, which, for most, was the first time they had been inside due to high ticket prices, were gleaned from sportswriter and social critic Dave Zirin's *Welcome to the Terrordome*, a text I have used in my sports communication course. Sports must also be greened; witness the Beijing Olympics, during which concerns over air quality led some athletes to wear masks, or concern from rowers who competed in sewage-fed waters in the Rio de Janeiro Olympics. And then there are issues such as travel to stadiums, consumption at stadiums, the need for green stadiums, and citizen tax money paying for stadiums instead of green infrastructure while team "owners" reap the rewards.

p. 282: The dire predictions from Bateson are from Peter Harrie-Jones's *A Recursive Vision: Ecological Understanding and Gregory Bateson.* An introduction to a new edition of *Steps to an Ecology of Mind*, written by his daughter, the author Mary Catherine Bateson, also explores Bateson's concern with the future of humanity. Of course, one can also find dire predictions in his own work, like in the following from *Steps*:

> [A]s you arrogate all mind to yourself, you will see the world around you as mindless and therefore not entitled to moral or ethical consideration. The environment will seem to be yours to exploit. Your survival unit will be you and your folks or conspecifics against the environment of other social units, other races and the brutes and vegetables…. If this is your estimate of your relation to nature and you have an advanced technology, your

likelihood of survival will be that of a snowball in hell. You will die either of the toxic by-products of your own hate, or, simply, of overpopulation and overgrazing. The raw materials of the world are finite (462).

p. 283: Mark Z. Jacobsen's views can be found in *No Miracles Needed: How Today's Technology Can Save Our Climate and Clean Our Air*. Jacobson discusses the basic arguments from his book with Andrew Keen in his "Keen On" podcast, which can be found on lithub.com. I am quite fond of Jacobsen's book and his argument that transitioning to wind, water, and solar (WWS) energy is possible. In an April 24, 2024, article in *Scientific American*, "A Golden Age of Renewables is Beginning, and California is Leading the Way," he writes that California, the fifth-largest economy in the world, "has experienced a record-breaking string of days in which the combined generation of wind, geothermal, hydroelectric and solar electricity has exceeded demand on the main electricity grid from anywhere from 15 minutes to 9.25 hours a day." This is encouraging and hopeful news. However, Jacobsen does not write about Jevons' paradox, in which technological efficiencies lead to more consumption. In other words, citizen-consumers end up using more energy, potentially canceling out the benefits of the improved technologies, especially if renewables support a growth economy (see Jem Bendell's *Breaking Together: A Freedom-Loving Response to Collapse* for analysis of Jevons' Paradox). Also, Jacobsen does not consider that a switch to electric cars, for example, does nothing to combat sprawl and strip malls, habitat destruction, absurd amounts of roadkill, nature deficit disorder, and sensory disengagement, or to encourage biking infrastructure and a life informed by sauntering.

p. 283: The possibilities of collapse, and why switching to renewable energy is not enough in response, is explored in Pablo Servigne and Raphael Stevens's *How Everything Can Collapse*. In *Bright Green Lies: How the Environmental Movement Lost Its Way and What We Can Do About It*, Derrick Jensen, along with Lierre Keith and Max Wilbert, argues that "bright green energy" is not a sufficient response to climate crisis. Paul Hawken supplies plenty of climate solutions in *Regeneration: Ending the Climate Crisis in One Generation* that go "well beyond solar, electric vehicles, and tree planting" (as stated on the back of the book).

My views on societal collapse are influenced by Jared Diamond's *Collapse: How Societies Choose to Fail or Succeed*. A provocative, and rather grim, book is Wes Jackson and Robert Jensen's *An Inconvenient Apocalypse: Environmental Collapse, Climate Crisis, and the Fate of Humanity*. Jackson and Jensen agree with Diamond's basic definition of collapse as drastic decline in population and societal complexity, but they disagree with the claim that our response is simply a conscious choice, arguing instead that we are largely led by our "human carbon nature": our evolutionary big-brained biology led to the pursuit of carbon energy, which, of course, has led to climate crisis.

Another important and early thinker on collapse is Joseph Tainter, the author of *The Collapse of Complex Societies*, which came out in 1988. Ben Ehrenreich's 2020 *New York Times Sunday Magazine* article "How Do You Know When Society Is about to Fall Apart?: Meet the Scholars Who Study Civilizational Collapse" summarizes

Tainter's arguments, which include the claim that complexity is both a driver of civilization and its collapse when things get too complex, too unstable.

p. 284: The material from Christopher Bache's *Dark Night, Early Dawn* is from "The Great Awakening" (213–56). Bache has explored nonordinary states of consciousness, including via LSD, and he shares his discoveries in relation to education and sustainability and our collective becoming. In the preface, he acknowledges most academics may find his views, and the source influencing his views, as "unacceptably radical" (xvii). Regardless, he provides much that is worth considering. The Jung quotation on humans being the "makeweight" that may "tip the scales" of a positive future is from *Dark Night, Early Dawn* (244).

pp. 285–286: Ken Wilber's views in *The Religion of Tomorrow* on the possibility of a 10 percent change in consciousness among the collective population leading to significant material change can be found on page 321. He also discusses this possibility in *Trump and a Post-Truth World* and *Wicked and Wise: How to Solve the World's Toughest Problems*, the latter written with Alan Watkins. I explore Wilber's work in relation to human development and possible glory or collapse in *An Ecology of Communication: Response and Responsibility in an Age of Ecocrisis*, especially in chapter 2, "Integral Meta-Theory: Ken Wilber and Spiritual Communication."

p. 286: To explore the possibility of collective crisis leading to a great awakening, collapse, gradual learning in steps, or something else, I show students TED talks by Peter Diamandis and Paul Gilding. Diamandis's talk, "Abundance Is Our Future," is filled with techno-optimism—we have a history of knocking down problems as they arise, and technology will lead the way as we knock down new problems. Gilding's talk, "The Earth Is Full," is full of harrowing facts about current and coming ecocrisis, including the likelihood of collapse.

Students tend to agree with Diamandis at first—it feels good to be optimistic and hopeful after always hearing so much bad news (Diamandis criticizes the media for having an "if it bleeds, it leads" attitude). Environmentalists have long been criticized for their pessimistic vision because it may kill our spirit and fails to empower us to act. On the other hand, being in denial about the state of the planet and not listening to Gilding is also a problem. There is a third video when they both come on stage and answer questions. Diamandis states that he does not have much faith in government, but he does have faith in people and small companies who are doing research and creating new technologies. Gilding acknowledges this good work but argues governments and corporations rule the world and we will need a crisis to truly wake up; we are on our way to a whopper. Of course, we have crises all the time, but he argues that we will have, and need, a *really* big one to finally get the message and transform ourselves and infrastructure. I ask students to notice the communication metaphor—messages are everywhere, but we are not listening. Isn't the Arctic speaking about climate disruption via melting ice and other signs?

Gilding's argument is that civilizations have collapsed in the past due to ecocrisis and that it will happen again, while adding some hope for a post-collapse, learned-our-lessons sustainable civilization. Diamandis's argument is that it won't happen again because conditions are different due to our advanced technology.

I often tell students that they are living in a combustible time of ongoing good and bad news. This good and bad news extends to the scientific data, but also the framing of that data.

In Hannah Ritchie's 2024 book, *Not the End of the World: How We Can Be the First Generation to Build a Sustainable Planet*, she wants to change the climate framing from thinking that we are doomed to embracing the current generation as the first sustainable one. Ritchie, a senior researcher in the Programme on Global Development at Oxford University, focuses on hopeful data such as examples of lower emissions despite rising GDP in several countries. She also wants to reframe sustainability by focusing on opportunity rather than sacrifice. In contrast, Johan Rockstrom, the director of the Potsdam Institute for Climate Impact Research, has been documenting planetary boundaries or tipping points, a subject Ritchie does not mention, and based on the data we have entered nine danger zones, including climate, biodiversity, and ocean acidification, from which civilization (as we know it) may not be able to recover.

Given their stellar scientific credentials, it is not a matter of believing Ritchie over Rockstrom, or vice-versa, but recognizing they study differing data sets and supply differing messages of our predicament. Said differently, we are dealing with a both/and situation, not an either/or one, and climate communicators must respect and find a way to incorporate the data and messaging of both Ritchie and Rockstrom in their own messaging. Also, the phrase, or frame, "tipping points" can be misleading, as it suggests a singular event. Instead, we are dealing with a super-wicked problem consisting of multiple danger zones that respond differently to human behavior over different time periods with some being reversible.

Ritchie and Rockstrom both have TED Talks that can be used in the classroom. Rockstrom's research is also the basis of the documentary, *Breaking Boundaries: The Science of Our Planet*.

This documentary is filled with plenty of bad news, but the good news is that Kate Raworth, in her book *Doughnut Economics*, has developed an economic model that responds to the nine planetary boundaries. Raworth's model maps out the boundaries on the outside of a circle and sustainable responses on an inner ring; her goal is to create economies that can thrive whether or not they grow. Raworth chose to call her model "doughnut economics" because of the circular shape, but also because she wanted to reframe economics and move beyond capitalism, socialism, and communism debates. More good news: Amsterdam and other cities have been implementing doughnut economics. The ongoing bad news: we continue to step further into the danger zones.

pp. 286-287: Thomas Berry's quotation that we have moved from "suicide to homicide to genocide to ecocide to geocide" is from *The Great Work: Our Way into the Future* (74). Given the title of the book, he does not advocate for giving up in response to his analysis; rather, we must do our part to bring forth what he calls the ecozoic era. Gary Greenberg writes about long-term grief in his *New York Times* article "In Grief Is How We Live Now."

pp. 287–289: It is helpful to consider the analyses of Janine Benyus, David Orr, Per Espen Stoknes, and Robin Wall Kimmerer in response to eco-social crises within the context of two 2015 documents, "An EcoModernist Manifesto" and "A Call to Look Past an Ecomodernist Manifesto: A Degrowth Critique." Both documents, available online, have multiple authors and see the perils of global warming, but their conclusions are quite different. Like Peter Diamandis, the ecomodernists have faith in technology, including nuclear power, and argue for more growth. Like Paul Gilding, the degrowth authors see growth, and faith in it, as the problem since we cannot solve problems with the same consciousness that produced them in the first place. Both documents are good for the classroom although, strangely, the "Ecomodernist Manifesto" has no footnotes, making one wonder about their sources. This debate has been going on for a while, and we are and will continue to play it out.

Thoreau, of course, makes a strong case for living simply and thus degrowth. I would argue that Benyus, Orr, Stoknes, and Kimmerer are also on the side of degrowth, but Benyus advocates for the growth of technologies that mimic nature's wisdom. A key question, then, is what needs to grow and what needs to stop growing or perhaps disappear? An excellent book is Jason Hickel's *Less is More: How Degrowth Will Save the World.*

p. 288: The quotation from Per Espen Stoknes on air as "a grand subject, to which we are subjected" is from *What We Think about When We Try Not to Think about Global Warming* (203). Stoknes is influenced by David Abram's 1996 *The Spell of the Sensuous,* in which he gathers ecopsychological insights from our animistic past, exploring perception, language, and especially bodily-based converse within a more-than-human world.

pp. 288-289: The Robin Wall Kimmerer quotations on plants as teachers are from "Mishkos Kenomagwen, the Lessons of Grass" in *Traditional Ecological Knowledge: Learning from Indigenous Practices for Environmental Sustainability* (28). This essay is full of insights, but one of the most provocative ones is that some plant species thrive more through harvest, if done properly, or what is called "honorable harvest" (43). In other words, while leaving nature alone may be the best strategy for the restoration of some plant species, for others, humans using them via proper practices is best. Kimmerer argues that in many cases plants need humans to accept their gifts for them to thrive; humans should reciprocate by giving gifts in return, living in the spirit of gratitude, and creating a gift economy. Kimmerer's views on the many gifts of mosses and mosses as a measure of success are from "Ancient Green: Moss, Climate, and Deep Time" in *Emergence Magazine* online.

p. 289: The quotations from Rachel Carson's commencement address in 1962 are from Maria Popova's *Figuring* (487–88).

p. 290: Not surprisingly, the quotation "In the long run we find what we expect; we shall be fortunate, then, if we expect great things" is taken from Kevin Dann's *Expect Great Things* (258).

p. 290: Thich Nhat Hanh states that the Bodhisattva listens to the suffering of the world and responds with compassion in many of his books. In my The Voice of Nature course, I have used *The World We Have: A Buddhist Approach to Peace and Ecology*, a slim volume that is easy for students to read while providing provocative insights that stimulate class discussion. Students do not completely agree with Hanh, nor do I; agreeing is not the point. Being challenged by his ideas is the point. I mention that I am not trying to turn students into Buddhists, but I also say that Buddhism can be interpreted more as psychology, which is useful no matter our religious faith or spiritual interests.

pp. 290-291: The journal quotation on Thoreau's weeklong job of hard surveying work making him "more susceptible than usual to the finest influences, as music and poetry" is from Celeste Healey's "On Pencils and Purpose" in *Now Comes Good Sailing: Writers Reflect on Henry David Thoreau* (234). Healy argues that Thoreau searched for and eventually found balance between his spiritual and work life, with his early writing being more against work and his later writings being more pro-work. However, Thoreau's last essay, "Walking," has some caustic passages about work, including the line about his fellow townsfolk not knowing what their legs are for since they spend their days busy with business. Still, this is an insightful essay in part because Healey writes about how Thoreau made leisure productive. She makes it clear that Thoreau was no slacker.

p. 291: Thoreau's September 7, 1851, journal entry on always being on "the alert to find God in nature" and extracting "honey from the flower of the world" were shared via the Thoreau Society Facebook group.

pp. 295-296: The Emerson quotation on the possibility of heaven when we are "raised above ourselves by the power of principles" can be found in Barry Andrews's *American Sage: The Spiritual Teachings of Ralph Waldo Emerson* (64). Its original source is Emerson's speech and essay, "Man the Reformer." Emerson's claim that "We are incompetent to solve the times" and the resulting question: "How shall I live?" can also be found in *American Sage* (144–45), and the original source is Emerson's essay "Fate." The last quotation, "One of the illusions is that the present hour is not the critical decisive hour. Write it on your heart that every day is the best day of the year. No man has learned anything rightly until he knows that every day is Doomsday," is from *American Sage* (146), and the original source is his essay "Works and Days." Emerson, of course, can be of differing minds in differing essays; in *The American Scholar* he writes, "man hopes: genius creates" (56).

p. 296: Richard B. Primack's descriptions of changes to the land, pond, and New England bioregion in *Walden Warming: Climate Change Comes to Thoreau's Woods* are from pages 215–17.

p. 296: The loss of Walden ice, including for skating, is detailed in George Howe Colt's "Thoreau on Ice" in *Now Comes Good Sailing: Writers Reflect on Henry David Thoreau* (175). Despite the bad news on the loss of ice, this is a fun piece on Thoreau's love of ice skating, and winter generally, and reveals Thoreau as a seeker of fun. He had a deep sense of purpose but also loved to play.

p. 297: The material from Fast Company and recruiter.com on Thoreau's influence on our pandemic world comes from Brent Ranalli's column, "Notes & Queries," in a 2021 *Thoreau Society Bulletin*, a newsletter sent out to members.

p. 297: Thoreau's influence on the environmental movement is explored in Michael Zizer's "The Modern Environmental Movement." His influence on tiny houses is explored in April Anson's "The Patron Saint of Tiny Houses." And his influence on popular culture is explored in Carl H. Sederholm's "Popular Culture." All three essay are from *Henry David Thoreau in Context*.

p. 297: Rebecca Solnit's "The Thoreau Problem" is from *Orion* magazine and can be found online. Solnit also wrote "Mysteries of Thoreau, Unsolved" for *Orion* magazine, in which she takes on the silly accusation propagated online that Thoreau is a hypocrite because his mother supposedly did his laundry when he was living at Walden Pond. The truth is that we don't know who did Thoreau's laundry, but that his whole family may have had their laundry done by a well-treated maid because their home was also a boardinghouse. Regardless, Solnit points out that no one cares about the laundry of any other author, and they should not care about Thoreau's laundry. Instead, they should address his ideas, which he did fine job of living. He also helped considerably at home and with the family pencil business, especially after his father died, paid rent to stay in his attic room, and had a close relationship with his mother and sisters.

pp. 298–299: My final thoughts on the spirituality of being lost were influenced by Rebecca Solnit's excellent *A Field Guide to Getting Lost*. Solnit references the Thoreau quotation from which the title of this book is taken but does not explore Thoreau much. She is a fan, however, defending him in her *Orion* articles and speaking to the 2022 Thoreau Society Gathering in Concord, Massachusetts. I am a big fan of Solnit's books and journalism, and I share with students her 2021 *Guardian* piece "Ten Ways to Confront the Climate Crisis without Losing Hope."

In 2023, Solnit, along with Thelma Young Lutunatabua, published *Not Too Late: Changing the Climate Story from Despair to Possibility*, in which they argue that our climate outcome is not decided. There is a history of collapse but also a history of small steps leading to big change. We need to embrace possibility and take those steps.

In a 2023 *Guardian* article "We Can't Afford to Be Climate Doomers," Solnit acknowledges that things are getting worse; she also argues there is plenty of good news: more solutions, including tech solutions, more information and engagement, more climate activism, and more significant victories. By not celebrating that good news, and only focusing on the bad, "doomers" undermine the hope needed to sustain and grow a climate movement. In a response in *Medium*, Renaee Churches argues that the climate battle is already lost and that we need to accept that reality. Churches, a proponent of Deep Adaptation and self-described "doomster" (again, see Jem Bendell's work and the Deep Adaptation Facebook Group), states that views like Solnit's are what keeps us from the real work of adaptation because wealthy elites and new technologies will not save us.

This debate reflects another question of our time worth exploring in the classroom. It should be noted, however, that climatologist Michael Mann argues that every fraction of a degree of warming is worth preventing, and both Solnit and Deep Adaptation proponents advocate for doing good work in community, or great work, answering with our actions the questions thrust upon us in climate crisis times. In doing so, we may return to Emerson's claim that humans hope, but inner genius creates, along with Thoreau's many responses to our eco-spiritual lostness, including expecting great things.

Works Cited

Abram, David. *The Spell of the Sensuous: Perception and Language in a More-Than Human World*. New York: Pantheon, 1996.

Alexander, Bryan. *Universities on Fire: Higher Education in the Climate Crisis*. Baltimore: Johns Hopkins University Press, 2023.

Andrews, Barry. *Transcendentalism and the Cultivation of the Soul*. Amherst: University of Massachusetts Press, 2017.

———. *Emerson as Spiritual Guide: A Companion to Emerson's Essays for Personal Reflection and Group Discussion*. Boston: Skinner House Books, 2003.

———. *American Sage: The Spiritual Teachings of Ralph Waldo Emerson*. Amherst: University of Massachusetts Press, 2021.

Anson, April. "The Patron Saint of Tiny Houses." In *Henry David Thoreau in Context*, edited by James S. Finney, 331–41. Cambridge, England: University of Cambridge Press, 2017.

Athanasiou, Tom. *Divided Planet: The Ecology of Rich and Poor*. Athens: University of Georgia Press, 1998.

Bache, Christopher. *Dark Night, Early Dawn: Steps to a Deep Ecology of Mind*. Albany: SUNY Press, 2000.

———. *The Living Classroom*. Albany: SUNY Press, 2008.

Balcombe, Jonathan. *What a Fish Knows: The Inner Lives of Our Underwater Cousins*. New York: Farrar, Strauss, & Giroux, 2016.

Baldwin, James. *The Evidence of Things Not Seen*. 1985. Reissue. New York: Henry Holt & Company, 2023.

Balthrop-Lewis, Alda. *Thoreau's Religion: Walden Woods, Social Justice, and the Politics of Asceticism*. Cambridge, England: Cambridge University Press, 2021.

Bateson, Gregory. *Mind and Nature: A Necessary Unity*. New York: Bantam, 1979.

———. *Steps to an Ecology of Mind*. New York: Ballantine, 1972.

Bateson, Gregory, and Mary Catherine Bateson. *Angels Fear: Toward an Epistemology of the Sacred*. New York: Bantam Books, 1987.

Bendell, Jem. *Breaking Together: A Freedom-Loving Response to Collapse*. Bristol, England: Good Works: 2023.

Berkes, Fikret. *Sacred Ecology*. New York: Routledge, 2012.

Berry, Thomas. *The Dream of the Earth*. Oakland: Sierra Club Books, 1990.

———. *The Great Work*. New York: Bell Tower, 1999.

———. *Evening Thoughts: Reflecting on Earth as a Sacred Community*. San Francisco: Sierra Club Books, 2006.

Berry, Thomas, and Brian Swimme. *The Universe Story*. San Francisco: HarperCollins, 1992.

Berry, Wendell. *What Are People For?* San Francisco: North Point Press, 1990.

————. *Home Economics*. San Francisco: North Point Press, 1987

————. "Whose Head Is the Farmer Using? Whose Head Is Using the Farmer?" In *Meeting the Expectations of the Land*, edited by Wes Jackson, Wendell Berry, and Bruce Colman, 19–30. San Francisco: North Point Press, 1984.

Berryman, Phillip. *Liberation Theology*. New York: Pantheon Books, 1987.

Black Elk, and John Neihardt. *Black Elk Speaks*. Lincoln: University of Nebraska Press, 1988.

Boff, Leonardo. *Cry of the Earth, Cry of the Poor*. Maryknoll, NY: Orbis Books, 1997.

Botkin, Daniel B. *No Man's Garden: Thoreau and the New Vision for Civilization and Nature*. Washington, DC: Island Press, 2001.

Boyd, Daniel. *I Want a Better Catastrophe: Navigating the Climate Crisis with Grief, Hope, and Gallows Humor*. Gabriola Island, British Columbia: New Society Publishers, 2023.

Bragg, Billy. "Waiting for the Great Leap Forward." *Workers Playtime*. Go! Discs, 1990.

Bridgman, Richard. *Dark Thoreau*. Lincoln: University of Nebraska Press, 1982.

Buber, Martin. *I and Thou*. Edited by Walter Kaufmann. New York: Scribner's, 1970.

————. *Pointing the Way*. Harper & Row, 1963.

Buehrens, John A. Conflagration: *How the Transcendentalists Sparked the American Struggle for Racial, Gender, and Social Justice*. Boston: Beacon Press Books, 2020.

Buell, Lawrence. *Emerson*. Cambridge: Harvard University Press, 2003.

————. *Henry David Thoreau: Thinking Disobediently*. Oxford, UK: Oxford University Press, 2023.

Buell, Lawrence, ed. *The American Transcendentalists: Essential Writings*. New York: Modern Library, 2006.

Carbaugh, Donal. "'Just Listen': 'Listening' and Landscape among the Blackfeet." In *Cultures in Conversation*, 110–19. New York: Routledge, 2005.

Carr, Nicholas. "Is Google Making Us Stupid?" *Atlantic Monthly* (July/August 2008).

Carson, Rachel. "The Pollution of Our Environment." In *Lost Woods: The Discovered Writing of Rachel Carson*, edited by Linda Lear, 227–45. Boston: Beacon Press, 1999.

Case, Kristen. "Following Thoreau." In *Now Comes Good Sailing: Writers Reflect on Henry David Thoreau*, edited by Andrew Blauner, 149–58. Princeton: Princeton University Press, 2021.

————. "Thoreau's Vulnerable Resistance." In *Thoreau in an Age of Crisis: Uses and Abuses of an American Icon*, edited by Kristen Case, Rochelle Johnson, and Henrik Otterberg, 249–62. Paderborn, Germany: Brill-Fink, 2021.

Catala, Rafael. *Mysticism of Now*. Lakeland, CO: Acropolis Books, 1997.

Chenoweth, Erica. *Civil Resistance: What Everyone Needs to Know*. London: Oxford University Press, 2021.

Chodron, Pema. *No Time to Lose: A Timely Guide to the Way of the Boddhisattva*. Boston: Shambhala Publications, 2005.

Colt, George Howe. "Thoreau on Ice." In *Now Comes Good Sailing: Writers Reflect on Henry David Thoreau*, edited by Andrew Blauner, 161–75. Princeton: Princeton University Press, 2021.

Cope, Stephen. *The Great Work of your Life*. New York: Bantam Books, 2012.

Cramer, Jeffrey S. *Solid Seasons: The Friendship of Henry David Thoreau and Ralph Waldo Emerson*. Berkeley, CA: Counterpoint, 2029.

Cronon, William. *Changes in the Land: Indians, Colonists, and the Ecology of New England*. New York: Hill and Wang, 2003.

Dann, Kevin. *Expect Great Things: The Life and Search of Henry David Thoreau*. New York: TarcherPerigee, 2017.

———. *The Road to Walden: 12 Lessons from a Sojourn to Thoreau's Cabin*. New York: TarcherPerigee, 2018.

Deloria, Vine, Jr. *Spirit and Reason*. Colorado: Fulcrum Publishing, 1999.

———. *God Is Red*. New York: Putnam Publishing Group, 2003 (1973).

Diamond, Jared. *Collapse*. New York: Penguin, 2005.

Dossey, Larry. *One Mind: How Our Individual Mind Is Part of a Greater Consciousness and Why It Matters*. Carlsbad, CA: Hay House, 2013.

Early, Gerald. "*Walden* and the Black Quest for Nature." In *Now Comes Good Sailing: Writers Reflect on Henry David Thoreau*, edited by Andrew Blauner. Princeton: Princeton University Press, 2021.

Eastman, Charles (Ohiyesa). *The Soul of the Indian*. Lincoln, NE: Bison Books, 1980 (1911).

Eckert, Allan W. *A Sorrow in Our Hearts: The Life of Tecumseh*. New York: Bantam Books, 1992.

Einstein, Albert. *Ideas and Opinions*. New York: Three Rivers Press, 1982.

Elgin, Duane. *Promise Ahead*. New York: Quill, 2001.

Emerson, Ralph Waldo. *The Portable Emerson*. Edited by Carl Bode and Malcolm Cowley. New York: Penguin Books, 1981.

———. *The Political Emerson*. Edited by David M. Robinson. Boston: Beacon Press, 2004.

Emerson, R. W., and H. D. Thoreau. *Nature/Walking*. Edited by John Elder. Boston: Beacon Press, 1991.

Euripides. *The Bacchae*. Cambridge: Cambridge University Press, 2000.

Farnham, Susan, et al. *Listening Hearts: Discerning Call in Community*. Harrisburg, PA: Morehouse Publishing, 2011 (1991).

Feuerstein, Georg. *Holy Madness*. New York: Penguin Books, 1992.

Fischer, Louis. *Gandhi: His Life and Message to the World*. New York: Penguin Books, 1982 (1954).

Flood, Alison. "Scientists use Thoreau's journal notes to track climate change: Researchers use Walden author's tables of flowering dates in 1840s Massachusetts to show temperature has risen 2.4C." *Guardian*, May 12, 2012.

Foucault, Michel. *"What Is Enlightenment?"* In *The Foucault Reader*, edited by Paul Rabinow. New York: Pantheon Books, 1984.

Freedman, Andrew, and Chris Mooney. "Major new climate study rules out less severe global warming scenarios." *Washington Post*, July 22, 2020.

Freire, Paulo. *Pedagogy of the Oppressed*. New York: Continuum, 1990.

Fromm, Erich. *The Sane Society*. New York: Henry Holt & Co., 1990 (1955).

Fuller, Margaret. *The Portable Margaret Fuller*. Edited by Mary Kelly. New York: Penguin Books, 1994.

Furlong, Monica. *Zen Effects: The Life of Alan Watts*. Woodstock, VT: Skylight Paths Publishing, 2001.

Gagliano, Monica. *Thus Spoke the Plant: A Remarkable Journey of Groundbreaking Scientific Discoveries and Personal Encounters with Plants*. Berkeley, CA: North Atlantic Books, 2018.

Gardner, Howard. *Intelligence Reframed: Multiple Intelligences for the 21st Century*. New York: Basic Books, 1999.

Gatto, John Taylor. "Against School." *Harper's Magazine* 307/1840 (September 2003): 33–38.

Geldard, Richard. *The Spiritual Teachings of Ralph Waldo Emerson*. Great Barrington, MA: Lindisfarne Books, 2001.

Gelderloos, Peter. *The Failure of Nonviolence*. Seattle: Left Bank Books, 2015.

Gillis, Justin. "Naomi Oreskes: A Lightning Rod in a Changing Climate." *New York Times*, June 15, 2015.

Goldsmith, Joel. *The Thunder of Silence*. New York: Harper & Row, 1961.

———. *Invisible Supply*. San Francisco: HarperSanFrancisco, 1994 (1983).

Gould, Rebecca Kneale. "The Whiteness of Walden." In *Thoreau in an Age of Crisis: Uses and Abuses of an American Icon*, edited by Kristen Case, Rochelle Johnson, and Henrik Otterberg, 161–80. Paderborn, Germany: Brill-Fink, 2021.

Gutierrez, Gustavo. *A Theology of Liberation: History, Politics, and Salvation*. Maryknoll, NY: Orbis Books, 1971.

Green, Tova, et al. *Insight and Action: How to Discover and Support a Life of Integrity and Commitment to Change*. Gabriola Island, British Columbia: New Society Publishers, 1994.

Greenberg, Gary. "In Grief Is How We Live Now." *New York Times*, May 7, 2022. https://www.nytimes.com/2022/05/07/opinion/grief.html.

Greenway, Robert. "The Wilderness Effect and Ecopsychology." In *Ecopsychology: Restoring the Earth, Healing the Mind*, edited by Theodore Roszak, Mary E. Gomes, and Allen D. Kanner, 122–35. San Francisco: Sierra Club Books, 1995.

———. "Healing by the Wilderness Experience." In *Wild Ideas*, edited by David Rothenberg, 182–93. Minneapolis: University of Minnesota Press, 1995.

Gross, Robert A. *The Transcendentalists and Their World*. New York: Farrar, Strauss and Giroux, 2021.

Hadot, Pierre. *Philosophy as a Way of Life*. Hoboken: Blackwell Publishing, 1995.

———. *What Is Ancient Philosophy?* Cambridge: Harvard University Press, 2004.

Hanh, Thich Nhat. *The World We Have: A Buddhist Approach to Peace and Ecology*. Berkeley, CA: Parallax Press, 2008.

Harpur, Patrick. *Daimonic Reality*. New York: Penguin, 1994.

Harries-Jones, Peter. *A Recursive Vision: Ecological Understanding and Gregory Bateson*. Toronto: University of Toronto, 1995.

Harris, Michael. *The End of Absence: Reclaiming What We Have Lost in an Age of Constant Connection*. New York: Penguin, 2014.

Hawken, Paul. *Blessed Unrest: How the Largest Social Movement in History is Restoring Grace, Justice, and Beauty to the World*. New York: Penguin Books, 2008.

———. *Regeneration: Ending the Climate Crisis in One Generation*. New York: Penguin Books, 2021.

Healey, Celeste. "On Pencils and Purpose." In *Now Comes Good Sailing: Writers Reflect on Henry David Thoreau*, edited by Andrew Blauner. Princeton: Princeton University Press, 2021.

Heidegger, Martin. *Discourse on Thinking*. Translated by John M. Anderson and E. Hans Freund. New York: Harper and Row, 1966.

———. *The Question Concerning Technology*. New York: Harper & Row, 1977.

Hickel, Jason. *Less Is More: How Degrowth Will Save the World*. London: William Heinemann, 2020.

Hillman, James. *The Soul's Code: In Search of Character and Calling*. New York: Warner Books, 1996.

———. *Re-Visioning Psychology*. New York: Harper & Row, 1975.

Hillman, James, and Michael Ventura. *We've Had a Hundred Years of Psychotherapy—and the World's Getting Worse*. New York: HarperCollins, 1993.

Hixson, Lex. *Coming Home*. New York: Larsen Publications, 1995.

Homestead, William. *The Path of My Soul: Journey to the Center of Self*. Lakeland, CO: Acropolis Books, 1999.

———. "The Language that All Things Speak." *Voice and Environmental Communication*. New York: Palgrave MacMillan, 2014.

———. *An Ecology of Communication: Response and Responsibility in an Age of Ecocrisis*. Lanham, MD: Lexington Books, 2021.

———. "Robin Wall Kimmerer and Deep Listening: Practicing an Ecology of Communication." *About Place Journal*, October 2023. https://aboutplacejournal.org/article/robin-wall-kimmerer-and-deep-listening/. Accessed February 8, 2024.

hooks, bell. *Teaching to Transgress: Education as the Practice of Freedom*. New York: Routledge, 1994.

Howarth, William. "Reading Thoreau at 200." *American Scholar*, June 3, 2017. https://theamericanscholar.org/reading-thoreau-at-200/. Accessed February 8, 2024.

Jackson, Wes. *The New Roots of Agriculture*. Lincoln: University of Nebraska Press, 1980.

———. *Consulting the Genius of the Place: An Ecological Approach to a New Agriculture*. Berkeley, CA: Counterpoint, 2010.

Jackson, Wes, and Robert Jensen. *An Inconvenient Apocalypse: Environmental Collapse, Climate Crisis, and the Fate of Humanity*. South Bend: University of Notre Dame Press, 2022.

Jacobsen, Mark Z. *No Miracles Needed: How Today's Technology Can Save Our Climate and Clean Our Air*. Cambridge, England: Cambridge University Press, 2023.

———. "The Golden Age of Renewables is Beginning, and California is Leading the Way." *Scientific American* (April 24, 2024). Available online: https://www.scientificamerican.com/article/a-golden-age-of-renewables-is-beginning-and-california-is-leading-the-way/

James, William. *The Varieties of Religious Experience*. New York: Penguin Books, 1982.

Jayakar, Pupul. *J. Krishnamurti: A Biography*. New York: Penguin Books, 1986.

Jensen, Derrick, Lierre Keith, and Max Wilbert. *Bright Green Lies: How the Environmental Movement Lost Its Way and What We Can Do About It*. Rhinebeck, NY: Monkfish Books, 2021.

Jung, C. G. *Memories, Dreams, Reflections*. New York: Vintage Books, 1989 (1961).

———. *Psychology and Alchemy*. New Jersey: Princeton University Press, 1980 (1953).

Kant, Immanuel. "What is Enlightenment?" In *Kant: Political Writings*. Cambridge: Cambridge University Press, 1991 (1970).

Kaza, Stephanie. *The Attentive Heart: Conversations with Trees*. New York: Ballantine, 1993.

Kaza, Stephanie, and Kenneth Kraft, eds. *Dharma Rain: Sources of Buddhist Environmentalism*. Boston: Shambhala Publications, 2000.

Kendall, Henry. "Union of Concerned Scientists' Warning to Humanity." In *Life Stories*, edited by Heather Newbold, 198–202. Berkeley: University of California Press, 2000.

Kimmerer, Robin Wall. *Gathering Moss: A Natural and Cultural History of Mosses*. Corvallis: Oregon State University Press, 2003.

———. *Braiding Sweetgrass: Indigenous Wisdom, Scientific Knowledge, and the Teachings of Plants*. Minnesota: Milkweed, 2013.

———. "Mishkos Kenomogwen: The Lessons of Grass." In *Traditional Ecological Knowledge: Learning from Indigenous Practices for Environmental Sustainability*, edited by Melissa K. Nelson and Dan Shilling, 27–56. Cambridge, England: Cambridge University Press, 2018.

Klein, Ezra. "Your Kids Are Not Doomed." *New York Times*, June 5, 2022.

Kramer, Joel, and Diana Alstead. *The Guru Papers*. Berkeley, CA: Frog Books, 1993.

Krech, Shepard. *The Ecological Indian: Myth and History*. New York: Norton, 1999.

Kripal, Jeffrey J. *The Flip: Epiphanies of Mind and the Future of Knowledge*. New York: Bellevue Literary Press, 2019.

Krishnamurti, J. *Think on These Things*. New York: Harper & Row, 1964.

Kucich, John J. "Thoreau's Indian Problem: Savagism, Indigeneity, and the Politics of Place." In *Thoreau in an Age of Crisis: Uses and Abuses of an American Icon*, edited by Kristen Case, Rochelle Johnson, and Henrik Otterberg, 127–45. Paderborn, Germany: Brill-Fink, 2021.

Lanham, J. Drew. *The Home Place: Memoirs of a Colored Man's Love Affair with Nature*. Minneapolis: Milkweed, 2016.

Lebeaux, Richard. *Young Man Thoreau*. Amherst: University of Massachusetts Press, 1977.

Leloup, Jean-Yves. *The Gospel of Thomas: The Gnostic Wisdom of Jesus*. Rochester, VT: Inner Traditions, 2005.

Lemire, Elise. *Black Walden: Slavery and Its Aftermath in Concord, Massachusetts*. Philadelphia: University of Pennsylvania Press, 2009.

Levoy, Gregg. *Callings: Finding and Following an Authentic Life*. New York: Three Rivers Press, 1997.

Lewis, Anthony. *Make No Law: The Sullivan Case and the First Amendment*. New York: Random House, 1991.

Malm, Andreas. *How to Blow Up a Pipeline*. Brooklyn: Verso Books, 2021.

Marcuse, Herbert. *One Dimensional Man*. Boston: Beacon Press, 1991 (1964).

———. *An Essay on Liberation*. Boston: Beacon Press, 1969.

———. *Counter-Revolution and Revolt*. Boston: Beacon Press, 1972.

———. *The Aesthetic Dimension*. Boston: Beacon Press, 1978.

Marshall, Megan. *Margaret Fuller: A New American Life*. New York: Mariner Books, 2013.

Maslow, Abraham. *Toward a Psychology of Being*. New York: Wiley, 1968.

May, Rollo. *Love and Will*. New York: Dell Publishing, 1969.

McKibben, Bill. *The End of Nature*. New York: Anchor Books, 1999.

———. *Maybe One*. New York: Simon & Schuster, 1998.

———. *Eaarth*. New York: Henry Holt & Co., 2010.

———. "What Exxon Knew About Climate Change." *New Yorker*, September 18, 2015.

Momaday, N. Scott. *The Ancient Child*. New York: HarperPerennial, 1990.

Mooney, Chris. "30 years ago scientists warned Congress on global warming. What they said sounds eerily familiar." *Washington Post*, June 11, 2016. https://www.washingtonpost.com/news/energy-environment/wp/2016/06/11/30-years-ago-scientists-warned-congress-on-global-warming-what-they-said-sounds-eerily-familiar/. Accessed February 8, 2024.

————. "Some Like It Hot." *Mother Jones*, May/June 2005. https://www.motherjones.com/environment/2005/05/some-it-hot/. Accessed February 8, 2024.

————. *Unscientific America*. New York: Basic Books, 2009.

————. *The Republican War on Science*. New York: Basic Books, 2006.

Moore, Jason W., ed. *Anthropocene or Capitalocene? Nature, History, and the Crisis of Capitalism*. Oakland, CA: PM Press, 2016.

Mukherjee, Rudrangshu, ed. *The Penguin Gandhi Reader*. New York: Penguin Books, 1993.

Myers, Gerald E. *William James: His Life and Thought*. New Haven: Yale University Press, 1986.

Newbold, Heather. *Life Stories: World Renowned Scientists Reflect on their Lives and the Future of Life on Earth*. Berkeley: University of California Press, 2000.

Oreskes, Naomi, and Erik M. Conway. *Merchants of Doubt: How a Handful of Scientists Obscured the Truth on Issues from Tobacco Smoke to Global Warming*. New York: Bloomsbury, 2010.

————. *The Collapse of Western Civilization: A View from the Future*. New York: Columbia University Press, 2014.

Oreskes, Naomi, and Geofrey Supran. "What Exxon Mobil Didn't Say about Climate Change." *New York Times*, August 22, 2017.

Orr, David. *Earth in Mind: On Education, Environment, and the Human Prospect*. Washington, DC: Island Press, 1994.

————. *The Nature of Design*. Oxford: Oxford University Press, 2004.

————. *Dangerous Years: Climate Change, the Long Emergency, and the Way Forward*. New Haven: Yale University Press, 2016.

Ortega y Gasset, José. *The Revolt of the Masses*. New York: W. W. Norton & Co., 1993 (1932).

————. *The Dehumanization of Art*. Princeton: Princeton University Press, 1972 (1968).

Painter, Nell Irvin. *The History of White People*. New York: W. W. Norton and Co., 2010.

Palmer, Parker. *Let Your Life Speak: Listening for the Voice of Vocation*. San Francisco: Jossey-Bass, 1999.

Petrulionis, Sandra Harbert. "Between 'That Farthest Western Way' and 'The University of the West.'" In *Thoreau beyond Borders: New International Essays on America's Most Famous Nature Writer*, edited by Francois Specq, Laura Dassow Walls, and Julien Negre, 195–212. Amherst: University of Massachusetts Press, 2020.

Pirsig, Robert. *Zen and the Art of Motorcycle Maintenance*. New York: Bantam Books, 1975.

Plato. *The Republic of Plato*. Translated by Frances MacDonald Cornford. London: Oxford University Press, 1966.

Plec, Emily, ed. *Perspectives on Human-Animal Communication: International Communication*. New York: Routledge, 2014.

Popova, Maria. *Figuring*. New York: Vintage Books, 2020.

Postman, Neil. *Building a Bridge to the 18th Century*. New York: Vintage Books, 2000.

———. *Technopoly*. New York: Vintage Books, 1993.

Primack. Richard B. *Walden Warming: Climate Change Comes to Thoreau's Woods*. Chicago: University of Chicago, 2014.

Quinn, Daniel. *Ishmael*. New York: Bantam Books, 1992.

Radin, Dean. *Supernormal: Science, Yoga, and the Evidence for Extraordinary Psychic Abilities*. New York: Random House, 2013.

Raleigh, M. J. "Restorative Environments and Human Well-Being." *Ometeca* (2010): 294–300.

Ramsey, R. Eric. *The Long Path to Nearness: A Contribution to a Corporeal Philosophy of Communication and the Groundwork of an Ethics of Relief*. Atlantic Highlands, NJ: Humanity Books, 1998.

Ramsey, R. Eric, and David James Miller, eds. *Experiences between Philosophy and Communication*. Albany: SUNY Press, 2003.

Ramsey, R. Eric, and Linda Weiner. *Leaving Us to Wonder: An Essay on the Questions Science Can't Ask*. Albany: SUNY Press, 2005.

Ranalli, Brent. "Henry David Thoreau's Lifelong Indian Play." In *Thoreau in an Age of Crisis: Uses and Abuses of an American Icon*, edited by Kristen Case, Rochelle Johnson, and Henrik Otterberg, 145–60. Paderborn, Germany: Brill-Fink, 2021.

———. "Notes & Queries." *Thoreau Society Bulletin* 315 (Fall 2021): 15–20.

Raworth, Kate. *Doughnut Economics: 7 Ways to Think Like a 21st Century Economist*. White River Junction, VT: Chelsea Green Publishing, 2017.

Richardson, Robert D. *Henry Thoreau: A Life of the Mind*. Berkeley: University of California Press, 1986.

———. *Emerson: The Mind on Fire*. Berkeley: University of California Press, 1996.

———. *Three Roads Back: How Emerson, Thoreau, and William James Responded to the Greatest Losses of Their Lives*. Princeton: Princeton University Press, 2023.

Rilke, Rainer Maria. *Letters to a Young Poet*. New York: Vintage Books, 1986.

Ritchie, Hannah. *Not the End of the World: How We Can Be the First Generation to Build a Sustainable Planet*. New York: Hachette Book Group, 2024.

Robinson, David M. *Natural Life: Thoreau's Worldly Transcendentalism*. Ithaca: Cornell University Press, 2004.

Romero, Oscar. *The Violence of Love*. Compiled and translated by John Brockman. New York: Orbis Books, 1970.

Roszak, Theodore. *The Voice of the Earth*. New York: Simon & Schuster, 1992.

Ruffing, Janet K., ed. *Mysticism and Social Transformation*. Syracuse: Syracuse University Press, 2001.

Samraj, Adi Da. *The Knee of Listening*. Loch Lomond, CA: Dawn Horse Press, 1972.

Sattelmeyer, Robert. "The Evolutions of Thoreau's Science." In *Thoreau in an Age of Crisis: Uses and Abuses of an American Icon*, edited by Kristen Case, Rochelle Johnson, and Henrik Otterberg, 25–40. Paderborn, Germany: Brill-Fink, 2021.

Schrag, Calvin O. *The Resources of Rationality*. Bloomington: Indiana University Press, 1992.

Schulz, Kathryn. "Pond Scum." *New Yorker*, October 19, 2015.

Sederholm, Carl H. "Popular Culture." In *Henry David Thoreau in Context*, edited by James S. Finney. Cambridge, England: University of Cambridge Press, 2017.

Servigne, Pablo, and Raphael Stevens. *How Everything Can Collapse*. Cambridge, England: Polity Press, 2020.

Shankara. *Crest-Jewel of Discrimination*. Translated by Swami Prabhavananda and Christopher Isherwood. Hollywood, CA: Vedanta Press, 1978 (1947).

Shepard, Paul. *Nature and Madness*. Athens: University of Georgia Press, 1998 (1982).

———. *Coming Home to the Pleistocene*. Washington, DC: Island Press, 1997.

———. "The Unreturning Arrow." In *Talking on the Water*, edited by Jonathan White. San Francisco: Sierra Club Books, 1994.

———. "A Post-Historic Primitivism." *Limited Wants, Unlimited Means*, edited by John Gowdy, 281–325. Washington, DC: Island Press, 1998.

Silko, Leslie. *Ceremony*. New York: Penguin Books, 1977.

Singer, June. *Boundaries of the Soul*. New York: Anchor Books, 1994 (1972).

Smith, Harmon. *My Friend, My Friend: The Story of Thoreau's Relationship with Emerson*. Amherst: University of Massachusetts Press, 2001.

Snow, C. P. *The Two Cultures and a Second Look*. Cambridge: Cambridge University Press, 1959.

Soelle, Dorothy. *The Silent Cry: Mysticism and Resistance*. Minneapolis: Fortress Press, 2001.

Solnit, Rebecca. *A Field Guide to Getting Lost*. New York: Penguin Books, 2005.

———. "The Thoreau Problem." *Orion* (May/June 2007). https://orionmagazine.org/article/the-thoreau-problem/.

———. "Ten Ways to Confront the Climate Crisis Without Losing Hope." *Guardian*, November 18, 2021.

———. "We Can't Afford to Be Climate Doomers." *Guardian*, July 26, 2023.

Solnit, Rebecca, and Thelma Young Lutunatabua. *Not Too Late: Changing the Climate Story from Despair to Possibility*. Chicago: Haymarket Books, 2023.

Speth, James Gustave. *The Bridge at the End of the World: Capitalism, the Environment, and Crossing the Bridge from Crisis to Sustainability*. New Haven: Yale University Press, 2008.

———. *They Knew: The US Federal Government's Fifty-Year Role in Causing the Climate Crisis*. Cambridge: Massachusetts Institute of Technology Press, 2021.

Stoknes, Per Espen. *What We Think about When We Try Not to Think about Global Warming.* White River Junction, VT: Chelsea Green, 2015.

Stoneham, Michael. "Remeasuring Thoreau: *The Maine Woods* and Thoreau's Evolving Appreciation of the Racial Other." *Concord Saunterer: A Journal of Thoreau Studies* 27 (2019): 68–88.

Sullivan, Robert. *The Thoreau You Don't Know.* New York: HarperCollins, 2009.

Thomas, Leah. "Why Every Environmentalist Should Be Anti-Racist." *Vogue* (June 8, 2020). https://www.vogue.com/article/why-every-environmentalist-should-be-anti-racist.

Thoreau, Henry David. *The Heart of Thoreau's Journals.* Edited by Odell Shepard. New York: Dover, 1961

———. *Letters to a Spiritual Seeker.* Edited by Bradley P. Dean. New York: W. W. Norton & Company, 2004.

———. *The Portable Thoreau.* Edited by Carl Bode. New York: Penguin Books, 1975.

———. *Thoreau on Water: Reflecting Heaven.* Edited by Robert Lawrence France. New York: Mariner Books, 2001.

———. *Thoreau on Education: Uncommon Learning.* Edited by Martin Bickman. New York: Mariner Books, 1999.

Thorson, Robert. *The Boatman: Henry David Thoreau's River Years.* Cambridge: Harvard University Press, 2017.

Trahant, Mark. "How Colonization of the Americas Killed 90 Percent of Their Indigenous People—and Changed the Climate." *Yes!* February 13, 2019. https://www.yesmagazine.org/opinion/2019/02/13/how-colonization-of-the-americas-killed-90-percent-of-their-indigenous-people-and-changed-the-climate.

Trungpa, Chogyam. *Cutting through Spiritual Materialism.* Boston: Shambhala, 1987.

Turner, Jack. *The Abstract Wild.* Tucson: University of Arizona Press, 1996.

Tye, Larry. *The Father of Spin: Edward L. Bernays and the Birth of Public Relations.* New York: Henry Holt, 1998.

Underhill, Evelyn. *Practical Mysticism.* New York: E. P. Dutton, 1915.

Van der Braack, Andre. *Enlightenment Blues: My Years with an American Guru.* Rhinebeck, NY: Monkfish Books, 2003.

Waldman, Scott, and Benjamin Hulac. "This is when the GOP turned away from climate policy." *E&E News*, December 5, 2018. https://www.eenews.net/stories/1060108785.

Walls, Laura Dassow. *Henry David Thoreau: A Life.* Chicago: University of Chicago Press, 2017.

———. *Seeing New Worlds, Henry David Thoreau and Nineteenth-Century Natural Science.* Madison: University of Wisconsin Press, 1995.

———. "Introduction." In *Material Faith: Thoreau on Science*, edited by Laura Dassow Walls. New York: Houghton-Mifflin, 1999.

————. "Counter Frictions: Thoreau and the Integral Commons." In *Thoreau beyond Borders: International Essays on America's Most Famous Nature Writer*, edited by Francois Specq, Laura Dassow Walls, and Julien Negre. Amherst: University of Massachusetts Press, 2020.

————. "Technology." In *Henry David Thoreau in Context*, edited by James S. Finley. Cambridge, England: Cambridge University Press, 2017.

Walsh, Roger. *The Spirit of Shamanism*. New York: Tarcher/Putnam, 1990.

————. *Essential Spirituality: The Seven Central Practices to Awakening Heart and Mind*. New York: John Wiley & Sons, 1999.

Watts, Alan. *The Supreme Identity*. New York: Pantheon Books, 1972.

————. *Nature, Man and Woman*. New York: Vintage Books, 1992.

Weatherford, Jack. *Indian Givers*. New York: Three Rivers Press, 1988.

Weber, Renee. *Dialogues with Scientists and Sages: The Search for Unity*. Oxfordshire, England: Routledge, 1986.

Welch, James. *Fools Crow*. New York: Penguin Books, 1986.

Welwood, John. *Toward a Psychology of Awakening: Buddhism, Psychotherapy, and the Path of Personal and Spiritual Transformation*. Boston: Shambhala Pub., 2002.

Wilber, Ken. *A Brief History of Everything*. Boston: Shambhala, 1996.

————. *Grace and Grit: Spirituality and Healing in the Life and Death of Treya Killam Wilber*. Boston: Shambhala, 1991.

————. *Integral Spirituality*. Boston: Shambhala, 2007.

————. *The Religion of Tomorrow*. Boston: Shambhala, 2017.

————. *Sex, Ecology, Spirituality: The Spirit of Evolution*. Boston: Shambhala Publications, 1995.

Wilber, Ken, ed. *Quantum Questions*. Boston: Shambhala Publications, 1984.

Wildcat, Daniel R. *Red Alert! Saving the Planet with Indigenous Knowledge*. Golden, CO: Fulcrum Publishing, 2009.

Wilshire, Bruce. *Wild Hunger: The Primal Roots of Modern Addiction*. Lanham, MD: Rowman & Littlefield, 1998.

————. *The Primal Roots of American Philosophy*. Philadelphia: University of Pennsylvania Press, 2000.

————. *The Moral Collapse of the University*. Albany: SUNY Press, 1990.

Wink, Walter, ed. *Peace is the Way*. New York: Orbis Books, 2000.

Wirzbicki, Peter. *Fighting for the Higher Law: Black and White Transcendentalists against Slavery*. Philadelphia: University of Pennsylvania Press, 2021.

Yenner, William. *American Guru: A Story of Love, Betrayal, and Healing—Former Students of Andrew Cohen Speak Out*. Rhinebeck, NY: Epigraph Books, 2009.

Zirin, Dave. *Welcome to the Terrordome*. Chicago: Haymarket Books, 2007.

Zizer, Michael. "The Modern Environmental Movement." In *Henry David Thoreau in Context*, edited by James S. Finney, 342–48. Cambridge, England: University of Cambridge Press, 2017.

About the Author

WILLIAM HOMESTEAD is an associate professor and the author of *An Ecology of Communication: Response and Responsibility in an Age of Ecocrisis* (Lexington Books, 2021). Homestead had a long association with the Ometeca Institute, a nonprofit devoted to the integration of the sciences and the humanities. His work with Ometeca, along with his interdisciplinary degrees (MA in Communication Studies, MS in Environmental Studies, MFA in creative nonfiction writing), study with a spiritual teacher, and hiking experiences, provide much of the insight and inspiration for his writing. Homestead is a member of the International Environmental Communication Association (IECA), the National Communication Association (NCA), and the Thoreau Society.